AFRICAN AMERICANS IN THE VISUAL ARTS

Revised Edition

Steven Otfinoski

Facts On File
An imprint of Infobase Publishing

African Americans in the Visual Arts, Revised Edition

Facts On File, Inc.
An imprint of Infobase Publishing
132 West 31st Street
New York NY 10001

Library of Congress Cataloging-in-Publication Data
Otfinoski, Steven.
  African Americans in the visual arts / Steven Otfinoski. — Rev. ed.
    p. cm. — (A to Z of African Americans)
  Includes bibliographical references and index.
  ISBN 978-0-8160-7840-0
  1. African American art. 2. African American artists—Biography—Dictionaries.
  I. Title.
  N6538.N5O86 2010
  704.03'9607300922—dc22
  [B]   2009027202

Facts On File books are available at special discounts when purchased in bulk quantities for businesses, associations, institutions, or sales promotions. Please call our Special Sales Department in New York at (212) 967-8800 or (800) 322-8755.

You can find Facts On File on the World Wide Web at http://www.factsonfile.com

Excerpts included herewith have been reprinted by permission of the copyright holders; the author has made every effort to contact copyright holders. The publishers will be glad to rectify, in future editions, any errors or omissions brought to their notice.

Text design by Joan M. Toro
Composition by Newgen Imaging Systems Pvt. Ltd.
Cover printed by Sheridan Books, Ann Arbor, Mich.
Book printed and bound by Sheridan Books, Ann Arbor, Mich.
Date printed: February 2011
Printed in the United States of America

10 9 8 7 6 5 4 3 2 1

This book is printed on acid-free paper.

CONTENTS

LIST OF ENTRIES

ACKNOWLEDGMENTS

The author would like to especially thank the following people for their help and support in putting together this book: photographer Anthony Barboza; Dr. Judy Larson, director, and Sharon M. Wasserman, director, of the National Museum for Women in the Arts; and Kathleen Adrian and Joan Stahl of the Smithsonian American Art Museum.

I would also like to thank the following visual artists and their representatives for providing photographs and information about themselves: Benny Andrews, Xenobia Bailey, John Bankston, Stephen Bentley, Garry Bibbs, Ray Billingsley, Barbara Brandon-Croft, Yvonne E. Buchanan, Robb Armstrong, Adger Cowans, Renee Cox, Charles Harris, Barkley L. Hendricks, Dolores Johnson, Dindga McCannon, Aaron McGruder, Charnelle Holloway, Marilyn Nance, John Pinderhughes, Adrian Piper, Martin Puryear, Herbert Randall, Winfred Rembert, Faith Ringgold, Alex Simmons, Renee Stout, Kara Walker, Shawn Walker, and Ernest C. Withers.

INTRODUCTION

African Americans have probably faced more obstacles to their success in the visual arts than in any other creative arena. That black men and women could create painting, sculpture, and other works of fine art was largely rejected by white America until the 20th century. But such resistance only strengthened the resolve of many a black artist. It was, in fact, a newspaper article in 1867 that claimed blacks might appreciate fine art but could never produce it that made Edward Mitchell Bannister all the more determined to succeed as an artist. Today, Bannister is considered one of the finest American landscape painters of the late 19th century.

But before Bannister there were black artisans going back to the earliest days of slavery who were creating beautiful craft items, including ceramics, furniture, and signs. Only a few of them are remembered by name today, including the slave known as Dave the Potter.

The prejudice against African-American artists continued into the 20th century. Black women, members of two oppressed minorities, had a doubly difficult time succeeding as professional artists. Sculptor Edmonia Lewis was unjustly put on trial for attempted murder while in college. Nancy Elizabeth Prophet's career thrived for a short time, and then she drifted into impoverished obscurity. Augusta Savage largely gave up her own promising career as a sculptor and dedicated herself to teaching and guiding younger black artists, many of whom became successful.

Beginning with the great 19th-century painter Henry O. Tanner, many African-American artists found they could escape the racism of America and achieve their artistic dreams in Europe, especially in Paris, France. Some stayed briefly; others, such as painter Beauford Delaney, never left Europe except for brief visits home. Of those who struggled at home to create art, many could not make a living as artists and were forced to spend much, if not all, of their careers in other employment, from custodial to social work.

What kind of art did they pursue? Some of the earliest black artists, such as Bannister and Robert Scott Duncanson, looked to the rich tradition of European art for their models. However, in the early decades of the 20th century many African-American artists were turning to their ancestral home of Africa for their inspiration, rediscovering the great traditions and art forms of that continent. Some, such as Hale Woodruff and John Biggers, incorporated African designs and motifs into their own highly personal work. Others, such as Xenobia Bailey, Renee Stout, and the folk artist Mr. Imagination (whose real name is Gregory Warmack), to name only a few, wholly adopted styles and unique genres of African arts and crafts and blended them with their own experiences.

Perhaps no branch of the tree of African-American art is as rich, evocative, and dramatic as folk art. Many black folk artists found inspiration for their untaught but deeply creative art only in old age. (Bill Traylor was 85 when he created his first drawing.) Others found solace in their highly eccentric art while in prison, and still others as part of a religious mission. A deep spiritual faith is reflected in many of their works, although so is the earthy energy of rural life as lived by thousands of black southern Americans in a simpler time.

While the largest number of the 192 individuals in this volume are fine artists (painters, sculptors, ceramists, mixed media artists, etc.), there is a good representation of the other visual arts, including illustration, cartooning, photography, filmmaking, and architecture. The author has tried to represent not only the full range of the visual arts but has attempted to balance historical figures with contemporary ones. It has been easier to accomplish some sense of completeness in those fields where the number of blacks who have risen to prominence has been relatively small, not because of a lack of talent but a lack of opportunity. For example, there remain only a handful of syndicated cartoonists of color today and a relatively small, but growing, number of successful black filmmakers, illustrators, and architects.

The fine-art field, on the other hand, has seen an explosion of black artists in recent decades. As with any biographical work, the author faces the dilemma of who to include and who to leave out. Realizing that some artists will stand the test of time and others will not, the author has chosen few artists born after 1960 and only two born after 1970. Of those artists now in their prime, many of them have been largely ignored by the white press, and their names cannot be found in many general biographical works on American artists. Some of them do not even appear in the most current editions of *Who's Who in American Art,* a definitive reference source.

It is hoped that if the reader is interested in a particular artist, he or she will read further about that person in one of the books, articles, or Web sites listed at the end of each biographical entry in Further Reading or find a video or DVD about the artist listed in Further Viewing. This work is not intended to be definitive but a resource for the general reader who may not have a strong background in the visual arts. As such, the dramatic lives of some of these artists have been given as much space as their artistic achievements, although some evaluation of their work and its importance has been attempted in every instance.

While social concerns, especially racial ones, have been central to the work of many of these visual artists in whatever medium they have chosen, few of them would choose to be identified as African Americans first and artists second. Whether social realists or abstract expressionists, portrait painters or genre artists, all of these creative individuals have used the visual medium to express their vision, a vision that ultimately strives for the universal appeal that is the hallmark of all great art.

Alexander, William
(1916–1991) *filmmaker, film producer*

A pioneer independent black producer and director of the 1940s and 1950s, William Alexander made a wide range of black films, including documentaries, dramas, musicals, and the first newsreels aimed specifically at a black audience.

Little is known of his early life; he was born in 1916 somewhere in Missouri and played football in high school. Alexander attended Colorado State University, now the University of Northern Colorado, where he was a gymnast. In 1941, he moved to Washington, D.C., where the Office of War Information hired him. Together with producers Claude Barnett and Emmanuel Glucksman, Alexander made a series of newsreels designed to encourage blacks to enlist in the service during World War II. Called *All-American News,* these were the first theatrically shown newsreels aimed specifically at African Americans.

Like OSCAR MICHEAUX and other African-American filmmakers before him, Alexander wanted to make fictional films about real black people that broke the stereotypes long presented by the Hollywood studios. After the war, he founded Alexander Productions and turned out several short musical films in 1946, including *The Vanities; Flicker,* starring bandleader and jazz singer Billy Eckstein; and *Jivin' in Be-Bop,* the first film to feature jazz musician Dizzy Gillespie and his band, codirected by SPENCER WILLIAMS. The following year, Alexander directed the feature film *That Man of Mine,* which introduced black actress Ruby Dee to film audiences. Dee also costarred with heavyweight fighter Joe Louis in the Alexander-produced *The Fight Never Ends* (1949), a crime drama set in the world of boxing.

Alexander reached the pinnacle of his commercial success with *Souls of Sin* (1949), a realistic contemporary drama set in Harlem, a black community in upper Manhattan. It starred actor and future documentary filmmaker WILLIAM GREAVES as a transplanted southern blues singer. Like all of Alexander's films, it was shown only in black-owned movie theaters for a primarily black audience.

Alexander made perhaps his greatest contribution to black cinema in the mid-1950s when he produced a second series of black-oriented theatrical newsreels, *By-Line Newsreel.* Realizing that mainstream newsreels paid little if any attention to current events within the black community, Alexander and his small crew crossed the United States reporting on black news, particularly the events of the growing Civil Rights movement. Alexander himself served as the narrator and interviewer for *By-Line Newsreel,* which he produced from 1953 to 1956.

To survive tough financial times, Alexander moved his operation to London, England, in the late 1950s and produced a string of documentary films for ABC-TV in the United States about seven newly independent African nations. For his documentary work, he received a United Nations award.

Alexander's last effort, and the only big-budget Hollywood film he ever produced, was *The Klansman* (1974), based on a novel by William Bradford Huie. The film was about the effects of the Ku Klux Klan, a white racist group, on a small southern town. Despite a cast that included Richard Burton, Lee Marvin, and O. J. Simpson in his first film role, *The Klansman* was panned as exploitative and proved a box office disaster.

William Alexander, who will be remembered for his better efforts, died of cancer on November 18, 1991, in the Bronx, New York.

Further Reading

Jones, G. William. *Black Cinema Treasures: Lost and Found.* Denton: University of North Texas Press, 1997, pp. 36–38.

Moon, Spencer. *Reel Black Talk: A Sourcebook of 50 American Filmmakers.* Westport, Conn.: Greenwood Press, 1997, pp. 3–6.

"William Alexander," The Internet Movie Database. Available online. URL: http://us.imdb.com/name/nm0018796. Downloaded February 25, 2009.

Further Viewing

Jivin' in Be-Bop (1946). Storyville Records/Naxos, DVD, 2008.

Alston, Charles H.

(Charles Henry Alston)
(1907–1977) *painter, muralist, sculptor, illustrator, educator*

One of the most far-ranging, accomplished, and under-appreciated African-American artists of the 20th century, Charles H. Alston expressed his restless, creative spirit in a number of mediums and styles.

He was born Charles Henry Alston on November 28, 1907, in Charlotte, North Carolina, the youngest of five children. His father, an Episcopalian minister, died when he was three. His mother then married Harry Bearden, the uncle of another celebrated black artist, ROMARE BEARDEN.

Alston exhibited his artistic abilities at an early age. As a boy, he would take the red clay in his yard and mold it into animals. The family moved to New York City in about 1915, and Alston attended DeWitt Clinton High School, where he became the art editor of the school magazine. He entered Columbia University in 1925 and earned a Bachelor of Arts degree and later a Master of Fine Arts degree from Columbia Teachers College. Although they allowed him to study art at Columbia, the college authorities did not think it proper for Alston, as a black, to draw from a nude female model with the white students.

He did not allow such racist policies to hold him back, however, and in 1930 Alston illustrated and lettered the poem "Weary Blues" by black writer Langston Hughes for a term project. Hughes was impressed by Alston's work and the two became friends.

After graduating from Columbia, Alston taught art at the Harlem Art Center, the Harlem Artists Workshop, and The Utopia Children's Center. Among his students at the Children's Center was 10-year-old JACOB LAWRENCE, who already showed signs of being a superb painter. As the Great Depression of the 1930s deepened, Alston and other black artists formed a group called 306. The name came from the address of Alston's apartment, 306 West 141st Street, where they would meet.

Alston was hired by the federally operated Works Progress Administration to paint, teach, and create murals in public buildings. He proved to be a masterful muralist, giving his large monumental figures a strong sculptural look that reflected his interest in African art.

His most famous and controversial murals were *Primitive Medicine* and *Modern Medicine,* commissioned by Harlem Hospital in 1937. The murals' geometrically shaped, elongated figures showed the influence of the modern Italian artist Amedeo Modigliani in Alston's work. At first, the public was shocked by the African figures Alston depicted, but in time these murals were considered among the most famous in the city. When Harlem Hospital was remodeled 35 years later, the trustees asked Alston to create a new mosaic mural.

While working on these murals, Alston met Myra Logan, a female hospital intern, whom he later married. She went on to become a surgeon. Alston created many more impressive murals in New York City at the Harriet Tubman School, the Hall of Forestry in the Museum of Natural History, City College of the City University of New York, and Abraham Lincoln High School in Brooklyn.

Alston was drafted into the infantry during World War II at age 36. He was transferred to the Office of War Information in Washington, D.C., where he drew cartoons for publication in black newspapers. After the war, he worked for a time as a commercial artist to earn money. He illustrated the book jackets of works by southern novelist Eudora Welty and black poet Countee Cullen. A great lover of jazz music, Alston illustrated numerous record album covers. His illustrations also enlivened the pages of such magazines as the *New Yorker, Redbook,* and *Fortune.*

In 1950, Alston was one of 4,000 artists who entered paintings for the Metropolitan Museum of Art's first exhibition of contemporary art. His painting was one of the few chosen by the museum, and he was paid $1,500 for it. The same year, he became the first black artist to be invited to teach at the renowned Art Students League in New York. Alston was one of three representatives from the Museum of Modern Art and the State

Charles H. Alston, seen here in his Harlem studio, was among the most versatile of African-American artists. *(Photographs and Prints Division, Schomburg Center for Research in Black Culture, the New York Public Library, Astor, Lenox and Tilden Foundations)*

Department sent to the Brussels World's Fair in Belgium in 1958.

About this time, Alston painted what he called "protest paintings" depicting the African-American bus boycott in Birmingham, Alabama, and other events in the Civil Rights movement. His bronze head of Martin Luther King, Jr., is considered one of the finest likenesses of the great civil rights leader.

Alston won many awards and prizes during his nearly 50-year career, including a Rosenwald fellowship in painting, first prize at the Atlanta University Annual Exhibit, and a National Institute of Arts and Letters grant. He was named to the Advisory Board of the National Council of the Arts in 1967 and was a member of the National Society of Mural Painters. Charles Alston died of cancer on April 27, 1977.

Alston's very prolificity and his refusal to stick with one signature style are two reasons why he may not be as well remembered today as other black artists of his era. "I can't see this business of repeating and repeating and repeating," he once said. "I believe in developing or exploring an idea until you've gotten out of it everything you can, and beyond that, let's look for unexplored areas."

Further Reading

Alston, Charles Henry. *Portraits in Black: Charles Alston's Drawings of African Americans*. Washington, D.C.: National Archives & Record Service, 1992.

Bearden, Romare, and Harry Henderson. *A History of African-American Artists: From 1792 to the Present*. New York: Pantheon Books, 1993, pp. 260–271.

Bill Hodges Gallery and Charles Alston. *Charles "Spinky" Alston: Works of Art 1936–1969*. New York: Bill Hodges Gallery, 2004.

Riggs, Thomas, ed. *St. James Guide to Black Artists*. Detroit, Mich.: St. James Press, 1997, pp. 8–10.

Wardlaw, Alvia J. *Charles Alston* (The David C. Driskell Series of African American Art). Petaluma, Calif.: Pomegranate Communications, 2007.

Amaki, Amalia

(Linda Faye Peeks)
(1949–   ) *collagist, mixed-media artist, photographer, quilter, writer, curator, educator, art historian*

An artist who explores the public images and private lives of black women, Amalia Amaki has used everything from family photographs to button-encrusted objects to enrich her expressive art.

Amaki was born Linda Faye Peeks on July 8, 1949, in Atlanta, Georgia, the fourth of six daughters. Her father, Norman, was a caterer and musician with the group the Deep South Boys from Macon, Georgia. She developed a talent for writing and drawing as a child and majored in journalism and psychology at Georgia State University, graduating with a Bachelor of Arts degree in 1971. She earned a second B.A. in photography and art history from the University of New Mexico in Albuquerque, where she worked in the university art museum as an assistant for two years. She changed her name to Amalia Amaki in 1974.

Amaki received a Master of Arts degree in modern European and American art (1992) and a Ph.D. in 20th-century American art and culture (1994) from Emory University's Institute of Liberal Arts in Atlanta. In such exhibitions as *Buttons and Blues* (1994) at the Atlanta Financial Center and *When Duty Whispers, Pt. 2* (1999–2000) at the Hammonds House Gallery, she has attempted to create portraits of African-American women, families, and heritage through assemblages of photographs, fabrics, household buttons, music, and storytelling.

Her 10-year retrospective, *Boxes, Buttons, and the Blues* (2005) at the National Museum for Women in the Arts, in Washington, D.C., was an assemblage of art works, which one reviewer called "subtle commentaries on our image-obsessed culture." Elaborate button-encrusted candy boxes and handheld fans used by southern women in church combined feelings of domesticity and spirituality. "Amika's intricately patterned assemblages purposefully resemble folk art, reliquaries, and shrines, and, thanks to her use of the Stars and Stripes, make clear the fact that African American culture is as American as apple pie," wrote Donna Scamon in a review of a book based on the exhibition in *Booklist*.

Amika taught art history at a number of Georgia colleges and universities from 1987 to 2000, including Spelman and Morehouse Colleges in Atlanta. In 2001, she was named curator of the Paul R. Jones Collection of Art and assistant professor of art in the art history and black studies departments at the University of Delaware in Newark. Amaki was a scholar-in-residence at Spelman College for the 2005–06 school year.

Since 2007, she has been a professor of modern and contemporary art and art history at the University of Alabama at Tuscaloosa. She has worked as an art critic, written many articles for periodicals, and is a contributing author of the book *Hale Woodruff, Nancy Elizabeth Prophet and the Academy* (2007).

Further Reading

"Amalia Amaki Biography." The History Makers. Available online. URL: http://www.thehistorymakers. com/biography/biography.asp?bioindex=1256 &category=ArtMakers&occupation=Artist %2C%20Educator%20%26%20Curator&name= Amalia%20Amaki. Downloaded March 18, 2009.

Barnwell, Andrea D., Gloria Wade Gayles, and Leslie King-Hammond. *Amalia Amaki: Boxes, Buttons, and the Blues.* Washington, D.C.: National Museum of Women in the Arts, 2005.

Lewis, Samella. *African American Art and Artists.* Berkeley: University of California Press, 2003, pp. 319–321.

Amos, Emma

(1938–   ) *mixed-media artist, muralist, painter, printmaker, weaver, educator*

An artist of great range and diversity, Emma Amos has woven racial, social, and cultural themes through her paintings for five decades.

She was born on March 16, 1938, in Atlanta, Georgia. Her father owned a drugstore at Atlanta University Center. She graduated from Antioch College in Yellow Springs, Ohio, in 1958 and studied at the London Central School of Art in England. Amos later moved to New York City and received a Master of Arts degree from New York University. In the 1960s, Amos joined Spiral, a group of African-American artists who met regularly to discuss the role of black art amid the decade's social unrest. Of Spiral's 15 original members, who included ROMARE BEARDEN and NORMAN LEWIS, Amos was the only female.

The philosophy of Spiral, which saw art as a means of communication and social change, greatly influenced Amos's work, although her various styles are wholly her own. A strong feminist, she acknowledged the contributions of other black women artists in the series *Women Artists* (1991). In the painting *Elizabeth Catlett, India, and Emma,* she pays tribute to sculptor ELIZABETH CATLETT. The intriguing work compares the theme of mother-daughter in Catlett's work with Amos's relationship with her own daughter India. Amos has incorporated photographs into such well-known works as *X Flag* (1993) and *Confederate* (1994). Both these works feature the Confederate flag, a potent symbol for many African Americans of the long heritage of racial discrimination in the South.

Her best-known paintings focus on figures falling or floating against a usually abstract backdrop. These works, according to art historian Regenia Perry, explore "individual freedom and fear through [their] imaginative arrangements of human figures." One of Amos's most ambitious works is the mosaic mural *The Sky's the Limit* (1995), which hangs from the ceiling of the circular lobby of a Manhattan public school at 167th Street and Jumel Place.

Such public works intrigue the artist. "Most public art is a collaborative art, like making good theater," Amos said in 1997. "With public art we hope the applause lasts forever."

Amos was represented in the show *Art by African Americans: A Selection from the Collection* at the New Jersey State Museum in Trenton, New Jersey, in 2002. Her solo exhibition, *Head First,* was mounted at the Flomenhaft Gallery in New York City in early 2008. Amos was part of the group show *If I Didn't Care: Multigenerational Artists Discuss Cultural Histories* at the Richman Gallery in Baltimore, Maryland, in 2009. Emma Amos was professor of art at the Mason Gross School of the Arts at Rutgers University in New Brunswick, New Jersey, from 1980 until her retirement in 2008.

Further Reading

Amos, Emma. *Emma Amos: The Water Series.* New York: Parker/Bratten Gallery, 1987.

Gouma-Peterson, Thalia, and Kathleen McManus Zurko. *Emma Amos: Paintings and Prints 1982–1992.* Wooster, Ohio: College of Wooster Art Museum, 1993.

Official Web site of Emma Amos. Available online. URL: http://emmaamos.com/. Downloaded February 25, 2009.

Riggs, Thomas, ed. *St. James Guide to Black Artists.* Detroit, Mich.: St. James Press, 1997, pp. 11–14.

Further Viewing

Emma Amos: Action Lines (1996). L & S Video, VHS, 1999.

Andrews, Benny

(1930–2006) *painter, collagist, illustrator, educator*

A leading African-American artist, Benny Andrews created work that reflected his strong commitment to the poor and disenfranchised and his opposition to what he saw as the racism and hypocrisy of American society.

He was born on November 13, 1930, in Plainview, Georgia, near the city of Madison, the second of 10 children. His parents were sharecroppers who could barely scrape a living off their small farm. "There was never any money, or any prospect of getting any," Andrews recalled years later. "You were always behind, and just surviving was an accomplishment." His father was a self-taught painter, and Andrews painted as a child on brown paper bags, using his father's hogs' hair brushes and pigments squeezed from berries.

At his mother's insistence, Andrews was the first member of his family to complete high school. He got a scholarship to study at Fort Valley State College in Fort Valley, Georgia, for two years and then joined the U.S. Air Force. He served in the Korean War and attained the rank of staff sergeant. After his discharge, Andrews went on to study at the School of the Art Institute of Chicago in 1954, where he quickly gained a reputation as an independent spirit. To help pay his expenses, he found work designing art for such jazz artists as Duke Ellington and the Ramsey Lewis Quartet. He graduated with a Bachelor of Fine Arts degree from the Art Institute in 1958.

In 1958, Andrews moved to New York City and lived in near-poverty for years on the Lower East Side. His first one-man show took place in 1960, not in New York but at the Paul Kessler Gallery in Provincetown, Massachusetts. His early paintings had the three-dimensional look of sculpture, enriched by his experiments with the use of such

Benny Andrews, modern master of the collage painting, is shown at work in his studio. *(John Groo)*

materials as paper and cloth. He once wrote that "collage caused me to look for those symbols that I'd wanted to identify and merge into my work . . . burlap, ropes, chains, gunnysacks, and other haunting textures and materials that stayed in my conscience though I'd left the environment [the South] where they predominated." His first work to incorporate such materials was *Janitors at Rest* (1958), which used tissues and paper towels for its abstract shapes.

Andrews had one-man shows at the Forum Gallery in New York in 1962, 1964, and 1966. He won a John Hay Whitney Fellowship in 1965. He used the money to return to his native Georgia, where he renewed his family ties and interviewed members of his family. This research inspired him to create several series of paintings based on themes. The first, and one of the most ambitious of these, was a six-part *Bicentennial Series* that was a bitter critique of American society in the 1970s. He completed it during the United States' bicentennial year of 1976. Other series were more celebratory, such as *Southland,* which recalled events from his childhood; the *Langston Hughes Series,* which paid tribute to the African-American poet and writer; and *Musical Interlude,* dedicated to another of Andrews's passions, popular music.

An artist of restless energy and far-ranging interests, Andrews was also an illustrator of novels, children's books, and an anthology of African-American poetry called *I Am the Darker Brother: An Anthology of Modern Poems by African Americans* (1997). Among his last children's books are *The Hickory Chair* (2001), for which he created memorable folk-style paintings, and *Delivering Justice: W. W. Law and the Fight for Civil Rights* (2008).

In 1969, Andrews helped found the Black Emergency Cultural Coalition, an organization whose goal is to challenge the exclusion of African-American artists from mainstream American art museums, such as the Whitney Museum of American Art in New York. He also served as visual arts director of the National Endowment for the Arts from 1982 to 1984. Andrews retired in 1996 after 29 years as an art professor at Queens College in New York City.

He was elected to the National Academy of Design in 1999. Andrews formed the Benny Andrews Foundation, a not-for-profit publicly funded organization dedicated to supporting the arts, in 2002. The foundation is located in Connecticut. Early in 2006, Andrews went to the Gulf Coast to work in an art project with children displaced the previous year by Hurricane Katrina.

Benny Andrews's second wife was the sculptor Nina Humphrey. He had three children from his first marriage. His son Thomas is a glass artist. Another son Christopher is an architect, and his daughter, Julia, is a midwife. Andrews maintained studios in New York City and Litchfield, Connecticut.

Benny Andrews died of cancer on November 10, 2006, at his home in Brooklyn, New York. He was 75.

"If I can continue to reach humanity both through my paintings and through my missionary kind of teaching, then I will have made some small contribution," he once said.

Further Reading

Andrews, Benny. *Between the Lines: 70 Drawings and 7 Essays.* New York: Pella Publishing Co., 1988.
———. *Benny Andrews: Selections from a Life in Art.* New York: Bill Hodges Gallery, 1997.
Gruber, J. Richard. *American Icons: From Madison to Manhattan, the Art of Benny Andrews, 1948–1997.* Jackson: University Press of Mississippi, 2005.
Haskins, Jim and Benny Andrews. *Delivering Justice: W. W. Law and the Fight for Civil Rights.* Somerville, Mass.: Candlewick Press, 2008.
Studio Museum in Harlem Staff. *The Collages of Benny Andrews.* New York: Studio Museum in Harlem, 1988.

Further Viewing

Benny Andrews: The Visible Man. L & S Video, VHS, 1999.

Armstrong, Robb

(1962–) *cartoonist, illustrator, writer*

One of the few nationally syndicated African-American cartoonists is Robb Armstrong, whose comic strip *Jump Start* appears daily in more than 400 newspapers.

He was born on March 4, 1962, in West Philadelphia, Pennsylvania, the youngest of five children. Raised by a single mother, Armstrong began drawing cartoons at age three, copying Charlie Brown and his dog Snoopy from Charles Schulz's *Peanuts* comic strip. He attended Syracuse University in New York State and drew a comic strip called *Hector* for the school newspaper. He graduated with a Bachelor of Fine Arts degree in 1985 and went to work in the advertising field.

Armstrong developed the strip *Cherry Top*, about two police officers, in the late 1980s. It eventually evolved into *Jump Start*. The comic was picked up by United Media Feature Syndicate for distribution in October 1989. *Jump Start* revolves around Joe and Marcy Cobb, a young African-American couple, and their two children, Sunny and Jojo. Besides the central characters, the strip includes an interracial couple and Benny, Jojo's white preschool buddy. While humorous, *Jump Start* is noted for its positive and upbeat view of today's black family. The strip's appeal is heightened by Armstrong's loose style with thick, rounded edges on panels that sometimes have no borders and dialogue balloons that often run up against the borders.

"Nearly every married couple I know is like Joe and Marcy," Armstrong has said of his comic characters. "The image of young blacks is skewed, so false. I don't know anybody who's carjacking, playing basketball, rapping."

The strip has struck a chord with both black and white readers. In 1995, Armstrong received the Religious Public Relations Council's Wilbur Award for demonstrating "excellence in the communication of religious issues, values, and themes." The cartoonist has let his characters be used for such worthy causes as the American Diabetes Association and the American Cancer Society's "Great American Smokeout." A popular motivational speaker for companies and businesses, Armstrong also frequently visits schools and libraries to talk to young people about his career and how they too can succeed by excelling at something they love to do. He has said: "I hope some kid who doesn't know he could ever hope to be a professional cartoonist sees my strip and says, 'I could do that too!'"

Armstrong has written a number of young-adult books that combine cartoons and comics with narrative fiction. His popular series of books about the African-American boy Drew Taylor include *Drew and the Bub Daddy Showdown* (1996), *Drew and the Filthy Rich Kid* (1997), and *Drew and the Homeboy Question* (1997).

Robb Armstrong has been a member of the board of directors for the National Cartoonists Society and Syracuse University. He lives in Philadelphia with his wife and two children.

Further Reading

Armstrong, Robb. *Drew and the Homeboy Question.* New York: HarperCollins Children's Books, 1997.
———. *Twins—Twice the Fun.* Avon Park, Fla.: Journey Publications, 2008.
Jump Start, Comics.com. Available online. URL: http://comics.com/jump-start/. Downloaded February 25, 2009.
Robb Armstrong's Official Web site. Available online. URL: http://www.robbarmstrong.com/. Downloaded March 23, 2009.

Artis, William E.

(William Ellisworth Artis)
(1919–1977) *sculptor, ceramist, educator*

A sculptor whose work focuses on black children and youth, William E. Artis was also a masterful potter who helped raise ceramics to new artistic heights in the 1940s.

He was born on February 2, 1919, in Washington, North Carolina. He moved with his family to New York City when he was eight. The African-American arts movement known as the Harlem Renaissance was in full bloom during his youth. Artis got a job through a grant from the College Art Association to teach soap carving to children in neighborhood centers. About the same time, he studied sculpture with master teacher and artist AUGUSTA SAVAGE. Artis was one of Savage's most devoted disciples, and his photographs of some of her works are the only record of these lost pieces.

Artis received a Bachelor of Science degree from Nebraska State Teachers College in Chadron, Nebraska. His earliest known sculpture, *Head of a Girl,* received the John Hope Prize in Sculpture in 1933 from the Harmon Foundation, an organization devoted to encouraging and recognizing black artists. Soon after, he was awarded a scholarship to study and work at the prestigious Art Students League in New York City.

Some of Artis's best work was in terra-cotta, a hard, brownish-red clay. Among his most representative works is *Head of a Boy* (1940), a terra-cotta sculpture that shows the influence of African art on his work. During World War II, he served in the army as a technical sergeant. After the war, he studied at Syracuse University in Syracuse, New York, with Yugoslavian sculptor Ivan Mestrovic. During this time, Artis developed a strong interest in pottery and began to design artistically beautiful ceramic jugs, vases, and other functional objects.

He became an associate professor at his alma mater, Nebraska State Teachers College, in 1954 and remained there until 1965. From 1966 to 1975, he taught at Mankato State College in Minnesota. Artis was named Outstanding Educator of America in 1970.

In 1971, Fisk University in Nashville, Tennessee, mounted a retrospective of Artis's work with the paintings of ELLIS WILSON. William E. Artis died in April 1977 in Northport, New York.

"His restatement of the values and traditions derived from his culture's history is far more than simple repetition; it is the accomplishment of an artist whose pride in his racial heritage is equaled by his skill," wrote black artist and writer DAVID C. DRISKELL.

Further Reading

"Digital Archive—William E. Artis." Paul R. Jones Collections. Available online. URL: http://www.del.edu/museums/jones/archive/archive-pages/artist-pages/artis.html. Downloaded March 23, 2009.

Johnson, Robert P. "William Ellisworth Artis: Afro-American Sculptor, Ceramist and Teacher." *Minority Voices: An Interdisciplinary Journal of Literature and the Arts,* spring 1977, pp. 42–52.

Pendergraft, Norman E. *Heralds of Life: Artis, Bearden, and Burke, 4–30 November 1977: an Exhibition.* Durham: Museum of Art, North Carolina Central University, 1977.

Riggs, Thomas, ed. *St. James Guide to Black Artists.* Detroit, Mich.: St. James Press, 1997, pp. 22–23.

B

Bailey, Radcliffe
(1968–) *collagist, painter, mixed-media artist, sculptor*

One of the most prominent and successful African-American artists of his generation, Radcliffe Bailey has combined vintage photographs, found objects and bright swatches of color to create artworks that both define and transcend the African-American experience.

He was born in 1968 in Bridgeton, New Jersey, into a family with African-American and Native American ancestry. He moved with his family to Atlanta, Georgia, when he was five. As a child, Bailey built birdhouses with his grandfather, who was a blacksmith. This experience later inspired him to include common objects in his art. Bailey entered the Atlanta College of Art in 1987 and graduated in 1991 with a Bachelor of Fine Arts degree.

Success came quickly for the young artist. In 1994, he participated in a group exhibition, *Equal Rights and Justice*, at the High Museum of Art in Atlanta. The following year he had his first solo show at Atlanta's prestigious Fay Gold Gallery. The centerpiece of this exhibition was *The Magic City*, a large mixed-media work that resembled a rundown shack marked with branding irons and an emblem of an old Negro League baseball team, displaying both negative and positive images of the Old South that is typical of his work.

One of his murals was chosen to be exhibited in a hall in Atlanta's Hartsfield International Airport during the 1996 Summer Olympics in that city. The previous year, Bailey signed with the David Beitzel Gallery in New York City, which mounted a show in 1997. The large pieces showed his creativity and imagination to its best advantage. *Black and Tan* was sculptured in the shape of a grand piano with flickering electric candles for the keyboard. *Mound Magic*, another tribute to Negro League baseball, was in the shape of a baseball diamond with baseballs embedded in it. The art critic David Ebony praised the show, calling Bailey's artwork "exhilarating music for the eye." *Radcliffe Bailey: The Magic City*, exhibited at the Birmingham Museum of Art in Alabama and the Forum for Contemporary Art in St. Louis, Missouri, was held in 2000. A 2008 exhibit at the Arthur Roger Gallery in New Orleans, Louisiana, included sculptures of slave ships, a new element in his work. In June 2009, Bailey married actress, dancer, and author Victoria Rowell.

The writer Crystal Britton has referred to Bailey's art as a "spiritual divining rod, [that] connects him to his ancestors. Serving as stationary altars, the works house their souls." Bailey himself has said, "Growing up, I spent a lot of time with my grandparents and great-grandparents, and I feel like that's lost in most families today. In my art I try to restore some of the lost kinship between people."

Further Reading

Bailey, Radcliffe. *The Magic City*. Birmingham, Ala.: Birmingham Museum of Art, 2001.

Lewis, Samella. *African American Art and Artists*. Berkeley: University of California Press, 2003, pp. 321–322.

"Radcliffe Bailey." Answers.com. Available online. URL: http://www.answers.com/topic/radcliffe-bailey. Downloaded March 18, 2009.

Bailey, Xenobia

(1958–   ) *decorative artist, installation artist, mixed-media artist, doll maker, storyteller*

Hats, hair braiding, clothes, and other objects of adornment have become statements of ethnic and cultural pride in the skillful hands of Xenobia Bailey. Her "Paradise Under Reconstruction in the Aesthetic of Funk" is a cultural project that has been under construction since she was in nursery school and first discovered the power, beauty, and importance of aesthetics through personal expression.

She was born in Seattle, Washington, on April 5, 1958, and studied ethnomusicology at the University of Washington and apparel design at Seattle Community College. She later attended the Pratt Institute in Brooklyn, New York, where she earned a Bachelor of Arts degree in 1977. She worked at the Black Arts West Community Theater in Seattle designing costumes, masks, and puppets, which inspired her Black Doll Collection. Bailey was the first African American in the Pacific Northwest to braid hair as a decorative art form in the 1970s, and she created a series of African-inspired decorative crochet hats between 1986 and 1998. Her distinctive hats were in *Elle* magazine and ad campaigns for the Benetton

Multitalented artist Xenobia Bailey models one of her elaborate, African-inspired headdresses. *(Photo courtesy of the artist)*

clothing line and Absolut Vodka and appeared on television's *The Cosby Show* and in SPIKE LEE's film *Do the Right Thing*. Her crowns were commissioned for Disney World's Animal Kingdom theme park.

Bailey's hat series later developed into elaborate headdresses, garments, mythological tales, wall hangings, floor coverings, and full-size crochet tents. These have been exhibited at the Studio Museum in Harlem, Rush Arts, and the Stephen Stux Gallery, all in New York City. Her work has also been displayed at the Seattle Art Museum, the Johnson Museum at Cornell University in New York State, the Allentown Textile Museum in Pennsylvania, and the Bronx Museum in New York City. Bailey's work resides in the permanent collections of the Schomburg Center for Research in Black Culture, the American Craft Museum in New York City, the Allentown Textile Museum in Pennsylvania, and the investment firm of Neuberger & Berman. In 2008, Bailey's solo exhibit *(Re)Possess Exhibit* was mounted at the Jersey City Museum in New Jersey, and she was part of the group show *S & M: Shrines and Masquerades in Cosmopolitan Times* at New York University Steinhardt's 80 Washington Square East Galleries.

Using her background in ethnomusicology, apparel, and industrial design, Bailey is developing the visual aesthetic of her longtime project "Paradise Under Reconstruction in the Aesthetic of Funk," which involves the visual art of urban masking, a derivative of the music of enslaved Africans that survived the Atlantic Middle Passage. "This is a therapeutical and self reviving aesthetic that is designed to deliver descendants of enslaved Africans from a culture of trauma," Bailey has said.

"My purpose," Bailey has said, "is to inspire African Americans to culturally recreate themselves . . . [to] spread this idea of cultural recreation and personal adornment . . . and have this way of being to become a way of everyday life."

Further Reading

Garnett, Joy. "Into Africa," Artnet.com. Available online. URL: http://www.artnet.com/magazine/reviews/garnett/garnett12-12-00.asp. Downloaded February 25, 2009.

Rozelle, Robert V., Alvia Wardlaw, and Maureen A. McKenna, eds. *Black Art-Ancestral Legacy: The African Impulse in African-American Art.* Dallas, Tex.: The Dallas Museum of Art, 1989, pp. 202, 203, 260.

Rubiner, Joanna. "Xenobia Bailey," Answers.com Available online. URL: http://www.answers.com/topic/xenobia-bailey. Downloaded February 25, 2009.

Xenobia Bailey's Artist Journal. Available online. URL: http://xenobia.blogspot.com/. Downloaded March 23, 2009.

Ball, James P.
(James Presley Ball)
(1825–1904) *photographer*

One of the most successful and celebrated African-American photographers of the 19th century, James P. Ball chronicled the lives of both black and white Americans from Ohio to Washington State in a career that spanned more than five decades.

He was born in Virginia on July 28, 1825 and raised in Cincinnati, Ohio. The first modern photographs, called daguerreotypes, were taken in France by Joseph Nicephore Niepce the year after Ball's birth. Ball met John B. Bailey, a black daguerreotypist, in the mid-1840s, and he taught the teenager how to create daguerreotypes. Eager to make pictures, Ball set up a small studio in Cincinnati in 1845. Business was poor, and the studio closed in three months. He became a traveling daguerreotypist, working out of temporary studios in one town after another.

Ball opened a second permanent studio in Richmond, Virginia, in 1846. This time it was a success. Families, couples, and individuals flocked to his studio to have their photographs taken. Ball moved back to Cincinnati, and on New Year's Day, 1851, he opened a large, lavish studio. He grandly called it "Ball's Great Daguerrian Gallery of the West." It was the western equivalent of the New York studio of the great Civil War photographer Mathew Brady. Among Ball's nine employees in the early 1850s was famed landscape artist ROBERT SCOTT DUNCANSON, who hand-tinted photographs for Ball, adding color to them.

In 1855, Ball hired a group of African-American artists to paint a 2,400-square-yard panorama that bore the unwieldy title *Ball's Splendid Mammoth Pictorial Tour of the United States Comprising Views of the African Slave Trade; of Northern and Southern Cities; of Cotton and Sugar Plantations; of the Mississippi, Ohio, and Susquehanna Rivers, Niagara Falls, & C.* The panorama was a wild success and was shown at several venues, including Boston's Armory Hall.

One measure of Ball's success was the number of famous people who came to be photographed at his studio. Among his subjects was the black abolitionist and newspaper editor Frederick Douglass. Ball took countless pictures of Union soldiers during the Civil War. After the war, competition in the photographic field grew intense, and he moved his operation west.

Around 1871, Ball set up a studio in Minneapolis, Minnesota, and in 1888 moved to the frontier community of Helena, Montana. He became one of Helena's leading citizens and played an active role in helping to make the city the state capital. He was the president of the statewide Afro-American Club and was the first black to be nominated for county coroner, an official who investigates any death not resulting from natural causes. Ball's photographs chronicled the people and events of Helena, documenting everything from public hangings to the laying of the cornerstone of the capitol building.

But Ball's restless spirit drove him further west to Seattle, Washington, where he opened the Globe Photo Studio in 1900. John P. Ball died May 3, 1904, in Honolulu, Hawaii, where he had gone to seek relief from arthritis.

The few Ball daguerreotypes that have survived are rare. In 1992, one sold at a New York gallery auction for $58,000—a world record for a daguerreotype.

Further Reading

"July 28." African American Registry. Available online. URL: http://www.aaregistry.com/detail. php?id=1840. Downloaded March 23, 2009.

Sullivan, George. *Black Artists in Photography, 1840–1940.* New York: Cobblehill Books, 1996, pp. 38–57.

Willis, Deborah. *J. P. Ball, Daguerreon and Studio Photographer.* New York: Routledge, 1993.

———. *Reflections in Black: A History of Black Photographers from 1840 to the Present.* New York: W. W. Norton, 2002, pp. 4, 5–9, 12, 15, 20–22.

Bankston, John
(1963–) *painter*

John Bankston's intriguing paintings inhabit a world of dark fantasy and biting humor distilled through the bright, garish designs of a coloring book.

He was born in Benton Harbor, Michigan, on February 16, 1963. He attended the University of Chicago in Illinois, where he earned a Bachelor of Arts degree in biology. Drawn to art, he switched to the School of the Art Institute of Chicago, where he earned a Master of Fine Arts degree. Bankston moved to San Francisco, California, in 1994 and took a studio for his work at the artists' colony at Hunters Point Naval Shipyard.

His paintings were exhibited at the Yerba Buena Center for the Arts in 1999, where they were seen by Thelma Golden, deputy director of the Studio Museum in Harlem, New York City. Golden was researching a show for her museum featuring new black artists and was attracted to Bankston's work, which she called "irreverent, heartfelt, and very sincere."

The Harlem show, "Freestyle," opened in April 2001 and featured Bankston's 17-drawing series entitled *The Capture and Escape of Mr. M, Chapter 1.* The colorful narrative followed the progress of Mr. M, an Everyman fond of alcohol, who is abducted by space aliens, only to be rescued by a menagerie of animals right out of a folk tale by the Brothers Grimm. The work, according to the artist, draws on both the world of the Internet and the tradition of slave narratives, which he compares to an "out-of-body experience."

The coloring book outline of his characters gives Bankston's work a pop culture look. "I like the way they combine painting and drawing, figurative and abstract," Bankston says of coloring books. "The line delineates the form, and the color can work with or against it."

He received a 2001 Art Council Grant and was the recipient of a 2002 SECA Award from the San Francisco Museum of Modern Art. The exhibit *John Bankston: Locating Desire,* an installation of 20 works on paper, was mounted at San Francisco's de Young Museum in 2006. In 2009, Bankston was Jack Drake Visiting Artist at the University of Alabama in Birmingham. Bankston's work—humorous and thoughtful, innocent and knowing—has made him one of the more interesting contemporary African-American painters. "I like to think of fantasy as a way of re-imagining our world," Bankston has said. "It is a means of stepping outside of one's known territory and breaking boundaries."

Further Reading

Camhi, Leslie. "Satyrs, Slaves, and Monsters in the Colors of Childhood." *New York Times,* March 18, 2001, Arts and Leisure Section, p. 36.

Cornell, Daniell. "John Bankston: Locating Desire." Available online. URL: http://tfaoi.com/aa/6aa/6aa245.htm. Downloaded March 25, 2009.

"John Bankston: Temptation and Desire." Absolute arts.com. Available online. URL: http://www.absolutearts.com/artnews/2002/03/201/29758.html. Downloaded February 28, 2003.

San Francisco Museum of Modern Art. *2002 SECA Art Award: John Bankston, Andrea Higgins, Chris Johnson, Will Rogan.* San Francisco Museum of Modern Art, 2003.

Bannister, Edward Mitchell
(1828–1901) *painter*

A major American landscape painter of the second half of the 19th century, Edward Mitchell Bannister created work that exudes a tranquility and strength and reflects his determination in the face of prejudice and racism.

He was born in November 1828, the exact date of his birth being unknown, at St. Andrews in New Brunswick, Canada. His father was a black man from the Caribbean island of Barbados. His mother was possibly a white Canadian. Bannister liked to draw as a child, and he would copy family portraits on fences and barn doors. After completing school, he went to sea as a ship's cook. His experiences at sea fostered a deep love of the ocean, which is reflected in some of his finest paintings.

By 1850, he was living in Boston, Massachusetts, where he worked as a janitor in a barbershop, a hairdresser, and a handyman. In his free time, Bannister pursued painting, studying at the Lowell Institute and taking a studio in the Boston Studio Building. The white students at Lowell ignored him and at times made his life miserable. But he refused to give up on a career as a painter and studied privately with sculptor and anatomist Dr. William Rimmer of the Art Academy. Bannister sold his first painting, *The Ship Outward Bound,* to African-American physician John V.

One of the first African-American artists to gain wide recognition, Edward Mitchell Bannister was a leading landscape painter of the late 19th century. *(The Anthony Barboza Collection)*

DeGrasse in 1854. However, he could not yet earn a living as an artist, so he kept working at other jobs.

In 1857, he married wigmaker and hairdresser Christiana Cartreaux, a Narragansett Indian. After years of struggling to be a successful artist, Bannister read an article in *The New York Herald Tribune* in 1867 that distressed him greatly. The author declared that "the Negro seems to have an appreciation for art while being manifestly unable to produce it." Bannister was determined more than ever to prove the falseness of such statements.

He and his wife moved to Providence, Rhode Island, in 1870, hoping to make a fresh start in his career. Bannister quickly became an active member of the art community and was one of seven founding members of the Providence Art Club in 1873, which is still in existence today. It is the oldest art club in the country, out of which grew the Rhode Island School of Design, one of the most prominent art schools in the United States. Christiana Bannister took a keen interest in social work and helped found the Bannister Nursing Care Center, also still in existence.

In 1876, Bannister entered his monumental landscape *Under the Oaks* in the Philadelphia Centennial Exhibition. The painting, which depicted cows and sheep taking shelter under oak trees during a storm, won the exhibition's bronze medal. But when the joyful Bannister arrived in Philadelphia to collect his prize, the judges were flabbergasted to learn their winning artist was a black man. They quickly decided to withdraw his prize and give it to another painter. When the other artists in the exhibition heard this, they threatened to withdraw their work unless Bannister was given his rightful due. The judges relented and gave him the bronze medal.

The prize gained Bannister the recognition he had long sought. He was suddenly in great demand as an artist and received numerous commissions. For the first time in his life, he was financially secure enough to devote himself full-time to painting. He earned enough money to buy a yacht and sail across Narragansett Bay, sketching the sea. *Under the Oaks*, which was sold for $1,500 to John Duff of Boston, unfortunately disappeared sometime around 1900 and is now lost.

As Bannister's fame grew, his art matured. The romantic landscapes of earlier years were replaced by bolder, highly impressionistic paintings with few details. Yet Bannister's landscapes remained for the most part depictions of nature at peace. Humans rarely appeared, and when they did they were tiny figures, all but lost in the rich panorama of nature's world. Bannister's work bears not a hint of racial identity, but the very act of a black artist rising to the top of his profession was statement enough. His total output is estimated at 1,000 paintings.

Edward Bannister died from a heart attack on January 9, 1901, during a prayer meeting at his church. The members of the Providence Art Club held an exhibition of 101 of his paintings shortly afterward as a tribute to their friend and colleague. "This pure and lofty soul . . ." reads the monument at his grave, "who, while he portrayed nature, walked with God."

Today, Bannister's majestic landscapes and other works can be viewed at the Rhode Island School of Design, the Providence Art Club, and the Howard University Art Gallery in Washington, D.C.

Further Reading

Bearden, Romare, and Harry Henderson. *A History of African-American Artists: From 1792 to the Present.* New York: Pantheon Books, 1993, pp. 40–51.

"Edward Mitchell Bannister." Rhode Island College Web site. Available online. URL: http://www.ric.edu/BANNISTER/about_emb.php. Downloaded February 26, 2009.

Jennings, Corrine. *Edward Mitchell Bannister.* New York: Whitney Museum, 1992.

Lewis, Samella. *African American Art and Artists.* Berkeley: University of California Press, 2003, pp. 29–33.

Perry, Regenia A. *Free Within Ourselves: African-American Artists in the Collection of the National Museum of American Art.* San Francisco: Pomegranate Communications, 1992, pp. 22–27.

Barboza, Anthony
(1944–) *photographer*

A self-taught photographer with wide-ranging interests, Anthony Barboza has excelled in the worlds of documentary, commercial, fashion, and editorial photography.

He was born on May 10, 1944, in New Bedford, Massachusetts. Interested in photography in his youth, he studied under ROY DeCARAVA at the Kamoinge Workshop for black photographers in 1964 and served as a photographer in the U.S. Navy from 1965 to 1968. After his discharge, Barboza opened a commercial photography studio in New York City in 1969. By the 1970s, he was a leading commercial and fashion photographer, counting among his clients Coca-Cola, Adidas, Miramax Films, and the United Negro College Fund.

Barboza was awarded New York State Council on the Arts grants in 1974 and 1976. A National Endowment for the Arts grant in 1980 allowed him to self-publish his acclaimed collection of black-and-white portraits *Black Borders*, with a text by his brother Steven Barboza and the writer Ntozake Shange. Among the celebrities pictured and bordered in black, hence the title, were African-American jazz musicians like Lester Bowie and writers such as James Baldwin and Amiri Baraka. Anthony Barboza was the recipient of a New York Foundation for the Arts grant in 2002.

Barboza's work as a fashion and editorial photographer has appeared in *Sports Illustrated, New Yorker, Harpers Bazaar, Life, Vogue,* and *New York Times Magazine.* His images are in the permanent collection of the Museum of Modern Art in New York and the Museum of Fine Arts in Houston, Texas, among others. His photographs have also been featured in numerous published works,

Anthony Barboza has successfully combined a career as a commercial and a fine art photographer. *(Eccles)*

including *African Americans* (1993), *Jazz* (2000), *Committed to the Image* (2001), and *Day in the Life of Africa* (2002). Barboza is currently president of the Kamoinge Workshop.

"All photography is autobiographical," Barboza has said. "If you look beyond the subject matter, the photo reveals more about the photographer."

Photographs from his latest project, "Black Dreams/White Sheets," were exhibited at the Bill Hodges Gallery in New York City in late 2010. "These images possess—psychologically and spiritually—the essence of us, living in America," Barboza says. "They don't try to answer all questions but they are meant to demand a response, whether positive or negative."

Further Reading
"Anthony Barboza." Answers.com. Available online. URL: http://www.answers.com/topic/anthony-barboza. Downloaded March 24, 2009.

Barboza, Anthony, and Carol Patterson, photographers, Marlene Perchinske, ed. *Commitment: Fatherhood in Black America*. Columbia: University of Missouri Press, 1998.

Barboza Studio Web site. Available online. URL: http://www.barbozastudio.com/. Downloaded March 24, 2009.

The Candid Frame 96—Anthony Barboza. Available online. URL: http://www.thecandidframe.com/. Downloaded August 10, 2010.

Barthé, Richmond
(1901–1989) *sculptor*

Perhaps the most successful African-American sculptor of the 20th century, and one of the first black artists to support himself solely by his art, Richmond Barthé was a master of capturing the human figure in all its beauty and dynamism.

He was born on January 28, 1901, in Bay St. Louis, Mississippi. His father died when he was an infant. He showed an early aptitude for art and was painting by age six. In his teens, Barthé went to New Orleans, Louisiana, where he worked for a wealthy family he had known in Bay St. Louis. Denied admission to an art school in New Orleans because he was black, he later attended the School of the Art Institute of Chicago in 1924. His tuition was paid by a Roman Catholic priest who believed in his talent. At first, Barthé was a painter, but he switched to sculpture after a teacher encouraged him to make some clay models to strengthen his painting.

A sensitive, handsome young man who worked in a realistic style that the general public could appreciate, Barthé quickly gained commissions for portraits and busts from wealthy Chicagoans. He was one of the first black artists to focus on black people as his main subject. This made him popular during the Harlem Renaissance, a flowering of black art, music, and literature in the 1920s.

Barthé favored famous people in his work and was praised for his portraits in clay of Haitian revolutionary Toussaint Louverture and such contemporary blacks as educator Booker T. Washington and scientist George Washington Carver. He was also strongly attracted to the theater and dance. He even joined a modern dance troupe to get a better understanding of the art. Barthé's many sculptures of dancers flow with energy and movement. Perhaps his best-known piece, however, is *The Boxer* (1942), which shows the dance-like agility of a prizefighter.

Rarely did social issues surface in Barthé's work. An outstanding exception is *Supplication* (1939), which depicts a black woman holding the body of her lynched son. It was exhibited at the 1939 New York World's Fair and unfortunately was destroyed a year later in a shipping accident.

During World War II (1939–45), Barthé reached the peak of his fame, held up by white society as an example of how a black man could succeed in the United States in spite of racism and segregation. Barthé's celebrity and his fondness for social status alienated him from many other black artists who were more critical of American society.

Many American sculptors turned to abstract forms after the war, and Barthé's traditional sculpture fell out of style. He continued to work, however, creating an ambitious series of sculptures of famous actors in their signature roles. The series was not well-received by critics or the public. Many people found the spark of personality and expressiveness exhibited in his earlier work missing in these sculptures.

Disillusioned and overstressed by life in New York City, Barthé moved to Jamaica in the West Indies, where he lived contentedly among such old friends as English playwright Noel Coward. He continued to sell his sculptures to wealthy tourists and his home became an island landmark.

In the 1960s, Barthé moved to Florence, Italy, but grew lonely in his old age for the United States. He moved to Southern California, where, unable to obtain Social Security because he never had a regular job, Barthé lived in genteel poverty.

He was befriended by actor James Garner, who helped pay his rent and his hospital bills when the artist became terminally ill. One of the last sculptures Barthé completed was a portrait of Garner, to whom he willed all his work. Richmond Barthé died at age 88 on March 5, 1989.

Garner turned over Barthé's sculptures to the director of the newly opened Museum of African American Art in Los Angeles. Although Barthé is no longer considered one of the greatest of black artists, his sculptures retain their power and beauty.

"All of my life I have been interested in trying to capture the spiritual quality I see and feel in people," he once wrote, "and I feel that the human figure as God made it is the best means of expressing this spirit in man."

Further Reading

Bearden, Romare, and Harry Henderson. *A History of African-American Artists: From 1792 to the Present.* New York: Pantheon Books, 1993, pp. 136–146.

Black, Patti Carr. *American Masters of the Mississippi Gulf Coast: George Ohr, Duysti Bonge, Walter Anderson, Richmond Barthé.* Jackson: University Press of Mississippi, 2008.

Kranz, Rachel, and Philip J. Koslow. *The Biographical Dictionary of African Americans.* New York: Facts On File, 1999, pp. 21–22, 155.

Vendryes, Margaret Rose. *Barthé: A Life in Sculpture.* Jackson: University Press of Mississippi, 2008.

Basquiat, Jean-Michel

(1960–1988) *graffiti artist, painter*

One of the most celebrated and influential African-American artists of the 1980s, Jean-Michel Basquiat began spray-painting his art on the walls of buildings and ended up selling his paintings in the finest galleries in the United States and Europe.

He was born in Brooklyn, New York, on December 22, 1960. His father was a Haitian and his mother was of Puerto Rican descent. Contrary to what Basquiat led the world to believe, his family was upper middle class, not poor. He attended an alternative high school for gifted but troubled students and left home a year before graduating. He lived with friends in lower Manhattan, selling hand-painted postcards and T-shirts on the streets. His main activity, however, was spray-painting graffiti on buildings and in subway cars with his friend Al Diaz. Their work was cryptic and consisted of weird stick figures, African-like face masks, and crowns, often accompanied by unexplained words and phrases. They signed their work SAMO, and it quickly attracted the interest of the New York art world.

When Basquiat's identity was finally revealed, he was embraced as a new, rising artist and a leader of the neoexpressionist movement of painting. In 1980, he participated in his first group exhibit in a vacant building in the Times Square district of Manhattan. In 1982, poet and artist Rene Ricard published an article about Basquiat called "The Radiant Child" in *Artforum* magazine that gained national attention. Basquiat gradually abandoned his graffiti and painted his figures on canvas, selling them from his tenement apartment.

Many critics hailed him as a genius whose work contained biting social commentary on black and white relations. Other critics dismissed him as a fraud whose celebrity owed more to the unusual circumstances surrounding his discovery and his skin color. They attributed his success to good marketing, not artistic excellence. But the controversy only made Basquiat more famous and successful. He had solo shows in New York and Europe, and his paintings sold for huge sums. He became friends with pop artist Andy Warhol, and they collaborated on a series of paintings.

As Basquiat's fame grew, his art became less daring and his stark stick people were replaced by cartoon figures. "Largely linear with shapes colored in," wrote art critic Laurie Fitzpatrick, "these canvases boldly go nowhere."

Jean-Michel Basquiat began his meteoric career as a graffiti artist on the streets of New York City, as seen in this still from the documentary film *Downtown 81.* *(Photofest)*

Basquiat traveled to Africa in 1986 and had a show in Abidjan, Ivory Coast. Another major exhibition was held at a museum in Hannover, Germany, where he was the youngest artist ever to be exhibited.

The outlaw lifestyle that helped thrust Basquiat into the limelight finally caught up with him. Unable to deal with his sudden fame and the money it brought, Basquiat became more reckless in his use of drugs. Taking drugs made him paranoid; he constantly feared that art dealers were cheating him and that people wanted to steal his paintings. He finally died of an overdose of cocaine and heroin on August 12, 1988, at age 27.

Basquiat's art and his short but event-filled life continue to fascinate. The biographical film *Basquiat,* directed by his friend and fellow artist Julian Schnabel, was released in 1996. Actor Jeffrey Wright played the artist, and rock singer David Bowie portrayed Andy Warhol. A documentary *Jean-Michel Basquiat: The Radiant Child,* directed by Tamra Davis, was released in 2010.

While critical opinion on Basquiat's work is still sharply divided, the power of his paintings, especially in the early stages of his career, is widely acknowledged. "Their collective energy, and in many cases, their explanation of an African American people, entitle them to serious study," writes art historian Richard J. Powell.

Further Reading

Chiappini, Rudy. *Jean-Michel Basquiat.* Milan, Italy: Skira, 2005.

Cortez, Diego, and others. *Jean-Michel Basquiat, the Studio of the Street.* New York: Chantal Deitch Projects, 2007.

Hoban, Phoebe. *Basquiat: A Quick Killing in Art.* New York: Penguin, 1999.

Marshall, Richard. *Jean-Michel Basquiat.* New York: Abrams, 1992.

Mayer, Marc, Jean-Michel Basquiat, and Fred Hoffman. *Basquiat.* London: Merrell, 2005.

O'Brien, Glenn, and Annette Lager. *The Jean-Michel Basquiat Show.* Milan, Italy: Skira, 2007.

Further Viewing

Basquiat (1996). Miramax Home Entertainment, VHS/DVD, 1998/2002.

Downtown 81 (1981). Zeitgeist Films, VHS/DVD, 2002.

Battey, C. M.

(Cornelius Marion Battey)
(1873–1927) *photographer*

Considered the first African-American photographer to raise photography from a craft to a fine art, C. M. Battey created idealized photographs of both famous and ordinary black people that are still treasured today.

He was born Cornelius Marion Battey in 1873, in Augusta, Georgia, but his family moved north when he was still a child. His first professional job was working in an architect's office in Indianapolis, Indiana. Interested in photography, which was still a new medium, Battey got a job in a Cleveland, Ohio, photography studio. He later moved to New York City, where for six years he was superintendent of the Bradley Photographic Studio on Fifth Avenue. He went to work at the city's most famous photographic company, Underwood and Underwood, where he was put in charge of the retouching department.

Battey finally got the opportunity to work on his own. With a partner he opened the Battey and Warren Studio in New York. Battey's pictures were characterized by their use of soft focus and his painstaking retouching of prints and negatives with pencil or pen. The retouching enhanced the portrait and gave it a clean and soft look. The photographers working in this style were known as pictorialists, and Battey was one of the best pictorialists in New York City.

His work led him into a valuable friendship with black author and educator W. E. B. DuBois, one of the founders of the National Association for the Advancement of Colored People (NAACP). DuBois was also editor of the NAACP's official magazine, *The Crisis.* Soon Battey's portraits of well-known black leaders were appearing regularly on the covers of *The Crisis.*

In 1916, Battey was invited to take over the photography department of the Tuskegee Institute in Tuskegee, Alabama. The first black institute of higher learning in the nation, Tuskegee was founded by famed educator and social thinker Booker T. Washington in 1881. Washington saw Tuskegee as a place where young black people could learn a trade or profession that would make them economically independent. He established a photography department for this purpose. "A colored man would have almost as good an opportunity to succeed as a white man . . . [in the field of photography]," he wrote in a letter to photographic inventor George Eastman.

Washington died the year before Battey arrived at Tuskegee, and Battey photographed the construction and dedication of a monument erected to the school's founder. At Tuskegee, Battey not only taught photography but also chronicled in pictures the life of the campus. His hundreds of photographs of Tuskegee included candid shots of students in class, on the playing fields, and in job training classes. His photographs serve today as an invaluable record of black university life in the early 20th century.

Battey's growing fame as a photographer led him to take portraits of such national figures as President Calvin Coolidge and Chief Justice of the Supreme Court William Howard Taft. While at Tuskegee, he published *Our Heroes of Destiny,* a series of portraits of outstanding African-Americans, including abolitionist and statesman

Frederick Douglass, Booker T. Washington, and poet Paul Laurence Dunbar. These portraits were later mass-produced in postcard format and sold to thousands of black people across the nation.

Battey died at Tuskegee in 1927 at age 54. The black journal *Opportunity* summed up his artistic achievement in an editorial that described his life "as one increasing struggle to liberate, through a rigid medium, the fluid graces of an artist's soul. For paintbrush and palette, he used a lens and shutter."

Further Reading

Sullivan, George. *Black Artists in Photography, 1840–1940.* New York: Cobblehill Books, 1996, pp. 71–82.

Willis, Deborah. *Reflections in Black: A History of Black Photographers from 1840 to the Present.* New York: W. W. Norton, 2002, pp. 14, 37, 38–39, 44–45, 46, 47, 49–53.

Bearden, Romare
(Fred Romare Howard Bearden)
(1911–1988) *painter, collagist, printmaker, art historian*

A major innovator in American 20th-century art, Romare Bearden plumbed the African-American experience in a wide range of styles from social realism to abstract expressionism to his own unique collage-paintings.

He was born Fred Romare Howard Bearden on September 2, 1911, into a middle-class black family in Charlotte, North Carolina. The family moved to New York City when he was nine and settled in the Harlem section. His father was a sanitation inspector for the city, and his mother Bessye was the New York editor of the *Chicago Defender,* the nation's leading African-American newspaper.

Bessye Bearden was also a social activist, an intellectual, and the first president of the Negro Women's Democratic Association. The Bearden apartment was a gathering place for leading members of the Harlem Renaissance, a rebirth of African-American arts. They included actors, jazz musicians, and such artists as AARON DOUGLAS and CHARLES H. ALSTON.

Bearden's initial interests lay in different directions. He was an outstanding baseball player in high school and enrolled in New York University, where he majored in mathematics. He also enjoyed drawing, and was a cartoonist for the school humor magazine. After graduating in 1935, he decided to pursue a career as an artist and joined the Harlem Artists Guild and a group of black artists who called themselves 306. The group's unusual name came from the address of their gathering place, Charles H. Alston's apartment at 306 West 141st Street. Bearden also studied with renowned German-born artist George Grosz at New York's Art Students League.

To support himself, Bearden took a job as a social worker for the city of New York. He would remain in this position until 1966. His early paintings were realistic depictions of Harlem street life and scenes from his southern childhood. In 1940, he had his first solo exhibition at 306 and became recognized as one of the leading African-American artists in New York.

In 1942, Bearden enlisted in the army and served in World War II (1939–45). On his discharge in 1945, he returned to painting. His series *Passion of Christ* was exhibited in his first solo show in a Manhattan art gallery. In the busy postwar art world, he began to lose his footing, unable to decide on what direction his work should take or even if he should continue as an artist at all. In 1950, Bearden went to Paris, France, where he studied philosophy for a year. He returned to New York to pursue a career as a songwriter and had some success.

In 1953, still uncertain of his future, Bearden suffered a nervous breakdown. He recovered and married the dancer and choreographer Nanette Rohan. She encouraged him to return to painting. He embraced abstract expressionism, a nonrepresentational style of painting based largely on spontaneous expression, in the late 1950s. However,

A major figure in 20th-century American art, Romare Bearden also cowrote a definitive history of African-American art. *(Anthony Barboza)*

Bearden was not satisfied with this style and looked for a strong philosophy to base his art on. He finally found it in Spiral, a group of 15 black artists who came together in 1963. They believed artists should use their talents to better society.

Inspired by this idea, Bearden began to create collages, pasting different materials to the surface of his paintings to create a unique effect. He cut up photographs and combined them in intricate designs, often with acrylic paintings and drawings. In other works, he enlarged photographs to life-size. "Bearden's choppy photocollages of the 1960s and 1970s," wrote art historian Crystal Britton, "were the visual metaphors of struggle—both the African American's and the black artist's."

Bearden had strong ideas about what the goals and methods of the African-American artist should be, and he began to explain his ideas in articles and books. *The Painter's Mind: A Study of the Relation of Structure and Space in Painting* (1969), his first book, was written with artist Carl Holty. Bearden also became a chronicler of the history of African-American art, which was largely ignored by the white establishment. He wrote two books on black artists with journalist Harry Henderson, devoting 15 years of research and writing to the second, the monumental *A History of African-American Artists*. The book was completed by Henderson after Bearden's death in 1988.

Bearden's own work grew more monumental in the late 1970s. He produced several splendid series of paintings. *The Odysseus* (1977) reinterpreted the ancient Greek myth of Odysseus, who suffers through various adventures on his sea journey home, using one dominant color. His *Jazz* series (1980) dealt with great black jazz musicians whom Bearden admired. A trip to his wife's home island of St. Martin in the West Indies resulted in an important series of colorful watercolors of Caribbean people, landscapes, and seascapes.

By now, Bearden was considered one of the masters of African-American art and its leading spokesperson. He was elected to the American Academy of Arts and Letters and the National Institute of Arts and Letters in 1966. In 1987, he received the president's National Medal of the Arts. He died the following year in March of cancer at age 77. In 2003–04, the National Gallery of Art held a major retrospective.

"My intention," Romare Bearden once said about his art, "is to reveal through pictorial complexities the life I know."

Further Reading

Bearden, Romare, and Carl Holty. *The Painter's Mind: A Study of the Relation of Structure and Space in Painting.* New York: Garland Publishing, 1981.

Fine, Ruth E. *The Art of Romare Bearden.* New York: Harry N. Abrams, 2003.

O'Meally, Robert, and Romare Bearden. *Romare Bearden: A Black Odyssey.* New York: A.C. Moore Gallery, 2008.

Schwartzman, Myron. *Romare Bearden: Celebrating the Victory.* London: Franklin Watts, 2000.

Trout, Victoria. *Conjuring Bearden.* Durham, N.C.: Duke University Press, 2006.

Further Viewing

The Art of Romare Bearden (2003). Homevision DVD, 2004.

Bey, Dawoud

(David Edward Smikle)
(1953–) *photographer, educator*

One of today's leading portrait photographers, Dawoud Bey captures the psychological makeup of his subjects in large-scale color photographs.

Born David Edward Smikle on November 25, 1953, in Jamaica, Queens, New York, he knew he wanted to be a photographer after viewing the landmark exhibition *Harlem on My Mind* at the Metropolitan Museum of Art in Manhattan at age 15. He was particularly impressed by the photographs of black photographer JAMES VAN DER ZEE. Barely out of his teens, Smikle began photographing African Americans on the streets of Harlem. This would become his own tribute to that New York City neighborhood. He changed his name to Dawoud Bey in the early 1970s. In 1979, *Harlem, USA* became his first solo exhibition at the Studio Museum in Harlem. Already an established photographer praised for capturing the personality of ordinary people in his pictures, Bey began attending Empire State College, part of the State University of New York system in, 1986. He graduated with a Bachelor of Arts degree in photography in 1990. He went on to earn a Master of Fine Arts degree from Yale University's School of Arts in New Haven, Connecticut, in 1993.

The previous year, Bey began to photograph students from different high schools during a residency at the Addison Gallery of American Art on the campus of Phillips Academy in Andover, Massachusetts. He was interested in exploring through portraiture the differences and commonalities among students from different social, economic, and ethnic backgrounds. For the next 15 years, Bey crossed the nation, visiting various high schools for several weeks to photograph students

Dawoud Bey uses his photography to both reflect and contest the stereotypes and images that exist in popular culture. *(Anthony Barboza)*

in classrooms in 45-minute sessions. Before starting each session, he had each subject write a brief autobiographical statement. Text and photographs accompanied each other in an exhibition, *Class Pictures*, mounted as a four-year-long traveling show beginning in 2007. The exhibition was published as a book that same year. "My interest in young people has to do with the fact that they are the arbiters of style in the community; their appearance speaks most strongly of how a community of people defines themselves at a particular historical moment," Bey has said.

His photographs are part of the permanent collections of the Brooklyn Museum; the Schomburg Center for Research in Black Culture, Manhattan; and the Bibliotheque Nationale, in Paris, France. He is a professor of photography at Columbia College in Chicago, where he lives. Bey was the commencement speaker at the Yale University School of Art 2010 graduation.

Further Reading

Bey, Dawoud, Jacqueline Terrassa, Stephanie Smith, and Elizabeth Meister. *Dawoud Bey: The Chicago Project*. Chicago: Smart Museum of Art, the University of Chicago, 2004.

Bey, Dawoud, Jock Reynolds, and Taro Nettleton. *Dawoud Bey: Class Pictures*. New York: Aperture, 2007.

Coleman, A. D., and Dawoud Bey. *Dawoud Bey: Portraits 1975–1995*. Minneapolis, Minn.: Walker Art Center, 1995.

"Dawoud Bey." Museum of Contemporary Photography. Available online. URL: http://www.mocp.org/collections/permanent/bey_dawoud.php. Downloaded March 18, 2009.

"What's Going On?—Dawoud Bey's Blog." Available online. URL: http://whatsgoingon-dawoudbeysblog.blogspot.com/2008_07_01_archive.html. Downloaded March 19, 2009.

Bibbs, Garry

(1960–) *printmaker, sculptor, educator*

A playful surrealist who mixes the fantastic with the everyday in his colorful monoprints and fantastical sculptures, Garry Bibbs is the creator of a style he calls "funk art."

He was born in Athens, Alabama, on January 26, 1960, the first of five children. His father, Willie Dean Bibbs, is a bricklayer and carpenter who taught him how to work with his hands. The family moved to Louisville, Kentucky, when Bibbs was still very young. He later played football at Seneca High School in Louisville and for a time wanted to be both a pro football player and an artist.

He attended Kentucky State University in Frankfort on an art scholarship and earned a Bachelor of Science degree in 1983. While at Kentucky State, he took a course from a professor from California that changed the direction of his art. "His [the professor's] California influence suddenly opened my eyes," he has said. "It was really bright, real active and colorful; just some things that I could really relate to."

Bibbs received a Master of Fine Arts degree from the University of Kentucky in Lexington in 1985. The following year he attended the School of the Art Institute of Chicago, where he studied under sculptor RICHARD H. HUNT. Soon he was creating monoprints rich in color with characters and landscapes from his fertile imagination. A typical work is *House Party* (1988), which, according to artist and writer SAMELLA LEWIS, "adopts a playful, emotional approach creating figures that float, dance and play against a graffiti environment."

Bibbs has created a number of public sculptures in Louisville, including the Kentucky Civil Rights Hall of Fame sculpture in 2000 for the 40th anniversary of the Kentucky Commission on Human Rights. His print *They've Killed the King* was featured in the Smithsonian Institution's traveling exhibit *In the Spirit of Martin: The Living Legacy of Dr. Martin Luther King, Jr.* in 2001. He said the inspiration for the print came to him while visiting the Lorraine Motel in Memphis, where the civil rights leader was assassinated in 1968. Bibbs's solo exhibition, "Bibbs, Black Steel and Color," was held at Louisville's Gallerie Hertz the same year.

In 2003, Bibbs was awarded a commission by the Kentucky Arts Council to create a public sculpture in downtown Louisville to represent the spirit of transportation. The work, *Now Get*, composed of an arched gateway topped by a flying automobile, was completed in August 2006.

Garry Bibbs has been associate professor and head of the sculpture department at the University of Kentucky since 1990. He is also director of graduate studies, Art Studio, and served on the Arts Administrative Advisory Council from 1997 to 2000.

"You do not walk up to my stuff, look and walk away," he said in an interview. "That's the strength of a fine arts piece, if you ask me."

Further Reading

Davis, Merlene. "His Heart's in His Work: Garry Bibbs Reveals Himself Through Art." *Lexington Herald-Leader,* April 28, 2002, p. J3.

Garry Bibbs Official Web site. Available online. URL: http://www.garrybibbsart.com/pages/welcome.html. Downloaded March 29, 2009.

Lewis, Samella. *African-American Art and Artists.* Berkeley: University of California Press, 2002, p. 275.

Biggers, John
(John Thomas Biggers)
(1924–2001) *painter, sculptor, muralist, illustrator, educator*

One of the first African-American artists to regularly visit Africa and incorporate its art into his own work, John Biggers was a leading contemporary artist and teacher for more than five decades.

He was born on April 13, 1924, in Gastonia, North Carolina, the youngest of seven children. His father was a teacher and shoemaker. When Biggers first attended Hampton Institute in Virginia in 1941, it was with the idea of becoming a plumber. But an art course taught by art chairman Viktor Lowenfeld steered him toward fine art. Lowenfeld became his mentor, encouraging Biggers to delve deeply into his African-American cultural roots for inspiration. He went on to Pennsylvania State University in 1946, following Lowenfeld there, and earned a Bachelor of Arts degree and Master of Arts degree in art education. In 1948, Biggers married his wife Hazel, a fellow student.

In 1949, at age 25, Biggers was offered the rare opportunity to start an art department at Texas State University for Negroes in Houston, Texas, later to become Texas Southern University (TSU). It was at TSU that Biggers first developed as an artist. In 1950, he began the first of four ambitious murals in African-American communities in Texas. He went on to create more than 20 major murals, many of them in the Southwest. He also illustrated a collection of African-American Texan folklore, *Aunt Dicey Tales.*

Biggers traveled to West Africa under a United Nations Educational, Scientific and Cultural Organization (UNESCO) fellowship in 1957. It was a trip that would alter his life and art. He visited Ghana, Dahomey, Nigeria, and Togo, absorbing the art and culture of each nation and its people. He wrote about his experience in *Ananse, Web of Life in Africa* (1962), a pioneering work in African-American literature. "*Ananse* became a means by which African Americans learned about, and took pride in, their heritage and armed themselves for cultural battle," wrote art critic Alvia J. Wardlaw. Among his murals that reflect the artist's fascination with African symbols and signs is *The Rites of Passage,* commissioned by the Houston Music Hall. Among the everyday symbols he used in this and other works are such domestic items as an anvil, iron washbasin, and fireplace. Biggers also became a major collector of African art, as well as African-American folk art and crafts.

Following a five-year bout with a serious illness in the early 1970s, he returned to painting, his work becoming more noticeably abstract. He retired from TSU after 36 years in 1983 and devoted himself to painting. The influence of African art can be clearly seen in such works as *Starry Crowns* (1987), which refers to both the beautifully colorful headdresses of the African women depicted and the title of a Negro spiritual.

In 1990, Biggers returned to his alma mater, now named Hampton University, as an artist-in-residence and moved back to his hometown of Gastonia. He was the recipient of the Harbison Award for Distinguished Teaching (1968).

"The role of art is to express the triumph of the human spirit over the mundane and material," Biggers wrote. "It is also to express the universal myth and archetypes of the universal family of man." John Biggers died of a heart attack on January 25, 2001, at his home in Houston. He was 75 years old.

Further Reading

Biggers, John. *Ananse: The Web of Life in Africa*. Austin: The University of Texas Press, 1996.

———. *John Biggers: My America: The 1940s and 1950s—Paintings, Sculpture and Drawings*. New York: Michael Rosenfeld Gallery, 2004.

Perry, Regenia A. *Free Within Ourselves: African-American Artists in the Collection of the National Museum of American Art*. San Francisco, Calif.: Pomegranate Communications, 1992, pp. 36–39.

Theisen, Olive Jensen, and John Biggers. *A Life on Paper: The Drawings of John Thomas Biggers*. Denton: University of North Texas Press, 2006.

Wardlaw, Alvia J., ed. *The Art of John Biggers: View from the Upper Room*. New York: Harry N. Abrams, 1995.

Billingsley, Ray
(1957–) *cartoonist*

Creator of the popular comic strip *Curtis*, about an 11-year-old black boy and his family, Ray Billingsley uses humor to humanize the black urban experience.

He was born in Wake Forest, North Carolina, on July 25, 1957, and later moved with his family to the Harlem section of New York City. A precocious artist, Billingsley got his first professional job at age 12 as an artist for *Kids* magazine. He attended the High School of Music and Art in New York and won a full scholarship to the prestigious School of Visual Arts there. He studied with the legendary comic book artist Will Eisner, creator of the visual masterpiece *The Spirit*.

After graduating, Billingsley got a job as an intern at the Walt Disney Studio in California. He created his first comic strip, *Lookin' Fine*, in 1978 when he was 21. It was syndicated by United Features Syndicate and ran for nearly three years. After that Billingsley became a freelance artist and created television commercials and animation for advertisers. One night he got the idea for his second comic strip. "It was 3:30 or 4, I didn't even turn on a light," he recalls. "I just sketched a little boy, and the next morning, there he was: Curtis."

The comic was picked up for syndication by King Features in 1988 and now appears in more than 250 newspapers seven days a week. In the strip, Curtis and his younger brother Barry live with their parents, Greg and Diana Wilkins, in a large American city. Other characters include Curtis's bizarre friend Gunk, a white transfer student from Flyspeck Island in the Bermuda Triangle; Michelle, the spoiled girl he loves; and Gunther, the know-it-all barber.

Billingsley bases *Curtis* on his own memories of growing up black. The tone and atmosphere of

One of only a handful of nationally syndicated African-American cartoonists, Ray Billingsley is the creator of *Curtis,* a funny but realistic comic strip about a black family in urban America. *(King Features Syndicate)*

the strip is grittier and more realistic than other African-American comic strips such as *Jump Start* and *Herb & Jamaal*. In one story line, Curtis's dad sets the family couch on fire with a cigarette. Every December, Billingsley departs from his regular story line and creates an original African folktale in honor of the African-American celebration of Kwanzaa.

Educators praise Billingsley for his warmth and humor as well as his honest handling of such inner-city problems as drug abuse and crime. He "always tries to influence his young readers in positive ways," says a spokesperson for King Features, "and presents an accurate picture of a family's struggle to survive the hardships of modern life."

In recognition of his story lines in which Curtis tries to get his father to quit smoking, Billingsley was presented with the American Lung Association's President's Award in 2000 during the American Lung Association/Canadian Lung Association conference in Toronto, Canada. The President's Award, which was first given in 1983, was created to acknowledge an individual, or nonprofit or commercial organization, responsible for an outstanding contribution in an area of importance to the goals of the American Lung Association. Billingsley also received the Humanitarian Award from the American Lung Association of Southeast Florida in 1999.

Two book-length collections of *Curtis* have been published. Billingsley, who is single, also enjoys painting, movies, music, time for quiet contemplation, and traveling (although he has a fear of flying). He is outspoken on the difficulties that he and other African-American cartoonists have in getting their work published in book form. His last *Curtis* collection appeared in 1993. "[A]n editor once told me that it was thought that blacks don't read and what white person would buy this for their kids?" Billingsley said in an 2007 interview. "We're appreciated, we're just not respected."

Ray Billingsley is the only black cartoonist to have had two syndicated comic strips about the black experience.

Further Reading

Andelman, Bob. "Mr. Media Interviews: Ray Billingsley." Available online. URL: http://www.media.com/2007/04/fridays-with-mr-media-ray.html. Downloaded June 22, 2008.

Billingsley, Ray. *Curtis.* New York: Ballantine Books, 1993.

———. *Curtis: Twist and Shout.* New York: Ballantine Books, 1993.

"Curtis." King Features Web site. Available online. URL: http://www.kingfeatures.com/features/comics/curtis/about.htm. Downloaded March 2, 2009.

Birch, Willie
(1942–) *mixed-media artist, muralist*

A creator of often complicated three-dimensional works that range from churches to courtyards, Willie Birch draws on the symbols and signs of African art and culture to express his feelings about the contemporary African-American experience.

He was born on November 26, 1942, in New Orleans, Louisiana. Birch first attended Southern University in Baton Rouge in 1960, but he did not earn his Bachelor of Arts degree until 1969 at Southern University's New Orleans campus, where he had his first individual exhibition in 1968. He received a Master of Fine Arts degree in 1973 from the Maryland Institute in Baltimore, Maryland.

Birch settled in Brooklyn, New York, and was artist-in-residence at the Studio Museum in Harlem in 1977 and 1978. He created two-dimensional collages of images and text and murals. Two of his better-known murals are in an Upper Manhattan subway station and the Philadelphia International Airport.

By the 1990s, he was creating three-dimensional works mostly out of papier-mâché, a substance made of paper pulp mixed with glue and other materials. Many of his works deal with racism and slavery, such as "Oppression Anywhere Is Oppression Everywhere," which features a nailed boot crushing the head of a black man.

Birch has traveled widely, and his trips to Africa, especially the nation of Kenya, led him to incorporate African culture and mysticism into his work. He uses clay figures of the Igbo people, called *mbair;* Kenyan cultural dress; and other features of African culture and religion to deepen the social and spiritual meaning of his art. He often incorporates text, signs, and found objects into his works as well.

One of Birch's most ambitious works is a courtyard with a mosaic flooring at the Crossroads Juvenile Center in Brooklyn, New York, completed in 1997. Called *If You Don't Know Where You Come From, How Do You Know Where You Are Going?* after a Ghanaian proverb, the work includes benches, tablets, and a circular map of the world. Birch meant the work to create a sense of hope and positive action for the center's youth and staff. Much of Birch's art contains this social message, going beyond racism and cultural differences to true communion. According to art critic A. M. Weaver, Willie Birch is "a modern-day shaman [tribal spiritual leader] . . . [who] combines multiple African traditions within an individual piece in an attempt to make contact with the spiritual realm."

Birch's most recent work focuses on his hometown of New Orleans, which he returned to in 1997 after living in New York City for two decades. His series of large charcoal drawings, *Celebrating Freedom* (2006), is a tribute to the culture of New Orleans and its people. His *Prospect 1*, a multipanel work of drawings, celebrates the people of his own Seventh Ward, a section of the city hit hard by Hurricane Katrina in 2005, and resides in the grand foyer of the New Orleans Museum of Art.

Birch is the recipient of a grant from the National Endowment for the Arts, a Lila Wallace International Artist fellowship, and a Guggenheim fellowship. His artworks are found in many museums, including the Metropolitan Museum of Art in New York City, the New Orleans Museum of Art, the Smith-Mason Gallery and Museum in Washington, D.C., and the Wilfredo Lam Center in Havana, Cuba.

Further Reading

Csaszar, Tom. "Willie Birch." *Sculpture*, April 15, 1996, pp. 59–60.
Riggs, Thomas, ed. *St. James Guide to Black Artists.* Detroit, Mich.: St. James Press, 1997, pp. 54–56.
Rubin, David. *Celebrating Freedom: The Art of Willie Birch.* Manchester, Vt.: Hudson Hills Press, 2006.
Thompson, Nato, Willie Birch, and others. *Waiting in New Orleans: A Reader by Paul Chan.* New York: Creative Time, 2008.

Blackburn, Bob

(Robert H. Blackburn)
(1920–2003) *printmaker, educator, arts administrator*

Bob Blackburn was a master printmaker whose Printing Workshop was a training ground and source of inspiration for black artists for five decades.

He was born Robert H. Blackburn on December 10, 1920, in Summit, New Jersey. He later moved with his family to New York City where he attended public schools. One of his English teachers was black poet Countee Cullen. While in junior high school, Blackburn got a job working at the Harmon Foundation, one of the most important benefactors of African-American artists in the 1930s and 1940s. After high school, Blackburn studied at the Art Students League and with sculptor AUGUSTA SAVAGE at her Harlem Community Art Center. Here he developed a strong interest in lithography, a method of producing an image on a flat prepared stone and taking ink impressions of the work. Part of his attraction to printmaking was that it provided a way to make original copies of an artwork and sell them inexpensively to people who could not afford the high price of a one-of-a-kind drawing or painting.

In February 1939, some of Blackburn's prints appeared in the group show "Contemporary Negro Art" at the Baltimore Museum of Art, a landmark show for black artists. His prints are noted for their fine detail and sharp observations. During the 1940s, he moved from the Harlem section of New York City downtown to the Chelsea section. Unable to find opportunities to show and sell his work, he founded the Bob Blackburn Printmaking Workshop on West 17th Street in 1948. The nonprofit workshop attracted other black artists who wanted to learn the various techniques of printmaking, including lithography, etching, and woodcut.

Blackburn was hired to teach art at the City College of New York in 1949. He went on to teach at many New York schools, including New York University, the Pratt Institute, and the School of Visual Arts. In 1970, he became a professor of art at Columbia University and remained there for 20 years.

Among the many awards Blackburn received are the Purchase Award of the Library of Congress, a Creative Artists Program Award, and the first Augusta Savage Memorial Award. In 1992, he was awarded a MacArthur Fellowship for lifetime achievement. His prints have been shown in many individual shows, including the IBM Gallery in New York City; the Howard University Gallery in Washington, D.C.; the Appalachian Gallery in Maryland; and the Asilah Festival in Morocco in Northern Africa.

Bob Blackburn died on April 20, 2003 in New York City. As an artist, teacher, and administrator, he was a guiding light in the world of American printmaking.

Further Reading

Barnet, Will. *Will Barnet, Bob Blackburn: An Artistic Friendship in Relief.* La Grange, Ga.: Cochran Collection, 1997.

Berlind, Robert. "Bob Blackburn: Interview." *Art Journal,* spring 1994.

"Fifty Years of Robert Blackburn's Printmaking Workshop." Creative Space. Available online. URL: http://www/loc.gov/exhibits/blackburn/. Downloaded March 2, 2009.

Parrish, Nina, and Harriet Green. *Robert Blackburn: A Life's Work.* New York: Alternative Press, 1990.

Riggs, Thomas, ed. *St. James Guide to Black Artists.* Detroit, Mich.: St. James Press, 1997, pp. 56–59.

Williams, Dave, and Reba Williams. *Alone in a Crowd: Prints of the 1930s and 1940s by African-American Artists from the Collection of Dave and Reba Williams.* Newark, N.J.: Newark Museum and Equitable Gallery, 1992.

Bond, J. Max, Jr.
(1935–2009) *architect, educator*

One of the few black architects to achieve national fame for buildings he designed from Ghana to Atlanta, Georgia, J. Max Bond, Jr., was also an inspiring teacher who served as a model for a new generation of minority architects.

He was born into a prominent African-American family on July 17, 1935, in Louisville, Kentucky. His father, J. Max Bond, Sr., was president of the University of Liberia in Africa in the 1950s. His mother Ruth was an educator and well-known quilter.

Bond attended Harvard University in Cambridge, Massachusetts, where he earned a Bachelor of Arts degree in 1955 and a Masters of Arts degree in 1958. While there, racists burned a cross outside his dormitory. This moved a faculty member to counsel him not to pursue his dream of becoming an architect. "There have never been any famous, prominent black architects," the teacher told him. "You'd be wise to choose another profession." But Bond, who had worked for a summer for black West Coast architect PAUL R. WILLIAMS, knew otherwise and continued doggedly with his studies.

One of a small number of prominent African-American architects, Max Bond, Jr., designed buildings throughout the United States and Ghana. *(Anthony Barboza)*

After leaving Harvard, Bond found few opportunities to work in his field and went to France, where he worked with architect Andre Wagenscky. He eventually found work with a New York architectural firm but traveled abroad again in 1964 to Ghana where for three years he designed buildings for the government. The most celebrated of these is the Bolgatana Regional Library, whose table-top roof provided natural ventilation without air-conditioning in the hot African climate.

Returning to America, Bond and Donald P. Ryder formed the firm Bond Ryder and Associates in 1970 in New York City. They became known for taking on projects that reflected Bond's African-American heritage and commitment to civil rights. These included the Martin Luther King, Jr., memorial and crypt in Atlanta, Georgia, and the Birmingham Civil Rights Institute in Alabama. But Bond became most associated with the many buildings he designed in the city where he worked and lived—New York. These include the Schomburg Center for Research in Black Culture and the redesigned Audubon

Ballroom—where Malcolm X was assassinated in 1965—both in Harlem. He also helped plan the September 11 memorial and designed the museum that was part of the project.

A brilliant teacher, Bond taught at Columbia University, where he was chairman of the architectural division at the Graduate School of Architecture and Planning from 1980 to 1984. He moved to City College in 1985 where he was dean of the School of Architecture and Environmental Studies until 1992.

J. Max Bond, Jr., died of cancer on February 18, 2009, in New York City at age 73. Socially committed to the poor and underprivileged, he said in a 2003 interview that "Architecture inevitably involves all the larger issues of society."

Further Reading

Craven, Jackie. "J. Max Bond, Jr. New York Visionary." About.com Architecture. Available online. URL: http://architecture.about.com/od/greatarchitects/p/bond.htm. Downloaded March 19, 2009.

Dunlap, David W. "J. Max Bond Jr., Architect, Dies at 73." *New York Times*, February 19, 2009, p. A20 [obituary].

Solomon, Nancy B., ed. *Architecture: Celebrating the Past, Designing the Future: Commemorating the 150th Anniversary of the American Institute of Architects.* New York: Visual Reference Publications, 2008, pp. 70–71, 84.

Booker, Chakaia
(1953–) *sculptor*

Calling herself "a narrative environmental sculptor," Chakaia Booker has used the discarded materials of contemporary life to comment on race, genre, and other issues.

Born in 1953 in Newark, New Jersey, she attended Rutgers University in New Brunswick and earned a Bachelor of Arts degree in sociology in 1976. She settled on a career as an artist in the East Village of New York City. Finding burning cars in her neighborhood was the inspiration for her best-known work. The burned tires of the cars fascinated her. "Once they would burn, you would get different effects," she said in a 2009 interview. "I would go by these cars after they cooled and just begin to scrape off what I could." She started to assemble the strips and pieces of burnt tires into complex sculptures. She discovered in their design and textures a parallel with the complex patterns in African textiles. The worn treads of rubber tires also symbolized for her the difficult, worn lives of many African Americans as well as their resiliency and ability to survive. Soon Booker was combining tires with other discarded materials to create intriguing works such as *Dorothy Shoes* (1994), which evokes the magical shoes from *Wizard of Oz*, without the magic. Her 20-foot-high tire relief, *It's So Hard to Be Green*, was featured at the 2001 Whitney Museum of American Art Biennial. Other works have a more feminist focus, such as *Wench (Wrench) III* (2001), which features a mechanics wrench (masculine) being transformed into a feather boa (feminine).

Booker has transformed some of her tire art into clothes, such as vests and necklaces that she hopes to someday sell as part of her own fashion line.

Recent solo exhibitions include *Chakaia Booker* (2007) at Marlborough Chelsea Gallery in New York and *Inside Out* (2008–09) at the Elmhurst Art Museum in Elmhurst, Illinois, a collaboration with sculptor Bob Emser. Booker was one of seven African-American artists showcased in *Provocative Visions: Race and Identity* at the Metropolitan Museum of Art in New York from August 2008 to March 2009.

She earned a Master of Fine Arts degree from the City College of New York in 1993 and was artist-in-residence at the Studio Museum in Harlem in 1995–96. Booker was the recipient of a Guggenheim Fellowship in 2005. She lives and works in New York City and Allentown, Pennsylvania, where she rips apart old tires for her sculptures in her studio, a converted laundry factory.

Further Reading

Booker, Chakaia, and Bob Emser. *Inside Out.* Elmhurst, Ill.: Elmhurst Art Museum, 2008.

Cook, Christopher. *Rubbermade: Sculpture by Chakaia Booker.* Kansas City, Mo.: Kemper Museum of Contemporary Art, 2008.

Lewis, Samella. *African American Art and Artists.* Berkeley: University of California Press, 2003, pp. 321–322.

The Official Chakaia Booker Web site. Available online. URL: http://www.chakaiabooker.com/. Downloaded March 18, 2009.

Shuster, Robert. "Chakaia Booker is a Radial Radical." *Village Voice.* Available online. URL: http://www.villagevoice.com/2009-03-18/art/spring-guide-chakaia-booker-is-a-radial-radical/. Downloaded April 8, 2009.

Bowser, David Bustill
(1820–1900) *painter*

A commercial artist whose bold colors and designs enlivened the signs and banners of 19th-century America, David Bustill Bowser was one of the first successful African-American artists in the United States.

He was born on January 16, 1820, in Philadelphia, Pennsylvania. A member of the black middle class, he attended a private school operated by his cousin, Sarah Mapps Douglass. Bowser showed a natural talent for art and in 1833 apprenticed to another cousin, sign painter Robert Douglass, Jr.

Unable at first to make a living as a painter, Bowser became a hairdresser and then worked as a barber on Mississippi steamboats. When he returned to Philadelphia a few years later, he devoted himself to his art. He received the first-prize medal of the Colored American Institute's exhibitions in 1851 and 1852 for marine and landscape paintings.

But sign and banner painting became the bread and butter of Bowser's career as an artist.

Elaborate, decorative signs were a primary form of advertising in 19th-century America and were much in demand. Another avenue of work for Bowser involved the many volunteer fire companies operating at the time. Each had their own distinctive art on their hose reels, engine panels, banners, and various apparel they wore and carried in parades and processions. For several decades Bowser painted these materials, as well as signs and emblems for fire insurance companies and military units in Philadelphia and other cities. His work was always outstanding and characterized by bold, vibrant colors; clean, effective design; and dramatic presentation.

Bowser was also a landscape and portrait painter. Among his most famous subjects was the abolitionist John Brown, who was a guest in Bowser's home when he painted his portrait, and President Abraham Lincoln. Bowser painted 21 oil paintings and retouched photographs of the president, one of which Lincoln himself is said to have bought. Bowser kept the check Lincoln wrote for the painting, and it became a treasured family heirloom for years.

During the Civil War, Bowser created pictorial flags for 10 troops of black Union soldiers. Among his most stirring works, the flags depict heroic black soldiers in battle with such captions as "Rather Die Freeman than Live to Be Slave."

Bowser lived by the mottoes he painted. Before the war, he helped fugitive slaves escape to freedom and after the war he helped end segregation on streetcars in Philadelphia. Although few of his works survive, Bowser's achievement and reputation inspired other African Americans to becomes artists, including the greatest black painter of the 19th century, HENRY O. TANNER.

David Bustill Bowser died on July 2, 1900.

Further Reading

Lewis, Samella. *African American Art and Artists.* Berkeley: University of California Press, 2003, p. 20.

Riggs, Thomas, ed. *St. James Guide to Black Artists.* Detroit, Mich.: St. James Press, 1997, p. 66.

Brandon-Croft, Barbara
(1958–) *cartoonist, illustrator*

The first female African-American cartoonist to be nationally syndicated, Barbara Brandon-Croft is the creator of the weekly comic strip *Where I'm Coming From*, a witty mixture of social commentary and humor from the perspective of young black women.

She was born Barbara Brandon on Long Island, New York, November 27, 1958. She came by her cartooning talent naturally. Her father, Brumsic Brandon, Jr., was the creator of the comic strip *Luther* (1971–86). As a girl, Brandon assisted her father with his comic for allowance money. She entered Syracuse University's College of Visual and Performing Arts in 1976. A year after graduating, she decided to become a cartoonist like her dad and was hired by the black women's magazine *Elan*. Unfortunately *Elan* went out of business before Brandon's first strip was published. She moved on to another black women's magazine, *Essence*, where she worked as a fashion and beauty writer.

In 1989, Brandon created the comic strip *Where I'm Coming From*, based on herself and her circle of female friends. The strip first appeared in the *Detroit Free Press* that year and was picked up for syndication by Universal Press Syndicate in 1991.

The funny and topical strip was populated by a group of African-American women who talked about everything from politics and social issues to men and work. Each character had her own personality and interests. Lekesia was the social and political activist, while Nicole always had men on her mind.

Stylistically, *Where I'm Coming From* was noted for its minimal artwork. There were no backgrounds, and only the character's heads, arms, and hands were drawn. The dialogue was free of the traditional cartoon balloons, and the characters talk directly to the reader. "While she usually . . . [works] in a humorous context, Brandon does not suffer fools and injustice lightly," wrote comics historian Bill Crouch.

Brandon-Croft's illustrations have appeared in *Essence,* as well as such other publications as *The Village Voice* and *The Crisis,* published by the Association for the Advancement of Colored People (NAACP). She also has illustrated *Sista Girlfren' Breaks It Down . . . : When Mom's Not Around* (1994), a humorous guide to black teen girls by Franchestra Ahmen-Cawthorne. Brandon-Croft has created a popular line of African-American greeting cards for ZorbiZ Greeting Cards that feature her strip characters.

Discouraged that interest in her strip had fallen off and only seven newspapers still carried it, Brandon ended *Where I'm Coming From*'s 14-year run in March 2005.

Further Reading

"Barbara Brandon." African American Literature Book Club. Available online. URL: http://aalbc.com/authors/barbara.htm. Downloaded March 2, 2008.

Brandon-Croft, Barbara. *Where I'm Coming From.* Kansas City, Mo.: Andrews McMeel Publications, 1993.

———. *Where I'm Still Coming From.* Kansas City, Mo.: Andrews McMeel Publications, 1994.

Brown, Frederick J.
(1945–   ) *painter*

A painter whose expressive, colorful paintings have captured black folk heroes and blues musicians, Frederick J. Brown has moved from abstract art to more figurative works without losing the boldness of his style.

He was born on February 6, 1945, in Greensboro, Georgia. Later his family joined the black exodus north to find better jobs and moved to the South Side of Chicago, Illinois. As a youth, he met such legendary Chicago blues musicians and singers as Muddy Waters, Jimmy Reed, and Howlin' Wolf, who were friends of his father. Brown earned a Bachelor of Arts degree in art from Southern Illinois University and then taught art in Illinois public schools.

In 1970, he moved to New York City and taught part-time at the Brooklyn Museum and the School of Visual Arts in Manhattan while pursuing his painting. His first works were large, daring abstract paintings. Then in 1975 he befriended famed abstract expressionist Willem de Kooning, whose style had a profound effect on Brown. Gradually, his paintings became more figurative like de Kooning's, using strong, vibrant colors to express the emotional state of his subjects. He also painted folklike landscapes.

Brown painted such African-American folk heroes as the "steel-drivin' man" *John Henry* (1979) and *Stagger Lee* (1983). Like a number of other contemporary black artists, he was drawn to Leonardo da Vinci's famous painting *The Last Supper,* which he re-created in 1984. In his version of Christ at his last meal, Brown replaced Christ's 12 apostles with men who were important in his own life. The monumental work took the form of a collage, with photographs of the 12 people affixed to the painting.

In 1988, Brown became one of the first African-American artists to be given a retrospective exhibition at the National Museum of the Chinese Revolution in Tiananmen Square in Beijing, China. A year later, he researched a documentary film on blues singers in the American South. The experience inspired Brown to paint an ambitious series of portraits of great blues musicians. In the bold colors of the portraits, Brown successfully captures the power and intensity of their music. Perhaps the best-known of these portraits is *Junior Wells,* dominated by a huge, expressionistic hand holding a microphone.

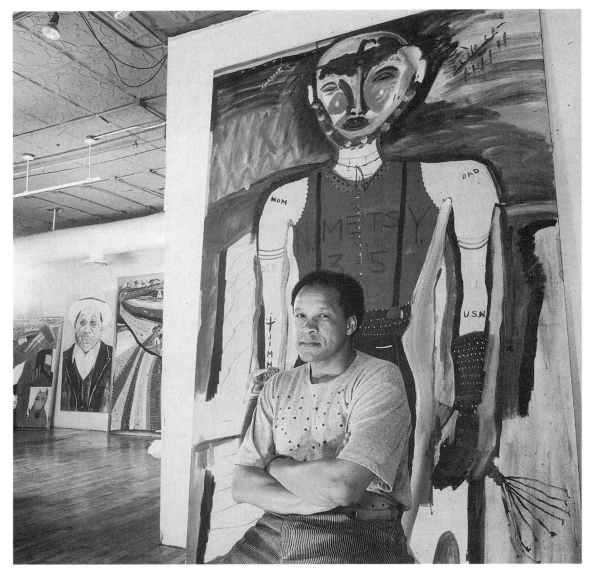

Painter Frederick J. Brown poses before one of his larger-than-life expressionistic portraits. *(Anthony Barboza)*

His solo show *Frederick J. Brown: Portraits in Jazz, Blues, and Other Icons* (2002–03) at the Kemper Museum in Kansas City, Missouri, featured more than 30 portraits from three decades. *New Portraits of Jazz Greats* (2009) at the New Orleans Museum of Art included Brown's renderings of Louis Armstrong, Billie Holliday, and Frank Sinatra. He anticipates when his monumental series of musicians is completed it will contain more than 300 works.

Frederick J. Brown lives in New York City and in Arizona, where he maintains a studio.

"Art is a religious experience," Brown has said. "It's not coming from you. It's coming through you."

Further Reading

Brown, Frederick J. *Frederick J. Brown: Portraits in Jazz, Blues, and Other Icons*. Kansas City, Mo.: Kemper Museum of Contemporary Art, 2002.

"Frederick J. Brown Paints Jazz." People'sWeekly World.org. Available online. URL: http://www. pww.org/article/articleview/1362/. Downloaded March 2, 2009.

Johnson, K. "An Adventure in Paint Attuned to the Beat and Offbeat of Jazz." *New York Times,* June 6, 2003, p. E34.

Perry, Reginia A. *Free Within Ourselves: African-American Artists in the Collection of the National Museum of American Art*. San Francisco: Pomegranate Artbooks, 1992, pp. 40–45.

Browne, Vivian E.

(1929–1993) *painter, educator*

An artist whose work powerfully expresses humankind's alienation from itself and the world of nature, Vivian E. Browne developed her own unique blend of realism and abstraction.

She was born in Laurel, Florida, on April 26, 1929, and moved to Long Island, New York, with her family as a child. She watched her father paint pictures in his spare time, but when she expressed interest in becoming an artist herself, her mother discouraged her. Browne graduated from Hunter College in New York City with a Bachelor of Science degree in 1950. Unable to get a teaching job, she worked for a year as a mail clerk at the National Board of the Young Women's Christian Association in New York. A year later she returned to the South and got a job as a fine arts teacher at Booker T. Washington High School in Columbia, South Carolina. In 1953, Browne moved back to New York and taught for more than a decade in public schools while pursuing her career as an artist. She received a Master of Fine Arts degree from Hunter in 1959. In 1966, she became a superintendent of art for the New York Board of Education.

Browne's work reflected the difficulty of human relations in the contemporary world. Such stirring, expressionistic paintings as *Seven Deadly Sins* (1967) with its haunting faces, *Two Men* (1961) with its distorted bodies, and *Dancer* (1968) with its disproportionate man dancing alone, all reflect a deep sense of alienation. Even nature was distorted in Browne's world. A number of her paintings combine trees and hulking, human-made metal communications towers.

"Browne's paintings show the vulnerable relationship between living things and their environments. . . [it] explores the constant struggle between the subjects and their imposed surroundings," wrote Christine Miner Minder.

Browne began teaching art at Rutgers University in Newark, New Jersey, in 1975, and remained there for many years. Two years earlier, she had helped establish SOHO 29, one of the first women's art cooperatives in Manhattan. Among the awards she received were the MacDowell Colony Painting Fellowship (1980), the Artist Honoree of the Year from the New York Fine Arts Institute (1988), and the Distinguished Teacher of Art from the College Artists Associations in 1989. Browne died of bladder cancer in New York City on July 23, 1993 at age 64.

"The statements I make in painting must be universal," she said in an interview in 1968. "I don't know that I've reached that or passed it yet but I think it's coming. And I think that I've made a very great inroad to it."

Further Reading

Browne, Vivian E., et al. *Racism Is the Issue: Heresies 15. Heresies* Collective, 1982.

Hamalian, Leo. "Talking to Vivian Browne." *Black Artists Literary Forum* 19, spring 1985, pp. 48–49.

"Oral History Interview with Vivian Browne, July 1, 1968," The Smithsonian Archive of American

Art Web site. Available online. URL: http://www.aaa.si.edu/collections/oralhistories/transcripts/browne68.htm. Downloaded March 2, 2009.

Riggs, Thomas, ed. *St. James Guide to Black Artists.* Detroit, Mich.: St. James Press, 1997, pp. 77–78.

Bryan, Ashley
(1923–) *illustrator, writer, educator, painter*

A children's book author and illustrator whose specialty is retelling folktales from around the world, Ashley Bryan is also a respected teacher who for many years headed the art department at Dartmouth College in Hanover, New Hampshire.

He was born on July 13, 1923, in the Bronx, New York. He grew up in a rough neighborhood and, in his own words, "learned from kindergarten that drawing and painting were the toughest assets I had to offer my community." He would illustrate books and then give them to schoolmates as gifts.

He attended the School of Art at the Cooper Union in New York City, but World War II (1939–45) interrupted his studies, when he served in the U.S. Army. After the war, Bryan returned to Cooper Union and then went on to Columbia University in New York City, where he studied philosophy.

Sometime after graduating, he opened an art studio in the Bronx and began illustrating. His second assignment was creating pictures for a collection of poems by Indian poet Rabindranath Tagore entitled *Moon, for What Do You Wait?* (1969). His next job was to illustrate a book of African folktales. When Bryan complained about the poor quality of the writing to his editor she replied, "Tell them in your own way." He did so and began a successful career as a writer-illustrator. In this first collection, *The Ox of the Wonderful Horns and Other African Folktales* (1971), he created illustrations that looked like woodcuts.

In other books, Bryan has matched his illustrative style to the nature of the story he is telling.

In *The Dancing Granny* (1977), which he based on a remembrance of his own feisty grandmother, he employed a Japanese-style brush-painting technique that accented movement. In *The Cat's Purr* (1985), he used sepia line drawing to suggest a spontaneous feeling.

Bryan's favorite works are his remarkable series based on Negro spirituals, including *Walk Together Children* (1981), *I'm Going to Sing* (1982), and *All Night, All Day—A Child's First Book of African-American Spirituals* (1991). This last volume was one of four of his works chosen as Coretta Scott King Honor Books. He has also illustrated books by such outstanding children's writers as Walter Dean Myers and Nikki Grimes.

Bryan was invited to come to Dartmouth for a semester as an artist-in-residence and ended up staying on as a member of the faculty. He later became the chairman of the art department. Now retired as a professor emeritus, Bryan lives and paints on an island in Isleford, Maine. His paintings have been exhibited in numerous one-man shows. In 2009, he published an autobiography, *Words to My Life's Song,* for children.

Further Reading
Bryan, Ashley. *Ashley Bryan: Words to My Life's Song.* New York: Atheneum, 2009.
———. *Beautiful Blackbird.* New York: Atheneum, 2003.
Bryan, Ashley, and David Manning Thomas. *All Night, All Day—A Child's First Book of African-American Spirituals.* New York: Atheneum, 1991.
Telgen, Diane, ed. *Something About the Author,* Volume 72. Detroit, Mich.: Gale Research, 1993, pp. 26–29.

Buchanan, Beverly
(1940–) *sculptor, painter, mixed-media artist, photographer*

An artist of diverse talents, Beverly Buchanan is best known for transforming the humble dwellings of poor black southerners into objects of enduring beauty.

She was born on October 8, 1940, in Fuquay, North Carolina. Her father, Walter Buchanan, was dean of the School of Agriculture at South Carolina University in Orangeburg, and she grew up on its campus.

In 1958, Buchanan enrolled in Bennett College in Greensboro, North Carolina, from which she earned a Bachelor of Science degree in art in 1962. She received a Master of Science degree from Columbia University in New York City in 1968.

By the 1970s, she was fascinated with structures and buildings and how they reflected the people who built and lived in them. This interest produced the series *Black Walls,* paintings on paper of rural walls and parts of walls.

Even more celebrated is her long-running obsession with the rundown houses, or shacks, of poor southern blacks, which she recalls from her childhood. Like the poor people who dwelt in them, Buchanan sees the shacks not as tawdry and ugly but as a reflection of their inhabitants' strength of character and ability to persevere.

"When Buchanan shows us these shacks," wrote Jontyle Theresa Robinson, "they are observed as architecture, but they also are presented as individualized 'portraits,' almost like people."

Originally depicted in oil paintings and then photographs, Buchanan's shacks eventually took on a three-dimensional life in sculptures and mixed-media works. Some of them are as large as a room. Many of the best examples of her work traveled around the country in the 1994 exhibition *Beverly Buchanan: Shack Works.* One of her shacks was so convincing that some people believed it was the real thing. Built in a park in Atlanta, Georgia, near Atlanta University Center, it was repeatedly vandalized before it was finally dismantled and removed.

A solo exhibit *Response and Memory: The Art of Beverly Buchanan* ran at the Morris Museum of Art in Atlanta, Georgia, from November 2009 to January 2010.

Beverly Buchanan has received Guggenheim and National Endowment for the Arts fellowships and an award from the National Conference of Women Sculptors. Her works can be found in the permanent collections of the High Museum of Art, Atlanta, Georgia; the Columbia Museum of Art, Columbia, South Carolina; and the Metropolitan Museum of Art, New York. In 2003, she was a visiting artist at Spring Island, South Carolina.

Further Reading

Buchanan, Beverly. *Beverly Buchanan* July 19–September 20, 1992. (Parameters Series). Norfolk, Va.: Chrysler Museum, 1992.

———. *Beverly Buchanan: Habitats and Shotgun Shacks.* Atlanta, Ga.: City Gallery East, 2000.

Beverly Buchanan's Official Web site. Available online. URL: http://www.beverlybuchanan.com/cv.html. Downloaded March 2, 2009.

Kohl, Mary Ann F., and Kim Solga. *Great American Artists for Kids.* Bellingham, Wash.: Bright Ring Publishing, Inc., 2008.

Riggs, Thomas, ed. *St. James Guide to Black Artists.* Detroit, Mich.: St. James Press, 1997, pp. 78–80.

Walker, Rebecca. *House and Home: Spirits of the South.* Seattle: University of Washington Press, 1994.

Buchanan, Yvonne E.
(1956–   ) *illustrator, video artist, educator*

An illustrator of childlike whimsy, Yvonne Buchanan creates drawings and watercolors that have graced children's books, American Express ads, and the editorial pages of some of the nation's leading newspapers.

She was born in New York City on November 14, 1956. As a child she got in trouble when she drew the Japanese cartoon character Astro Boy on the walls of her home. She studied at the High School of Art and Design in New York and earned a Bachelor of Arts degree in illustration from the Parsons School of Design in New York.

Buchanan started illustrating for newspapers such as *The Washington Post, Newsday,* and *The New York Times* with sharp-eyed editorial illustrations, cartoons, and caricatures. She began illustrating children's books in the 1980s. Many of the books she has worked on deal with African-American history. *Juneteenth Jamboree* (1992) tells about the celebration in a Texan town following the freeing of Texan slaves in 1865. *Follow the Drinking Gourd* (1998) is about the Underground Railroad, which helped slaves escape North in the years before the Civil War. Other books include *Fly, Bessie, Fly* (1998), a biography of Bessie Coleman, the first black woman aviator; and *God Inside of Me,* with text by actress and singer Della Reese, star of the television drama *Touched by an Angel.* Most of Buchanan's book illustrations are in bright watercolors.

She has been the recipient of the Showtime Achievement Award and the Parents' Choice Silver Honor and was nominated for an NAACP Image Award in 1999. Buchanan is assistant professor of illustration at Syracuse University in New York State. In recent years, she has created a number of digital videos.

"I am very interested in politics and the cultural values of this country and how it relates to the rest of the world," she said in one interview. "I have a fantasy about being in a room with a group of international artists who can only communicate visually. I believe we could cure the ills of the world."

Further Reading

Connelly, Bernadine, and Yvonne Buchanan, illustrator. *Follow the Drinking Gourd.* New York: Simon & Schuster, 1998.

Joseph, Lynn, and Yvonne Buchanan, illustrator. *Fly, Bessie, Fly.* New York: Simon & Schuster, 1998.

Reese, Della, and Yvonne Buchanan, illustrator. *God Inside of Me.* New York: Hyperion, 2005.

Wesley, Valene Wilson. "African-American Illustrators—Tom Feelings, Yvonne Buchanan, and Others." BNET. Available online. URL: http://findarticles.com/p/articles/mi_m1546/is_4_15/ai_65069609. Downloaded March 2, 2009.

Burke, Selma
(Selma Hortense Burke)
(1900–1995) *sculptor, educator*

Few African-American artists' work is as pervasive as that of Selma Burke. A sculptor of great power and expression, she is best known for her portrait of President Franklin Delano Roosevelt that adorns the U.S. dime.

She was born on December 31, 1900, in Mooresville, North Carolina. Although she was interested in art from an early age, her mother insisted she take up a more practical profession, so she studied nursing at the St. Agnes Training School for Nurses in Raleigh, North Carolina. She received her registered nurse diploma in 1924 and went on to attend the Women's Medical College in Philadelphia, Pennsylvania.

After several years in nursing, Burke had the good fortune to work as a private nurse for a rich heiress. This woman encouraged Burke's gift for sculpturing and later became her patron. Burke left nursing in the 1930s and moved to New York City to pursue sculpture. She helped found the Harlem Arts Guild and taught for a time at the Harlem Art Center. Burke was an art instructor at the Friends Council on Education in Philadelphia in 1930, a position she held for 19 years. While on sabbatical, she studied in Paris, France, under sculptor Oronzio Maldarelli and also worked in Germany and Austria.

Returning to the United States in 1940, she founded the Selma Burke School of Sculpture in New York's Greenwich Village. From her time in Europe she developed a neoclassicist style, based on ancient Greek and Roman sculpture. Burke earned a Master of Fine Arts degree from Columbia University in New York in 1941.

Sculpting in brass, wood, and stone, she was commissioned to do portraits and busts of famous people and historical figures. In 1944 President Franklin Delano Franklin sat for a bronze figure. When Roosevelt died suddenly in 1945, President Harry Truman unveiled the figure in Washington. The next year it was used on the face of the new dime struck to commemorate the late president.

While known for her busts of great Americans, including black educator Mary McLeod Bethune and Martin Luther King, Jr., one of Burke's finest sculptures is of an ordinary black man, simply called *Jim*. According to art critic Regina Holden Jennings, *Jim* "demonstrates her high level of skill in portraiture" with its strong, solid features and intense emotional depth. Among her other notable works are the dynamic *Falling Angel* and the tender, moving *Mother and Child*.

From 1963, Burke taught at a number of prestigious colleges, including Haverford College in Haverford, Pennsylvania; Swarthmore College in Swarthmore, Pennsylvania; and Livingston College in Salisbury, North Carolina. While at Livingston, she received her doctoral degree in 1970. She founded the Selma Burke Art Center in Pittsburgh, Pennsylvania, in 1968.

Selma Burke was awarded a citation for Contribution to Negro Art in America from President Jimmy Carter in 1979. She died of cancer on August 29, 1995 at age 94.

Further Reading

Jackson, Garnet, and Cheryl Hanna. *Selma Burke Artist.* Upper Saddle River, N.J.: Curriculum Press, 1994.

Riggs, Thomas, ed. *St. James Guide to Black Artists.* Detroit, Mich.: St. James Press, 1997, pp. 80–81.

Schwalb, Harry. "Without Color." *Art News,* September 1994, p. 24.

"Selma Burke." Answers.com. Available online. URL: http://www.answers.com/topic/selma-burke. Downloaded March 2, 2009.

Burnett, Charles

(1944–   ) *filmmaker, screenwriter, film producer*

One of the most respected and uncompromising of contemporary black filmmakers, Charles Burnett has created memorable movies about the black experience largely outside of the Hollywood studio system.

He was born on April 13, 1944, in Vicksburg, Mississippi. His father was in the military and the family resettled in Los Angeles, California, when Burnett was still a youth. After high school, he entered Los Angeles Community College to study electronics. He was drawn to filmmaking, however, as a way to tell stories about the people he knew growing up in South Central L.A.

Burnett studied film at UCLA. As his graduate thesis he directed the feature-length film *Killer of Sheep* (1977). This riveting film was about a black man who worked in a slaughterhouse killing sheep in South Central L.A. The man's grim profession numbs him to the life and people around him. The film was a hit at film festivals and on college campuses and launched Burnett's career. It won the Critics Prize at the Berlin International Film Festival in Germany in 1981.

Burnett's next film, *My Brother's Wedding* (1984), was about a man who must choose between going to his brother's wedding or a friend's funeral. It was not widely seen. His third movie would be his most celebrated, as well as his most frustrating. He wrote the original screenplay of *To Sleep with Anger* for Public Television, but he had artistic differences with the producers and withdrew the script. Burnett decided he would produce the film himself and spent the next two-and-a-half years raising money for the production. African-American actor Danny Glover liked the script and agreed to both star in the picture and help coproduce it.

To Sleep with Anger (1990) was the story of a transplanted black middle-class family originally from the South now living in Los Angeles. An old family friend, Harry Mention (Glover), arrives for a short visit that stretches on interminably. Harry stirs up trouble for the family, bringing back old memories of a macho past they thought they had left behind them in the South. Even in death, Harry's unwelcome corpse continues to plague them. The film was a fascinating study of the black family in turmoil and won the Special Jury Prize at the prestigious Sundance Film Festival in 1990. It was also awarded best screenplay from the National Critics Poll.

Unfortunately, the distributors of the film failed to market it appropriately. Few black people, who should have been its core audience, saw *To Sleep with Anger* or even knew about it. It died a quick death at the box office.

Burnett was bitter about the experience but continued to make films his own way. *The Glass Shield* (1994) was based on the real experiences of a black police officer in mostly white Orange County, California. The cast included rap artist and actor Ice Cube. More recently, Burnett has directed more commercial projects for television. He made the miniseries *The Wedding* (1998), produced by television magnate Oprah Winfrey. *Selma, Lord, Selma* (1999), made for Disney Television, was the honest and affecting story of an Alabama black schoolgirl caught up in the Civil Rights movement during the mid-1960s.

He also made the documentaries *Nat Turner: A Troublesome Project* and *The Blues: Warming by the Devil's Fire* (both 2003), part of a seven-part television series produced by Martin Scorsese. *Nambia: The Struggle for Liberation* (2007) was a historical epic of that African nation starring Danny Glover.

Charles Burnett received the Maya Deren Award for Independent Film and Video Artists from the American Film Institute (AFI) in 1991.

Further Reading

Alexander, George. *Why We Make Movies: Black Filmmakers Talk About the Magic of Cinema.* New York: Harlem Moon, 2003, pp. 183–195.
Bogle, Donald. *Toms, Coons, Mulattoes, Mammies, & Bucks: An Interpretive History of Blacks in American Films.* New York: Continuum, 1997, pp. 337–339.
Moon, Spencer. *Reel Black Talk: A Sourcebook of 50 American Filmmakers.* Westport, Conn.: Greenwood Press, 1997, pp. 39–46.

Further Viewing

The Glass Shield (1994). Miramax Home Entertainment, DVD, 2005.
Killer of Sheep: The Charles Burnett Collection. New Yorker. Video/Milestone Cinematheque, 2 DVDs, 2007.
To Sleep with Anger (1990). Columbia Tristar, VHS, 1995.

Burroughs, Margaret Taylor

(1917–2010) *printmaker, painter, illustrator, writer, educator, museum director*

One of the leading lights and tireless promoters of African-American art in her hometown of Chicago, Illinois, Margaret Taylor Burroughs combined a successful career as an artist with that of a teacher and museum director.

She was born Margaret Taylor on November 1, 1917, in St. Rose, Louisiana. Her family moved to Chicago when she was still a child. Burroughs earned a Bachelor of Arts degree and Master of Fine Arts degree from the School of the Art Institute of Chicago. She became an active member of the black artistic community and helped found the South Side Community Arts Center in 1939. It is one of the few projects of the federal Works Progress Administration from the 1930s still in operation today.

At first a painter, Burroughs created canvases full of color, and she often used storytelling in depicting her subjects. She could not live on the sale of her paintings, however, and turned to teaching art at Du Sable High School in Chicago in 1946. She remained there for 23 years.

In 1939, she married another artist, Bernard Goss. The marriage lasted eight years. With her second husband, Charles Gordon Burroughs, who she married in 1949, she founded the Du Sable Museum of Art in 1961 in their home to display the work of African-American artists. The Burroughses also included African art in their museum, which they seriously began collecting in the late 1950s. Margaret Burroughs was not shy about using her friends to enlarge the Du Sable's collection. "Every time anyone went over to Africa," she said, "we asked people to bring us something back." The Burroughs moved the museum into a separate building in 1971. She remained executive director of the museum until 1985.

In printmaking, Burroughs found a way to share her art with more people at reasonable cost, since many copies can be made from one original. She created her first print, *Face of Africa,* the portrait of an African woman, after her initial visit to Africa in 1965. Since then she has made numerous prints from woodcuts and linoleum, her favorite medium to work in. In 1947, Burroughs wrote and illustrated the children's book *Jasper the Drummin' Boy* and produced several other children's books, including *Did You Feed My Cow?* (1956) and *For Malcolm: Poems on the Life and Death of Malcolm X* (1967), which she coedited.

Burroughs also served as art director for the Negro Hall of Fame and received a National Communication Association (NCA) Award in 1963. She received honorary degrees from the School of the Art Institute of Chicago and DePaul University in Chicago, among other institutions. In 1989, Burroughs received the Paul Robeson Award.

Margaret Taylor Burroughs died on November 21, 2010, at age 95. On her death, President Barack Obama praised her "commitment to under-served communities through her children's books, art workshops and community centers that both inspired and educated young people about African-American culture."

Further Reading

Burroughs, Margaret Taylor. *Did You Feed My Cow? Street Games, Chants, and Rhymes.* River Grove, Ill.: Follett Corporation, 1969.

"Dr. Margaret Burroughs Celebrates Her Fifty Years as Artist." The *Chicago Defender,* May 14, 1992.

Margaret Taylor-Burroughs. AKA Authors. Available online. URL: http://dickinsg.intrasun.tcnj.edu/akaauthors2/Taylor.htm. Downloaded March 2, 2009.

Riggs, Thomas, ed. *St. James Guide to Black Artists.* Detroit, Mich.: St. James Press, 1997, pp. 85–87.

Byard, Carole
(1941–) *illustrator, mixed-media artist, muralist, painter, sculptor*

An award-winning illustrator of children's books, Carole Byard is committed to the interpretation of history—both African and American—through her dramatic drawings and other artworks.

Carole Byard has made her mark as both a leading children's book illustrator and a fine artist. *(Anthony Barboza)*

She was born on July 22, 1941, in Atlantic City, New Jersey. Her grandparents were from Barbados in the West Indies and her mother grew up in Panama. "My earliest memories of the power of creating began when I was seven years old," she says. "Drawing sent me to some kind of crawl space that gave me wings—allowed me to fly, float, drift and dance in the air."

Movement and action remain central to Byard's illustrative work and her life. To earn money to help her family, she once worked as a simulation pilot at the National Aviation Facilities Experimental Center near Atlantic City. She attended the New York Phoenix School of Design from 1964 to 1968 and then taught at the school for three years. Byard began her career doing magazine illustrations and was drawn to the performing arts. This interest eventually led to one of her first assignments as a children's book illustrator for a biography of Arthur Mitchell, African-American ballet dancer and the founder of the Dance Theatre of Harlem.

In 1971, Byard won a fellowship that allowed her to travel to Africa. She spent three months in various countries and painted a mural in a village temple. She returned a few years later to take part in the second Black and African Festival of Art and Culture held in Lagos, Nigeria. Byard's experiences in Africa lent strength and authenticity to her charcoal illustrations for *Three African Tales* (1979), written by Adjai Robinson. Byard has illustrated a total of 16 children's books, including the Coretta Scott King Award winners *Africa Dream* (1992), about a black girl who dreams of ancient Africa, and *Cornrows* (1997).

Another book that mixed fantasy and reality was *The Black Snowman* (1991), written by Phil Mendez. An African-American boy living in urban poverty comes to grips with his heritage through a magical snowman he builds out of black city slush. The reviewer in *Horn Book* noted that Byard's "pastel drawings have a dreamlike quality."

She was one of six African-American illustrators, including JERRY PINKNEY and FAITH RINGGOLD, who collaborated on *Jump Back, Honey: The Poems of Paul Laurence Dunbar* (1999), an anthology of the celebrated black poet's work.

Two of Byard's books were named Coretta Scott King Honor Books, and *Working Cotton* won the Caldecott Medal in 1993.

She is also a fine artist whose mixed-media works and sculptures reside in several leading museums. Her mixed-media work *The Perception of Presence* (1992), which is composed of earthen African heads and recorded interviews, was inspired by a racial incident involving her godson and New York City police. Another striking work is a "portrait" of black leader Malcolm X at the Walker Art Center in Minneapolis, Minnesota. This environmental work was a collaboration with photographer Clarissa Sligh, and it includes photographs as well as audio sounds of civil rights marches and the voices of such participants as civil rights leader Martin Luther King, Jr., and Montgomery, Alabama, police chief Bull Connor.

"History relies on whoever is telling the story to tell the story well," she said in an interview. "We must be responsible for our stories, our telling, our histories, our words, and our imagery."

Further Reading

Johnston, Tony, and Carole Byard, illustrator. *Angel City*: New York: Philomel, 2006.

Mendez, Phil, and Carole Byard, illustrator. *The Black Snowman*. New York: Scholastic, 2005.

Riggs, Thomas, ed. *St. James Guide to Black Artists*. Detroit, Mich.: St. James Press, 1997, pp. 87–90.

Williams, Sherley Anne, and Carole Byard, illustrator. *Working Cotton*. Boston: Sandpiper, 1997.

Campbell, E. Simms
(Elmer Simms Campbell)
(1906–1971) *cartoonist*

The first African-American cartoonist to gain national recognition, E. Simms Campbell helped to make *Esquire* and *Playboy* two of the most successful magazines in America through his drawings of svelte and sexy women.

He was born Elmer Simms Campbell on January 2, 1906, in St. Louis, Missouri. His father was an assistant high school principal, and his mother painted watercolors and taught him the fundamentals of art. Campbell attended Englewood High School in Chicago, Illinois, where he was a football halfback and editorial cartoonist for the school newspaper. He gained national recognition as a senior in 1926 with an Armistice Day cartoon that depicted a World War I soldier at his friend's grave telling him, "We've won, Buddy!"

After graduation, he entered the School of the Art Institute of Chicago. While there, Campbell drew for *College Comics* on a freelance basis. He signed his work E. Simms Campbell, because he disliked his first name. Completing his schooling, he moved in with an aunt in the Harlem section of New York City in 1932. He studied at the Art Students League, where his mentor was German-born artist and caricaturist George Grosz.

In 1933, Campbell got a chance to work for a new men's magazine, *Esquire*, on the recommendation of cartoonist Russell Patterson. *Esquire*'s first issue had a number of Campbell's single-panel color cartoons. His gags about curvaceous young women were just the kind of humor the magazine wanted in order to attract a large male readership. Campbell also created a big-eyed, mustached little man in evening clothes called "Esky," who became *Esquire*'s mascot.

The magazine signed the cartoonist to a long-term contact, and Campbell's cartoons appeared in every issue of *Esquire* for the next 25 years. When *Playboy*, a competitor of *Esquire*, began publication in the early 1950s, Campbell drew cartoons for it too. His work also appeared in such leading magazines as *The New Yorker*, *The Saturday Evening Post*, *Redbook*, and *Cosmopolitan*. During his most productive years he turned out as many as 500 cartoons and other pieces of art a year.

Although he never created a traditional comic strip, Campbell's single-panel cartoons produced two memorable characters. Cutie was a pretty redhead who appeared in a daily panel for King Features Syndicate starting in 1943. He said he made her a redhead because the color red reproduces well. The Sultan appeared in a richly colored, full-page panel in *Esquire* in the 1930s and later in *Playboy*. What made the Sultan so humorous was his great interest in food and toys and his lack of interest in the beautiful women who surrounded him in his harem. "His drawings had a spontaneity that often made the gag secondary," wrote cartoon historian Bill Crouch.

Despite Campbell's popularity, *Esquire* editors were careful to keep his race a secret. They were afraid that white males would be offended to learn that a black man drew all the gorgeous white women in their magazine.

Campbell rarely if ever drew a black person in his cartoons, and this disturbed members of the black community. His response was that he was a commercial artist meeting the demands of the marketplace. "I sell a commodity," he once said. "I sell what people want."

However, he did take pride in his black heritage and illustrated several children's books, including the classic *Popo and Fifina: Children of Haiti* (1932) by black writers Arna Bontemps and Langston Hughes. He also illustrated *We Who Die and Other Poems*, a collection of poetry by Haitian poet Binga Desmond.

In 1957, tired of the racial prejudice he experienced in the United States, Campbell and his wife moved to the tiny village of Neerach, Switzerland. "Out here in this little off-the-wall village we don't have to prove nothin' to nobody," he said in a 1966 interview. Campbell remained in Switzerland until his wife's death in October 1970. Then he returned to the United States and died of cancer at his home in White Plains, New York, on January 27, 1971.

Further Reading

Bontemps, Arna, Langston Hughes, and E. Simms Campbell, illustrator. Reprint: *Popo and Fifina: Children of Haiti.* New York: Oxford University Press, 2000.

Dismond, Binga, and E. Simms Campbell, illustrator. *We Who Would Die and Other Poems: Including Haitian Vignettes.* Whitefish, Mt.: Kessinger Publishing, 2008.

"E. Simms Campbell." Answers.com. Available online. URL: http://www.answers.com/topic/e-simms-campbell. Downloaded March 2, 2009.

Horn, Maurice, ed. *The World Encyclopedia of Cartoons.* New York: Chelsea House Publishers, 1980, p. 154.

Catlett, Elizabeth
(Alice Elizabeth Catlett)
(1915–   ) *sculptor, printmaker, educator*

One of the most important female African-American sculptors of the 20th century, Elizabeth Catlett has celebrated the indomitable strength and spirit of black women in the face of poverty and injustice in her work.

She was born into a middle-class Washington, D.C., family on April 15, 1915. Her grandfather worked on the railroad in North Carolina and saved enough money to buy a farm. Her father, who died before she was born, was a math professor at the Tuskegee Institute in Tuskegee, Alabama, one of the country's first private institutions of higher learning for African Americans. Catlett attended the Lucretia Mott Elementary School and Dunbar High School. She then applied to the Carnegie Institute of Technology in Washington but was denied admittance because she was black. Instead, she attended Howard University in Washington, another leading black college, where she studied drawing and design in the first black art department in the country. "I always wanted to be an artist," she told writer Elton C. Fax in 1971, "but for a long time, I thought I was going to be a painter."

Catlett graduated with honors in 1936 and went on to teach art in Durham, North Carolina. Already she was fighting injustice, working for equal salaries in Durham for black and white teachers. She left teaching to attend the University of Iowa, where she earned the first Master of Fine Arts degree given by the school in 1940.

At Iowa, Catlett studied with leading American painter Grant Wood, who encouraged her to sculpt and focus her work on her African heritage.

The same year she graduated, she was awarded first prize in sculpture for her work *Mother and Child* at the American Negro Exposition in Chicago, Illinois. Catlett married Chicago painter CHARLES WHITE in 1941, and the couple settled in the Harlem section of New York City. She got a job as promotion director in a community school for adults under the sponsorship of the federal Works Progress Administration. One of the school's students was photographer ROY DeCARAVA. White received a fellowship to go to the South, where he created a mural at Hampton Institute in Virginia. During their travels, Catlett taught at several southern schools, including Hampton.

On the couple's return to New York, Catlett continued to create sculptures of mothers and children, one of her most enduring themes. In 1946 the couple moved to Mexico City, Mexico, on a fellowship that she received. Catlett studied mural painting and printmaking and found artistic inspiration and a spiritual home in Mexico. She befriended Mexican artists, studied the country's culture, and created prints depicting Mexican life. Her marriage, however, did not survive the move, and she and White divorced in 1947. He returned to the United States, while she stayed in Mexico City and later married Mexican painter and engraver Francisco (Pancho) Mora. They had three sons together.

In Mexico, Catlett became a member of the Graphic Arts Workshop. She created posters and leaflets that promoted literacy in Mexican schools and made a series of linoleum-cut prints of black heroes.

Catlett's sculpture became less traditionally realistic and more abstract and simplified. This lent great power to such works as *Negro Woman* (1960) and prints such as *Sharecropper* (1968).

Catlett's politics reflected her art. She and Mora were social activists whose left-wing beliefs were investigated by the House Committee on Un-American Activities in the United States in the 1950s. Harassed by the U.S. government, Catlett became a naturalized Mexican citizen

Elizabeth Catlett, now in her 90s, is one of the deans of American sculptors. *(Photographs and Prints Division, Schomburg Center for Research in Black Culture, the New York Public Library, Astor, Lenox and Tilden Foundations)*

in 1962. About the same time she was refused admittance into the United States. Her visa privileges were finally restored nearly a decade later, in part due to the protest of many other African-American artists.

Catlett became the first woman professor of sculpture in 1960 at the National University in Mexico City, which boasts one of the oldest art schools in the Americas. She continued to sculpt, producing a nine-foot figure, "Olmec Bather," for the national Polytechnic Institute of Mexico in 1966. Her "Reclining Woman" was displayed in the Olympic Village during the 1968 Summer Olympics in Mexico City.

She eventually became the director of the School of Fine Arts Sculpture Department at the National University, a position from which she retired in 1976. Catlett continues to live in Mexico. A 50-year retrospective of her work consisting of 60 sculptures held at the Neuberger Museum in Purchase, New York, in 1998 restored her to her place as a leading American sculptor. The exhibition showed the wide range of her work and materials—including polished wood, marble, bronze and terra-cotta, a hard, brownish-red clay.

In May 2003, a bronze sculpture by Catlett was dedicated as a monument to writer Ralph Ellison in Riverside Park, near his former Harlem neighborhood. Among the many awards and honors Catlett has received are one from the Women's Caucus for Art and an international peace prize from the Graphic Arts Workshop, of which she is a founding member. Berkeley, California, has declared an Elizabeth Catlett Week.

"Art must be realistic for me, whether sculpture or print-making," she has said. "I have always wanted my art to service Black people—to reflect us, to relate to us, to stimulate us, to make us aware of our potential."

Further Reading

Catlett, Elizabeth. *Elizabeth Catlett; Sculpture: A Fifty-Year Retrospective*. Seattle: University of Washington Press, 1998.

Herzog, Melanie Anne. *Elizabeth Catlett: An American Artist in Mexico* (The Jacob Lawrence Series on American Artists). Seattle: University of Washington Press, 2005.

Lewis, Samella. *The Art of Elizabeth Catlett*. Prescott Valley, Ariz.: Snowfire Publishing, 2000.

———. *Elizabeth Catlett: In the Image of the People*. Chicago: Art Institute of Chicago, 2005.

Zeidler, Jeanne. *Elizabeth Catlett: Works on Paper*. Hampton, Va.: Hampton University, 1993.

Further Viewing

Elizabeth Catlett: Sculpting the Truth. L & S Video, VHS, 1999.

Chase-Riboud, Barbara
(1939–   ) *sculptor, novelist, poet*

One of the first African-American female sculptors to work on a monumental scale, Barbara Chase-Riboud is also one of the few American artists to have a career as a successful novelist and poet.

She was born Barbara Chase on June 26, 1939, in Philadelphia, Pennsylvania. Her father was a trained painter and frustrated architect. Her mother, a Canadian, earned a college degree in her forties.

Chase won her first art prize at age eight while a student at the Fletcher Art School in Philadelphia. At 15, she won *Seventeen* magazine's art contest with a woodcut and sold her first prints to the Museum of Modern Art in New York City.

She was the only black student at Temple University's art school in Philadelphia when she entered and earned her Bachelor of Fine Arts degree in 1957. Chase won a fellowship to study in Rome, Italy, for a year at the American Academy. Back in the United States, she was the only black woman accepted into the Yale School of Art and Architect in New Haven, Connecticut. While still a student, she received her first commission and created an aluminum fountain in Washington, D.C.

After earning her Master of Fine Arts degree from Yale in 1960, Chase returned to Europe. In Paris, France, she met and married journalist-photographer Marc Riboud. They traveled around Europe while he worked and she raised their two sons. Chase produced no more sculptures until 1967.

She entered her work in the Pan-African Festival in Algeria in North Africa in 1968 and experienced what she calls a "turning point" in her career. She learned a rope-wrapping technique that she incorporated into her sculptures. The ropes gave her work a flexibility and texture that was startlingly original. Back in Europe, she experimented with diverse, contrasting material, including silk and bronze, and bronze and wood, to create dynamic sculptures of great power.

In 1974, Chase-Riboud published her first collection of poetry. Interested in slavery and its role in American history, she published a historical novel, *Sally Hemings* (1979), based on the alleged relationship between President Thomas Jefferson and his slave Sally Hemings. The novel was praised by critics for its realism and thoughtfulness and won her the Janet Heidinger Kafka Prize for best novel by an American woman. To date, she has written five more novels, including *Echo of Lions* (1989), about the slave trade, and *The President's Daughter* (1994), a sequel to *Sally Hemings* that follows the life of Jefferson and Hemings's daughter Harriet into the Civil War period. In 1997, Chase-Riboud sued the movie production company Dreamworks for $10 million for allegedly plagiarizing her novel *Echo of Lions* in their film *Amistad* (1997). The suit ended in an undisclosed out-of-court settlement.

Chase-Riboud's art continues to be as bold and daring as her fiction. One of her most recent works, *Africa Rising,* a monumental sculpture, commemorates a colonial African-American burial ground in New York City. *Tantra* (1995), a Hindu word relating to a circular assembly of signs and symbols, is made of fabric in gold, silk, and bronze.

She is the recipient of the Academy of Italy Award Gold Medal (1978) and is a Knight of the Order of Arts and Letters of the French Republic (1996). Chase-Riboud holds honorary doctorate degrees from several universities, including her alma mater Temple University. A citizen of the world who divides her time between Paris and New York, Barbara Chase-Riboud sees herself as an independent and original black sculptor, much like her role model, pioneer woman sculptor EDMONIA LEWIS.

Further Reading

Chase-Riboud, Barbara. *Hottentot Venus*. New York: Anchor, 2004.

———. *Sally Hemings*. Reprint, Chicago: Chicago Review Press, 2009.

Jason, Anthony F., and Peter Howard Selz. *Barbara Chase-Riboud: Sculptor.* New York: Harry N. Abrams, 1999.

Munro, Eleanor C. *Originals—American Woman Artists.* New York: Da Capo Press, 2000.

Wells, Monique Y. "Barbara Chase-Riboud, Visionary Woman . . ." *Black Issues Book Review,* March 2005, p. 64.

Clark, Claude

(1915–2001) *painter, printmaker, educator, writer*

A leader in establishing an art curriculum that deals with the black experience, Claude Clark painted themes from African-American life in his native South with a bold expressiveness.

He was born on November 11, 1915, in Rockingham, Georgia, and attended the Philadelphia Museum School of Industrial Art in 1935. On leaving school, Clark worked with the Federal Arts Projects of the Works Progress Administration for several years, developing a simple style of painting that owed much to folk art. The first major exhibition of his work took place at the New York World's Fair in 1939. In 1945, he began teaching art in Philadelphia's public schools. Clark was hired as an assistant professor of art at Talladega College in Talladega, Alabama, in 1948, and remained there for the next seven years. In 1955 he moved to California and enrolled in Sacramento University, earning a Bachelor of Arts degree. He earned a Master of Arts degree at the University of California at Berkeley in 1962. Clark tried creating abstract art at Berkeley but later returned to figurative art. He brought a strong social consciousness to his paintings of African Americans, such as in the work "Slave Lynching." He painted scenes of Caribbean life as well as life in his native rural South.

"Clark's work achieves a tactile reality by means of the solidity of paint piled in ropes and mounds on the canvas with a palette knife," wrote fellow African-American artist DAVID C. DRISKELL.

Clark turned his attention to making the study of art more meaningful for African-American students while teaching at Merritt College in Oakland, California. In 1967, he developed an art curriculum there that focused primarily on black art and artists. It became the blueprint for other black art programs throughout the state of California.

In 1969, Clark wrote the textbook *A Black Art Perspective: A Black Teacher's Guide to a Black Visual Art Curriculum,* which became the prime text for educators across the country. He revised this valuable resource in the 1990s with his wife, Daima May Lockhart. Clark retired from Merritt College in 1981 and died on April 21, 2001 at age 85.

"Today [the black artist] has reached the phase of Political Realism where his art becomes even more functional," Clark wrote in a letter to David C. Driskell in 1972. "He not only presents the condition but names the enemy, and directs us toward a plan of action in search of our own roots and eventual liberation."

His son, Claude Lockhart Clark, is a well-known wood carver.

Further Reading

"Claude Clark *Slave Lynching,* 1946." Narratives of African American Art and Identity. Available online. URL: http://www.driskellcenter.umd.edu/narratives/exhibition/sec4/clar_c_01.htm. Downloaded March 24, 2009.

Riggs, Thomas, ed. *St. James Guide to Black Artists.* Detroit, Mich.: St. James Press, 1997, pp. 110–112.

Web site of Claude Clark. Available online. URL: http://www.claudeclark.com/index.html. Downloaded March 3, 2009.

Colescott, Robert
(1925–2009) *painter, educator*

An artist with a highly developed sense of humor and irony, Robert Colescott took masterworks of European art and populated them with contemporary black people in order to comment on the racism in American society today.

He was born on August 26, 1925, in Oakland, California. He studied art at the University of California, Berkeley, where he earned his Bachelor of Arts degree in 1949 and a Master of Arts degree three years later. Colescott studied in Paris, France, with leading French artist Fernand Léger for a year and spent two years in Cairo, Egypt, where he taught at the American University and discovered his African heritage.

On returning to the United States, Colescott began producing the works he is best known for—humorous configurations of European art as seen through a black sensibility. Among the European artists he parodied are Vincent van Gogh and Pablo Picasso. In more recent years, Colescott added another layer to his reinterpretative paintings—the often uneasy relations between the sexes, both in terms of black men and women and interracial relationships. His large charcoal drawings of sensuous women from the mid-1980s convey both humor and tenderness and reveal a strain of female liberation in his work.

Colescott was associate professor of art at Portland State University in Portland, Oregon, from 1957 to 1966 and taught at the San Francisco Art Institute from 1976 to 1985. He then became professor of art at the University of Arizona, Tucson. In 1990, he became regents' professor of art at Arizona. He retired in 1998 and was named professor emeritus. Colescott was the recipient of three National Endowment of the Arts grants and won a Guggenheim Fellowship in 1985. His work was part of group exhibitions over the last decade at the Museum of Modern Art and the Whitney Museum of Contemporary Art, both in New York City, and the Corcoran Gallery of Art in Washington, D.C. The city of Houston, Texas, honored him by declaring December 2, 1988, "Robert Colescott Day." Colescott was chosen to represent the United States at the 1997 Venice Biennale with works dating from 1987 to 1997.

He was the African-American artist to represent the United States there in a solo exhibition.

"Colescott transcended surface satire and provoked complex reactions, making people aware of the often absurd and racist patterns of American life," wrote art critic Udo Kultermann. *Robert Colescott: Troubled Goods: A Ten Year Survey (1997–2007)* was mounted at the Meridian Gallery in San Francisco in 2007. The exhibit *Robert Colescott: Works on Paper* was held at the Phyllis Kind Gallery in New York City in 2008. Robert Colescott died from the effects of Parkinson's disease on June 4, 2009, at his home in Tucson. He was 83.

Further Reading

Colescott, Robert. *Robert Colescott: Recent Paintings.* Buffalo, N.Y.: Thorner Press, 1997.

Selz, Peter. *Robert Colescott: Troubled Goods.* San Francisco, Calif.: Meridian Gallery, 2008.

Smith, Roberta. "Robert Colescott, 83, Artist Who Toyed with Stereotypes." *New York Times*, June 10, 2009, p. A27 [obituary].

Weiss, Katherine, and Susan Arnold. *The Eye of the Beholder: Recent Work by Robert Colescott: Another Judgment.* Richmond, Va.: University of Richmond Press, 1988.

Further Viewing

Robert Colescott: The One-Two Punch. L & S Video, VHS, 1999.

Commodore, Chester

(1914–2004) *cartoonist, editorial cartoonist*

For five decades the celebrated editorial cartoonist for the *Chicago Defender*, the nation's leading black newspaper, Chester Commodore was one of the few African Americans to make his mark nationally in this challenging and highly specialized genre of cartooning.

He was born in 1914 in Racine, Wisconsin and began cartooning at age five on his grandmother's dining room table under the tutelage of his uncle John Prophet. The family moved to Chicago, Illinois, when he was 13. Commodore attended Tilden Technical High School and after graduating worked at a variety of odd jobs, from chauffeur to Pullman railroad car cleaner.

In 1938, he was hired as a cartoonist for the *Minneapolis Star*, a newspaper in Minneapolis, Minnesota, on the recommendation of a well-known lawyer. But when Commodore showed up for work, he was dismissed because he was black. Undaunted, he continued to draw cartoons for his own pleasure and that of fellow workers.

In 1948, a national printers' strike led to a job on the *Chicago Defender*, then a weekly black newspaper. A friend hired him to help with printing and publishing the paper even though Commodore had no experience in this area. He did his job so well that he was soon hired as the paper's advertisement layout artist. He was later promoted to editorial artist and then layout designer for the entire paper. In 1950, when the paper's regular cartoonist died, Commodore took over and produced seven different cartoon features for each issue. Later the paper became a daily, and his workload doubled. He not only drew the established comic features but also created new ones, such as the family humor strip *The Sparks* and *Ravings of Professor Doodle*.

After more than two decades of this heavy workload, Commodore asked to be relieved of his duties to concentrate on drawing the newspaper's editorial cartoons. The focus in these cartoons was on the black community and the issues that affected them. The targets of his satire included loan sharks, white racists, and indifferent politicians.

In 1981, Commodore went into semiretirement and moved to Colorado, but he returned to drawing occasional editorial cartoons for the *Chicago Defender* in 1992.

Chester Commodore's editorial cartoons have earned him 12 nominations for the Pulitzer Prize. In 1973, he was named Best Editorial Cartoonist of the year by the magazine *Cartoon PROfiles* and received the Gold Medallion Award for his cartooning in 1976. The Prairie School in Commodore's hometown of Racine established a scholarship and Achievement Award for Creativity and Writing in his honor in 1985.

Chester Commodore died on April 10, 2004. The Chicago Public Library acquired his papers from his stepdaughter and family in the summer of 2007. The following year the library presented the exhibition, "Chester Commodore—1914–2004: Work and Life of a Pioneering Cartoonist of Color."

"You don't need a lot of words to make your point," Commodore once said about creating editorial cartoons. "You've already drawn the cartoon—it should say it all!"

Further Reading

"Bungleton Green: The Chester Commodore Years." Barnacle Press comics. Available online. URL: http://www.barnaclepress.com/?p=473. Downloaded March 3, 2009.

"Chester Commodore Interview," PBS website. Available online. URL: http://www.pbs.org/blackpress/film/transcripts/commod.html. Downloaded March 3, 2009.

"Commodore exhibit to run throughout 2008." The Association of American Editorial Cartoonists Web site. Available online. URL: http://editorialcartoonists.com/news/article.cfm/816/. Downloaded March 3, 2009.

Conwill, Houston

(1947–   ) *installation artist, mixed-media artist, painter, sculptor*

Houston Conwill is one of the leading lights of a generation of African-American artists intent on stretching the concept of what is a work of art. His installations combine traditional art forms with music, dance, narrative, song, and theater to create works that envelop the viewer with the art experience.

He was born in Lexington, Kentucky, on April 2, 1947. He earned his Bachelor of Fine Arts degree from Howard University in Washington, D.C., in 1973 and went on to earn a Master of Fine Arts degree from USC. Conwill began his career as a painter and sculptor but changed his direction largely through working with two older artists. Painter JEFF DONALDSON led him to look at art and the world as a black artist. SAM GILLIAM, for whom he later worked as an assistant, showed Conwill how painting could break free of its two-dimensional framework.

Out of these influences and his own original ideas, Conwill became an installation artist in Los Angeles in the late 1970s. Installation art is any artwork that encompasses an extended space and often incorporates different media to enrich the viewing experience.

One of Conwill's major contributions to installation art was the creation of scroll forms he called "petrigraphs," filled with African-American objects and placed in niches within a work. In a more elaborate scenario, he focused a live and taped performance of music and native rituals around West African juju bags, symbols of good luck.

Conwill moved to New York in 1980, where he enlarged the concept of the petrigraph and created the "cosmogram," a ceremonial ground drawing based on those of the Kongo people of Zaire in Africa. The cosmogram created an environment of movement and music around the artwork that further drew in the spectator.

Conwill took the unusual step in 1989 of forming a permanent collaboration with two other artists—his sister, artist and poet Estella Conwill Majozo, and architect Joseph De Pace. Their first three cosmograms together were put on exhibit in public libraries in New York, Chicago, and Charleston, South Carolina. Each work related to the history of the public site—*River* honored black

New York poet Langston Hughes. *DuSable's Journey* commemorated the life of black explorer and founder of Chicago, Jean-Baptiste Point DuSable. *The New Charleston* was a tribute to the popular 1920s dance named for the southern city.

In 1995, the trio created *The New Ring Shout*, after an 18th-century African-American burial ground discovered in New York City three years earlier. "Together," says Conwill, "we form an interdisciplinary team of collaborating artists concerned with the function of art in bringing meaning to our lives and serving as a catalyst for social change."

Further Reading

Conwill Houston. *Houston Conwill: Works: August 2– October 8, 1989.* Washington, D.C.: Hirshhorn Museum and Sculpture Garden, 1989.

"Houston Conwill Arc, 1986." York College's Online Gallery of Contemporary Art. Available online. URL: http://york.cuny.edu/compus-art/installation/houston-conwill.html. Downloaded March 3, 2009.

Lewis, Samella. *African American Art and Artists.* Berkeley: University of California Press, 2003, pp. 277–279.

Riggs, Thomas, ed. *St. James Guide to Black Artists.* Detroit, Mich.: St. James Press, 1997, pp. 118–121.

Cortor, Eldzier

(1916–) *painter, printmaker*

An uncompromising artist with a singular vision, Eldzier Cortor has celebrated the beauty and spiritual strength of black women in his painting and lithographs for more than five decades.

He was born on January 10, 1916, in Richmond, Virginia. His father was a self-taught electrician who moved his family to Chicago, Illinois, when Eldzier was still an infant. The senior Cortor opened a grocery store and appliance repair shop with his wife and later became one of the first black pilots in the United States. His son began copying comic strips as a boy and aspired to become a cartoonist. At Englewood High School, he met fellow student CHARLES WHITE, another future African-American artist.

Cortor dropped out of high school and went to work to help support his family. He continued, however, to pursue his interest in art in evening drawing classes at the Chicago Art Institute. He was finally able to attend the institute full-time at the age of 25. A white teacher from Texas exposed him to the exquisite sculpture of Africa and helped convince Cortor to pursue fine art. After finishing school he went to work in 1937 on federal arts projects for the Works Progress Administration. He also taught art at the South Side Community Arts Center.

Cortor was awarded a Rosenwald Fellowship and used the money to travel to the Sea Islands off the South Carolina coast. Here he lived among the native African Americans called Gullah, who had strong cultural ties to Africa. About this time he abandoned his earlier abstract art for a more representational style of painting that focused on African-American people. He later moved to New York and studied at the National Institute of Design and Columbia University, where he learned woodblock printing. Cortor mastered the art of lithography, in which prints are made from an original work of art. This allowed him to sell inexpensive copies of one painting and freed him from having to work with galleries to sell his artwork.

Cortor began to create the stunning, statuesque nude black women that he is best known for. Heavily influenced by African sculpture, his paintings of nudes have the shape and weight of sculptures with their full, elongated bodies. These strong women sometimes appeared within the crowded, sordid confines of an urban apartment. Rather than make them less noble, such surroundings only brought their power and dignity to the fore.

A photograph of one of Cortor's paintings appeared in *Life* magazine in 1946 and brought him national attention. It also earned him a Guggenheim Fellowship, which allowed him to travel to the West Indian islands of Cuba, Jamaica, and Haiti. He fell in love with the African-derived culture of Haiti and remained there for two years, teaching drawing at the Haitian Centre d'Art in the capital of Port-au-Prince.

On his return to the States, Cortor lived in Chicago and then New York City. When sales of his paintings fell off during the politically conservative 1950s, he lived in Mexico for several years. Returning to the United States, he grew tired of the politics involved in dealing with art galleries and sold his lithographs directly through the Associated American Artists of New York. The only other avenue for his work is competitive, juried museum shows. Eldzier Cortor has remained faithful to his nudes, which he refers to as his "classical compositions," and has not changed his style to take advantage of current art trends and fashions.

He created paintings that he has said "can fit into any period—not locked into a style that will go out of date. . . I very carefully try to keep things from being the latest style—the latest thing."

Back in 1940, he said, "I want to paint, never reach any set goals, always work towards an ideal." Now in his 90s, Eldzier Cortor is still working toward that ideal.

Further Reading

Bearden, Romare, and Harry Henderson. *A History of African-American Artists: From 1792 to the Present.* New York: Pantheon Books, 1993, pp. 272–279.

"Eldzier Cortor." Answers.com. Available online. URL: http://www.answers.com/topic/eldziercortor. Downloaded March 3, 2009.

Riggs, Thomas, ed. *St. James Guide to Black Artists.* Detroit, Mich.: St. James Press, 1997, p. 121.

Robinson, Jontyle Theresa, David Driskell and Others. *Three Masters: Eldzier Cortor, Hughie Lee-Smith, Archibald John Motley Jr.* New York: Kenkeleba Gallery, 1988.

Cowans, Adger

(1936–) *photographer, painter, educator*

One of the leaders in the movement to make photography a fine art in the United States, Adger Cowans brings passion and drama to every photograph he takes, from movie stills to documentary work.

He was born on September 19, 1936. He received a Bachelor of Fine Arts degree in photography from Ohio University in Athens, Ohio, in 1958 and served in the U.S. Navy as a photographer. Cowans later studied filmmaking at the School of Visual Arts in New York and gained a love of film that later brought him into the movie industry.

Cowans's first photography job was for *Life* magazine, where he worked with master photographer GORDON PARKS. He also worked with the fashion photographer Henri Clarke. With Parks, Cowans documented in photos the Civil Rights movement in the 1960s, particularly photographing events surrounding the Congress of Racial Equality and the Student Nonviolent Coordinating Committee. His strong images earned him first prize at the Yolo International Exhibition in 1963. Two years later he had his first one-man show at the Heliography Gallery in New York, one of the first American galleries to display photography as fine art. That same year Cowans was awarded a John Hay Whitney Fellowship.

Since the 1970s, he has made still pictures for publicity purposes for more than 30 motion pictures, including *The Way We Were, Dirty Dancing, The Cotton Club, On Golden Pond,* and *Boomerang.*

Cowans's photographs have appeared in many leading magazines, including *Life, Esquire, Harper's Bazaar,* and the African-American publications *Essence* and *Ebony.* His paintings are in the collections of the Schomburg Center for Research in Black Culture and the Studio Museum in Harlem, both in New York City. Cowans has traveled to Suriname in South America and taken memorable photographs of the native people

Adger Cowans has worked in a variety of styles as a photographer, from movie stills to fine art. *(Anthony Barboza)*

there. Photography historian and writer Deborah Willis has called his pictures of the people of Suriname "intimate as well as documentary in intention." Cowans's book-length collection *Sacred Bond: Black Men and Their Mothers* was published in 1998. Recent major exhibitions of his work include the Detroit Institute of Art's "Reflections in Black: Smithsonian African American Photography" (2001) and the New Jersey Institute of Technology's "Different Directions" in Newark, New Jersey (2002).

Adger Cowans is a founder of International Black Photographers and is a member of Afri-COBRA (Coalition of Black Relevant Artists) and the International Photographers of the Motion Picture Industry. He has lectured and taught photography at the Cleveland Institute of the Arts in Cleveland, Ohio, the University of Michigan, and Wayne State University in Detroit, Michigan. He is the recipient of the Lorenzo II Magnifico Alla Carriera, in recognition of a distinguished career, at the 2001 Florence Biennale of Contemporary Art. "I like exposing things that are seen all the time but not seen," Cowans has said.

Further Reading

"Art Works of Adger W. Cowans." Burgess Fine Arts. Available online. URL: http://www.burgessfinearts. com/Cowans.htm. Downloaded March 3, 2009.

Brown, Keith Michael, and Adger W. Cowans, photographer. *Sacred Bond: Black Men and Their Mothers.* Darby, Pa.: Diane Publishing Co., 2002.

Willis, Deborah. *Reflections in Black: A History of Black Photographers from 1840 to the Present.* New York: W. W. Norton, 2002, pp. 118, 156–157.

Cox, Renee
(1960–   ) *photographer, mixed-media artist*

One of the most controversial African-American artists working today, Renee Cox has used her own body, both nude and clothed, to celebrate black womanhood and criticize a society she often views as racist and sexist.

She was born on October 16, 1960, in Colgate, Jamaica, into a middle-class family who later settled in Scarsdale, New York. Cox's first ambition was to become a filmmaker. "I was always interested in the visual," she said in one interview. "But I had a baby boomer reaction and was into the immediate gratification of photography as opposed to film, which is a more laborious project."

From the very beginning, her work showed a deep concern for social issues and employed disturbing religious imagery. In *It Shall Be Named* (1994), a black man's distorted body made up of 11 separate photographs hangs from a cross, as much resembling a lynched man as the crucified Christ.

Renee Cox's often controversial photographs and mixed-media art have brought her both fame and notoriety. *(Photo courtesy of the artist)*

In her first one-woman show at a New York gallery in 1998, Cox made herself the center of attention. Dressed in the colorful garb of a black superhero named Raje, Cox appeared in a series of large, color photographs. In one picture, she towered over a cab in Times Square. In another, she broke steel chains before an erupting volcano. In the most pointed picture, entitled *The Liberation of UB and Lady J,* Cox's Raje rescued the black stereotyped advertising figures of Uncle Ben and Aunt Jemima from their products' labels. The photograph was featured on the cover of the French magazine *Le Monde.*

"These slick, color-laden images, their large format and Cox's own powerfully beautiful figure heighten the visual impact of the work, making Cox's politics clear and engaging," wrote one critic.

But her next photographic series would be less engaging for many people and would create a firestorm of controversy. In the series *Flipping the Script,* Cox took a number of European religious masterpieces, including Michelangelo's *David* and the *Pietà,* and reinterpreted them with contemporary black figures.

"Christianity is big in the African-American community, but there are no presentations of us," she said. "I took it upon myself to include people of color in these classic scenarios."

The photograph that created the most controversy when it was shown in a black photography exhibit at the Brooklyn Museum in New York City in 2001 was *Yo Mama's Last Supper.* It was a remake of Leonardo da Vinci's *Last Supper* with a nude Cox sitting in for Jesus Christ, surrounded by all black disciples, except for Judas who was white. Many Roman Catholics were outraged at the photograph and New York Mayor Rudolph Giuliani called for the forming of a commission to set "decency standards" to keep such works from being shown in any New York museum that received public funds.

Cox responded by stating "I have a right to reinterpret the Last Supper as Leonardo da Vinci created the Last Supper with people who look like him . . . The hoopla and the fury are because I'm a black female . . . It's about me having nothing to hide."

Renee Cox continues to push the envelope in her work, questioning society and the roles it gives to blacks and women with her elaborate scenarios. In the autobiographical *American Family* (2002), mounted at the Robert Miller Gallery in New York, Cox juxtaposed sexually charged self-portraits with old family album photographs and a video projection. In *Queen Nanny of the Maroons* (2005), also at the Miller Gallery, Cox posed as the Jamaican heroine Queen Nanny who led an 18th-century rebellion against the British. The exhibit won the Aaron Matalon Award at the Jamaican Biennial in 2007.

Further Reading

Cox, Renee, and Jo Anna Isaak. *Renee Cox: American Family.* New York: Robert Miller Gallery, 2002.

Official Web site of Renee Cox. Available online. URL: http://reneecox.org/. Downloaded March 3, 2009.

Williams, Monte. "Freedom of Expression: Renee Cox vs. William Donohue/'Yo Mama's Last Supper.'" *New York Times,* February 21, 2001, pp. A21, B3.

Willis, Deborah. *Reflections in Black: A History of Black Photographers from 1840 to the Present.* New York: W. W. Norton, 2000, pp. 188, 316–317.

Craft, Jerry

(1963–) *cartoonist, illustrator*

Creator of the syndicated comic strip *Mama's Boyz,* Jerry Craft is as talented an entrepreneur as he is a cartoonist, having self-published both his popular strip and a book-length collection.

He was born on January 22, 1963, in New York City. "I started off by tracing drawings from my comic books collection," he said in a 1996 interview, "then when I got older I started trying to draw on my own."

Craft attended the School of Visual Arts in New York City, where he did not take a single cartooning course, and received his Bachelor of Fine Arts degree in 1984. One day two years later, he was reading his local weekly paper and was appalled by the poor quality of its comic strip. Deciding he could do better, he created a strip called *The Outside View* and submitted it to the paper's editor. Just three weeks later his comic was running alongside the strip he had complained about. Craft sold *The Outside View* to several newspapers on his own, but was turned down when he brought it to King Features, one of the nation's biggest comic strip syndicates.

In 1990, Craft worked on several established comic books, including DC Comics' *Sweet Sixteen,* Harvey's *New Kids on the Block,* and Marvel's *Yuppies From Hell.*

In 1991, he created his own comic strip, *Mama's Boyz,* about two African-American teenage brothers and their mother. Craft took up the bold challenge of selling his comic strip himself directly to newspapers. He made his first sale to New York's *The City Sun* in November 1992. Soon *Mama's Boyz* was appearing in newspapers in half a dozen other cities. In 1995, King Features, which had originally rejected his work, agreed to distribute Craft's strip to more than 1,500 weekly and monthly newspapers as part of a package of features.

Mama's Boyz revolves around Pauline Porter, a single mom, and her two sons, Tyrell and Yusuf. Pauline's husband Virgil died of diabetes, and with the help of her boys, she supports the family with a bookstore that specializes in African-American literature. Other characters includes Uncle Greggo, who runs a computer software company; Gran'pa, a retired chef from Harlem in New York City; and pretty Keisha, who helps out in the bookstore.

While the strip is warm and funny, Craft takes the disease of diabetes seriously. The Porter family members are national spokescharacters for the American Diabetes Association, helping to fight a disease that is particularly prevalent among African Americans. Craft was presented with the Association's Outstanding Supporter Award for his work during National Diabetes Month in 1996. "I've looked at cartooning as entertainment and I've looked at it as a source of income," Craft has said, "but to think that my characters might actually help to save someone's life is amazing."

Encouraged by the comic's success, Craft self-published a book-length collection of the best of *Mama's Boyz* in 1997. This daunting task took him a year and a half of work, but he feels it was worth it. "I don't think that people realize how important it is to be able to see and relate to African-American cartoon characters, especially for kids," he has said. "That's why I decided to self-publish."

More recently, Craft has begun to create a line of products based on *Mama's Boyz,* including mugs, T-shirts, and hats. In 2006, Craft formed his own company, Mama's Boyz Inc. In June 2007, he was the recipient of a "Conversation Starter" award from the Washington, D.C., campaign to Prevent Teenage Pregnancy. He has illustrated two children's books *Hillary's Big Business Adventure* (2008) and *Looking to the Clouds for Daddy* (2009).

While he is proud to be one of only four black cartoonists out of some 300 syndicated cartoonists in the country, Craft would like to see that small number grow in the future. "It amazes me to think that you have to go back 25 years to Fat Albert and the Cosby Kids to find really popular black characters [in comic strips]," he has said.

Jerry Craft and his colleagues are busy changing that for a new generation of comics readers.

Further Reading

Craft, Jerry. *Mama's Boyz: As American as Sweet Potato Pie!* New York: American Publishing Company, 1997.

Horn, Maurice, ed. *The World Encyclopedia of Comics.* New York: Chelsea House Publishers, 1995, p. 218.

"Jerry Craft." African American Literature Book Club. Available online. URL: http://aalbc.com/authors/jerry.htm. Downloaded March 3, 2009.

Crews, Donald

(1938–   ) *illustrator, writer*

A children's book writer and illustrator who specializes in nonfiction, Donald Crews re-creates his subject matter for his readers in bold and vivid pictures.

He was born on August 30, 1938, in Newark, New Jersey. His father, Asa Crews, was a railroad trackman and his mother, Marshanna White, a dressmaker. Interested in art from an early age, Crews attended the Arts High School in Newark and then enrolled in the School of Art at The Cooper Union in New York City. After graduation, he worked for *Dance* magazine for a time until he was drafted into the U.S. Army in 1962. He served for 18 months in Germany, where he married Ann Jonas, a fellow student at Cooper Union.

While in the service, Crews created his first picture book, *We Read: A to Z*, in his spare time. He returned to the United States and civilian life in 1964 and worked as a freelance artist, doing book jackets and book illustrations. Publisher Harper & Row published *We Read: A to Z* in 1967. It won high praise from critics for its original and sophisticated approach to teaching children the alphabet. His next book, *Ten Black Dots* (1968), took a similar approach to counting numbers.

After illustrating several books written by other writers, Crews moved into the major league of children's book illustrators with *Freight Train* (1978). This exciting visualization of a train's journey across the land was inspired by Crews's childhood memories of watching trains pass by at his grandparents' farm in Cottondale, Florida. *Freight Train* was named a Caldecott Honor Book and an American Library Association (ALA) Notable Book. His next work, *Truck* (1981), brought the same visual excitement to a truck's journey and was also a Caldecott Honor Book. Over the years, Crews has continued to produce popular books for preschoolers about things and places in movement, including *Harbor* (1982), *Bicycle Race* (1985), *Night at the Fair* (1998), and *School Bus* (2002).

Some of his books have blended his nonfiction style with narrative fiction. Perhaps the best example is *Shortcut* (1996), about a group of boys that narrowly escapes an oncoming train, which *Horn Book* called "a superb example of the picture book as theater."

Donald Crews lives with his wife, Ann Jonas, a freelance artist and designer, in the Hudson River Valley of New York State.

"You have to find something that interests you, and create a visual interpretation that will excite people," Crews has written about his work. "[Books] should each have something different and be filled with your full creative range."

Further Reading

Bodmer, George. "Donald Crews: The signs and times of an American childhood—essay and interview." Bnet. Available online. URL: http://findarticles.com/p/articles.mi_m2838/is_n1_32/ai_20610477. Downloaded March 3, 2009.

Crews, Donald. *Freight Train*. New York: Tupelo, 1996 [board edition].

———. *Shortcut*. New York: Mulberry Books, 1996.

Giganti, Paul, and Donald Crews. *How Many Blue Birds Flew Away?: A Counting Book with a Difference*. New York: Greenwillow, 2005.

Telgen, Diane, ed. *Something About the Author, Volume 76*. Detroit, Mich.: Gale Research, 1994, pp. 41–45.

Crichlow, Ernest

(1914–2005) *painter, illustrator, muralist, printmaker, educator*

A social realist who is capable of delivering his message with expressive power, Ernest Crichlow was also one of the first successful African-American illustrators of children's books.

He was born on June 19, 1914, in Brooklyn, New York. His parents, Herbert and Irene Clark Crichlow, were from the West Indian island of Barbados. He demonstrated his talent for drawing in grade school and attended Hareen High School in New York City. His teachers believed in his gifts and helped him get a scholarship to the Commercial Illustration School of Art.

However, he first pursued a career as a fine artist, encouraged by the sculptors AUGUSTA SAVAGE and SELMA BURKE, whom he met at the Harlem Art Center in New York. While there he met other young artists, including JACOB LAWRENCE and CHARLES WHITE. Like these artists, Crichlow created paintings and prints with a strong social message. One of his best-known early works is the print *Lovers III* (1938), which depicts a black woman confronted in her bedroom by a white-hooded member of the Ku Klux Klan, a white racist group. Gabriel Tenabe has called it "an ominous lithograph, small but powerful . . . [that] is social commentary in the highest degree."

Crichlow's first children's book, *Two Is a Team*, written by Lorraine and Jerrold Beim, appeared in 1945. It was a story about the interracial friendship of two boys. After that he illustrated a number of books, including biographies of abolitionist Harriet Tubman and President Abraham Lincoln.

One of his most ambitious works is a 25-panel mural he created at the Boys and Girls High School in Brooklyn in 1976. It depicts people at work at various careers and trades, an inspiration for students to achieve excellence in their lives. Crichlow went to Lagos, Nigeria, in 1977 to participate in the Black and African Festival of African Countries. He has visited the West Indian island of Jamaica many times, and its cool Caribbean colors are reflected in his paintings.

Crichlow taught at numerous institutes of higher learning, including SUNY, New Paltz, City College of New York, and the Brooklyn Museum Art School. He founded the Cinque Gallery for young developing black artists in New York with ROMARE BEARDEN and NORMAN LEWIS in 1969. Crichlow was one of 10 black artists from the National Conference of Artists honored by President Jimmy Carter at the White House in the late 1970s. He participated in the Art Gala V at North Carolina Central University in Raleigh, North Carolina, in 2001.

Ernest Crichlow died of heart failure on November 10, 2005, at age 91.

Further Reading

Beim, Lorraine Levey, Jerrold Beim, and Ernest Crichlow, illustrator. *Two Is a Team* (1945). Reprint, New York: Harcourt Brace, 1974.

"Ernest Crichlow (1914–2005)," aviscafineart.com. Available online. URL: http://www.avisecafineart.com/Other_Artists/Ernest_Crichlow/ernest_crichlow.htm. Downloaded March 3, 2009.

New York, Skylight Gallery. *Ernest Crichlow: A Life in Art*. New York: Bedford Stuyvesant Restoration Corp., 2000.

Riggs, Thomas, ed. *St. James Guide to Black Artists*. Detroit, Mich.: St. James Press, 1997, pp. 122–123.

Sterling, Dorothy, and Ernest Crichlow, illustrator. *Freedom Train: The Story of Harriet Tubman*. New York: Doubleday, 1970.

Crite, Allan Rohan

(1910–2007) *painter, printmaker, illustrator, educator*

Faithful chronicler of the black Boston neighborhood where he lived most of his long life, Allan Rohan Crite was one of the first African-American artists to celebrate the lives of ordinary black Americans.

He was born on March 20, 1910, in Plainfield, New Jersey, the only child of Oscar and Annamae Crite. His father was an electrical engineer and his mother a homemaker who wrote poetry in her spare time. He attended the Boston English High School, then won a scholarship to the School of the Museum of Fine Arts, where he studied for six years. Even though Crite was already a budding artist, his loyalty to his parents proved stronger than to his career. When his father was seriously injured in an accident at work that year, Crite remained at home, helping his mother care for him for the next eight years until his father's death.

Through the 1930s, he painted the people in Roxbury and the South End, the main black communities of Boston. These works were characterized by their bold realism, meticulous detail, and warm feelings. The most famous of these paintings is *Parade on Hammond Street*, which depicts black families dressed up in their Sunday clothes viewing a passing parade.

"My intentions in the neighborhood paintings and some drawings," Crite wrote, "was to show . . . persons enjoying the usual pleasures of life with its mixtures of both sorrow and joys."

He called himself the "reporter-artist" of his neighborhood, and his paintings showed African-Americans not as symbols or stereotypes or exotics but as everyday people who enjoyed the same things white Americans did.

In 1940, Crite took a job as an engineering draftsman with the Boston Naval Shipyard and remained in that position for 30 years. All that time he continued to paint and draw. In the 1940s, he began creating religious works. A devout Christian and member of the Episcopalian Church, Crite drew and painted church banners, altarpieces, and Stations of the Cross at several churches. His religious artwork culminated in what many regard as his masterwork in the genre, *Three Spirituals from Earth to Heaven* (1948), a book of pen-and-brush illustrations that vividly visualized three well-known Negro spirituals.

Crite first turned to teaching at Oberlin College in Ohio in 1958 as a lecturer. He earned a Bachelor of Arts degree from Harvard University Extension School in Cambridge, Massachusetts, in 1968. He taught art at Roxbury Community College in New York in 1977.

He moved with his mother to a 150-year-old town house on Columbus Avenue in Boston in 1971. She died six years later.

Although his paintings became part of the permanent collections of many important museums across the country, Crite did little to promote his art and gave away numerous paintings or sold them for next to nothing.

"Allan's still undiscovered; he's still practically an unknown artist," said Michael Wentworth, curator of painting and sculpture at the Boston Athenaeum. "He would have been one of the most important black artists of his time, but he's always been indifferent to exhibiting or putting himself forward."

Despite this casual approach to his career, honors began to come his way by the 1980s. He received Harvard's 350th anniversary medal in 1986, and in the same year a square near his home was named after him.

Crite lived in his Boston town house with his wife, Jackie Cox, an art consultant whom he married in 1993. She was also his agent and the director of the Allan Rohan Crite Research Institute. Allan Rohan Crite died of natural causes on September 11, 2007, at age 97. In a 2002 review of his work the *Boston Globe* called him "the grand-daddy of the Boston art scene."

"I've only done one piece of work in my life," Crite said in a newspaper article in 2000. "I regard everything I've done since age six as part of one work. And I'll stop working on it only when I die."

Further Reading

Caro, Julie Levin, Barbara Earl Thomas, and Edmund Barry Gaither. *Allan Rohan Crite: Artist-Reporter of the African American Community.* Seattle, Wa.: Frye Art Museum, 2001.

Crite, Allan Rohan. *All Glory: Brush Drawing Meditations on the Prayer of Consecration.* Whitefish, Mont.: Kessinger Publishing, 2007.

———. *Three Spirituals from Earth to Heaven.* Cambridge, Mass.: Harvard University Press, 1948.

Eckel, Mike. "One Artist, One Story," Alumni Bulletin. Harvard University Extension School website. Available online. URL: http://www.dce.harvard.edu/pubs/alum/2000/03.html. Downloaded March 3, 2009.

Perry, Regenia A. *Free Within Ourselves: African-American Artists in the Collection of the National Museum of American Art.* San Francisco: Pomegranate Communications, 1992, pp. 50–53.

Cuffie, Curtis
(1955–2002) *folk sculptor*

A sculptor who once lived on the streets of New York City, Curtis Cuffie created strange, often fragile urban assemblages that amazed and enchanted passersby and brought this homeless artist fame and stability.

He was born in Hartesville, South Carolina, in 1955 and moved to Brooklyn, New York, at age 15 to live with two older brothers. His mother's death in 1983 deeply depressed Cuffie, and he soon found himself alone and living on the streets of Lower Manhattan. He began to take objects he found on the streets—wires, discarded furniture, scraps of clothing, and auto parts—and build them into original sculptors. One of his favorite motifs was mops turned upside down and draped in rags so that they looked like city scarecrows.

Cuffie exhibited his art works on sidewalks, along fences, and against walls. It did not seem to bother him that the sanitation department regularly removed or destroyed his art: He just kept creating more of it.

By the early 1990s, Cuffie's odd creations were attracting the attention of many people in the East Village—including artists like DAVID HAMMONS, who befriended Cuffie, and Carol Thompson, a former curator of the Museum for African Art in SoHo, another Manhattan neighborhood. Thompson and Cuffie became romantically involved, and he moved in with her in 1996, making the transition back to respectability and a permanent address. By then, Cuffie's sculptures were being reviewed in the *Village Voice* and other publications. His work was shown in various Manhattan galleries, including American Primitives and East Art and at the American Visionary Art Museum in Baltimore, Maryland.

Reviewing a one-man show of his work at Flamingo East, a New York supper club, Alan Moore wrote, "Flamboyant and poignant, Cuffie's works are fragile, tenuous in their hold on sculptural identity. They fall apart easily, and once they have been disassembled, they're junk again."

Cuffie's personality was as colorful as his assemblages. He was known for mixing performance with his art, often haranguing passersby with loud rantings and mystic statements. This led David Hammons to comment that he brought European curators to meet Cuffie "just to frighten them."

In May 2002, Cuffie was named artist-in-residence by the Lower Manhattan Cultural

Council and was given a studio. A stipend from the council supplemented his income from his job in the buildings and grounds department at the School of Art at the Cooper Union. Curtis Cuffie died four months later on September 13, 2002, of a heart attack in the apartment he shared with Thompson.

"I make sculpture for space that needs life," he once said. "You're got to be very deeply concerned about your creation. Not just what you make of your art, but how it affects others."

Further Reading

"Curtis Cuffie, 47, Artist of Life in the Streets," the *New York Times*, September 21, 2002, p. B7.

Moore, Alan. "Curtis Cuffie Flamingo East." Available online. URL: http://www.rovetv.net/cuffie-flamingo.html. Downloaded March 3, 2009.

Cummings, Pat
(Pat Marie Cummings)
(1950–   ) *illustrator, writer*

One of the leading illustrators of children's books today, Pat Cummings combines a strong sense of color and character with a wry sense of humor to create her best-selling books, many of which she also writes.

She was born Pat Marie Cummings on November 9, 1950, in Chicago, Illinois. Her father was an army serviceman and her mother was a librarian. While she was growing up, the family moved frequently from one military base to another. Some of her childhood was spent in Japan.

"The first thing I ever drew was . . . a scribble," she wrote in her book *Talking with Artists.* "And then I'd spend all afternoon coloring my scribbles."

Cummings used her talent for art to fit in at each new school she attended. She worked on the school yearbook, made hall posters, and drew pictures for her classmates. "In fifth grade, I had a healthy business during recess, selling drawings of ballerinas," she recalled.

Her parents encouraged her interest in art, and she attended the Pratt Institute in Brooklyn, New York, graduating with a Bachelor of Fine Arts degree in 1974. Before turning to illustration, Cummings worked with children's theater companies, creating everything from posters and advertisements to costumes and sets. Soon the limitless imagination and fantasy of children's books drew her to illustration.

The first book Cummings illustrated was *Good News* (1977) by Eloise Greenfield. Her mentor when she started illustrating was African-American illustrator TOM FEELINGS. *Just Us Women* (1982), with text by Jeannette Caines, was a Coretta Scott King Honor Book in 1983. The following year, Cummings received the Coretta Scott King Award for *My Mama Needs Me* by Mildred Pitts Walter. The first book that Cummings both wrote and illustrated was *Jimmy Lee Did It* (1985), which she based on the misadventures of her brother Artie.

Her bright, colorful, stylized pictures have a larger-than-life realism that appeals to both children and adults. Cummings often uses real people she knows as her models for characters, including her lawyer husband Chuckua Emeka Lee, her brother Artie, and even a fellow illustrator, Sheila Hamanaka. Among her other children's books are *Clean Your Room, Harvey Moon!* (1991), also based on growing up with her brother; *PURRRR* (1999), which received *Parents* magazine's Magic Reading Award; *Squashed in the Middle* (2005), with text by Elizabeth Winthrop, which received an American Library Association Notable Children's Books, Younger Readers award, and *Go Fish* (2009).

Her admiration for the work of her fellow illustrators in the children's book field led Cummings to write *Talking with Artists* (1992), a book of interviews with leading children's illustrators. She asked her colleagues the kinds of questions that she felt children would like to ask. Among the people she talked to are illustrators LEO DILLON and his wife, Diane, JERRY PINKNEY, and Tom Feelings. The book proved so popular that she has written two further volumes of interviews, the most recent one published in 1999.

Speaking of her own working method, Cummings has this to say: "Everything starts with the story. I read it repeatedly, swallow it whole, and live with it. I want to look around the world of the book and see the people in it, the setting. The style is suggested by the text."

Pat Cummings, who speaks several languages, lives in Brooklyn, New York, with her husband and their cat, Cash.

Further Reading

Cummings, Pat. *Clean Your Room, Harvey Moon!* New York: Aladdin, 1994.

———. *Harvey Moon, Museum Boy.* New York: Harper Collins, 2008.

———. *Talking with Artists, vol. 3: Conversations with . . .* Boston: Clarion Books, 1999.

"HarperCollins Listserv Subscribers' Interview with Pat Cummings." Available online. URL: http://www.manhattan.lib.ks.us/kail/cummiin.html. Downloaded January 2, 2002.

Hedblad, Alan, ed. *Something About the Author, Volume 107.* Detroit, Mich.: Gale Research, 1999, pp. 47–52.

Pat Cummings Official Web site. Available online. URL: http://patcummings.com/menu.html. Downloaded March 3, 2009.

Winthrop, Elizabeth, and Pat Cummings, illustrator. *Squashed in the Middle.* New York: Henry Holt, 2005.

D

Dash, Julie
(1952–) *filmmaker, screenwriter, film producer*

The first African-American female filmmaker to have a film in national theatrical distribution, Julie Dash makes challenging historical movies that chronicle the lives of African-American women.

She was born on October 22, 1952, in Long Island City, New York. Her uncle was St. Julian Dash, a jazz tenor saxophonist and composer. She first studied film at New York's City College and later at UCLA and the American Film Institute. She made her first short film, *Working Models of Success*, in 1973, and grew in strength and maturity with each subsequent effort. *Diary of an African Nun* (1977) was based on a short story by black author Alice Walker. It was followed by *Illusions* (1982), a drama about race relations set during World War II.

When this short film was released, Dash was already at work on her first full-length film, *Daughters of the Dust* (1991), a personal historical drama that no major studio wanted to produce. Dash, who also wrote the script, spent the next 10 years raising the money for and then shooting this film. *Daughters of the Dust* was filmed on St. Helena, one of South Carolina's Sea Islands, where the story takes place. Mosquitoes bit the actors and crew mercilessly. Sandstorms and Hurricane Hugo delayed filming several times. The project was so demanding that Dash decided against having her first child because she felt she did not have the time and energy for both challenges.

Daughters of the Dust takes place in the summer of 1902 when a group of island women belonging to the Gullah culture, originally from West Africa, are about to leave the island to live on the mainland. An unborn child narrates the complex, nonlinear story. Despite its complexities, the film was hailed for its originality and striking visual style. "Dash creates a rich, absorbing tableau in which the landscape itself is a presence and a character," wrote film historian Donald Bogle. "[This film] helped break the model in which black women have traditionally been portrayed."

Some critics found the film too dense and unconventional, but others praised it, and it has since become a cult classic. *Daughters of the Dust* received the Best Cinematography Award at the Sundance Film Festival in Utah in 1991 and was chosen the Film of the Century at the Newark Black Film Festival. In 2004, the film was placed in the National Film Registry by the Library of Congress.

The film's critical success has brought Dash into the mainstream, and in the 1990s she directed a number of made-for-television movies, including an episode of the HBO series *Subway*

Filmmaker Julie Dash worked for a decade on *Daughters of the Dust,* her astonishing film about the women of South Carolina's Sea Islands. *(Photofest)*

Stories: Tales from the Underground (1997). More recently, Dash directed the CBS-TV movie *The Rosa Parks Story* (2002), starring Angela Bassett as civil rights pioneer Rosa Parks and the feature film *Brothers of the Borderland* (2004) about slaves escaping from the pre–Civil War south along the Underground Railroads.

Further Reading

"About Julie Dash," African American Literary Book Club website. Available online. URL: http://aalbc.com/authors/julie.htm. Downloaded March 3, 2009.

Bogle, Donald. *Toms, Coons, Mulattoes, Mammies, & Bucks: An Interpretative History of Blacks in American Films.* New York: Continuum, 1997, pp. 300, 324, 344, 348.

"Julie Dash," The Internet Movie Database. Available online. URL: http://www.imdb.com/name/nm0201969/. Downloaded March 3, 2009.

Moon, Spencer. *Reel Black Talk: A Sourcebook of 50 American Filmmakers.* Westport, Conn.: Greenwood Press, 1997, pp. 79–86.

Further Viewing

Daughters of the Dust (1991). Kino International, VHS/DVD, 1996/2000.

The Rosa Parks Story (2002). Xenon, DVD, 2003.

Dave the Potter
(Dave Drake)
(ca. 1800–ca. 1864) *folk ceramist*

A slave craftsman of whom little is known other than his name, Dave the Potter created outstanding examples of stoneware pots, jugs, and jars that bear the unmistakable stamp of a true artist.

He was probably born around 1800 and spent his life in South Carolina. His first master is believed to have been Abner Landrum, owner of a stoneware pottery in Edgefield, South Carolina. Dave worked as a typesetter for Landrum's newspaper, *The Hive,* during which time he probably learned to read and write.

In 1831, Landrum gave Dave to his son-in-law, Lewis Miles, who owned a mill. Dave worked as a potter at Miles Mills for more than 20 years. He was one of many slaves and free blacks who worked in Edgefield's numerous stoneware factories. Dave's pots and jugs, however, stood out from the work of other potters in the region. They were incredibly large, capable of holding up to 40 gallons of liquid. They also had a distinctive widening near the top with a ridge that circled the pot's mouth.

While other potters, often illiterate, stamped their initials on their pots, Dave wrote out his name and the date the pot was made. This was an extremely daring thing to do at a time when it was forbidden by law for slaves to be taught to read and write. On some of his pots he even inscribed short rhyming verses. Some of these were innocent statements of fact, such as "Dave belongs to Mr. Miles/where the oven bakes and the pot biles [boils]." Other verses pointedly referred to his bondage and his hopes for a better future, such as: "I wonder where is all my relations/Friendship to all and every nation." Dave had reason to wonder about friends and family. Many fellow slaves were moved or sold to other states or regions, while Dave was kept in the Edgefield district most of his life because of his skill as a potter.

Dave is thought to have produced as many as 40,000 stoneware pieces between 1834 and 1864. The few of his pots to have survived have commanded high prices on the antique market, bringing as much as $50,000 each.

When he was emancipated with other slaves in 1862, Dave took the last name of Drake, possibly to honor the man who first taught him pottery. He died shortly thereafter.

Although his life remains largely a mystery, Dave the Potter's work speaks volumes about a slave and master potter who freely expressed his creativity and his personality through his work.

Further Reading

"Dave the Slave": Pottery and Poetry. Available online. URL: http://www.davetheslave.org/. Downloaded March 3, 2009.

Hill, Laban Carrick, and Bryan Collier, illustrator. *Dave the Potter: Artist, Poet, Slave.* New York: Little, Brown, 2010.

Koverman, Jill Beaute. *I Made This Jar: The Life and Works of the Enslaved African-American Potter, Dave.* Columbia: University of South Carolina Press, 1998.

Todd, Leonard. *Carolina Clay: The Life and Legend Of the Slave Potter Dave,* New York: W. W. Norton, 2008.

Day, Thomas

(1801–1861) *furniture maker*

The most successful furniture designer and maker in North Carolina in the first half of the 19th century, Thomas Day combined European style with African design to create memorable pieces that are treasured by collectors and museums today.

He was probably born a slave in 1801 in Dinwiddie County, Virginia, and was later freed by his master. Day was educated in Boston, Massachusetts, and Washington, D.C., and moved to North Carolina probably around 1817. A decade later he settled in the town of Milton, where he founded his furniture business.

Day personally designed furniture for some of North Carolina's best families. His furniture was even used in the governor's mansion in Raleigh. Day made most of his furniture from mahogany, but also worked in cherry, walnut, and rosewood. He added touches of his African heritage to his tables, chairs, and secretaries, such as a graceful S curve, which suggested the African symbol for *sankofa*. It is a West African word that means "one must return to the past in order to move forward."

By 1848, Day's furniture business was so successful that he bought the Union Tavern in Milton and converted it into a combination showroom and residence for himself, his wife, and three sons. A workshop was located in the building's rear.

To staff his factory, Day began in 1830 to buy slaves. By 1850 he had 14 slaves working for him. Why he decided to become a slave owner is not known, although he may have done so to stay in competition with white furniture makers who used slave labor to increase their production.

Day may have had ambivalent feelings about slavery. He sent his children to a Massachusetts school that advocated the abolition of slavery. He agreed to build the pews for the Milton Presbyterian Church on the condition that he and his family be allowed to sit downstairs rather than upstairs where blacks were usually restricted.

Day succeeded in besting the competition. In 1850 it is estimated that one-fourth of all furniture made in North Carolina came from the Day factory. His very success, however, eventually led to his undoing.

He bought a farm with his profits, overextended himself financially, and went bankrupt in 1858. Day's problems were made worse by a recession in 1857 and a sharp rise in the price of wood. It is believed he died in 1861, the year the Civil War broke out. His son Devereux carried on the family furniture-making business.

The Thomas Day House/Union Tavern was turned into a museum and named a National Historic Landmark in 1975. Partially destroyed by a fire in 1989, the site has since been fully restored.

Further Reading

Barfield, Rodney D., and Patricia P. Marshall. *Thomas Day—African American Furniture Marker.* Raleigh: North Carolina Office of Archives and History, 2005.

Lyons, May E. *Master of Mahogany: Tom Day, Free Black Cabinetmaker* (African-American Artists and Artisans). New York: Atheneum, 1994.

Thomas Day Education Project Web site. Available online. URL: http://www/thomasday.net/thames_day.html. Downloaded March 3, 2009.

DeCarava, Roy

(1919–2009) *photographer, educator*

Generally acknowledged as one of the finest photographers of the 20th century, Roy DeCarava was perhaps the first artist to photograph black people, in the words of his wife, as "a subject worthy of art."

He was born Roy Rudolph DeCarava on December 9, 1919, in Harlem, the black community in New York City. He was raised by his mother, Elfreda, an immigrant from Jamaica. His first artworks were chalk drawings of cowboys and Indians that he drew on the city sidewalks. DeCarava graduated from Textile High School, where he majored in art, in 1938 and found work as an artist with the federally funded Works Progress Administration making posters. At night he studied painting and lithography at the School of Art at the Cooper Union in New York.

The prejudice DeCarava faced at Cooper Union eventually caused him to leave there and study at the Harlem Art Center with such leading black artists as AARON DOUGLAS and AUGUSTA SAVAGE. He also studied under African-American artist CHARLES WHITE at the George Washington Carver Art School. White's belief that art should express social concerns greatly influenced DeCarava. He turned to photography in 1946 as a means of reference for his paintings and drawings. DeCarava eventually became interested in photography as an art form in itself, seeing it as a more immediate and direct way to capture life as it was lived.

Another photographer, seeing the sharp contrast of DeCarava's black-and-white photographs, suggested that he soften the tones in his images with a different printing technique. The process muted the tones to grays and brought viewers deeper into the photograph. It had the effect of making them active participants in the photograph as they tried to determine what was being conveyed.

DeCarava worked a day job and photographed mostly at night, roaming the streets of Harlem for people and places to photograph. His pictures were direct and unsentimental, but for that very reason were all the more moving. He had his first solo exhibit at a Manhattan gallery in 1950. Celebrated photographer Edward Steichen, who was curator of photography at the Museum of Modern Art (MOMA), attended the show and was deeply impressed. He bought two of DeCarava's prints for MOMA and urged him to apply for a Guggenheim fellowship. DeCarava took his advice and in 1952 became the first black artist in any field to be awarded a Guggenheim.

In 1955, firmly established as a photographer, DeCarava embarked on a unique collaboration with African-American writer Langston Hughes. Some 140 of his images accompanied Hughes's story of a black woman's life in Harlem. The book, *The Sweet Flypaper of Life*, became an instant classic.

DeCarava became a leading spokesperson for photography as well as one of its leading practitioners. In the mid-1950s, he opened Photographers Gallery in New York, one of the first galleries to treat photography as a fine art. In 1963, he cofounded the Komoinge Workshop for Black Photographers with SHAWN WALKER and others and became its first director. Over the years, Komoinge has nurtured such leading African-American photographers as Ming Smith and ANTHONY BARBOZA.

Roy DeCarava was one of the most celebrated African-American photographers. *(Anthony Barboza)*

DeCarava began teaching in 1969 as an adjunct professor of photography at Cooper Union in New York. In 1975, he became associate professor at Hunter College and in 1978 was named a professor of art there.

Through the 1960s, DeCarava's photos appeared in such leading magazines as *Time, Newsweek, Life,* and *Look.* He worked as a contract photographer for *Sports Illustrated* from 1968 to 1975.

A 1998 traveling retrospective of his work, featuring more than 200 of his images, was mounted by MOMA and curated by his wife, the art historian Sherry Turner DeCarava. His second volume of photographs, *The Sounds I Saw: Improvisation on a Jazz Theme* (2001), is a stunning collection of black-and-white images of Harlem nightlife in the 1950s and 1960s and such jazz musicians as Billie Holiday and John Coltrane, both of whom DeCarava knew well. He had planned the book 40 years earlier but could not find an interested publisher. The reviewer in the *New York Times Book Review* spoke of the book's images being "rooted in the experience of the urban underclass, and

they often forsake clarity of detail for an improvisational, emotionally provocative effect."

What DeCarava found important in a picture can be both startling and revelatory. Sometimes he focused on only a part of his subject's body—a hand, a pair of legs, or an extreme close-up of a face. *Bill and son* (1962) shows only Bill's black hands holding up his tiny son, dressed in terrycloth. The viewer senses the father's love all the more powerfully without seeing his face or that of the child.

In other photographs, there is no human figure in the lonely urban landscape. Simple objects take on new meaning in their surroundings—a dangling coat hanger amid the darkened booths of a diner, a white towel hanging mysteriously above a row of traffic directional arrows.

"My pictures are immediate and yet at the same time, they're forever," DeCarava said. "They present a moment so profoundly a moment that it becomes an eternity. . . It's like the pole vaulter who begins his run, shoots up, then comes down. At the peak there is no movement. He's neither going up nor going down. It is that moment I wait for, when he comes into an equilibrium with all the other life forces—gravity, wind, motion, obstacles. . . The moment when all the forces fuse, when all is in equilibrium, that's the eternal . . . that's jazz . . . and that's life."

Roy DeCarava was awarded the International Center of Photography's Master of Photography Infinity Award in 1998 and was the recipient of the National Medal of Arts in 2006. DeCarava died on October 27, 2009, just shy of his 90th birthday.

Further Reading

DeCarava, Roy. *The Sounds I Saw: Improvisation on a Jazz Theme.* New York: Phaidon Press, 2003.

Galassi, Peter, and Sherry Turner DeCarava. *Roy DeCarava: A Retrospective.* New York: Museum of Modern Art, 1996.

Hughes, Langston, and Roy DeCarava, photographer. *The Sweet Flypaper of Life.* 1955. Reprint, Washington, D.C.: Howard University Press, 1984.

" Roy DeCarava." Available online. URL: http://www.answers.com/topic/roy_decarava. Downloaded March 3, 2009.

Further Viewing

Charlie Rose with John Hume . . . Roy DeCarava (March 21, 1996). Charlie Rose, DVD, 2006.

Delaney, Beauford
(1901–1979) *painter*

One of the first artists to paint in the style known as abstract expressionism, Beauford Delaney spent the last 25 years of his life living and painting in Paris, France, thus earning the title "the dean of African-American painters living abroad."

He was born on December 31, 1901, in Knoxville, Tennessee. His parents named him after their hometown of Beaufort, South Carolina. His father was a circuit-riding Methodist preacher. Delaney took to drawing early and studied art with Knoxville artist Lloyd Bronson while working as a shoemaker's apprentice. Bronson encouraged him to go to Boston, Massachusetts, to study art. Delaney took his advice and studied at the Massachusetts Normal Art School and the South Boston School of Art.

In 1929, he moved to New York City, where the cultural rebirth of black art, literature, and music called the Harlem Renaissance was still in full swing. Delaney enthusiastically took in the city's cultural treasures. He got a job as a telephone operator and handyman at the Whitney Museum of American Art, then in the Greenwich Village section of Manhattan. He attended the opera and went to jazz clubs. He got to know many artists and writers, including author James Baldwin, who became a lifelong friend. Delaney had his first one-man art show at the 135th Street Branch of the New York Public Library in Harlem, the black section of New York.

His first paintings were street scenes and portraits of friends. But gradually he turned toward abstract paintings, filled with swirling colors that exploded with feeling. Years later these features would characterize the abstract expressionism school. Delaney, however, was too much of a free spirit ever to be part of an art movement. He was a gentle, charming man and a true bohemian who cared little about money and material things. If a friend or acquaintance expressed admiration for one of his paintings he would be so pleased he would likely give it to the person. As novelist Henry Miller wrote about him in one of his books, Delaney was "poor in everything but pigment. With pigment he was as lavish as a millionaire."

His friends were devoted to Delaney and helped him get a fellowship to Yaddo, an artists' community in Saratoga Springs, New York. In the early 1950s he decided to take a long-anticipated trip to Rome, Italy, to paint and study the great art of the past. On the way to Rome, however, Delaney stopped off in Paris and fell in love with the city. He never got to Rome but remained in Paris for the rest of his life, living in a modest hotel on the Left Bank. Among the American expatriates who were part of his close circle was his old friend James Baldwin.

Delaney's paintings, which had previously been known for the denseness of their thick paint, became lighter and more carefree in Paris. He sold many of them locally, but never made enough money to be financially secure. He received a grant in 1969 from the National Council of the Arts in the United States.

Delaney's bohemian lifestyle and his growing alcoholism, fueled by guilt over his homosexuality, finally caught up with him. In 1971, he experienced an emotional breakdown and had to be hospitalized. It was later learned he had Alzheimer's disease, which attacks the nervous system and brain. Delaney was well liked by the French, and the French government took the extraordinary measure of arranging for his hospital care, while holding his paintings in trust.

In 1978, a major retrospective of Delaney's work was held at the Studio Museum in Harlem, securing his reputation as a pioneer and leading artist of abstract expressionism. He died the following year on March 26, 1979, in a French insane asylum, and was buried in Paris. Years earlier, James Baldwin said of his friend, "Beauford's work leads the inner and the outer eye, directly and inexorably to a new confrontation with reality."

His brother JOSEPH DELANEY also was a successful artist.

Further Reading

Bearden, Romare, and Harry Henderson. *A History of African-American Artists: From 1792 to the Present.* New York: Pantheon Books, 1993, pp. 280–286.

Canterbury, Patricia Sue. *Beauford Delaney: From New York to Paris.* Minneapolis, Minn.: Minneapolis Institute of Arts, 2005.

Leeming, David Adams. *Amazing Grace: A Life of Beauford Delaney.* New York: Oxford University Press, 1998.

Powell, Richard J. *Beauford Delaney: The Color Yellow.* Atlanta, Ga.: The High Museum of Art, 2001.

Rosenfeld, Michael. *Stroke! Beauford Delaney, Norman Lewis and Alma Thomas.* New York: Rosenfeld Gallery, 2005.

Delaney, Joseph

(1904–1991) *painter, educator*

Younger brother of BEAUFORD DELANEY, Joseph Delaney was a gifted artist in his own right, best known for his deeply felt genre paintings of his adopted city of New York and his insightful portraits of women.

He was born in Knoxville, Tennessee, on September 13, 1904, the ninth of 10 children. His father, Samuel Delaney, was a poor Methodist minister who instilled a deep religious faith in Joseph.

He left home at age 18 and wandered around Kentucky and Illinois, living a hand-to-mouth existence. To gain some stability in his life, he joined the Illinois National Guard and served for three years. In 1930 he moved to New York City, where he followed his older brother's footsteps and pursued a career as an artist. To this end, he enrolled at the Art Students League, where he studied with painters Thomas Hart Benton and George Bridgeman. Benton taught him the importance of mastering the fundamentals of art and exploring the people and places he knew best. Bridgeman, who taught anatomy, instructed him on how bones and muscles helped define the human figure. Another influence was abstract expressionist painter Jackson Pollock, whom Delaney befriended.

In 1931, he became a regular participant at the annual Washington Square Outdoor Art Show in Lower Manhattan. As he sat at his easel, Delaney drew the passersby, including such celebrities as actress-singer Eartha Kitt. Later, Delaney would make a living by doing portraits of well-to-do New Yorkers. He was particularly fond of painting women of all ages and backgrounds. He was adept at capturing their personalities on canvas. To supplement his income during the difficult years of the Great Depression (1929–39), Delaney taught art for the College Art Association and worked for the Metropolitan Museum of Art on its Index of American Design project. In this position he recorded American decorative art from the early colonial era to the beginning of the 20th century.

Beginning in the 1940s, Delaney painted his celebrated series of paintings of the people and places of New York City. Such works as *VJ Day Times Square, Easter Parade, Central Park Skating,* and *Waldorf Cafeteria* captured the heart and soul of the city's life with fluid, expressive lines.

When his brother died in Paris, France, in 1979 after years of mental illness, Joseph Delaney traveled there and brought back a number of Beauford's paintings to the United States.

He himself returned home to Knoxville in 1986 to be part of the statewide celebration "Homecoming '86." He never left, becoming an artist-in-residence at the University of Tennessee.

He remained in that position until his death on November 24, 1991.

Never as famous as his brother, Joseph Delaney was philosophical about it. "Beauford and I were complete opposites," he once said, "me, an introvert, and Beauford, an extrovert."

Further Reading

"Joseph Delaney." University of Tennessee Web site. Available online. URL: http://sunsite.utk.edu/del aney/delaney.htm. Downloaded March 4, 2009.

Painting the Town: Paintings from the Museum of the City of New York. "Harlem Parade (Adam Clayton Powell, Jr. Passing in a Car)," The Museum of the City of New York website. Available online. URL: http://www.mcny.org/museum-collections/ painting-new-york/pttcat104.htm Downloaded March 4, 2009.

Riggs, Thomas, ed. *St. James Guide to Black Artists.* Detroit, Mich.: St. James Press, 1997, pp. 137–138.

DePillars, Murry N.
(Murry Norman DePillars)
(1938–2008) *painter, printmaker, illustrator, educator, arts administrator*

A founding father of the black artists' movement in Chicago in the 1960s, Murry N. DePillars successfully combined the career of a politically committed artist with that of teacher and administrator.

He was born on December 21, 1938, in Chicago, Illinois. After high school, he served for two years in the U.S. Army. He attended Kennedy-King Community College in Chicago in 1966 and went on to earn his Bachelor of Arts degree and Master of Arts degree in urban studies from Roosevelt University, Chicago. In 1976 DePillars earned his doctoral degree in art education from Pennsylvania State University in University Park, Pennsylvania.

The political turmoil brought on by the Civil Rights movement and the anti–Vietnam War movement in the 1960s exploded in Chicago. "The decisive factor in my work is the social and political plight of blacks throughout the world," DePillars has said. One of his best-known paintings from the period is *Aunt Jemima* (1968), in which he transformed the stereotypical mammy figure from the pancake mix into a black revolutionary who wields her pancake spatula as a lethal weapon. Another example of his playing with racial stereotypes is *The People of the Sun* (1972), in which the African-American storyteller Uncle Remus is depicted escaping from a book of black folktales to a new life of independence from the racist past.

In the mid-1980s, DePillars joined the black art movement African Commune of Black (or Bad) Relevant Artists (AfriCobra). This group, founded in the 1960s by black artist JEFF DONALDSON and others, is dedicated to social commitment in the black community, the development of a new African-American aesthetic, and the furthering of racial pride. DePillars's work became less social and more inspired by traditional African artwork and crafts. His Queen Candance series conjured up the ancient Nubian kingdom of Cush in Africa, represented by a pregnant woman of royal bearing.

DePillars was dean and art professor at the Virginia Commonwealth University School of the Arts in Richmond, Virginia, from 1976 to 1995. He then became executive vice president of Chicago State University. As educator and administrator, Murry DePillars worked to bring African-American artists into the college curriculum.

Among his more unusual awards is the Man of Excellence plaque given him by the Republic of China's Ministry of Education. He also received the Award for Excellence in the Education, Preservation and Promotion of Jazz from the Richmond Jazz Society (1982) and the Virginia Commonwealth University's Presidential Medallion (1996). Murry DePillars died on May 31, 2008, at his Richmond home. He was 69 years old.

Further Reading

Lewis, Samella. *African-American Art and Artists.* Berkeley: University of California Press, 2003, p. 247.

Madhubuti, Safisha, and Murry DePillars, illustrator. *The Story of Kwanzaa.* Chicago, Ill.: Third World Press, 1989.

Riggs, Thomas, ed. *St. James Guide to Black Artists.* Detroit, Mich.: St. James Press, 1997, pp. 141–144.

Slayton, Jeremy. "Murry DePillars, retired dean of VCU's art school dies." *Richmond Times-Dispatch,* June 2, 2008 [obituary].

Dillon, Leo

(1933–) *illustrator*

The first African-American artist to win the Caldecott Award, the highest honor for the illustrator of a children's picture book, Leo Dillon has been collaborating for more than four decades with his wife Diane on everything from paperback covers of science fiction novels to record album covers.

He was born on March 2, 1933, in Brooklyn, New York. His father ran a trucking business and his mother was a dressmaker. After high school, Dillon joined the U.S. Navy and served for three years. In 1953, on his discharge, he enrolled at the Parsons School of Design in New York City. While there he met white student Diane Sorber, whose work he quickly came to admire.

"We spent a lot of time and energy trying to prove ourselves to each other," he recalled. "In the midst of all this, born of the mutual recognition of our respective strengths, we fell in love. We tried to keep our relationship a secret because in those days interracial couples were not easily accepted." Nevertheless, Leo and Diane got married in 1957.

Dillon worked for a year as an art editor for West Park Publishers in New York before launching a freelance career as an artist and illustrator with Diane. He attended the School of Visual Arts in 1958 and returned there as an instructor in illustration from 1969 to 1977.

Through the 1960s, the Dillons illustrated book covers, from paperback classics to best-selling novels. They worked on the cover art for many science fiction novels, especially those by Harlan Ellison and Terry Carr. For their work on Carr's *Ace Specials* series, they were awarded the Hugo Award from the International Science Fiction Association in 1971. One of their first children's books, *Hakan of Rogen's Saga* (1963), was named the *New York Herald Tribune*'s Children Spring Book Festival Award honor book.

By the 1970s, the Dillons were concentrating on illustrating children's books. They won their first Caldecott Medal in 1976 for their illustrations for the African folktale *Why Mosquitoes Buzz in People's Ears* and won it again the following year for *Ashanti to Zulu* (1977), an African alphabet book. No other illustrators to date have won the Caldecott twice in a row.

The Dillons' style of illustration is characterized by careful attention to detail, clean lines, an enriched sense of humanity, and exacting accuracy. It also is based on adapting the medium and style that best serves the text that they are working on. They will change their technique and style completely if something new and different is called for in the story. They have even been known to create an entirely new technique to tell a story.

Their working collaboration is a unique one. "After we receive a manuscript, we sit and talk about it for days and weeks," says Diane, "until we hit on something we agree upon. Then one of us takes it."

As each illustration is completed, they pass it back and forth, working and reworking it, until the collaboration is so seamless that they cannot tell where one's work began and the other's ended.

"There is the challenge of reading the manuscript over and over again until we get a feel for what needs to be shown, what is not said, and what the author means," Diane has said.

"What's interesting to us, as to many other artists, is that we look and we interpret," Leo added.

The Dillons have illustrated more than 30 picture books and 20 chapter books. They have shown particular interest in books about folktales, African-American history, classic literature, and biblical stories. *The People Could Fly: American Black Folktales* (1986) was their first of five stunning collaborations with the late celebrated children's writer Virginia Hamilton. It won the Coretta Scott King Award and was named a *New York Times* Best Illustrated Book. Their second compilation, *Her Story: African-American Folktales, Fairy Tales, and True Tales* (1995), is a fascinating collection of tales that focus on African-American women. Their fourth collaboration, *Many Thousand Gone: African Americans from Slavery to Freedom* (2002), contained, according to one reviewer for *Kirkus Reviews*, "powerful black-and-white illustrations of heroic figures of monumental simplicity, handsomely set in dramatically spare compositions." Their last collaboration with Hamilton, a picture book version of *For the People Could Fly* (2004), won a Coretta Scott King Illustrator Honor Award. The couple's *Jazz on a Saturday Night* (2007), their tribute to such jazz greats as Ella Fitzgerald and Miles Davis, is also a Coretta Scott King Honor Book.

The Dillons have won the Hamilton King Award and the Gold Medal for Children's Book Illustration from the Society of Illustrators. In 1996 they were the U.S. nominees for the Hans Christian Andersen Award, an international illustration prize. They received the New York Library Association's Knickerbocker Award for their body of work in 2006 and the World Fantasy Convention's Life Achievement Award in 2008.

Further Reading

Commire, Anne, ed. *Something About the Author, Volume 106.* Detroit, Mich.: Gale Research, Inc., 1997, pp. 56–65.

Cummings, Pat, ed. *Talking with Artists: Conversations with Victoria Chess, Pat Cummings, Leo and Diane Dillon, etc.* New York: Simon & Schuster, 1992.

Dillon, Leo, and Diane Dillon. *Mother Goose Numbers on the Loose.* Orlando, Fla.: Harcourt Children's Books, 2007.

Hamilton, Virginia, and Leo and Diane Dillon, illustrators. *The People Could Fly: American Black Folktales.* New York: Knopf, 1993.

Preiss, Byron, ed. *The Art of Leo & Diane Dillon.* New York: Ballantine Books, 1981.

Dixon, Ivan
(1931–2008) *filmmaker, television director, actor*

One of the most underrated African-American film actors of the 1960s, Ivan Dixon went on to become one of the busiest directors in television in the 1970s and 1980s.

He was born in New York City on April 6, 1931. He attended North Carolina Central University in Durham, North Carolina, and earned a scholarship to Case Western Reserve University in Cleveland, Ohio. Dixon intended to study law at Case, but got sidetracked into acting when he auditioned for a play at Karamu House, an African-American cultural center.

Dixon returned to New York to study acting at the American Theater Wing, where one of his classmates was actor James Earl Jones. After landing several roles off-Broadway, he went to Hollywood, California, where he was hired as a stunt double for black actor Sidney Poitier. He made his film debut in the South African drama *Something of Value* (1957) and played supporting roles in such films as *Porgy and Bess* (1959) and *A Raisin in the Sun* (1961). In 1964, he played the lead role of a black drifter fighting the racist system in the South in the excellent drama *Nothing But a Man* (1964). Dixon's totally honest and moving performance is generally considered one of the finest by a black actor in the 1960s.

Unfortunately, he rarely got a chance to stretch his acting muscles to such an extent again. In 1965, Dixon took the role of Sergeant Ivan

A talented screen actor, Ivan Dixon found greater satisfaction as a film and television director. *(Photofest)*

Kinchloe, a member of a group of World War II prisoners of war, in the hit television situation comedy *Hogan's Heroes*. Although it was frustrating for him playing the show's token black character, Dixon learned how to direct by observing the show's director at work week after week. "It [acting] was something I could do, but directing was always my ambition," he has said.

He got the opportunity to direct a benefit theatre performance of the play *The Blacks* in Los Angeles, California. His friend the actor and comedian Bill Cosby was impressed and encouraged him to try directing for television. Dixon was soon one of the first blacks to direct in prime-time television. One of his first assignments was a Bill Cosby special.

Dixon made his film directorial debut with *Trouble Man* (1972), a black crime film starring Robert Hooks and Paul Winfield. It was one of the era's many so-called blaxploitation films. The following year he directed *The Spook Who Sat by the Door*, a picture he also produced. This intriguing story of a black CIA operative who becomes a revolutionary did not find an audience on its initial release. It went on, however, to become something of a cult film, especially on college campuses and was released on DVD in 2004.

Dixon returned to television and directed more than 200 episodes of television series, mostly in the action/crime genre. The shows he worked on include *Get Christie Love!* (1975), the first television show to star a black policewoman, *The Rockford Files, Starsky and Hutch, Quincy, Magnum P.I.*, and *In The Heat of the Night*, based on the hit movie starring Sidney Poitier.

Dixon continued to act sporadically in films and television through the 1970s. In 1995, he quit directing and bought radio station KONI-FM in Hawaii. It is the number one station on the island of Maui.

Ivan Dixon was inducted into the Black Filmmakers Hall of Fame in 1980 and won five Image Awards from the NAACP for his directing and acting. He died of complications of kidney disease on March 11, 2008, in Charlotte, North Carolina. Dixon was 76 years old.

Further Reading

Bogle, Donald. *Prime Time Blues: African Americans on Network Television*. New York: Farrar, Straus and Giroux, 2001, pp. 98–100, 113–115.

"Ivan Dixon." Internet Movie Database. Available online. URL: http://www.imdb.com/name/nm0228853/. Downloaded March 4, 2009.

Moon, Spencer. *Reel Black Talk: A Sourcebook of 50 American Filmmakers*. Westport, Conn.: Greenwood Press, 1997, pp. 87–94.

Further Viewing

Nothing But a Man (1964). Cinema V, DVD, 2004.

The Spook Who Sat by the Door (1973). Monarch Video, DVD, 2004.

Donaldson, Jeff

(Jeff Richardson Donaldson)
(1932–2004) *painter, printmaker, illustrator, muralist, educator, arts administrator*

Cofounder of the historic black art movement African Commune of Black (or Bad) Relevant

Artists (AfriCobra), Jeff Donaldson was a key figure in the development of a new black aesthetic in the 1960s and 1970s, both as a spokesperson and an artist.

He was born on December 15, 1932, in Pine Bluff, Arkansas. After high school, he attended the University of Arkansas at Pine Bluff and earned a Bachelor of Arts degree in studio art. He enlisted in the army in 1955 and served a two-year stint. Then he earned a Master of Science degree in art education from the Institute of Design at the Illinois Institute of Technology in 1963. He later got his doctoral degree in art history from Northwestern University in Evanston, Illinois.

While teaching at Northwestern in the late 1960s, Donaldson and other black artists were caught up in the new militant politics of the black power movement. African Americans were struggling to find a new identity separate from white America. Donaldson believed that this identity demanded a new black aesthetic that looked to African culture and the diaspora, or scattering of African peoples caused by the slave trade. Thus, along with fellow artist Wadsworth Jarrell, Donaldson founded AfriCobra in 1968 in Chicago. Two years later he wrote the group's manifesto, which contained four major objectives. They were to develop a new African-American aesthetic, become involved as artists in the local black community, make a strong commitment to be socially responsible, and foster pride and a sense of self-identity as blacks. Donaldson originated the phrase "Trans Africa" to link the culture and independence movements going on in the United States, Africa, and the Caribbean.

As an artist, he created Chicago's *Wall of Respect* (1967), a public mural that depicted important African Americans of the past and present. It became a model for a series of such murals in cities across the United States. In more recent years, Donaldson's art had become more abstract but no less socially relevant. In *Jam Packed and Jelly Tight* (1988), he used African-inspired patterns of color to celebrate the music of the progressive jazz group the Association for the Advancement of Creative Musicians.

In 1970, Donaldson became associated with Howard University in Washington, D.C., the country's most prominent black institution of higher learning. He served as art professor, associate dean, and, from 1990 to 2004, as the dean of the College of Fine Arts. He also served as director of the Black and African Festival of Art and Culture in Lagos, Nigeria, from 1975 to 1980. Jeff Donaldson died on February 29, 2004, of prostate cancer in Washington D.C., at age 71.

Further Reading

"Jeff Donaldson." Available online. URL: http://www. answers.com/topic/jeff_donaldson. Downloaded March 4, 2009.

Lewis, Samella. *African American Art and Artists.* Berkeley: University of California Press, 2003, pp. 266–267.

Riggs, Thomas, ed. *St. James Guide to Black Artists.* Detroit, Mich.: St. James Press, 1997, pp. 152–154.

Douglas, Aaron

(1899–1979) *painter, muralist, illustrator, educator*

Considered the foremost artist of the Harlem Renaissance, a flourishing of black culture and art in the 1920s and 1930s, Aaron Douglas remains one of the best-known and most popular African-American artists of the 20th century.

He was born on May 26, 1899, in Topeka, Kansas. He was attending the University of Nebraska in Lincoln, Nebraska, and studying art when the United States entered World War I (1914–18). Douglas served for a time in the Student Army Training Corps and then returned to school. He studied drawing with Blanche O. Grant and received his first art prize for general excellence in drawing. He earned a Bachelor of Fine Arts degree from the University of Nebraska in 1922.

Douglas then became the first art teacher in a Topeka, Kansas, high school.

He moved to New York City in 1925, inspired by the illustrations and writing in the black journals *The Crisis* and *Opportunity*. He settled in Harlem, the black section of the city, where the Harlem Renaissance was getting under way. Douglas met and studied with German-born artist and designer Winold Reiss, who urged him to explore his African background in his work. He did so and quickly developed a unique style, combining modernism with traditional African art and folk art. His drawings and paintings were filled with elongated and angular silhouetted figures that celebrated both African culture and the African-American experience.

W. E. B. DuBois, a founder of the NAACP, and Charles S. Johnson, editor of *Opportunity*, hired Douglas to create illustrations for both that journal and *The Crisis*. Based on the recognition he received from this exposure, Douglas began to illustrate the covers of books by such Harlem Renaissance writers as poets Countee Cullen and Langston Hughes and novelist James Weldon Johnson. After doing the cover for Johnson's novel *The Autobiography of an Ex-Coloured Man*, Douglas was hired to illustrate his new book, *God's Trombones*, a collection of seven folk sermons that dealt with events from the Bible. Douglas's striking illustrations perfectly captured the religious and mystical nature of Johnson's sermons, and the two created a literary classic.

"I tried to portray everything not in a realistic but [an] abstract way," Douglas wrote about this experience. "I used the starkness of the old spirituals as my model—and at the same time I tried to make my painting modern."

In 1927, Douglas turned his artistic talents to murals, creating one of the first of this genre by an African-American artist for the New York Ebony Club. Douglas's outstanding design for the mural attracted other leading black artists to the genre for decades to come. The money earned from the mural enabled Douglas and his wife, whom he had married a year earlier, to travel to Paris, France.

Here the artist met one of his heroes, expatriate black artist HENRY O. TANNER.

On his return to the United States, Douglas created murals for the Harlem YMCA and a series of four murals based on African-American history for the Countee Cullen Branch of the New York Public Library in Harlem. Called *Aspects of Negro Life*, these murals traced the migration of African Americans from the South to the North in the early decades of the 20th century. Completed in 1934, *Aspects of Negro Life* is today considered one of the landmark works of the Harlem Renaissance.

This portrait of artist Aaron Douglas by Betsy Grave Reyneau hangs in the National Portrait Gallery in Washington, D.C. *(National Portrait Gallery, Smithsonian Institution/Art Resource, NY)*

In 1939, Douglas was invited to start an art department at all-black Fisk University in Nashville, Tennessee. Founded in 1865, Fisk has since become a multiracial institution. Douglas remained chairman of the art department at Fisk for 29 years. During this time he taught and influenced several generations of African-American artists. Despite his heavy load of teaching and administrating, he continued to produce paintings, murals, and illustrations, many of them for the benefit of Fisk.

In 1944, Douglas was commissioned to paint an ambitious panel for Fisk's International Student Center. He called the work *Building More Stately Mansions*, a line from the poem *The Chambered Nautilus* by Oliver Wendell Holmes. The mural took as its theme no less than the story of civilization from the dawn of history to the present. Douglas used symbols to represent different cultures—a pyramid for ancient Egypt, a cathedral for medieval Europe, and a skyscraper for modern America. African Americans were featured prominently in the final section of the panel, expressing Douglas's optimism for the future of blacks in American society.

While Douglas was hailed for his striking murals and illustrations, he was also a skillful portrait painter. His portraits were in a more classical, traditional style and included a memorable portrait of the great black concert singer Marian Anderson.

Douglas retired from Fisk in 1966. In 1971, a major retrospective exhibition of his paintings was held at the university. Fisk gave him the honorary degree of doctor of arts in 1973. Douglas continued to create illustrations and paintings until his death in Nashville on February 2, 1979.

"Our problem," Douglas once wrote, "is to conceive, develop, establish an art era. Not white art painting black . . . let's bare our arms and plunge them deep through laughter, through pain, through sorrow, through hope, through disappointment, into the very depth of the souls of our people and drag forth material crude, rough, neglected."

Further Reading

Bey, Sharif. *Aaron Douglas and Hale Woodruff: The Social Responsibility and Expanded Pedagogy of the Black Artist.* Saarbrucken, Germany: VDM Verlag Dr. Muller, 2008.

Earle, Susan, ed. *Aaron Douglas: African American Modernist.* New Haven, Conn.: Yale University Press, 2007.

Johnson, James Weldon, and Aaron Douglas, illustrator. *God's Trombones: Seven Negro Sermons in Verse.* 1927. Reprint, New York: Penguin USA, 1990.

Kirschke, Amy Helene. *Aaron Douglas: Art, Race and the Harlem Renaissance.* Jackson: University Press of Mississippi, 1995.

Lewis, Samella. *African American Art and Artists.* Berkeley: University of California Press, 2003, pp. 60–64.

Driskell, David C.
(David Clyde Driskell)
(1931–) *painter, art historian, printmaker, museum curator, educator*

One of the world's leading authorities and scholars on African-American art, David C. Driskell is a talented abstract painter in his own right.

He was born David Clyde Driskell on June 7, 1931, in Eatonton, Georgia. He studied for a year at the Skowhegan School of Painting and Sculpture in Skowhegan, Maine, before enrolling at Howard University, in Washington, D.C. He earned a Bachelor of Arts degree in 1955 and had his first solo art exhibition the following year at the Savey Art Gallery in Talladega College in Talladega, Alabama. He taught at the college from 1955 to 1962.

Driskell's painting was heavily influenced by an art teacher at Howard, Morris Louis, who was a member of the abstract color-field school of painting. Unlike some of the color-field painters who worked on immense canvases, Driskell created compositions that were relatively small in scale. By the 1970s he was using bolder colors in his work and adding mixed-media materials, expanding the tight limits of pure abstract painting.

After leaving his teaching post at Talladega, Driskell taught art at Howard (1962–66), Fisk University in Nashville, Tennessee (1966–77), and finally settled at the University of Maryland, in College Park, in 1978. He taught for a year at the University of Ife (now called Obefemia Auolowo) in Ile-Ife, Nigeria, in Africa. He was chairperson of the art department at the University of Maryland until 1983 and is curator of the Aaron Douglas Collection and Amistad Research Center. He became cultural adviser in 1977 to comedian and actor Bill Cosby and his wife, Camille, as they built their extensive collection of African-American art.

Driskell retired as professor emeritus of art from Maryland in 1997 and three years later established the David C. Driskell Center for the Study of the African Diaspora on the campus. Its mission, as stated on its Web site, is "to nurture responsibility and creativity of the highest caliber, provide training for scholars on issues and methodologies in the study of the African Diaspora, and encourage the growth of future generations of artists and researchers who can bring new insights to the phenomenon of the African Diaspora and its influence."

Driskell is the author of numerous books, museum catalogs, and articles. He is married to Thelma G. Deloatch. In 2000, he was a recipient of the National Humanities Medal.

"With art I shall always be able to see a second time more than I saw when I first glanced the physical shape or form," Driskell has written. "This is why time and space can be as one in the lively sight of art. I want to share these experiences in my art."

Further Reading

Childs, Adrienne. *Evolution: Five Decades of Printmaking by David C. Driskell*. San Francisco, Calif.: Pomegranate Communications, 2007.

Driskell, David C., *African American Visual Aesthetics: A Postmodernist View*. Washington, D.C.: Smithsonian Institution Press, 1996.

Driskell, David C., Camille O. Cosby, and William H. Cosby Jr. *The Other Side of Color: African American Art in the Collection of Camille O. and William H. Cosby, Jr.* San Francisco: Pomegranate Communications, 2001.

McGee, Julie L. *David C. Driskell: Artist and Scholar*. San Francisco: Pomegranate Communications, 2006.

Riggs, Thomas, ed. *St. James Guide to Black Artists*. Detroit, Mich.: St. James Press, 1997, pp. 158–160.

Duncanson, Robert Scott
(ca. 1821–1872) *painter*

One of the first African-American artists to achieve international fame, Robert Scott Duncanson created vivid romantic landscapes that could rival those of the finest European painters of his day.

He was born in Seneca County, New York, in about 1821 into a biracial family. His father was Scottish Canadian and his mother was African American. He attended Canadian schools as a boy and took to sketching pictures as a teenager. At age 20, Duncanson moved to Mt. Healthy, Ohio, a refuge for blacks, located near the city of Cincinnati.

Working as a house painter to earn his living, Duncanson painted his pictures in his free time. His artistic ability soon attracted public attention and he had his first exhibition of paintings in Cincinnati in 1842. Upper-class abolitionists and businessmen were impressed by Duncanson's lush landscapes, and soon he was receiving commissions to paint portraits and landscapes for many of Cincinnati's leading citizens. "I had a great treat last evening in the view of some portraits and fancy pieces from the pencil of a Negro, who has had no instruction or knowledge of the art," wrote famed abolitionist and newspaper editor

William Lloyd Garrison in an article. Lawyer Nicholas Longworth hired Duncanson to paint huge landscape murals in the entrance hall of his house. The murals took him two years to complete. Today they are considered among the finest wall paintings in the United States.

Members of the Western Freedman's Aid Society, an abolitionist group, paid for Duncanson to go to Europe to study and paint in 1853. He was greatly impressed by England's landscape painters, especially J. M. Turner, whose impressionistic style would have a profound influence on his own painting. Duncanson's landscapes attracted much admiration in Europe. The *London Art Journal* in 1860 named him one of the greatest of contemporary landscape painters.

But he was also a competent portrait painter and an excellent painter of historical scenes. In England, he met poet Alfred, Lord Tennyson and proceeded to base several of his paintings on scenes from Tennyson's poems. His *Trial of Shakespeare,* about the life of another great English writer, is one of his best-known works.

More contemporary events, however, were making it difficult for a black artist to work in the United States. The Civil War broke out in 1861, and Duncanson moved to Canada to escape the turmoil. When the war ended in 1865, he returned to Europe, spending most of his time in England and his beloved Scotland. He came back to the United States in 1867. By then, Duncanson had rejected the romantic style of the Hudson River School of painters and was painting in a more realistic style. In 1869 and 1871, he exhibited his work in both the United States and Scotland, which he visited one last time. His paintings were selling for the impressive sum of $500 each. But financial and critical success did not bring happiness for the painter.

His biracial roots caused an identity problem that Duncanson never overcame. In the summer of 1872, his insecurities came to a head and he suffered a nervous breakdown. He was hospitalized at the Michigan State Retreat for three months. Duncanson died soon after of an unknown disease on December 21, 1872. Unfortunately, most of his paintings have since been lost or destroyed.

While Robert Scott Duncanson's career was a great achievement for him personally, it also showed a skeptical world that the firmly held belief that blacks were incapable of creating sophisticated art was a myth. In its obituary, the *Detroit Tribune* wrote: "He had acquired the idea that in all his artistic efforts he was aided by the spirits of the great masters."

Further Reading

Bearden, Romare, and Harry Henderson. *A History of African-American Artists: From 1792 to the Present.* New York: Pantheon Books, 1993, pp. 18–39.

Ketner, Joseph D. *The Emergence of the African American Artist: Robert S. Duncanson, 1821–1872.* Columbia: University of Missouri Press, 1994.

Lewis Samella. *African American Art and Artists.* Berkeley: University of California Press, 2003, pp. 24–29.

Lubin, David M. "Reconstructing Duncanson," in *Picturing a Nation: Art and Social Change in Nineteenth-Century America.* New Haven, Conn.: Yale University Press, 1994, pp. 107–157.

Perry, Regenia A. *Free Within Ourselves: African-American Artists in the Collection of the National Museum of American Art.* San Francisco: Pomegranate Artbooks, 1992, pp. 58–63

"Valley Pasture (1857)." Smithsonian American Art Museum and the Renwick Gallery. Available online. URL: http://americanart.si.edu/collections/search/artwork/?id=7615. Downloaded March 25, 2009.

Edmondson, William
(ca. 1870–1951) *folk sculptor*

The first African-American artist to have a one-person show in a major museum, William Edmondson created elemental sculptures of astonishing power in a career that spanned the last 15 years of his life.

He was born near Nashville, Tennessee, in Davidson County, sometime between 1863 and 1870; a fire destroyed the family Bible in which his birth date was recorded. His parents were freed slaves, and his father died when he was quite young. His mother supported her six children by working in the fields. With little education, Edmondson soon went to work as a farmhand and a groom at a racing stable. He then worked for 25 years at the all-white Women's Hospital in Nashville as an orderly and handyman.

In 1931, in his sixties, he either quit or was let go from the hospital and retired to a brick cottage where he lived alone, never having married. By chance, Edmondson got a job as a stonemason's helper and learned the craft of stone carving. The work fascinated him and he began to salvage abandoned limestone curbstones being replaced by the city with concrete ones. Using chisels he fashioned from old railroad spikes, he began to make tombstones and sold them to local black families.

Edmondson was soon making traditional tombstone figures of doves and lambs. He then began carving small figures of other animals—horses, dogs, lions, and imaginary creatures of his own fancy that he called "varmints." Finally, he added human figures to his limestone gallery—preachers, biblical characters, and even black sports figures such as the heavyweight boxer Jack Johnson.

With no formal art training whatsoever, and strictly limited to small blocks of limestone that most professional sculptors would have rejected, Edmondson created simple, archaic figures that expressed a deep religious faith, a sharp and unexpected sense of humor, and an astonishing modernity of design and form.

Slowly, word started to get around about the old black man and his yardful of sculptured treasures. In 1936, top fashion photographer Louise Dahl-Wolfe came upon Edmondson's work while visiting a friend in Nashville and took photographs of it. Her pictures eventually came to the attention of Alfred Barr, director of the Museum of Modern Art (MOMA) in New York City. Barr was so taken with Edmondson's work that he arranged for an exhibition of 12 of his sculptures at MOMA in 1937. Thus, William Edmondson, an illiterate black man who never left Nashville except for one short trip to Memphis, became the first black artist to have his work exhibited at one of the nation's most prestigious museums.

William Edmondson of Nashville, Tennessee, is flanked by one of his primitive but powerful sculptures. *(Photograph by Louise Dahl-Wolfe)*

The exhibition made Edmondson into something of a media celebrity, and he was interviewed by newspapers and magazines, including *Time*. The press in general took him to be an untutored, intuitive, ignorant artist, a role that Edmondson craftily played along with. Whatever he really thought about his art, he did not see himself as an artist and never expected to make money from what he called his "miracles." "I is just doing the Lord's work," he said in a 1941 interview. "I didn't know I was no artist till them folks come tole me I was."

What makes Edmondson's achievement all the more impressive was the fact that he never made preliminary sketches or models of his sculptures but painstakingly carved them directly out of stone, giving them an elemental design far more powerful than the more sophisticated and detailed works of many professional sculptors.

His New York show, however, did little to further his career. Edmondson received a year's work from a federal government arts program, the Works Progress Administration, in 1939 and had another show, the only other one in his lifetime, at the Nashville Art Gallery in 1941.

When he began to lose his health to cancer and no longer had the strength to carve in his workshop, Edmondson continued to carve with tiny blocks of limestone, the only material he could ever afford. He died of a heart attack on February 7, 1951. Ironically, this master carver of tombstones is buried in an unmarked grave, its location no longer known, in Mt. Ararat Cemetery on the outskirts of Nashville.

"I can't help carving, I just do it," Edmondson told *Time* in 1937. "Jesus has planted the seed of carving in me."

Further Reading

Cheekwood Museum of Arts. *The Art of William Edmondson.* Jackson: University of Mississippi Press, 2000.

Fuller, Edmund L. *Visions in Stone: The Sculpture of William Edmondson.* Pittsburgh, Pa.: University of Pittsburgh Press, 1973.

Livingston, Jane, and John Beardsley. *Black Folk Art in America 1930–1980.* Jackson: University Press of Mississippi, 1989, pp. 86–91.

Spires, Elizabeth. *I Heard God Talking to Me: William Edmondson and His Stone Carvings.* New York: Farrar, Straus and Giroux, 2009.

Edwards, Melvin
(Mel Edwards)
(1937–) *sculptor, educator*

Perhaps the most prolific contemporary African-American sculptor, Melvin Edwards welds together scrap metals and found objects to create sculptures that conjure up the slavery era and racist past, while pointing to a better future.

He was born on May 4, 1937, in Houston, Texas. His mother, Thelmarie, was a seamstress and his father, Melvin, Sr., worked by day as a waiter and at night as a photographer in nightclubs. He attended USC, where he earned a Bachelor of Fine Arts degree. Beginning in 1964, he taught at several California schools, including San Bernardino Valley College and Orange County Community College.

In 1963, Edwards began his best-known series, *Lynch Fragments*. These small but powerful wall sculptures consisted of chains, scissors, hammers, padlocks, spikes, gears, wrenches, and axes, all welded together in different combinations. They were grim reminders of the lynching of hundreds of blacks in the South during the 19th and 20th centuries. The artist claims that "in the United States we're the only people to actually come out of the lynching experience. . . It's documented and it's not over yet." But the chains that served as a recurring motif in these and other works are not only meant to symbolize the shackles of slavery but also the important link between African Americans and their ancestral land of Africa. Edwards revived the *Lynch Fragments* series in 1973 and once more in 1978.

The sculptor is also known for his many large, outdoor sculptures in public spaces. Many of these works continue his use of old, discarded materials in new ways, an African-American tradition. Such innovative works as *Pyramid Up, Pyramid Down* (1969) constructed of barbed wire and chains, uses linear space rather than the three-dimensional space that most sculptures occupy.

Edwards has taught art at Rutgers University's Mason Gross School of the Arts in New Brunswick, New Jersey, since 1972. He had traveled and worked in Africa many times and is one of the few African-American sculptors whose work resides in the government collections of such African countries as Benin and Ghana. "I go to Africa every chance I get," he has said. "I've probably been there more times since 1970 than I've been to my home state of Texas."

Some of his large, public works reflect an African influence. *Gate of Ogun* (1983) is a stainless steel structure that is a tribute to the deity Ogun, the Yoruba god of metal.

In 1993, a 30-year retrospective of Edwards's work was held at the Neuberger Museum at SUNY at Purchase. His work resides in many museum collections, including the Brooklyn Museum of Art, New York, the Los Angeles County Museum, California, and the Wadsworth Atheneum, Hartford, Connecticut. He is the recipient of a National Endowment for the Arts Fellowship (1984) and a Fulbright Fellowship to Zimbabwe in Africa (1988–89).

As writer Josephine Gear has observed: "Edwards, without fanfare, has long forged cross-cultural influences to produce some of the most powerful and bracing sculpture of our time."

Further Reading

Gedeon, Lucinda H., ed. *Melvin Edwards Sculpture: A Thirty-Year Retrospective, 1963–1993*. Seattle: University of Washington Press, 1993.

Lewis, Samella. *African-American Art and Artists*. Berkeley: University of California Press, 2003, pp. 210–211.

"Melvin Edwards Biography." Bookrags.com. Available online. URL: http://www.bookrags.com/biography/melvin-edwards/. Downloaded March 4, 2009.

Riggs, Thomas, ed. *St. James Guide to Black Artists*. Detroit, Mich.: St. James Press, 1997, pp. 170–172.

Evans, Minnie
(1892–1987) *folk painter*

A self-taught artist who did not start painting until the age of 43, Minnie Evans used her art to depict her religious visions with the hallucinogenic power of a psychedelic trip.

She was born on December 12, 1892, in Long Creek in Pender County, North Carolina, near Wilmington, where she moved with her parents as an infant. The only child of poor farmers, she attended school through the sixth grade. At age 15 she married Julius Evans and had three sons with him. A great lover of flowers, she was for many years a gatekeeper at Wilmington's Airlie Gardens.

Evans began painting after experiencing a religious vision on Good Friday, 1935, in which she claimed God commanded her to draw. Her first paintings, made with wax crayons, supposedly depicted religious visions she had experienced since childhood. Evans's paintings are swirling spirals of luscious plant life, animal shapes, and eyes out of which often emerges a human face. God appears frequently in her paintings and is usually depicted with wings and a rainbow halo. The eyes symbolize the all-seeing nature of God.

Evans sold her first paintings for 50 cents apiece. A folk art specialist and photographer befriended her and agreed to help sell her paintings at better prices.

Art experts have called her work surrealistic, visionary, and even psychedelic. Full of religious mysteries, Evans herself confessed she was not always sure of their meaning. "When I get through with them I have to look at them like everybody else. They are just as strange to me as they are to anybody else."

She felt her pictures were too personal to share with the public and did not do so until 1961, when she had her first one-person exhibition, at the Little Gallery in Wilmington (now St. John's Museum). She had subsequent exhibitions during her lifetime in London, England; at the Whitney Museum of American Art, New York City; and the North Carolina Museum of Art, Raleigh. In the 1960s Evans began to experiment with mixed media, cutting out designs and pasting them onto canvas board on which she painted with watercolors or oils.

Minnie Evans died on December 16, 1987, in Wilmington, North Carolina. Her work continues to intrigue and haunt the art world and general public. "My whole life has been dreams," she once said, "[and] sometimes day visions. . . No one taught me about drawing. No one could because no one knows what to teach me. No one has taught me to paint; it came to me."

Further Reading

Kahan, Mitchell. *Heavenly Visions: The Art of Minnie Evans.* Chapel Hill: University of North Carolina Press, 1986.

Lyons, Mary E. *Painting Dreams: Minnie Evans, Visionary Artist.* Boston: Houghton Mifflin, 1996.

Perry, Regenia A. *Free Within Ourselves: African-American Artists in the Collection of the National Museum of American Art.* San Francisco: Pomegranate Communications, 1992, pp. 68–71.

Wharton, Fred. *The Bottle Chapel at Airlie Gardens: A Tribute to Minnie Evans,* Wilmington, N. C.: Publishing Laboratory of UNC. Wilmington, 2008.

F

Feelings, Tom
(1933–2003) *illustrator, writer, educator*

The prizewinning illustrator of more than 20 books, Tom Feelings artistically expressed a spiritual connection between African Americans and their homeland of Africa, where he visited and lived.

He was born on May 19, 1933, in the Bedford-Stuyvesant section of Brooklyn, New York. He studied art at the George Westinghouse Vocational High School and attended the School of Visual Arts in New York on a scholarship. In 1953, Feelings left school and joined the U.S. Air Force, working as staff illustrator in the Graphics Division in London, England. On his discharge four years later, he returned to the School of Visual Arts. The following year, 1958, he created the comic strip *Tommy Traveler in the World of Negro History* for the black journal *New York Age*.

As a freelance artist, Feelings drew pictures of black street life for the African-American magazines the *Liberator* and *Freedomways*. *Look* magazine published some of his drawings of black people in New Orleans that he completed on a trip there in 1961.

In 1964, Feelings was invited to Ghana in West Africa, where he illustrated the *African Review*, a monthly magazine published by the Ghanaian Government Publishing House. He returned to the United States in 1966, determined to become an illustrator of children's books. His goal was to provide African-American children with the kinds of positive images he saw among the children of Africa.

Feelings wrote several books with his wife Muriel, who had lived and taught in East Africa. *Moja Means One* (1972) was a counting book for children, explaining numbers in the Swahili language of East Africa. Feelings's soft, charcoal drawings earned him a Caldecott Honor Award, the first time an African-American artist had won this prestigious prize in children's literature.

Three years later the husband-wife team produced *Jambo Means Hello,* an alphabet book explaining Swahili words. It earned them a second Caldecott Honor Award.

Feelings spent two years in Guyana in South America in the early 1970s, directing the Guyanese Ministry of Education's children's book project. After illustrating the words of others for years, Feelings wrote and illustrated *Black Pilgrimage* (1972), which described his travels in Africa.

By now he was illustrating books for black Americans of all ages, such as *Soul Looks Back in Wonder* (1992), an anthology of poetry by Langston Hughes, Maya Angelou, and Margaret Walker. Feelings's full-color painting illustrations earned him his third Coretta Scott King Award.

In 1995, Feelings published his most ambitious book yet, *The Middle Passage: White Ship/ Black Cargo.* It took him 20 years to complete the book's 64 pages of textless illustrations in pen, ink, and tempera. The pictures told the grim journey of a slave ship's journey from West Africa to the New World. "I clearly did this book for black people so it would be something that inspires them," Feelings said. "The book is also for the whites who claim they can't recognize what racism feels like. They will be able to go through the experience, too." *The Middle Passage* earned Feelings his fourth Coretta Scott King Award as well as an American Library Association Award. In *Souls Look Back in Wonder* (1999), Feelings elicited and edited the poems of 13 African-American writers and illustrated them. His last book, published posthumously, *I Saw Your Face* (2004), coauthored by poet Kwame Dawes, is a celebration of the black diaspora.

Feelings taught book illustration at the University of South Carolina in Columbia from 1989 to 1995. Having divorced his first wife, Muriel, in 1974, he married Diane Johnson in 1992. In 1996, he received an honorary doctoral degree from his alma mater, the School of Visual Arts. He also won eight certificates of merit from the Society of Illustrators and was the recipient of a National Endowment for the Arts Visual Artists Fellowship Grant in 1982.

"When asked what kind of work I do, I say that I am an illustrator, a storyteller in picture form who tries to interpret life as I see it," Feelings wrote. "When asked who I am, I say I am an African born in America." He died of cancer on August 25, 2003, at age 70.

Further Reading

Feelings, Muriel, and Tom Feelings, illustrator. *Jambo Means Hello: Swahili Alphabet Book.* New York: Dial Books, 1974.

Feelings, Tom. *Black Pilgrimage.* New York: Lothrop Lee & Shepard, 1972.

———. *The Middle Passage: White Ship/Black Cargo.* New York: Dial Books, 1995.

Feelings Tom, and Kwame Dawes. *I Saw Your Face.* New York: Dial, 2004.

Rockman, Connie C. *Eighth Book of Junior Authors and Illustrators.* New York: H. W. Wilson, 2000, pp. 142–146.

"Tom Feelings Biography." Available online. URL: http://biography.jrank.org/pages/2346/Feelings-Tom.html. Downloaded March 4, 2009.

Franklin, Carl
(1949–   ) *filmmaker, screenwriter, actor*

One of the most talented if unheralded African-American filmmakers to emerge in the 1990s, Carl Franklin has exhibited the skill and vision of a major film director.

He was born on April 11, 1949, in Richmond, California, and attended the University of California at Berkeley on a football scholarship. When he took a drama course to fill an English requirement, he fell in love with theater and decided to become an actor. After leaving Berkeley, Franklin found work in regional theaters in Washington, D.C., and New York City. He accompanied a friend to a film audition, not intending to try for a role himself, and ended up being cast. The film was the black family comedy *Five on the Black Hand Side* (1973).

Franklin moved to Los Angeles, California, where he landed recurring roles on several television series, including the police dramas *Caribe* (1975) and *McLain's Law* (1981–82). Disillusioned with acting, he entered the master's program at the American Film Institute (AFI) in Los Angeles (L.A.) in 1986 to study film directing. Before leaving AFI, he directed the impressive short film *Punk* (1986), about a black child who kills a child molester.

Like many fledgling filmmakers, Franklin found work with B-movie master Roger Corman. He directed two cheap, exploitative films for Corman before landing his first major assignment, the film noir thriller *One False Move* (1991). This tightly directed film tells the story of a trio of L.A. drug dealers and killers who drive cross-country to one member's hometown in rural Arkansas. Filled with a foreboding atmosphere, sharp characterizations, and nerve-tingling suspense, *One False Move* starred Billy Bob Thornton, (who cowrote the script), Michael Beach, Cynda Williams, and Bill Paxton. Largely ignored at the time of its release, the film has since achieved cult status on television and video.

Four years passed before the release of Franklin's next film, *Devil in a Blue Dress* (1995), his first big-budget Hollywood movie. Set in post–World War II L.A., it starred black actor Denzel Washington as novice private detective Easy Rawlins. The film was cowritten by Walter Mosley, who adapted his own novel. Rawlins followed a trail of murder and corruption as he searched for a missing white woman. The film was praised for its authentic recreation of 1940s L.A., offbeat characters, and skillful use of suspense and violence. Like its predecessor, however, *Devil in a Blue Dress* failed to find a wide audience.

Franklin's next feature film was a change of pace, the domestic drama *One True Thing* (1998), adapted from an Anna Quindlen novel and starring Meryl Streep, William Hurt, and Renee Zellweger. Although some critics criticized Franklin's superimposing of a mystery element on the plot, writer Leonard Maltin praised the film for its "superb acting and the constant ring of truth."

His next film, *High Crimes* (2002), a courtroom thriller starring Morgan Freeman and Ashley Judd, was poorly received by critics. *Out of Time* (2003), a crime thriller that reunited him with Denzel Washington, was better received. Franklin has recently directed for television, including part of the World War II miniseries, *The Pacific* (2009).

A filmmaker of acknowledged insight and skill, Carl Franklin still waits for the big, successful mainstream film that will bring him widespread fame.

"I usually look for universal truths of some kind, you know," he said in a 1995 interview, "certain kinds of thematic universal principles that somehow reach me on an emotional, visceral level. And then usually I start to see the film."

Further Reading

Alexander, George. *Why We Make Movies: Black Filmmakers Talk About the Magic of Cinema.* New York: Harlem Moon, 2003, pp. 419–441.

"Carl Franklin," The Internet Movie Database. Available online. URL: http://www.imdb.com/find?s=nm&q=Carl+Franklin&x=12&y=5. Downloaded March 4, 2009.

Harris, Erich Leon. "A Conversation with Carl Franklin." Available online. URL: http://www.moviemaker.com/directing/article/carl_franklin_3167/. Downloaded March 4, 2009.

Moon, Spencer. *Reel Black Talk: A Sourcebook of 50 American Filmmakers.* Westport, Conn.: Greenwood Press, 1997, pp. 111–114.

Further Viewing

Devil in a Blue Dress (1995). Sony, VHS/DVD, 1998/1999.

One False Move (1991). Sony, VHS/DVD, 2000/1999.

Out of Time (2003). MGM Home Entertainment, DVD, 2004.

Fuller, Meta Vaux Warrick
(1877–1968) *sculptor*

An important precursor of the black cultural movement known as the Harlem Renaissance, Meta Vaux Warrick Fuller created sculptures that celebrated the African roots of the "new Negro" in the 20th century.

She was born Meta Vaux Warrick on June 8, 1877, in Philadelphia, Pennsylvania. Her family was middle class, and she received a scholarship in 1894 to attend the Pennsylvania Museum School of Industrial Art, later to become the University of the Arts. Her first clay sculpture, *Head of Medusa,* earned her an award.

Encouraged by her teachers, Warrick went to Paris, France, to study and sculpt. She entered her work in several exhibitions, including one at the Paris Salon. Famed French sculptor Auguste Rodin visited her studio and was impressed by her sculptures. Rodin's monumental style and strong sense of drama had a great effect on Warrick's work.

After her return to the United States, she was commissioned by the Jamestown Tercentennial Exposition in Virginia in 1907 to create a sculpture that would depict the efforts of blacks in American history. She was the first black female artist to receive a federal commission. She came up with 14 tableaux, or scenes, containing 150 figures on the theme. The work was displayed at the Exposition's Negro Pavilion and earned Warrick a gold medal.

In 1909, Warrick married Liberian-born neurologist and Harvard University professor Solomon Fuller, and they settled in Framingham, Massachusetts. She continued to sculpt and joined the Wellesley Society of Artists and the Boston Art Club. At the same time, she was drawn to the theater and worked with both black and white theater companies in the Boston area. She built theater sets, created costumes and props, and even wrote plays, but under a pseudonym. While making the costumes for a black show in Boston she met LOIS MAILOU JONES. She encouraged Jones to pursue a career in art. Years later, Jones claimed that Fuller's marriage robbed her work of much of the strength and emotion her earlier sculptures had exhibited. Very possibly Fuller felt pressure as a professor's wife to support her husband's work to the detriment of her own.

To make matters worse, a warehouse fire in 1910 destroyed the sculptures Fuller had made in Paris. Nonetheless, she continued to create memorable pieces. At the request of W. E. B. DuBois, she created the three-figure group *The Spirit of Emancipation* (1913). The sculpture commemorated the 50th anniversary of President Abraham Lincoln's Emancipation Proclamation, which freed many slaves.

Among her best-known works is *Ethiopia Awakening* (1914), which depicts a black woman in Egyptian-like garb, who, writes Crystal Britton, "powerfully symbolize[s] the emergence of Black life and culture in America." Another impressive piece was *Mary Turner* (1919), which commemorated the lynching of a black woman.

Fuller continued to sculpt until her husband became seriously ill and then nursed him until his death in 1953. By then, Fuller herself was seriously ill, having contracted tuberculosis in about 1950. She recovered her health in 1956 and returned to sculpting. She became deeply involved with the Civil Rights movement in the 1960s and even donated money from the sales of her art to benefit the cause of black equality. Her sculpture *Crucifixion* was a tribute to the four young girls killed in the bombing of a Birmingham, Alabama, black church in 1963. After a long and eventful life filled with both happiness and sorrow, Meta Vaux Warrick Fuller died on March 18, 1968, at age 90. Today, her surviving sculptures reside at the Cleveland Museum of Fine Art, the Schomburg Collection at the 135th Street Branch of the New York Public Library, and Howard University's Gallery of Art, among other collections.

Fuller's best work expressed the pain and suffering of the world's disenfranchised peoples as well as the hopes and promise of a new era in which African Americans would find their place in the world.

Further Reading

Lewis, Samella. *African American Art and Artists.* Berkeley: University of California Press, 2003, pp. 51–53.

"Meta Vaux Warrick Fuller," Bridgewater State College Hall of Black Achievement website. Available online. URL: http://www.bridgew.edu/HOBA/fuller.htm. Downloaded March 4, 2009.

Perkins, Kathy. "The Genius of Meta Warrick Fuller." *Negro American Literature Forum,* September 1990, pp. 65–72.

Riggs, Thomas, ed. *St. James Guide to Black Artists.* Detroit, Mich.: St. James Press, 1997, pp. 203–204.

G

Gilchrist, Jan Spivey
(Janice Spivey Gilchrist)
(1949–) *illustrator, painter, educator*

A painter for 20 years before illustrating her first children's book at age 39, Jan Spivey Gilchrist has since then enhanced more than 35 children's books with her warm and intimate pictures of black children and their families.

She was born Janice Spivey on February 15, 1949, in Chicago, Illinois. Her father, Charles Spivey, was a minister, and her first drawings were copies of pictures from an illustrated Bible. Her mother, Arthric Jones, was a homemaker.

As a young child, Spivey suffered from a bone disease that prevented her from going outside to play with other children.

"I felt very lonely," she once explained. "And then I picked up my pen and picked up my pencil and I realized that I could do something because I had been drawing since I was little . . . and people would come and sit on the porch and I would draw them."

Encouraged by her parents to pursue art, Spivey entered Eastern Illinois University in 1969, where she received a Bachelor of Science degree. She married Arthur Van Johnson, an auditor, in 1970. He did not encourage her to work at her art, and they divorced in 1980. Spivey worked as a substitute teacher in Illinois for three years. Then she attended the University of Northern Iowa, where she received a Master of Fine Arts degree in painting in 1979.

While making a living at teaching, Spivey gained some notice for her paintings that were exhibited in local galleries around her home in Glenwood, Illinois. In 1983, she married administrator Kelvin Keith Gilchrist.

Attracted to the writing of African-American poet Eloise Greenfield, Gilchrist approached her at a party and impressed her with her work. Through Greenfield, she was introduced to her publisher and invited to illustrate a book written by Greenfield's mother, Lessie Jones, *Children of Long Ago* (1988). A reviewer in the *New York Times Book Review* said, "the soft pastel drawings . . . of people going about their activities but caught in a golden light are a perfect complement to the text."

Gilchrist next created illustrations for Greenfield's poetry collection *Nathaniel Talking* (1988), which dealt with the thoughts and feelings of a young black boy growing up. She drew the pictures in pencil, and they won her the Coretta Scott King Award for Illustration. Since then, she has collaborated on more than a dozen books with Greenfield, making them one of the most prominent African-American author/illustrator teams in children's literature today. They both won the Coretta Scott

King Award in 1992 for *Night on Neighborhood Street.*

Gilchrist created her first complete book—both illustrations and text—*Indigo and Moonlight Gold,* in 1997. Other recent titles include *In the Land of Words—New and Selected Poems* (2003) and *The Friendly Four* (2006), both with text by Greenfield. *My America* (2007), which Gilchrist wrote and co-illustrated with ASHLEY BRYAN, was a Parents' Choice Award winner.

The vivid realism of Gilchrist's work comes partly from her painstaking use of live models for her characters. She sees her positive approach to the African-American experience as important for her black audience. "I want my readers to feel that they are important," she has said. "I want them to see that the work is honest, that it's very positive, and that they—when they put the book down—feel that there is hope."

Jan Spivey Gilchrist received the Distinguished Alumni Award from Eastern Illinois University in 1992. She was inducted into the International Literary Hall of Fame for Writers of African Descent in 2000 and the Society of Illustrators in 2001. She has also created illustrations for the *New York Times,* the *Washington Post,* and *Ebony* magazine.

She lives in suburban Chicago with her husband and their two children.

Further Reading

Gilchrist, Jan Spivey, illustrator, and Ashley Bryan, illustrator. *My America.* New York: HarperCollins, 2007.

Greenfield, Eloise, and Jan Spivey Gilchrist, illustrator. *How They Got Over: African Americans and the Call of the Sea.* New York: HarperCollins Juvenile Books, 2003.

Johnson, James Weldon, and Jan Spivey Gilchrist, illustrator. *Lift Every Voice and Sing.* New York: Scholastic, 2002.

Telgen, Diane, ed. *Something About the Author, Volume 72.* Detroit, Mich.: Gale Research, 1993, pp. 81–88.

Gilliam, Sam

(1933–   ) *painter, educator*

The first artist to hang an unsupported canvas on a museum wall, Sam Gilliam is one of the leading artists of the abstract movement known as color-field painting.

He was born on November 30, 1933, in Tupelo, Mississippi, the seventh of eight children. His father worked on the railroad and moved the family to Louisville, Kentucky, when Sam was still an infant. By the fifth grade, Gilliam was determined to become an artist and took a special arts course in junior high school. After graduating from high school, he attended the University of Louisville and earned a Bachelor of Arts degree in fine arts in 1955. His graduate studies at Louisville were interrupted by a two-year hitch in the U.S. Army, but he returned to the university and earned a Master of Fine Arts degree in 1961.

Gilliam married journalist Dorothy Butler in 1962, and they relocated to Washington, D.C.,

Sam Gilliam changed the very nature of what a painting is with his distinctive draped canvases. *(Anthony Barboza)*

which remains their home today. His painting style at first was patterned after the German expressionists, who focused on recognizable figures in an abstract setting with dark, emotionally intense colors. Gilliam gradually moved to a new school of art, color-field painting, which emerged in New York City in the late 1950s. The color-field artists were abstract artists who reveled in simple compositions full of clear, bright colors.

Gilliam literally poured colors onto his canvases. He would fold a still wet painting onto itself to imprint new forms and shapes on it. Then in 1965 he tried something even more innovative. From his studio, he saw women hanging their laundry on clotheslines to dry. He wondered why a painting couldn't hang as freely, without benefit of frame or bar supporters. So he began to drape his loose canvases on walls and suspend them from ceilings. Folded and wrinkled, the canvas itself became part of the artwork. For this revolutionary technique Gilliam was dubbed "father of the draped canvas" and became the most prominent African-American artist of the color-field school.

"Color is the most tantalizing element in painting," Gilliam has said, "but I'm very much involved with structure and shape . . . whether the painting is on a structure or hanging free in space, or whether it is a found object or a proper sculpture on a pedestal, it is still a statement."

In 1975, he created his most extravagant draped canvas. *Seahorses* covered several hundred feet of paint-stained canvas and stretched across the outside walls of two museum wings of the Philadelphia Museum of Art in Philadelphia, Pennsylvania.

In the late 1970s, Gilliam developed a new style of painting. Inspired by the jazz music of such musicians as Dizzy Gillespie and Miles Davis, he began to create geometric collages and patchwork-quilt-like canvases using multiple layers of thick paint. In recent years, he has continued to create large, monumental works across the country. A major retrospective of his work was mounted at the Corcoran Gallery of Art in Washington, D.C.,

in 2005. He donated his silkscreen print *Museum Moment* to the Smithsonian Institution in 2009.

For more than 30 years, Sam Gilliam has taught in both public schools and universities, including the University of Maryland in College Park and Carnegie Mellon University in Pittsburgh, Pennsylvania. He was named the 2006 Alumnus of the Year by his alma mater, the University of Louisville. Gilliam lives in Washington, D.C., with his wife, who writes a syndicated column for the *Washington Post*. They have three daughters.

"I am a better artist today in that I am obviously a better teacher," he has said. "Whether I am teaching or making art, the process is fundamentally the same: I am creating."

Further Reading

Binstock, Jonathan P. *Sam Gilliam: A Retrospective*. Berkeley: University of California Press, 2005.

Driskell, David C. *Contemporary Visual Expressions: The Art of Sam Gilliam, Martha Jackson-Jarvis, Keith Morrison, William T. Williams: Inaugural Exhibition, Anacosti*. Washington, D.C.: Smithsonian Institution Press, 1987.

Middendorf Gallery. *Sam Gilliam: Small Drape Paintings 1970–1973. February 24–March 24, 1990*. Washington, D.C.: Middendorf Gallery, 1990.

Perry, Regenia A. *Free Within Ourselves: African-American Artists in the Collection of the National Museum of American Art*. San Francisco: Pomegranate Communications, 1992, pp. 72–79.

"Sam Gilliam." Available online. URL: http://www.answers.com/topic/sam-gilliam. Downloaded March 26, 2009.

Greaves, William
(William Garfield Greaves)
(1926–) *documentary filmmaker, film producer, screenwriter, actor*

Known as the leading African-American documentary filmmaker, William Greaves has been a part of the independent black film industry as

Documentary filmmaker William Greaves is seen here on the set of *Black Journal* with executive editor Lou Potter (left). Greaves helped create and host this groundbreaking television newsmagazine in the 1960s. *(Photofest)*

actor, director, producer, and writer for more than five decades.

He was born on October 8, 1926, in New York City. He attended City College in New York and later joined an African dance company. He soon turned to acting on the stage and was in the original Broadway production of the musical *Finian's Rainbow.* Greaves made his film debut in the black independent film *Sepia Cinderella* (1947). Over the next several years he appeared in a number of black films, including *Souls of Sin* (1949), produced by pioneering black filmmaker WILLIAM ALEXANDER. In the early 1950s, discouraged by

the lack of opportunities for blacks in mainstream filmmaking, Greaves moved to Canada, where he worked for the National Film Board. Between 1956 and 1959, he edited and did the sound for more than a dozen Canadian short films, learning every aspect of filmmaking in the process. Many of these works were public service films with such titles as *Fast Fire Suppression* (1956) and *Profile of a Problem Drinker* (1957). He also worked on a series of nature documentaries in the Canadian wilderness.

Greaves returned to the United States and raised enough money to direct his first documentary,

Emergency Ward (1959). During the 1960s he found work in television and served as executive producer and cohost of the groundbreaking Public Broadcasting Service (PBS) series *Black Journal,* for which he won an Emmy in 1968. This program is generally considered among the first to use a news magazine format. From 1969 to 1982 he taught film acting at New York's Strasberg Theatre Institute.

In 1967, Greaves wrote, directed, and produced a unique experimental film about the making of a movie, with the strange title *Symbiopsychotoxiplasm: Take One.* The film was poorly received and was not seen again until it was rediscovered 24 years later in 1991 and shown during a retrospective of Greaves's work at the Brooklyn Museum in New York City. At that time, it was hailed as an extraordinary exploration of the nature of filmmaking. In 2005, Greaves made a sequel, *Symbiopsychotoxiplasm: Take 2½.*

Greaves produced three documentaries during the 1970s—*The Voice of La Raza* (1972), about the radical Latino organization; *From These Roots* (1974), which dealt with the Harlem Renaissance of the 1920s; and *Ali, the Fighter* (1975), about the Muhammad Ali–Joe Frazier heavyweight fight.

In a rare foray into commercial filmmaking, Greaves served as executive producer of the Richard Pryor movie *Bustin' Loose* (1981). He reemerged after a long dry spell in 1990 with several important projects. He directed and hosted *That's Black Entertainment,* a retrospective look at African Americans in movies, and produced *Ida B. Wells: A Passion for Justice,* a biographical film about the great black educator. This latter film won 19 film festival awards and was nominated for an Image Award in 1990 from the National Association for the Advancement of Colored People.

Greaves's most recent film, another biography, is *Ralph Bunche: An American Odyssey* (2000), about the life of the undersecretary-general of the United Nations and the first African American to win a Nobel Prize for Peace. Narrated by actor Sidney Poitier, *Ralph Bunche* was shown on PBS and has won the Golden Award at two international film festivals.

William Greaves was inducted into the Black Filmmakers Hall of Fame in 1980 and received a Life Achievement Award from the Association of Independent Video and Filmmakers in 1986. He is a member of the board of directors of the Actors Studio in New York.

Speaking of his life in documentary film, Greaves has said, "I'm one of those individuals who gravitate towards knowledge, information, expansion of my consciousness."

Further Reading

Alexander George. *Why We Make Movies: Black Filmmakers Talk About the Magic of Cinema.* New York: Harlem Moon, 2003, pp. 28–45.

Knee, Adam, and Charles Musser. "William Greaves, Documentary Filmmaking and the African-American Experience." *Film Quarterly* 45, 1992, pp. 13–25.

Moon, Spencer. *Reel Black Talk: A Sourcebook of 50 American Filmmakers.* Westport, Conn.: Greenwood Press, 1997, pp. 123–130.

"William Greaves," The Internet Movie Database. Available online. URL: http://www.imdb.com/name/nm0337348/.Downloaded March 4, 2009.

William Greaves Productions Web site. Available online. URL: http://www.williamgreaves.com/. Downloaded March 4, 2009.

Further Viewing

Ali, the Fighter (1975). Starz/Anchor Bay, DVD, 2005.
Symbiopsychotoxiplasm: Two Takes. Criterion Collection (1968). Criterion, 2 DVDs, 2006.

Gunn, Bill
(William Harrison Gunn)
(1934–1989) *filmmaker, screenwriter playwright, actor*

A screenwriter of sensitivity and rare insight into the black experience, Bill Gunn directed only three films in his relatively short life, one of which is today considered a landmark of African-American cinema.

He was born William Harrison Gunn on July 15, 1934, in Philadelphia, Pennsylvania. He started, as so many black filmmakers have, as an actor. Through the 1960s Gunn appeared in episodes of such television series as *Naked City*, *The Outer Limits*, and *The Fugitive*. He turned to writing in the late 1960s and wrote stage plays and the screenplays for two eccentric films, both released in 1970. *The Angel Levine* was a fantasy starring Harry Belafonte and Zero Mostel, based on a short story by the Jewish-American writer Bernard Malamud. *The Landlord*, the first film directed by film editor Hal Ashby, was based on a novel by black writer Kristin Hunter. This film, about an unusual interracial triangle, starred Beau Bridges, Diana Sands, and Louis Gossett Jr. Barely noticed on its first release, *The Landlord* remains one of the most honest and penetrating looks at racial relations to come out of Hollywood in the 1970s. "Much of *The Landlord*'s strange, moody, dreamy tone and its perceptive, deeply felt depiction of ghetto life, can be attributed to . . . Gunn's sensitive screenplay," wrote film historian Donald Bogle.

Gunn's success as a screenwriter led to an opportunity to direct a film, *Stop* (1970). His second film, *Ganja and Hess* (1972), was supposed to be a cheap, exploitative horror film with black audience appeal. But in Gunn's creative hands it became something very different. The plot revolved around a wealthy black anthropologist played by Duane Jones, a black actor who was the star of the cult classic *The Night of the Living Dead* (1968). Jones's character unearths a wooden knife that belonged to an extinct Nigerian people. When he is accidentally stabbed by it, he turns into a blood-sucking immortal monster. From this unpromising premise, Gunn fashioned an extraordinary film that used vampirism as a symbol for everything from addiction to racism.

The film's intended audience was bewildered by its sophisticated narrative and art-house direction, and *Ganja and Hess* closed within days of its New York City release. The producers frantically reedited the movie, effectively destroying Gunn's creation in the process. They released it on video under no less than seven different titles, including *Black Evil*, *Black Vampire*, and *Vampires of Harlem*.

Gunn's achievement might have been completely lost if not for a single print of his original cut that was stored at the Museum of Modern Art in New York and later shown there. Through the museum's showings and a released DVD, *Ganja and Hess* became a cult classic.

Unfortunately Gunn only directed one more film in his lifetime, *Personal Problems* (1980), with a screenplay by black writer Ishmael Reed. He also wrote several more screenplays, including the one for *The Greatest: The Muhammad Ali Story* (1977). He died at age 55 on April 5, 1989, of encephalitis. The following day his last play, *The Forbidden City*, opened at New York's Public Theater.

Further Reading

"Bill Gunn," The Internet Movie Database. Available online. URL: http://www.imdb.com/name/nm0348155/. Downloaded March 4, 2009.

Bogle, Donald. *Toms, Coons, Mulattoes, Mammies, & Bucks: An Interpretative History of Blacks in American Films*. New York: Continuum, 1997, pp. 232, 233, 256.

Further Viewing

Ganja and Hess: The Complete Edition. (1972). Image Entertainment, DVD, 2006.

The Landlord (1970). MGM Home Entertainment, DVD, 2010.

H

Hammons, David

(1943–   ) *mixed-media artist, installation artist, painter, printmaker, video artist*

One of the most original and innovative mixed-media artists of his generation, David Hammons has incorporated everything from the American flag to human hair in his eye-arresting assemblages.

He was born on July 24, 1943, in Springfield, Illinois. He studied at Los Angeles Trade Technical City College in California in 1964–65 and later attended the Chouinard Art Institute and the Otis Art Institute of the Parsons School of Design, both in Los Angeles.

In about 1970, Hammons began to create unique body prints that brought him immediate fame. He covered his body and clothing with grease and then pressed himself against a large sheet of illustration board. Next he would fix the image of his body permanently on the board by sifting powdered paint onto it. He would sometimes add other elements to the body print, processing it with a silk screen or adding such three-dimensional objects as the American flag.

In these prints, wrote Crystal Britton, "the body serves as the actual printing plate and in the transfer to a paper surface is purposely distorted as part of the statement." Hammons used the American flag through the politically turbulent 1960s as a symbol not of patriotism but of the hypocritical racism of American society. In the "Spade series," which he began in 1973, he used a spade or shovel to symbolize African Americans, inspired by the racist phrase "as black as the ace of spades." Hammons's spades were imprisoned in chains, run over by cars, and even buried.

In 1976, Hammons moved from Los Angeles to Harlem, the black section of New York City. His work took a dramatic turn as he created assemblages from the most unlikely of found objects, collected directly from the black community. He used shopping bags, bottle caps, fried chicken wings, and even barbecue ribs to make social statements about African Americans in American society. In one extraordinary series of works, he collected hair from an African-American barbershop and wove the hairs together with wire rods. The final product was then attached to stone heads, returned to the barbershop for another haircut, and then photographed.

In another pointed installation aimed at black youth, he attached goals onto telephone poles in a Harlem neighborhood and decorated them with bottle caps. The goals were meant to show black teens the unattainability of becoming professional basketball stars. However, it also urged them to reach for even higher goals that require a good education.

Artist David Hammons is at home on the streets of Harlem, where he has found inspiration for many of his imaginative mixed-media works. *(Anthony Barboza)*

In recent years Hammons has created a number of video pieces such as *Phat Free* (2004), a collaboration with artist Alex Harsley that was shown at the Whitney Museum Biennial in New York City. Other recent solo exhibitions include *Media Series* (2006) at the St. Louis Art Museum in Missouri and *David Hammons* (2007) at L & M Arts in New York City.

Since 1987, Hammons has divided his time between Rome, Italy, his favorite city, and New York.

"Hammons is fundamentally a political artist," wrote Michael Kimmelman in the *New York Times*, "whose works address issues of black history, African culture, racism, drug addiction and poverty with the compassion and something of the complexity demanded by these issues. He is one of the most engaging and interesting artists working today."

Further Reading

Dammons, David. *David Hammons: Rousing the Rubble.* Cambridge, Mass.: MIT Press, 1991.

Hassan, Salah M., and Cheryl Finley. *David Hammons, Maria Magdalena Campos-pons, Pamela Z.: Three Artists, Three projects, Dakar Biennale: Diaspora, Memory, Place.* Munich, Germany: Prestel USA, 2008.

Ligon, Glenn. "Black Light: David Hammons and the Poetics of Emptiness." *Art Forum,* September 2004, BNET. Available online. URL: http://findarticles.com/p/articles/mi_m0268/is_1_43/ai_n7069057/. Downloaded March 26, 2009.

Powell, Richard J. "African American Postmodernism and David Hammons: Body and Soul," in *African American Visual Aesthetics: A Postmodernist View.* Washington, D.C.: Smithsonian Institution Press, 1995.

Sill, Robert. *David Hammons in the Hood.* Springfield, Ill.: Illinois State Museum Society, 1995.

Hampton, James
(1909–1964) *folk installation artist, millenarian*

In the curious gallery of eccentrics, visionaries, and originals that make up African-American folk artists, James Hampton stands alone. His claim to artistic fame rests on a single work that almost defies description and was only discovered by an astonished world after his death.

He was born on April 8, 1909, in Elloree, South Carolina, one of four children. His father, a Baptist minister and gospel singer, abandoned the family when he was a child. At 19, Hampton moved to Washington, D.C., where a brother was living. He worked as a short-order cook for a few years before joining the U.S. Army during World War II. On his discharge in 1945, Hampton returned to Washington and took a job as a janitor with the General Services Administration, a job he would keep for the rest of his life.

A quiet loner who never married, he lived in a small apartment and had few friends. But underneath Hampton's gentle, self-effacing exterior, a religious fervor burned in him that would lead him to create his single, extraordinary work of art. In around 1950 he rented an unheated brick garage not far from where he lived and began to construct his own personal vision of heaven. Hampton built his vision, a kind of chancel for worship, out of the most unlikely materials—old furniture, burnt-out lightbulbs, electric cables, jelly glasses, and a host of other discarded objects that he found on the street or in buildings where he worked.

Every object was meticulously wrapped in silver and gold tinfoil. When completed after more than a decade of work, there were 180 separate objects all arranged around an altar, offertory tables, chairs, pulpits, and a throne where Hampton, calling himself "St. James," presumably sat during his personal devotionals.

Hampton grandly called his religious installation *The Throne of the Third Heaven of the Nations Millennium General Assembly.* A sign above the central throne read "FEAR NOT." Numerous other inscriptions decorated the work, often in an undecipherable writing that he invented and that may never be decoded. A book he left behind quotes scripture, especially from the New Testament's Book of Revelation, and makes strange religious predictions. As a millenarian, Hampton believed that Jesus Christ would return to earth and reign for a thousand years.

After Hampton died of cancer on November 4, 1964, at age 53, the garage was opened and his work discovered. Art experts were as mystified as they were astonished by the throne's power and its singular testimony to the religious faith of a simple, uneducated janitor.

The work was eventually put on permanent display at the National Museum of American Art in Washington, D.C., where it resides today. This awesome, unearthly vision remains one of the most intriguing and extraordinary works in the history of American folk art.

Further Reading

Hartigan, Lynda Roscoe. *James Hampton—The Throne of The Third Heaven of the Nations Millennium General Assembly,* Museum of Fine Arts, Boston—October 19–February 13, 1976. Boston: Museum of Fine Arts, 1976.

Livingston, Jane, and John Beardsley. *Black Folk Art in America 1930–1980.* Jackson: The University Press of Mississippi, 1989, pp. 92–95.

Perry, Regenia A. *Free Within Ourselves: African-American Artists in the Collection of the National Museum of American Art.* San Francisco: Pomegranate Communications, 1992, pp. 80–85.

Walsh, Mike. "The Miracle of St. James Hampton." Available online. URL: http://missioncreep.com/tilt/hampton.html. Downloaded March 26, 2009.

Harper, William A.
(1873–1910) *painter, sculptor*

An important transitional figure in American art as it moved from the traditionalism of the 19th century to the modernism of the 20th century, William A. Harper exhibited a mastery of form and style in his brief career.

He was born in Cayuga, Canada, on December 27, 1873. At age 10, he moved with his family to Petersburg, Illinois, and then to Jacksonville, Illinois, when he was 18. In 1895, Harper enrolled at the School of the Art Institute of Chicago and graduated in 1901. He then moved to Houston, Texas, where he made a living as a drawing instructor. With the money he was able to save, Harper traveled in 1903 to Paris, France, the mecca of American artists. During his two-year stay, he and fellow institute graduate William E.

Scott studied and worked with African-American expatriate artist HENRY O. TANNER. Harper and Scott may have influenced Tanner's later work as much as he influenced them. Harper greatly admired the naturalistic paintings of the French Barbizon School, and he began to paint landscapes in the regions of Provence and Brittany in this style. His paintings were technically brilliant and colorfully impressionistic. They included such works as *Landscapes with Poplars* (1905), *Provencial Landscape* (1908), and *The Banks of the Laing* (not dated).

Harper's talents were noticed by his alma mater and a number of his paintings were exhibited at the Art Institute after 1903. "Harper had a technical command and poetic vision," wrote Cedric Dover in *American Negro Art* (1960), "alert to new trends, which should have brought a lively mind and master's palette into the resurgence of American art after the first World War."

But this was not to be. Harper developed tuberculosis—in those years, often deadly—and went to Cuernavaca, Mexico, in 1908 to recuperate and continue painting. The disease grew worse, however, and he died in Mexico on March 27, 1910.

More than 20 of Harper's landscapes and other paintings were displayed in a posthumous exhibition at the Art Institute of Chicago the year of his death. Since then, few of his paintings have been seen outside of the collections of the Carver Museum at the Tuskegee Institute, in Tuskegee, Alabama; the Oregon Public Library in Oregon, Illinois; and Chicago's Provident Hospital.

Further Reading

Bearden, Romare, and Harry Henderson. *A History of African-American Artists: From 1792 to the Present.* New York: Pantheon Books 1993, pp. 117, 338.

"December 27." African American Registry. Available online. URL: http//www.aaregistry.com/detail. php?id=2082. Downloaded March 26, 2009.

Riggs, Thomas, ed. *St. James Guide to Black Artists.* Detroit, Mich.: St. James Press, 1997, pp. 232–233.

Harrington, Ollie
(Oliver Wendell Harrington)
(1912–1995) *cartoonist, editorial cartoonist, writer*

Called America's most popular black cartoonist by his friend the writer Langston Hughes, Ollie Harrington attacked racial prejudice and injustice of all kinds in his satirical drawings for more than 50 years.

He was born Oliver Wendell Harrington on February 14, 1912, in Valhalla, New York, and started drawing cartoons while in school. Some of his first caricatures were of a prejudiced teacher. Harrington went to the Yale School of Fine Arts and graduated with a Bachelor of Arts degree. Later he attended the National Academy of Design in New York.

One of his first jobs was drawing cartoons for the black New York newspaper the *Amsterdam News.* In May 1935 he created a single-panel comic strip he called *Dark Laughter* that revolved around the misadventures of Bootsie, whom Harrington called a "jolly, rather well-fed but soulful character." *Dark Laughter,* which he continued to draw for nearly 30 years, expressed Harrington's feelings about racism in the United States and the problems of the poor. It is generally acknowledged to be the first black comic strip in the United States to receive national recognition.

During World War II (1939–45), Harrington was a reporter and artist for the *Pittsburgh Courier,* another prominent black newspaper. As a war correspondent, he expressed the often-ignored perspective of the African-American serviceman, who suffered at the hands of the segregated, racist armed forces. After the war, Harrington found new issues to take a stand on, particularly the resistance to new antilynching laws in the South. His political views got him into such trouble with the Federal Bureau of Investigation that in 1951 he left America and moved to Paris, France. Harrington lived there for a decade, becoming a member of an expatriate circle of black writers that included Richard Wright and Chester Himes.

In 1961, Harrington moved to what was then East Berlin, the part of the German city controlled by the Communist Soviet Union. From his home there, he continued to draw his political cartoons for newspapers in America and Europe. Ollie Harrington died in a free Berlin after the fall of communism on November 2, 1995, at the age of 84.

"His drawings," wrote Mel Watkins in the *New York Times Book Review,* "often transcend mere caricature even as they convey the impressionistic vigor and ironic thrust demanded by the genre. As his essays and cartoons demonstrate, much of his life and work was shaped by outrage at the way he and other blacks were treated."

Further Reading

Harrington, Oliver W. *Why I Left America and Other Essays.* Jackson: University Press of Mississippi, 1994.

———. *Soul Shots: Political Cartoons by Ollie Harrington.* New York: Longview Publishing, 1972.

Inge, M. Thomas, ed. *Dark Laughter: The Satiric Art of Oliver W. Harrington.* Jackson: University Press of Mississippi, 1993.

"Ollie Harrington Photo Gallery." pbase.com. Available online. URL: http://www.pbase.com/csw62/harrington. Downloaded March 4, 2009.

Harris, Charles
("Teenie" Harris)
(1908–1997) *photographer*

An untrained news photographer who never considered himself an artist, Charles "Teenie" Harris created possibly the largest and most complete documentation of African-American urban life ever conceived. He did so with the eye of a true artist.

He was born on July 2, 1908, in Pittsburgh, Pennsylvania, where he would remain for all his life. In his youth he became fascinated with photography and eventually became a studio photographer, taking portraits of people and families in the Hill District, the heart of Pittsburgh's black community. In 1931, he was hired by the *Pittsburgh Courier,* one of the nation's leading black independent weekly newspapers. The *Courier* covered news of interest to the African-American community that was usually ignored by the established white press. It had several editions, covering the nation as well as Africa, the Caribbean, and the Philippines.

Harris quickly became the *Courier's* leading photographer. He also took pictures for a black-run magazine called *Flash.* The city's mayor, David L. Lawrence, nicknamed Harris "One Shot," because the photographer rarely had to take more than one picture of a person or event, while the competition took seven or eight. Harris's other nickname, "Teenie," came from a cousin who called him "Teeny Little Lover." "After I grew up, they took the 'Lover' off," Harris said in an interview.

Harris photographed every celebrity who passed through Pittsburgh, including presidents, jazz musicians, athletes, and politicians—many of them black. But he also chronicled in his photographs the everyday life of the black community and its citizens. He was particularly fond of photographing women, children, and families. His pictures celebrated the positive in black life but also showed the restrictions of segregation and racism that African Americans lived under.

"He was not just a photographer but a real photojournalist," recalled former *Courier* city editor Frank Bolden, "because every picture he took had a story behind it."

Harris took thousands of pictures, many of which never made it into the paper's pages, and he saved every negative he ever took. After his retirement in 1975, he looked for a way to preserve his invaluable photo archive. In 1986, Harris sold his entire collection of 84,000 negatives to a local Pittsburgh photograph dealer for $3,000 and the promise of more money in royalties for his photographs. A decade later, Harris had received no more money and was unhappy with the arrangement. He took the dealer to court to get his archive back. The case was not settled when Harris died in 1997 at age 89. But three years later a federal jury ruled in his favor, claiming the dealer had violated his copyright on the photographs.

Harris's family temporarily turned the archive over for storage to Pittsburgh's Carnegie Museum of Art. The museum staff was astonished to see the quality and scope of Harris's work. "He had a great eye for composition, and he was extremely good at showing the character of an event or place or person," says museum curator Louise Lippincott. "His work is fascinating and compelling to look at."

Some experts in the field of photography go even further and place Harris in the front ranks of 20th-century African-American photographers. "This has got to be by far the largest documentation of African-American urban life in existence anywhere," claims University of Pittsburgh history teacher Laurence A. Glasco. "There's nothing that approaches it in depth and variety of topics."

The first public exhibition of Harris's work took place in 2001 at the Westmoreland Museum of American Art in Greensburg, Pennsylvania. Called *Spirit of a Community: The Photographs of Charles "Teenie" Harris*, the exhibition featured 82 images selected from the archive, some which had been printed for the first time.

Filmmaker Kenneth Love made an hour-long documentary of Harris's life and career in 2001. It includes an interview with Harris himself three months before his death. For Harris's centennial birthday in 2008, the August Wilson Center for African American Culture in Pittsburgh displayed a selection of his photographs in their gallery. As of 2006, 18,000 negatives of Harris's photographs have been scanned and 20,000 catalogued by the Carnegie Museum of Art.

Further Reading

Crouch, Stanley. *"One Shot" Harris: The Photographs of Charles "Teenie" Harris*. New York: Harry N. Abrams, 2002.

Harris, Charles A., and others. *Spirit of a Community: The Photographs of Charles "Teenie" Harris*. Greensburg, Pa.: Westmoreland Museum of American Art, 2001.

Kinzer, Stephen. "Black Life, in Black and White." The *New York Times*, February 7, 2001, p. E1.

"Teenie chronology." Carnegie Museum of Art Web site. Available online. URL: http://www.cmoa. org/teenie/bio.shtm. Downloaded March 4, 2009.

Willis, Deborah. *Reflections in Black: A History of Black Photographers from 1840 to the Present*. New York: W. W. Norton, 2000, pp. 90, 106–107.

Further Viewing

One Shot: The Life and Work of Teenie Harris. California Newsreel, VHS, 2001.

Harris, Lyle Ashton
(1965–   ) *photographer, mixed-media artist, educator*

An artist whose goal is to challenge and confront his audience, Lyle Ashton Harris uses images to express both his blackness and his homosexuality.

He was born on February 6, 1965, in New York City. Harris's first one-person show, *The Good Life*, was mounted in 1994. It included large-scale self-portraits that explored representation, gender, and ethnicity. "What distinguishes Harris' work from many other artists exploring similar subject matter is the inherently positive tone in his pieces," wrote critic Jack Shamama.

This is not to say Harris shrinks from the controversial. *Brotherhood, Crossroads, Et cetera*, a triptych, shows Harris and his brother Thomas Allen, whom he often collaborates with, posing nude and embracing and kissing in front of an African flag. There is little eroticism in their pose, which questions cultural taboos about male bonding more than about homosexuality.

In *Mirage: Enigmas of Race, Difference, and Desire* (1995), Harris collaborated with fellow photographer RENEE COX, who posed as a black love goddess in *Hottentot Venus 2000*. The work explores black female sexuality, juxtaposing Cox's own body with metallic appendages. "I am playing with what it means to be an African diasporic artist producing and selling work in a culture that is by and large narcissistically mired in the debasement and objectification of blackness," Harris has written.

His 1998 *Alchemy*, another collaboration with his brother, was an ambitious multimedia work that explored African cosmologies or worldviews using huge color photographs, video, and music. It drew on Harris's extensive knowledge of the African cultures of Yoruba, Santeria, and Voudou, among others.

Blow Up, Harris's first major retrospective, originated at the Scottsdale Museum of Contemporary Art in Arizona in 2008 and then traveled to several other museums. "Two decades into his career, Harris still concerns himself with the game of appearance and perceptions: how we present ourselves in public, how our bodies—and the meanings they carry—are received by others, [and] how gender and race are constructed," Jessica Dawson wrote in a review in the *Washington Post*. Harris has taught part of the year at the New York University extension in Accra, Ghana, since 2005.

Lyle Ashton Harris is the coauthor of several books, including *Rrose Is a Rrose Is a Rrose: Gender Performance in Photography* (1997), *In This World* (1992), and *Blow Up* (2008).

Further Reading

Cablentz, Cassandra, and Lyle Ashton Harris, photographer. *Blow Up.* New York: Gregory R. Miller & Company, 2008.

Cotter, Holland. "Art in Review: Lyle Ashton Harris." *New York Times* (April 1, 2010), p. C27.

Lyle Ashton Harris Web site. Available online. URL: http://www.lyleashtonharris.com/. Downloaded March 5, 2009.

Smith, Anna Devere, and Lyle Ashton Harris, photographer. Available online. URL: http://www.lyleashtonharrise.com/. Downloaded March 5, 2009.

Willis, Deborah. *Reflections in Black: A History of Black Photographers from 1840 to the Present.* New York: W. W. Norton, 2000, pp. 187–188, 292–293.

Hathaway, Isaac Scott

("The Dean of Negro Ceramists")
(1872–1967) *ceramist, sculptor, illustrator, educator*

The first African American to design a U.S. coin, Isaac Scott Hathaway made ceramics that enriched the black experience and brought the craft into the mainstream of African-American arts.

He was born on April 4, 1872 in Lexington, Kentucky, one of three children. His father was a minister, and his mother died when he was three. When Hathaway was nine, his father took him to a museum where they viewed the busts of famous Americans. The boy asked why there was no bust of the great black statesman Frederick Douglass. His father explained that the museum, as far as he knew, had no blacks to make such sculptures. The young Hathaway became determined to become the first such artist.

He attended Chandler College in Lexington and studied ceramics, the art of making products from clay, at Pittsburg Normal College in Pittsburg, Kansas. Hathaway continued his art studies at the Cincinnati Art Academy in Cincinnati, Ohio, then taught elementary school in Kentucky. He created plaster of paris models for science classes. His success with these led him to start a company to produce sculptured busts of famous African Americans to be displayed in schools and other public buildings. He called his firm the Afro Art Company, later changing it to the Isaac Hathaway Art Company.

Hathaway's busts included those of Frederick Douglass, black poet Paul Laurence Dunbar, and Richard Allen, the first black bishop in the United States. Besides his plaster busts, he made a more expensive line in bronze metal, as well as plaques and face masks of famous black and white Americans. Hathaway's business thrived, and he decided to bring ceramic arts into the curriculum of black colleges. He went to the Tuskegee Institute in Tuskegee, Alabama, in 1937 and became a founding member of the department of ceramics. He taught there for a decade.

In 1946, President Harry Truman authorized Hathaway to design a 50-cent commemorative coin to honor black educator and Tuskegee Institute founder Booker T. Washington. Although sculptor SELMA BURKE had designed the Roosevelt dime the same year, her bust of the late president was based on a sculpture she had made two years earlier while Roosevelt was still alive. Hathaway's design was the first originally made for an U.S. coin by an African American. Five years later he designed another 50-cent piece to commemorate black scientist George Washington Carver.

Isaac Scott Hathaway's achievements in ceramics, both as an artist and an educator, earned him the title "dean of Negro ceramists." He died at age 93 on March 12, 1967. The Isaac Scott Hathaway Museum, dedicated to exhibiting the lives and work of "distinguished African American artists, writers and others contributing to the community," is located in the Lexington History Center. "The art of a people," Hathaway once said, "not only conveys their mental, spiritual, and civic growth to posterity, but convinces their contemporaries that they can best portray in crystallization their feelings, aspirations, and desires."

Further Reading

"April 4." African American Registry. Available online. URL: http://www.aaregistry.com/detail. php?id=2482. Downloaded March 26, 2009.

"Isaac Scott Hathaway," African-Americans in the Visual Arts, a Historical Perspective. Available online. URL: http://www.liu.edu/cwis/cwp/library/ aavaahp.htm#hathaway. Downloaded March 5, 2009.

Isaac Scott Hathaway Museum. Available online. URL: http://www.hathawaymuseum.org/. Downloaded March 5, 2009.

Hayden, Palmer C.
(Peyton Cole Hedgeman)
(1890–1973) *painter*

The first African-American artist to win the prestigious Harmon Foundation prize for black achievement in the fine arts, Palmer C. Hayden earned both praise and criticism for his naive, folklike paintings during his long career.

He was born Peyton Cole Hedgeman on January 15, 1890, in Widewater, Virginia, the fifth of 10 children. Although he showed a talent for drawing as a child, art was secondary to his life until he was in his mid-twenties. As a young man, Hedgeman worked at a number of menial jobs. He was a drugstore errand boy in Washington, D.C., and later crossed the country with a traveling circus as a roustabout, setting up the circus tents and doing other manual labor. In his spare time he drew pictures of the clowns and other circus performers.

Hedgeman joined the U.S. Army in 1917 and served during World War I. His white sergeant gave him the name Palmer Hayden because he couldn't pronounce his real name. While in the army, Hayden took a correspondence art course, his first formal training. After his military discharge, Hayden moved to New York City, where he attended the School of Art at Cooper Union. He worked in the post office for five years and painted at night in his Greenwich Village apartment.

In 1926, he entered the first competition of the Harmon Foundation, set up to encourage the work of African-American artists. Almost a complete unknown, Hayden won first prize for a picture of a fishing boat he painted in Portland, Maine, while at the Boothbay Art Colony. When it was discovered that Hayden had been recently working as a janitor at the Harmon Foundation building, the press hailed him as the "janitor painter." A decade later, he produced *The Janitor Who Paints* (1937), one of his best-known works, which he claimed was not about him but an older friend whose art was not taken seriously because of his day job.

With his prize money, Hayden took a dream trip to Paris, France, where he studied at the École des Beaux-Arts and met the dean of black artists, HENRY O. TANNER. He stayed in Paris for five years, developing a consciously naive, flat style of painting that resembled folk art. In *Fétiche et Fleurs* (1926) he created one of the first paintings by an African American to incorporate African artifacts (a Fang mask from Gabon and a Bakuba raffia cloth from the Congo). At the same time Hayden claimed he felt little affinity for either African art or most modern art. "We're a brand-new race, raised and manufactured in the United States," he said of African Americans, adding, "I do like to paint what they did."

On his return to the United States, Hayden was hired by the Harmon Foundation to help in preparing exhibitions to be sent to African-American schools. He even starred in a film made by the foundation entitled *How to Paint a Picture,* intended for student audiences. During much of this time he also worked as an artist for the federally funded Works Progress Administration.

Hayden's interest in contemporary black life led to such paintings as *Midsummer Night in Harlem* (1938), which showed Harlemites enjoying the night life from their crowded tenement houses. While many admired Hayden's folkloric depictions, others, including leading black art historian JAMES A. PORTER, saw them as cruel caricatures of black people. Hayden responded by saying, "I just tried to tell it like it is. . . Some people are too thin-skinned."

He was also drawn to the black past—both historical and legendary. One figure who particularly fascinated him was the black folk hero John Henry, the "steel-driving man" who helped build the railroads. Hayden was surprised to learn that a real John Henry had lived in West Virginia and helped build the Big Bend Tunnel there in 1870. With his wife, schoolteacher Miriam Hoffman, he traveled to the Big Bend Tunnel and soaked up the local history while sketching the landscape. Hayden returned to New York and set about working on his most ambitious project, a series of 12 paintings depicting the life and death of John Henry, using lines from the "Ballad of John Henry" as his text.

This monumental work was first exhibited at Sarah Lawrence College in Bronxville, New York, in 1947 and many years later was given by Hayden's widow to the Museum of African American Art in Los Angeles, California. Teeming with life and the power of his naive but artful style, the *John Henry* series is perhaps Hayden's greatest work.

Through his long career, he continued to draw on the black experience. Many of his paintings dealt with the rural Southern life he recalled from his childhood and included such works as *The Baptizing Day* and *Milking Time.* In the 1970s Hayden executed a series of paintings about African-American soldiers that was commissioned by the New York Creative Arts Public Service Program.

Hayden continued to paint right up until shortly before his death at age 83 on February 18, 1973. In 1988, the Museum of African American Art held a major retrospective of his work entitled "Echoes of the Past: The Narrative Artistry of Palmer C. Hayden."

An artist with deep working-class roots, Hayden was always humble about his achievements.

He was asked once which was his favorite of all his paintings. "I haven't painted it yet," he replied. "I always hope I'll do better. The truth is, I never thought much of my own work. I never was satisfied with it."

Further Reading

Bearden, Romare, and Harry Henderson. *A History of African-American Artists: From 1792 to the Present.* New York: Pantheon Books, 1993, pp. 157–167.

Gordon, Allan M. *Echoes of our Past: The Narrative Artistry of Palmer C. Hayden.* Los Angeles: Museum of African American Art, 1988.

"Palmer C. Hayden Papers." Smithsonian Archives of American Art. Available online. URL: http://www.aaa.so.edui/collectionsonline/haydpalm/. Downloaded March 5, 2009.

Perry, Regenia A. *Free Within Ourselves: African-American Artists in the Collection of the National Museum of American Art.* San Francisco: Pomegranate Communications, 1992, pp. 86–89.

Hendricks, Barkley L.

(Barkley Leonnard Hendricks)
(1945–) *painter, educator, photographer*

Best known for his extraordinarily realistic, life-size portraits of black men and women, Barkley L. Hendricks vividly expressed the "black is beautiful" movement of the 1970s in his work.

He was born on April 16, 1945, in Philadelphia, Pennsylvania, and studied at the Pennsylvania Academy of the Fine Arts. After graduating in 1967 he went on to Yale University in New Haven, Connecticut, where he received his Master of Fine Arts degree in 1972. While at Yale, Hendricks met famed photographer Walker Evans, who interested him in the art of photography. This interest produced Hendricks's famous series of large figures, which have the detailed realism of photographs. Sometimes painting with a combination of oil and acrylic paints, Hendricks used his friends and students for most of his subjects. The dynamic force of each portrait is often accented by a flat monochrome background.

"Part of their success," said the artist in an interview with the *New York Times* in 2001, "is that I was able to get people at just the right scale so that they confront the viewer rather aggressively at times."

When he obtained a part of a human skeleton, Hendricks was inspired to create what he called his American Anatomy Series. These powerful pastel drawings of skeletons are executed on black paper, and many have a piece of human hair attached to them.

In the 1990s, Hendricks spent some time on the island of Jamaica and created a series of impressionistic landscapes. He is also a lover of black music, especially soul and rock. His painting *The Dead Fathers Clubs* is a tribute to the soul singer Marvin Gaye, who was shot to death by his father in 1984. When the Lyman Allyn Art Museum in Lyme, Connecticut, held a retrospective of his work in 2001, Hendricks called it "The Barkley L. Hendricks Experience" after the 1960s rock group the Jimi Hendrix Experience.

The Birth of the Cool, a five-decade retrospective of Hendricks's work, opened at the Nasher Museum at Duke University in North Carolina in early 2008 and then traveled to four other major museums around the country. The most recent paintings in the exhibit showed the artist returning to his large figurative paintings of the 1980s. In a review of the show, *New York Times* art critic Ken Johnson felt that "Mr. Hendricks's most memorable achievement remains his early pictures of coolness personified."

Hendricks has taught at the Pennsylvania Academy of the Fine Arts and has been a visiting artist at more than 20 schools. Since 1972 he has taught at Connecticut College in New London, Connecticut, where as a professor of art

Barkley L. Hendricks poses before some of the photo-realistic, life-size paintings that first brought him to prominence in the art world. *(Professor Dred Productions)*

he teaches drawing, illustration, watercolors, and photography.

Further Reading

Hendricks, Barkley L. *The Barkley L. Hendricks Experience: April 13 through June 17, 2001.* New London Conn.: Lyman Allyn Museum of Art, Connecticut College, 2001.

Johnson, Ken. "Slick and Stylish: Provocative Poses." *New York Times.* December 5, 2008, C33.

Riggs, Thomas, ed. *St. James Guide to Black Artists.* Detroit, Mich.: St. James Press, 1997, pp. 241–242.

Schoonmaker Trevor, ed. *Barkley L. Hendricks: Birth of the Cool.* Durham, N.C.: Nasher Museum of Art at Duke University, 2008.

Zimmer, William. "On The Trail of Art and Its Inspiration." The *New York Times,* May 6, 2001, Connecticut section, p. 11.

Higgins, Chester, Jr.
(1946–) *photographer*

A leading contemporary African-American photographer, Chester Higgins Jr. has brought sensitivity and an artistic sensibility to such subjects as black women, the African diaspora, and the aged.

He was born on November 6, 1946, in Lexington, Kentucky. He studied photography with famed black photographer P. H. POLK at the Tuskegee Institute in Tuskegee, Alabama. While still a student, Higgins had his first photographs published in the *Negro Digest.* He was one of the leading photographers of the Civil Rights movement in the 1960s and early 1970s. In 1975, Higgins got a job as staff photographer for the *New York Times* and has remained there to date. Besides his work for the *Times,* his photographs have appeared in such periodicals as *Newsweek, Fortune, Ebony,* and *Black Enterprise.*

Higgins's sense of composition and compassion for people has placed him in the tradition of such African-American photographers as GORDON PARKS and ROY DeCARAVA. His work has been featured in one-person exhibitions at the National Museum of African Art at the Smithsonian Institution in Washington, D.C., the International Center of Photography (ICP) in New York City, and the Newark Museum in Newark, New Jersey.

Higgins has published more book-length collections of his images than has almost any other African-American photographer. His books include *Black Women, Drums of Life,* and *Feeling the Spirit: Searching the World for the People of Africa.* The latter book was 30 years in the making, during which time Higgins traveled to more than 30 countries tracing the African diaspora, or geographic migration, brought about by the slave trade.

In *Elder Grace: The Nobility of Aging* (2001), Higgins said "I set out to discover how our parents and grandparents did it; how they survived and, yes, flourished. . ." His most recent book is *Echo of the Spirit: A Photographer's Journey* (2004).

Chester Higgins Jr. has received grants from the Ford Foundation, the Rockefeller Foundation, and the ICP. He was one of five African-American male artists and musicians who were featured in the Public Broadcasting Service documentary *BrotherMen* (2002) for "transmit[ting] the historical, political, and cultural revelations of the African-American experience." Recent solo exhibits of Higgins's work have been mounted at Philadelphia's African American Museum (2003) and the New York State Museum in Albany (2005). He lives in Brooklyn, New York, with his second wife, the magazine journalist Betsy Kissam.

Further Reading

"Chester Higgins, Jr.: Official Web site. Available online. URL: http//www.chesterhiggins.com/. Downloaded March 5, 2009.

Higgins, Chester, Jr. *Echo of the Spirit: A Photographer's Journey.* New York: Doubleday, 2004.

Higgins, Chester, Jr., and Betsy Kissam. *Elder Grace: The Nobility of Aging.* New York: Bulfinch Press, 2001.

Holloway, Charnelle
(1957–   ) *dollmaker, mixed-media artist, jewelry designer, metalsmith, educator*

A maker of exquisite dolls and jewelry, Charnelle Holloway brings a modern sensibility and concern to the ancient arts of her ancestral Africa.

She was born on September 15, 1957, in Atlanta, Georgia. She comes naturally by her artistic abilities; her mother Jenelsic Walden Holloway, a skilled painter, was chairperson of the department of art at Spelman College in Atlanta for two decades. Charnelle is also distantly related to famed African-American painter HENRY O. TANNER.

Holloway graduated cum laude from Spelman, one of the leading colleges for black women, in 1979 and earned a Master of Fine Arts degree in jewelry design and silversmithing from Georgia State University in 1986.

In 1983, she began to create the tiny dolls she is best known for. Holloway made her dolls out of metal and cloth. She crafted the humanlike faces through chasing and repoussé, a process whereby a design is raised in relief by hammering on the front and reverse sides of sheet metal. The hands and feet were created using the lost wax casting technique, and the metal, springy hair was curled by hand. She completed each doll by dressing it in hand-sewn miniature clothes.

"It wasn't just a doll anymore," she said after finishing the first one. "It had a mystical aura about it—a spirit or an angel—that I didn't know I was doing [in creating the work.]"

Some of her dolls convey a definite social message. *Fertility Belt for the Career Woman* (1995) is covered with jewelry, chimes, braided silk rope, and cowrie shells, an Ashanti symbol of fertility. Fashioned after the religious dolls of the Ashanti people of Africa, this modern-day fetish doll-belt is meant for contemporary women who are not certain they want children or want to put off having them until they have succeeded in their careers. The doll also links today's black woman to a distant ancestral African past.

Holloway returned to Spelman College to teach art in 1988 and was hired as a lecturer in 1990. Since 1999, she has been an associate professor of art. Her alma mater awarded her the Alumnae Achievement Award in 1997. She has also designed and created works for Spelman College, the National Black Arts Festival, Atlanta Hartsfield Airport, as well as many private commissions. Holloway is a member of The American Craft Council, the Organization of Black Designers, and has been included in the Smithsonian/Cooper-Hewitt African American Design Archives.

"My training as an artist of functional objects d'art," Holloway has said, "has led me to a place that merges the functionality of a familiar object with the ritual purpose of the object."

Further Reading

Britton, Crystal A. *African American Art: The Long Struggle.* New York: New Line Books, 2006, pp. 98–99.

"Charnelle Holloway Artist's Statement." Available online. URL: http://www.spelman.edu/academics/programs/art/faculty/charnelle.htm. Downloaded March 5, 2008.

Riggs, Thomas, ed. *St. James Guide to Black Artists.* Detroit, Mich.: St. James Press, 1997, pp. 250–251.

Honeywood, Varnette

(Varnette P. Honeywood)
(1950–2010) *painter, collagist, printmaker, illustrator, educator*

Perhaps the first African-American artist to have her work featured on a popular television situation comedy, Varnette Honeywood used various media to spread the word of her colorful and uplifting paintings, collages, and posters.

She was born in Los Angeles, California, on December 27, 1950. Her grandfather was the victim of a Ku Klux Klan cross burning. Honeywood's parents were elementary school teachers who often tried out their class art projects on her and her sister Stephanie. Honeywood took her first art lessons at the Chouinard Art Institute in Los Angeles and was a skillful artist. However, when she first attended Spelman College in Atlanta, Georgia, it was as a history major. Drawing instructor Joe Ross persuaded her to continue with her art and she changed majors. After graduation, she returned to L.A. and earned a master's degree at the University of Southern California. She taught art to black students and other minorities for five years.

In 1977, Honeywood's work was accepted at the Black and African Festival of Arts and Culture in Nigeria. While there, she was strongly influenced by African art and culture. Returning to the United States in 1978, she formed a partnership with her sister to produce and distribute her artwork on posters, note cards, and other products. Much of Honeywood's work celebrates African-American history. Its positive thrust brought her to the attention of comedian and actor Bill Cosby and his wife, Camille. They not only bought some of Honeywood's work but also put a reproduction of her painting *Birthday* (1974) in the living room of the Huxtable family in Cosby's hit television series *The Cosby Show.*

It was the beginning of a long and fruitful friendship. In the 1990s, Honeywood began to illustrate Cosby's series of Little Bill books for beginning readers. Each volume deals with a social issue affecting young children and illustrates how best to handle the situation. In 1996, Honeywood created the collage painting *Lifelong Learning* for the dedication of the Camille Olivia Hanks Cosby Academic Center at Spelman, her alma mater. The six figures represented in the work included Camille Cosby, African-American poet Phillis Wheatley, and Spelman president Johnetta Betsch Cole. In 2005, Honeywood received an honorary doctorate in fine art from Spelman.

Honeywood, according to artist and writer Samella Lewis, "approaches her subjects with empathy that stems from deep-seated spiritual convictions, and also manages to capture both the serious and humorous aspects of a situation."

Honeywood died of cancer on September 12, 2010, in Los Angeles.

Further Reading

Cosby, Bill, and Varnette P. Honeywood, illustrator. *The Day I Saw My Father Cry: Little Bill Books for Beginning Readers.* New York: Cartwheel Books, 2000.

Hubbard, Guy. "Varnette Honeywood: A Woman to Learn From," *Arts and Activities,* June 1983, pp. 29–31.

Mattox, Cheryl W., and Varnette P. Honeywood and Barbara Joysmith, illustrators. *Shake It to the One That You Love the Best: Play Songs and Lullabies from Black Musical Traditions.* Nashville, Tenn.: JTG of Nashville, 1991.

Riggs, Thomas, ed. *St. James Guide to Black Artists.* Detroit, Mich.: St. James Press, 1997, pp. 251–252.

"Varnette P. Honeywood." Available online. URL: http://www.answers.com/topic/varnette-p-honeywood. Downloaded March 5, 2009.

Hooks, Kevin

(1958–) *filmmaker, television director, actor*

A gifted child actor of the 1970s, Kevin Hooks has developed into a filmmaker of talent and sensitivity.

He was born on September 19, 1958, in Philadelphia, Pennsylvania. His father is film actor Robert Hooks, who played leading African-American roles in movies of the late 1960s and 1970s. Following in his father's footsteps, Hooks began acting while still a boy and at age 11 starred in the CBS Children's House episode *J. T.* (1969),

about a black boy in Harlem who befriends a sick cat. In 1972, he played the older son of Great Depression-era tenant farmers in the South in the critically praised *Sounder.* Cicely Tyson and Paul Winfield, who played his parents, received Academy Award nominations for their roles, but Hooks was also singled out for giving one of the finest performances by a young African-American actor ever seen. His brother Eric played his younger brother in the film.

Hooks's next major role was opposite actress Irene Cara in the Romeo and Juliet love story *Aaron Loves Angela* (1975), directed by black filmmaker GORDON PARKS, JR. He appeared as a regular cast member on the TV basketball dramatic series *The White Shadow* (1978) and directed for the first time at age 24 an episode of the series *Fame* (1982). Hooks was soon devoting more energy to directing than acting and directed episodes on several top dramatic television series, including *St. Elsewhere, Alien Nation,* and the series *21 Jump Street.*

Hooks attracted critical attention as a director with the made-for-television movie *Heat Wave* (1990), a scorching retelling of the race riots in the Watts section of Los Angeles during the summer of 1965. The story is seen through the eyes of Robert Richardson, the first black reporter for the *Los Angeles Times.* Hooks's fine direction was coupled with outstanding performances from a gallery of black actors, including Blair Underwood, Cecily Tyson, and James Earl Jones. *Heat Wave* is considered by critics as one of the best and most honest depictions of race relations in the polarized 1960s.

The film got Hooks his first feature film assignment, the uninspired comedy *Strictly Business* (1991). This was followed by the action movie *Passenger 57* (1992), starring black actor Wesley Snipes and Hooks's father as a FBI agent. Film historian Donald Bogle praised this film because it "did not deracialize its black hero," unlike many other Hollywood films of the time.

Since then Hooks has concentrated on television work. He has directed episodes of such top-notch dramatic series as *Homicide, NYPD Blue,* and the medical drama *ER.* He directed five episodes of the Showtime cable television series *Soul Food* (2001–04) about a trio of black sisters, which was derived from the hit movie of the same name. More recently, Hooks has directed episodes of such television series as *Lost, Alias,* and *Prison Break.*

Future Reading

Bogle, Donald. *Toms, Coons, Mulattoes, Mammies, & Bucks: An Interpretative History of Blacks in American Films.* New York: Continuum, 1997, pp. 142, 241, 246, 248, 354.

"Kevin Hooks," The Internet Movie Database. Available online. URL: http://www.imdb.com/name/nm0393661/. Downloaded March 5, 2009.

Further Viewing

Heat Wave (1990). Turner Home Entertainment, DVD, 2006.

Passenger 57 (1992). Warner Home Video, VHS/DVD, 1995/1998.

Prison Break—Season One (2005). Fox Home Video, DVD box set, 2006.

Sounder (1972). Koch Vision, DVD, 2008.

Hudlin, Reginald

(Reginald Alan Hudlin, Reggie Hudlin)
(1961–) *filmmaker, film and television producer, director, screenwriter, actor*

The creator of one of the most successful films of the 1990s, Reginald Hudlin is the father of hip-hop teen movies and an accomplished comedic filmmaker.

He was born Reginald Alan Hudlin on December 15, 1961, in Centerville, Illinois, and grew up in East St. Louis. Rhythm and blues (R & B) artists Ike and Tina Turner were his neighbors. Growing up, Hudlin looked to his older brother Warrington as a role model. An actor, producer, and filmmaker, Warrington Hudlin was cofounder of the Black Filmmakers Foundation in 1978 and is curator of the Acapulco Black Film Festival.

Reginald enrolled in Harvard College in Cambridge, Massachusetts, in 1979. A film student, he made a 20-minute film about black teenagers, *House Party* (1983), as his senior thesis. After graduation, Hudlin headed for Hollywood. He found his first acting role in a bit part in SPIKE LEE'S first feature film, *She's Gotta Have It* (1986).

In 1990, Hudlin got the opportunity to make his own movie, an expanded version of his thesis film at Harvard. *House Party* (1990), a sparkling comedy about a young man named Kid (Christopher Reid) who sneaks out of the house to go to a friend's party, was the first and one of the best of the hip-hop teen movies that mixed comedy with rap music. It featured a marvelous performance by comic Robin Harris as Pop, Kid's father. It also introduced comic and future star Martin Lawrence to film audiences in a smaller role.

House Party, which cost $2.5 million to make, grossed $27 million at the box office. A huge commercial hit, it also earned praise from critics for its fresh view of black teen culture. At the prestigious Sundance Film Festival in Utah, the film won both the Filmmaker's Trophy and the best cinematography award. *House Party* spawned two sequels, one of which Hudlin wrote the screenplay for, and a Saturday morning cartoon series.

Hudlin's next film, a collaboration with comic actor Eddie Murphy, was the romantic comedy *Boomerang* (1992). Murphy played a playboy advertising executive who got his comeuppance from a new female boss (Robin Givens) and learned what love is all about from her assistant (Halle Berry). An uneven mix of high and low comedy, *Boomerang* was another hit for Hudlin and was accompanied by a double platinum soundtrack CD produced by Kenneth "Babyface" Edmonds.

After making the intriguing science fiction television anthology *Cosmic Slop* (1994) for cable television's Home Box Office, Hudlin returned to the big screen with a boxing satire, *The Great White Hype* (1996). Samuel L. Jackson played a boxing promoter who arranges a fight for his client (Damon Wayans) with the only fighter ever to beat him—a retired white boxer. The script was coauthored by Ron Shelton, who wrote and directed such classic sport comedies as *Bull Durham* and *Tin Cup*.

Hudlin's next film, *The Ladies Man* (2001), was based on a character created by Tim Meadows on TV's *Saturday Night Live*. In 2002 he directed his first "white" film, *Serving Sara*, starring Elizabeth Hurley as a wayward wife served with divorce papers and Matthew Perry of TV's *Friends* as the process server who gets involved with her revenge scheme.

Since then, Hudlin has concentrated his energies on television. He directed the pilot episode of the hit sitcom *Everybody Hates Chris* (2005) and was executive producer and a director of the *Bernie Mac Show* (2001–06). Hudlin is the first president of entertainment of Black Entertainment Television and has created 17 of the network's top 20 shows. He was executive producer of the animated series *The Boondocks* (2005–08), based on the satiric comic strip by AARON MCGRUDER. He currently produces the animated series *Black Panther*, based on the Marvel Comics black superhero.

Further Reading

Alexander, George. *Why We Make Movies: Black Filmmakers Talk About the Magic of Cinema*. New York: Harlem Moon, 2003, pp. 442–459.

Hudlin Entertainment. Available online. URL: http://hudlinentertainment.com/. Downloaded March 5, 2009.

"Reginald Hudlin," The Internet Movie Database. Available online. URL: http://www.imbd.com/name/nm0399737/. Downloaded March 5, 2009.

Further Viewing

Boomerang (1992). Paramount Home Video, VHS/DVD, 1994/2002.

The Great White Hype (1996). Fox Home Video, VHS/DVD, 1998/2004.

House Party 3-Pack (1990). New Line Home Video, DVD, 2000.

Humphrey, Margo
(1942–) *printmaker, sculptor, installation artist, illustrator, educator*

One of the first African-American female printmakers to be nationally recognized, Margo Humphrey has mined her life and her family's roots in her colorful, vibrant art.

She was born on June 25, 1942, in Oakland, California. A late starter, she earned a Bachelor of Arts degree at age 30 from the California College of Arts and Crafts in Oakland. Two years later she earned her Master of Fine Arts degree in printmaking from Stanford University in Palo Alto, California.

Humphrey's prints are filled with color, narrative power, and an often-irreverent sense of humor. They have also been called symbolic and surrealistic. A good example of her work is *The Last Bar-B-Que*, one of her most popular pieces. The lithograph is modeled after the Last Supper, the final meal Jesus Christ shared with his disciples before his death. In Humphrey's version, Christ and the disciples are black and the menu is extended to include chicken and watermelon, traditional fare of southern African Americans. A pyramid rising out of a starry sky in the background suggests Egypt and Africa. Despite its humorous touches, the artist insists that *The Last Bar-B-Que* "is a serious piece: a rewriting of history through the eyes of my ancestry, a portrayal of a savior who looks like my people."

The African influence can also be seen in the bright range of colors in many of Humphrey's prints and lithographs. She has observed African art and culture firsthand, having taught at the University of Benin in Nigeria and Makala University in Kampala, Uganda. She has also taught at the Tamarind Institute of New Mexico, where in 1974 she became the first African-American woman to have her prints published by the internationally known Atelier. Among her most recent lithographs are a 2007 series using Christian crosses.

Since 1989, Humphrey has been an associate professor of art at the University of Maryland in College Park, Maryland. She is the winner of a Ford Foundation Fellowship in 1981 and a National Endowment for the Arts Fellowship and Tiffany Foundation Grant, both in 1988. She has had major exhibitions at the Oakland Museum and the National Museum of Women in the Arts, Washington, D.C. The exhibition "Her Story: Margo Humphrey, Lithographs and Works on Paper" was mounted at the David C. Driskell Center in College Park in 2010. Humphrey is the author and illustrator of a children's book, *The River That Gave Gifts* (1995), and also has produced sculptures.

"I use color," Humphrey has said, "to provoke, to startle, to engage the viewer [through the] narrative process."

Further Reading

Humphrey, Margo. *The River That Gave Gifts: An Afro American Story.* Berkeley, Calif.: Children's Book Press, 1995.

Lewis, Samella. *African-American Art and Artists.* Berkeley: University of California Press, 2003, p. 263.

"Margo Humphrey." The Department of Art: The University of Maryland. Available online. URL: http://www.art.umd.edu/people/mhumphrey/mhumphrey.html. Downloaded March 5, 2009.

Riggs, Thomas, ed. *St. James Guide to Black Artists.* Detroit, Mich.: St. James Press, 1997, pp. 258–259.

Hunt, Richard H.
(Richard Howard Hunt)
(1935–   ) *sculptor, printmaker, educator*

A leading contemporary sculptor who can transform scrap metal into expressive art, Richard H. Hunt has created monumental sculptures that dot the American landscape from California to Connecticut.

He was born Richard Howard Hunt in Chicago, Illinois, on September 12, 1935. His father was a barber and his mother a librarian who instilled in him a love of reading. A precocious artist, Hunt began studying at the School of the Art Institute of Chicago at age 13. When he was 15, he turned his bedroom into a studio and began modeling in clay. He attended the University of Chicago in 1953 and was inspired by an exhibit of Spanish metal sculptor Julio Gonzalez to try his hand at welded-metal sculpture. In just two years, he taught himself this demanding technique and won his first award, the Mr. and Mrs. Frank G. Logan Prize for artistic achievement, when he was 21.

During this time Hunt worked in a zoology lab at the university and became intrigued by the way some animals undergo a physical transformation as they mature. He adapted this idea to his art, which he sees as a mixture of the natural and the human-made.

"One of the central themes in my work is the reconciliation of the organic and the industrial," Hunt has said. "I see my work as forming a kind of bridge between what we experience in nature and what we experience from the urban, industrial, technology-driven society we live in."

Hunt earned a fellowship to study and travel in Europe in 1957 and met his first wife, Betty Scott, in Rome, Italy. They returned to Chicago the following year, and he served a two-year stint in the U.S. Army. On his discharge, Hunt took a teaching position at the School of the Art Institute of Chicago while pursuing his sculpture. His work became more abstract as he raided junkyards for car fenders, bumpers, and other auto parts. He welded them into powerful, abstract sculptures, although he refused to call them that.

Abstract or not, Hunt instilled intense emotions and feelings into his works. In 1967 a commissioned work called *Play* was too large for his studio, and he moved the work into a metal fabrication shop. Here machinists and other workers assisted him in its assembly. This was the beginning of his career as a sculptor of public art.

Over the next couple of decades, Hunt created dozens of outdoor, public sculptures, many of them in the Chicago area. His works grace the grounds of universities, office buildings, apartment complexes, and libraries. One of the most impressive of these sculptures is *I Have Been to the Mountain,* a memorial to civil rights leader Martin Luther King, Jr. It is made of welded steel and stands in Memphis, Tennessee, the city where King was assassinated in 1968.

"Public sculpture," according to Hunt, "responds to the dynamics of a community, or of those in it, who have a use for sculpture. It is this aspect of use, of utility, that gives public sculpture its vital and lively place in the public mind."

In 1971, he became the first African-American sculptor to be honored by a retrospective of his work at the Museum of Modern Art in New York City. Since then, Hunt has had numerous exhibitions and shows at museums around the country. A 2008 show at the Sculpture Center in Cleveland, Ohio, focused on small welded-metal pieces, many of them studies for larger commissions. His works can be found in museums from Milwaukee, Wisconsin, to Israel. Among his dozen or so honorary degrees is one he received in 1997 from Governors State University in Park Forest, Illinois. In 1998, he was elected a member of the American Academy of Arts and Letters. Hunt received the International Sculpture Center's Lifetime Achievement Award in 2009.

Richard H. Hunt has taught at many schools and universities, including Utah State University, in Logan, Utah, Cornell University in Ithaca, New York, and the State University of New York at Binghamton, New York. Since 1997 he has been on the faculty of Michigan State University in East Lansing, Michigan.

Hunt is also a printmaker who works in lithographs. Some of his lithographs have served as studies for his sculptures. "It's just like you learn a language—you start to think in it," Hunt said in a 2008 interview. "I think in metal. The ideas just come to me."

Further Reading

Brower, Hatcher, Richard Hunt, and Judy Pfaff. *Presage of Passage—Sculpture for a New Century.* Provo, Utah: Brigham Young University Museum of Art, 1999.

Castro, Jan Garden. "Richard Hunt: Freeing the Human Soul," *Sculpture,* May/June 1998, pp. 34–39.

Chicago. Columbia College. *Outside In: Public Sculpture by Richard Hunt.* Chicago: Columbia College, 1986.

Hunt, Richard. *The Sculpture of Richard Hunt.* New York: Museum of Modern Art, 1971.

Litt, Steven. "Richard Hunt at the Sculpture Center: Superb Abstracts from a Survivor." *Cleveland Plain Dealer,* September 9, 2008.

"Richard Hunt: American Artist," Michigan State University website. Available online. URL: http://www2.h-net.msu.edu/~rhunt/begin.html. Downloaded November 9, 2010.

Hunter, Clementine

(Clementine Reuben Hunter, "The Black Grandma Moses")
(ca. 1887–1988) *folk painter*

One of the best-known and most prolific of southern black folk painters, Clementine Hunter celebrated in her art the everyday life on the Louisiana plantation where she lived and worked for most of her 101 years.

She was born Clementine Reuben in December 1886 or January 1887, at Hidden Hill Plantation in Natchitoches Parish, Louisiana. Her father, Janvier Reuben, was a Creole of Native American, African-American, French, and Irish descent. Her mother, Antoinette Adams, was descended from Virginia slaves. As a young girl Hunter attended a Catholic elementary school only briefly and soon went to work at Melrose Plantation, picking cotton. She married Charlie Dupree, a Creole, and they had two children. He died about 1914.

She married Emmanuel Hunter in 1924 and they had five children together. Clementine gradually worked her way up to a position in the laundry and finally got a job as a cook in the plantation's kitchen. In 1939, in her mid-fifties, Hunter came upon some paints and brushes left behind by a visitor to the plantation. Encouraged by François Mignon, historian and permanent guest at the plantation, she used them to paint her first picture on an old window shade.

Soon she was painting scenes from the life of the plantation blacks including such activities as cotton picking, pecan gathering, and clothes washing. Hunter also painted scenes from Saturday night parties and Sunday prayer meetings. "Paintings catch memories a-crossing my mind," she said. "Pictures of the hard part of living. The easy parts, too, like fishing and dancing."

Her style was flat, two-dimensional, and naive, but full of life and color. Her canvases were anything she could lay her hands on—cardboard boxes, brown paper bags, plastic milk jugs, and soap cartons. Her husband did not approve of her painting and felt it took time away from her work on the plantation. But this did not stop Hunter, who over the next 35 years painted more than 4,000 pictures. Illiterate, she could not sign her name to her paintings but copied the initials of the plantation owner, Cammie Henry, which were coincidentally her own.

Critics and collectors began to praise her work, and in 1955 Hunter became the first black and the first woman to have a one-person show at the Delgado Art Museum, now called the New Orleans Museum of Art. Some people called her the "Black Grandma Moses," comparing her to another famous elderly folk artist, Anna Mary Robinson Moses.

Over the next 32 years, Hunter's paintings were shown in more than 24 one-person exhibitions at Fisk University in Nashville, Tennessee, and the University of Texas at Arlington, among others. Her work was later featured at the Museum of American Folk Art in New York City. In 1986, this simple black woman received an honorary degree of fine arts from Northwestern State University in Natchitoches, Louisiana.

Hunter continued to paint into her 90s, only putting down her paintbrush a month before her death at age 101 on January 1, 1988.

"Clementine is definitely in the genius bracket," wrote François Mignon, "industrious to an unusual degree and gifted in any line of art and handcraft on which she may rivet her attack."

Further Reading

Cook, Sterling. *Two Black Folk Artists: Clementine Hunter and Nellie Mae Rowe*. Oxford, Ohio: Miami University Art Museum, 1986.

Gilley, Shelby R. *Painting by Heart: The Life and Art of Clementine Hunter, Louisiana Folk Artist*. Baton Rouge, La.: St. Emma Press, 2000.

Hunter, Clementine, and Mary E. Lyons. *Talking with Tebe: Clementine Hunter, Memory Artist*. Boston: Houghton Mifflin, 1998.

Lamothe, Eva. "A Visit with Clementine Hunter: Painter of Visions and Dreams." New Orleans Arts Quarterly 7, April/May/June 1985, pp. 32–34.

Whitehead, Kathy, and Shane Evans, illustrator. *Art from Her Heart*. Kirkwood, N.Y.: Putnam Juvenile, 2008.

Wilson, James Lee. *Clementine Hunter: American Folk Artist*. Gretna, La.: Pelican Publishing Co., 1988.

J

Johnson, Joshua
(ca. 1763–ca. 1832) *painter*

The first successful African-American artist and one of the finest of early American portrait painters, Joshua Johnson remains shrouded in mystery some 180 years after he lived.

The year and place of his birth are unknown, although historians speculate that he was born in the French West Indies and came to America as an indentured servant, living in Maryland. Once he served his time, he would have been freed and soon after pursued a career as a painter in Baltimore, Maryland. It is possible that Johnson studied portrait painting with a member of the celebrated Peale family, which lived in Baltimore at the time and produced many artists. Whatever his training, Johnson distinguished himself as a leading portrait painter by the late 1790s.

More than 80 paintings have been attributed to Johnson, although only one of them bears his signature. The striking characteristics of that signed painting with its stiffly posed subjects in three-quarter-view portrait have helped to identify the others. Johnson's portraits and other paintings have been praised by critics for their careful composition; flat, modern style; and inventive use of color.

Although there are few mentions of the artist in the historical record, it has been recorded that he owned property in three counties, a sign of his success as an artist. Records in a local Catholic Church show that he was married and had three children. Little else is known about Johnson; even the color of his skin is in some question. The only reference to him being black comes from an 1817 Baltimore city directory that lists him as a "Free Householder of Colour." In an advertisement printed in a newspaper nearly 20 years earlier, Johnson referred to himself as a "self-taught genius" who had surmounted "many insuperable obstacles in the pursuit of his studies." This comment may hint that he was a black man struggling to succeed in a white society.

Most of Johnson's known portraits are of well-to-do Baltimore families. One of the few works attributed to him of black people is matching portraits of two African-American clergymen, members of the Methodist church. The men are depicted with great dignity and humanity, again indicating that the portraitist may have himself been black.

How and when Joshua Johnson died is unknown. All that remains of this gifted artist are his paintings, but the detective work continues.

Further Reading
Bearden, Romare, and Harry Henderson. *A History of African-American Artists: From 1792 to the Present.* New York: Pantheon Books, 1993, pp. 2–17.

"Joshua Johnson." Maryland ArtSource. Available online. URL: http://www.marylandartsource. org/artists/detail_000000091.html. Downloaded March 5, 2009.

Perry, Regenia A. *Free Within Ourselves: African-American Artists in the Collection of the National Museum of American Art.* San Francisco: Pomegranate Communications, 1992, pp. 94–99.

Weekley, Carolyn J., Stiles Tuttle Colwill, Leroy Graham, and Mary Ellen Hayward. *Joshua Johnson: Freeman and Early American Portrait Painter.* Baltimore: Maryland Historical Society, 1987.

Johnson, Malvin Gray
(1896–1934) *painter*

A painter who quickly mastered the modern techniques of his day, Malvin Gray Johnson left his great promise unfulfilled at the time of his early death.

He was born in Greensboro, North Carolina, on January 28, 1896, and experienced a childhood of grinding poverty. His family moved to New York City while he was still young, and he showed an early talent for art. However, poverty prevented him from entering the National Academy of Design in New York until he was 25 years old. Once in school, Johnson interrupted his studies for several years as he worked at menial jobs to earn his tuition. After leaving the academy, Johnson found work as a commercial artist, allowing him to paint his serious work in the evenings.

He burst on the New York art scene in 1928 when his abstract interpretation of the Negro spiritual *Swing Low, Sweet Chariot* won the Otto H. Kahn Prize at an exhibition held by the Harmon Foundation for black artists. Over the next few years he painted more pictures named for spirituals, including *Mighty Day, Climb up the Mountain,* and *I Know the Lord Laid His Hands on Me.*

Johnson worked largely in isolation, spending little time with other African-American artists living in the Harlem section of New York City. His day job and long nights of painting left him little time for anything else.

By 1931, Johnson's style began to change as he absorbed the principles of reductionism, reducing figures and landscapes to simple geometric forms. In 1933, he traveled to Brightwood, Virginia, where for two months he made memorable watercolors of black southern people going about their rural lives—picking crops, washing clothes, and attending religious revival meetings. These sparse, masterfully executed watercolors and the oil paintings he later produced from them are considered his finest and most mature work.

A one-person show of Johnson's work was being planned in New York City when he died suddenly on October 4, 1934, at age 38. The show turned into a memorial that included 35 oil paintings and 18 watercolors. Sadly, most of these works have since disappeared and only survive in photographs taken at the time of the 1935 exhibition. Other paintings of his were exhibited at the Texas Centennial Exposition in Dallas in 1936 and at the American Negro Exposition in Chicago in 1940.

Although his career was short, Malvin Gray Johnson managed in a few years to make great strides in his art and pointed the way to a bolder, more modern style of painting for other African-American artists. "Johnson ranks as one of the promising innovative artists of his day," wrote artist ROMARE BEARDEN, "who, like Stuart Davis and Marsden Hartley [white artists], found a forceful personal style of expression." An extensive exhibition of Johnson's paintings was held at North Carolina Central University in 2002. It was the first public exhibit of his work since his death in 1934.

Further Reading
Bearden, Romare, and Harry Henderson. *A History of African-American Artists: From 1792 to the Present.* New York: Pantheon Books, 1993, pp. 181–184.

Lewis, Samella. *African American Art and Artists.* Berkeley: University of California Press, 2003, pp. 74–75.

"Malvin Gray Johnson (1896–1934) Symbolic Abstractionist." State of Florida's Task Force in African American History. Available online. URL: http://afroamfl.com/Artists.aspx. Downloaded March 5, 2009.

Johnson, Noble
(1881–1978) *film producer, actor*

One of the first African-American actors to receive screen credit in movies, Noble Johnson was also one of the first blacks to produce films that depicted African Americans honestly and realistically.

He was born on April 18, 1881, in Marshall, Missouri. His family moved to Colorado Springs, Colorado, when he was young. He went to school with future silent screen star Lon Chaney and the two became lifelong friends. After school Johnson moved to Hollywood, California, where he acted in his first silent film in 1915. A year later he formed a film company with his brother George in Nebraska. The segregation of movie theaters in the South and parts of the North led to the growth of black theaters in the second decade of the century. The Johnson brothers wanted to provide all-black movies for this growing African-American audience. Their Lincoln Motion Picture Company was only the second movie company in the United States owned and operated by blacks.

Their first film, released in 1916, was *The Realization of a Negro's Ambition*. Although crude by Hollywood standards, the film depicted black people as sensitive human beings and not as the stereotypically stupid or evil characters seen in most Hollywood films of the day. Over the next five years the Johnsons produced about 10 films, including *Trooper of Troop K*, about a historical massacre of black cavalry soldiers by Native Americans in the West.

Because they worked on a tight budget, the Johnsons' films were only 20 to 30 minutes long,

Better known today as a film actor, Noble Johnson and his brother George were pioneers in the independent black film industry. *(Photofest)*

about half the length of most Hollywood films of the day. Black audiences wanted longer films, but without money from white backers, the Johnson brothers could not make longer films. Unable to market their films and running low on funds, they shut down the Lincoln Motion Picture Company in 1922.

Noble Johnson, who resigned as company president in 1920, went on to a highly successful career as a leading black actor, appearing in dozens of silent films, only a handful of which survive. These include *The Ten Commandments* (1923), *The Thief of Baghdad* (1924), and *The Navigator* (1924), starring comedian Buster Keaton. Johnson went on to appear in many more films in the sound era, playing Boris Karloff's Nubian slave in *The Mummy* (1932), an African chieftain in *King Kong* (1933), and a Sikh in *Jungle Book* (1942). He was often cast as an American Indian in westerns. Johnson retired from feature films in

1950 and made his last appearance in a television movie in 1966. He died on January 9, 1978, in Yucaipa, California, at age 97.

An impressive actor with a striking physique who lent dignity to even the most stereotypical of roles, Noble Johnson also played an important, if often forgotten, role in the early development of the independent black cinema.

Further Reading

Bogle, Donald. *Bright Boulevards, Bold Dreams: The Story of Black Hollywood.* New York: One World/ Ballantine Books, 2005, pp. 18–24, 28, 30, 60–63, 359–360.

"Noble Johnson." The Internet Movie Database. Available online. URL: http://www.imdb.com/ name/nm0425903. Downloaded March 5, 2009.

Further Viewing

Jungle Book (1942). Unicorn, DVD, 2006.
The Thief of Baghdad (1924). A2ZCOS.com, DVD, 2009.

Johnson, Sargent

(Sargent Claude Johnson)
(1887–1967) *sculptor, ceramist, printmaker*

One of the most gifted yet underappreciated African-American sculptors of the first half of the 20th century, Sargent Johnson drew on the art of the non-Western world for his inspiration.

He was born on October 7, 1887, in Boston, Massachusetts, the third of six children. His father was white and of Swedish ancestry and his mother was part African American and part Cherokee Indian. His father died when Johnson was 10 and his mother died of tuberculosis five years later. The children lived for a time with their uncle, a high school principal in Washington, D.C. Their aunt, Mary Helen Jackson, was a professional sculptor who was known for her busts of famous African Americans. Through her, Johnson developed an interest in sculpture but was sent to live with his grandparents before he could

pursue it. When his grandparents could no longer care for the children, the boys and girls were sent to separate orphanages. Johnson and his brother went to an orphanage run by the Catholic Sisters of Charity in Worcester, Massachusetts.

He entered a music school in Boston but left to study art. He moved in with relatives in Chicago, Illinois, for a time and then, at age 28, moved to San Francisco, California, where the Panama Pacific International Exposition of 1915 was under way. Johnson, who could have passed for white like his two sisters, but refused to, experienced less prejudice in San Francisco than anywhere else he had lived. He soon married and, with no formal art training, worked as a fitter in a factory for three years. Then he got a job tinting photographs.

At age 32, Johnson went to the California School of Fine Arts where he studied under two respected sculptors, Robert Stackpole and Beniamino Bufano. After completing his studies, he worked as Bufano's assistant. In 1925, Johnson made a sculpture of his two-year-old daughter Pearl and entered it in the San Francisco Art Exhibition. The sculpture won a medal and led to an invitation to participate in the first West Coast exhibition of the Harmon Foundation for African-American Artists in 1926. In the late 1920s, Johnson's work won several prizes in the Harmon shows, the only California artist to be so honored.

Eastern art critics, however, were not impressed by Johnson's work. They criticized his combining of different materials and his unorthodox use of color and glazing in his wood and clay sculptures. They also said his work was too decorative and not "serious" enough.

Johnson's work was certainly different from most American sculptors of that time. Unlike them, he used the art of pre-Columbian America, Asia, and especially Africa as his model, not Greco-Roman art. "Sculpture was never meant to be colorless," he said in his defense. "There is no reason why it should be; most ancient sculpture, with the exception of the late Greek, was polychrome."

The 1930s were Johnson's most productive decade. He produced some of his finest sculptures, including *Forever Free* (1935), a wood sculpture of a black mother and her two children, and two monumental stone figures of Inca Indians on llamas, completed for the Golden Gate International Exposition in San Francisco in 1939. He worked for the federal Works Progress Administration in 1936 and rose to be unit supervisor in the San Francisco area.

Johnson's 1940 frieze, a decorative sculpture in low relief designed for a wall at George Washington High School's football field, won a competition held by the San Francisco Arts Commission. Beniamino Bufano was another contestant. On hearing he had lost to his former pupil, Bufano was so enraged that he severed all connections with Johnson. Then came another dark moment in Johnson's personal life. His wife was committed to a state hospital in the late 1930s. Although they were separated at the time, Johnson faithfully visited her until her death in 1964.

Johnson continued to experiment with new materials and forms throughout his life. In 1947, he began to work on enamel steel plates after meeting a man whose company made them. He completed more than a hundred panel plates and even was commissioned to make a plate for Harold's, a Reno gambling casino. This steel mural of pioneers heading west in a wagon train is the largest mural of its kind.

Johnson traveled twice to Mexico to study its art during the 1940s. In 1958, at age 71, he spent seven months in Japan studying Shinto shrines. Some of his last sculptures were made of diorite, a granular, igneous rock that he collected at Big Sur, California.

Sargent Johnson was living in a hotel in downtown San Francisco when he died of a heart attack on October 10, 1967, at age 80. A versatile creative artist with a restless spirit, Johnson received his first one-person exhibition posthumously in 1971 at the Oakland Museum in California. On speaking of his commitment to African-American art and culture, he said, "It is the pure American Negro I am concerned with, aiming to show the natural beauty and dignity . . . I wish to show that beauty not so much to the white man as to the Negro himself."

Further Reading

Bearden, Romare, and Harry Henderson. *A History of African-American Artists: From 1792 to the Present.* New York: Pantheon Books, 1993, pp. 216–225.

Lefalle-Collins, Lizzetta, and Judith Wilson. *Sargent Johnson: African American Modernist.* San Francisco: San Francisco Museum of Modern Art, 1998.

Lewis, Samella. *African American Art and Artists.* Berkeley: University of California Press, 2003, pp. 77–83.

"Oral history interview with Sargent Johnson, 1964, July 31." Smithsonian Archives of American Arts. Available online. URL: http://www.aaa.si-edu/collections/oralhistories/transcripts/johnso64.htm. Downloaded March 5, 2009.

Perry, Regenia A. *Free Within Ourselves: African-American Artists in the Collection of the National Museum of American Art.* San Francisco: Pomegranate Communications, 1992, pp. 100–105.

Johnson, William H.
(William Henry Johnson)
(1901–1970) *painter*

William H. Johnson was one of the most accomplished and innovative African-American artists of the first half of the 20th century. However, his all-too-brief career ended in abject tragedy.

He was born on March 18, 1901, in Florence, South Carolina, the eldest of five children. As a child, he would skillfully copy comic strips from the newspapers to the astonishment of his family. When he was 17, he left home with an uncle and moved to New York City, where the two of them worked as stevedores, loading ships with war supplies during World War I (1914–18). Johnson saved his money and three years later had enough to enroll in the National Academy of Design in New York. There he studied under the painter Charles Hawthorne, who recognized his ability and helped him raise the money to study and paint in Europe. In 1926 Johnson arrived in France and over the next three years worked and traveled in Belgium and Denmark.

On his return to New York, Johnson entered six of his impressionistic landscapes of Europe in the Harmon Foundation show of 1930. This foundation had been set up in 1922 by white real estate developer William E. Harmon to encourage the work of African Americans in business, education, literature, science, and the fine arts. Johnson was awarded the gold medal, the art show's highest prize, and his career was launched.

Soon afterward, he was painting a picture of an old hotel in his hometown when white policemen arrested him. The humiliation of having to spend time in jail for merely painting left Johnson bitter, and he quickly returned to Europe, where he remained for 14 years.

While traveling in the south of France, Johnson met Danish textile artist Holcha Krake. The two artists fell in love and were married in Denmark. They settled down in the small fishing village of Kerteminde. Here Johnson was accepted by the local people, whom he compared to the hardworking black southerners he grew up knowing. In Kerteminde, he painted vibrant scenes of village life and marine landscapes. But before long, he again felt the urge to travel, and the couple journeyed to North Africa in 1935. Johnson fell in love with the bright colors of African art and learned the art of ceramics.

The couple headed north again and crossed Norway on bicycles. They lived for a time in the Lofoten Islands off the coast of Norway but returned to the United States in 1938 as approaching war loomed over much of Europe.

Back in the United States, Johnson developed the style of painting for which he is best known today. He followed the lead of JACOB LAWRENCE and other black artists whose work reflected black history and the everyday life of contemporary African Americans. These new narrative paintings abandoned the heavy brushstrokes of his expressionistic period and were full of bright colors and flat figures. They were deliberately naive, almost folklike in technique. These paintings, including *Chain Gang* (ca. 1939–40) and *Going to Church* (ca. 1940–41), were immensely popular with the public but were also praised by art critics. Johnson also reinterpreted classic scenes of Christ's life and biblical stories from a black perspective in such powerful paintings as *Mount*

Mental illness cut short the promising career of William H. Johnson, who remains one of the most important African-American painters of the 20th century. *(Photofest)*

Calvary, Lamentation (both ca. 1939), and *Swing Low, Sweet Chariot* (ca. 1944). According to art historian and artist DAVID C. DRISKELL, "Johnson changed the course of artistic interpretations of Black American themes in Christianity."

Then in January 1944, Johnson's beloved wife died of cancer. Crushed by his loss, he returned home to South Carolina to find comfort with his mother and other family members. It was a peaceful time for him, and he spent much of it visiting with friends and family and painting their portraits. Johnson soon returned to New York and went to work in the Brooklyn Navy Yard to earn enough money to return to Denmark. He became obsessed with the idea of marrying Krake's widowed sister. In 1945, he painted a popular series of historical paintings he called *Fighters for Freedom*. In montage style, he included such famous freedom fighters as white abolitionist John Brown, black educator Booker T. Washington, and black scientist George Washington Carver.

The following year, Johnson returned to Denmark but Krake's sister rejected his proposal of marriage. He remained with her family, however, and exhibited a number of his paintings in Copenhagen, Denmark, in March 1947. It would be his last exhibition in his lifetime. His behavior became increasingly erratic, and he was found wandering the streets of Oslo, Norway. Johnson's mental illness was probably the result of syphilis, a venereal disease he contracted years before. Soon he was sent back to New York. His work was put in storage, and he was committed to the Central Islip State Hospital on Long Island, New York. He remained there for 23 years until his death. In all those years, he did not produce another painting.

Most of his hundreds of paintings, sketches, and other work was saved by the Harmon Foundation, which gave it to the National Museum of American Art in Washington, D.C. Ironically, Johnson died on April 13, 1970, as a major retrospective of his work was being prepared at the museum. The exhibit was the first this distinguished museum

had given to an African-American artist, and it returned Johnson to the status of a major black painter.

"Johnson's intense colors and expressive painting techniques catapult his self-image into a modern aesthetic, one riddled with formal dichotomies and underlying emotions," wrote art historian and critic Richard J. Powell.

Further Reading

Bearden, Romare, and Harry Henderson. *A History of African-American Artists: From 1792 to the Present.* New York: Pantheon Books, 1993, pp. 185–199.

Everett, Gwen. *Li'l Sis and Uncle Willie: A Story Based on the Life and Paintings of William H. Johnson.* New York: Hyperion, 1994.

Lewis, Samella. *African American Art and Artists.* Berkeley: University of California Press, 2003, pp. 88–95.

Powell, Richard J. *Homecoming: The Art and Life of William H. Johnson.* New York: W. W. Norton, 1993.

Turner, Steve, and Victoria Dailey. *William H. Johnson: Truth Be Told.* Los Angeles: Seven Arts Publishing, 1998.

"William H. Johnson." Kenyon College Web site. Available online. URL: http://northbysouth. kenyon.edu/1998/art/pages/whjohnson.htm. Downloaded March 27, 2009.

Further Viewing

The Life and Art of William H. Johnson. Reading & O'Reilly, VHS, 1991.

Jones, Frank
(Frank Albert Jones)
(ca. 1900–1969) *folk graphic artist*

A three-time loser who spent 20 years of his life in prison, Frank Jones found his salvation in his intricate drawings of ghosts and demons that either drove him to crime or simply tormented an innocent man.

He was born Frank Albert Jones in Red River County, Texas, near the town of Clarksville in about 1900. The exact date of his birth is unknown and the facts about his childhood are sparse but grim. His father, Edward Jones, abandoned the family when Frank was about three, and his mother, Sarah Clark, left him on a street corner a few years later, never to return.

Two neighbors, Willie Dean Baker and Della Gray, raised Jones as best they could. He never attended school and never learned to read or write. However, he believed he had a unique gift that almost no one else in Clarksville could lay claim to. A caul, part of the fetal membrane, covered his left eye and supposedly gave him the power to see spirits or, as the southern blacks called them, "haints." Jones claimed to see his first spirit when he was nine and drew a picture of one a year later.

In 1941, the mother of a young woman Jones had raised accused him of raping her daughter. The mother's motives were suspicious: She had abandoned the girl and now wanted her back, but Jones refused to give her up. He protested his innocence but was convicted and served a little more than two years in prison.

After his release, Jones seemed to be getting his life back together. He married Audrey Calberson in 1945. Four years later one of Calberson's sons from a previous relationship was arrested for robbing and killing Jones's "stepmother" Della Gray. The son implicated Jones in the killing, which he vigorously denied. But again he was found guilty and sentenced to life in prison. Nine years later, Jones was paroled and came back to Clarksville.

But his time of freedom was brief. His housecleaner accused him of raping her. Jones denied the charge, but his parole was revoked and he returned to jail.

In 1964, Jones began to make the strange drawings he became famous for. Using red and blue pencil stubs discarded by prison bookkeepers, he created elaborate drawings he called "devil houses." These were cross sections of buildings that contained legions of tiny demons and devils.

Drawn on cheap typing paper, these devils were rendered harmless because they were locked in their houses, much as Jones was locked up in his prison cell. He gave them such colorful titles as *Creepin' Crawlin' Blue Devil Spider, Flying Fish Devil House,* and *Hawaiian Humpty Dumpty Devil.*

A prison art show in 1964 gave Jones his first public exposure. A Dallas, Texas, art gallery owner saw Jones's work and immediately signed him on as a client. He also provided the prison artist with better pencils and paper. Jones's drawings were exhibited at two Art on Paper shows in 1965 and 1966 at the Weatherspoon Gallery at the University of North Carolina. They were later seen at the Exhibition of Southwestern Prints and Drawings at the Dallas Museum of Fine Arts and the Contemporary Drawings Show at the Fort Worth Art Center.

Jones, who in 15 years in prison had not had one visitor, enjoyed his new celebrity. He was interviewed by local reporters and treated with respect by the other inmates. With some of the money from the sales of his art he bought a gold watch, although it is said he could not tell time.

As his art matured, the devil houses more and more resembled his prison block. Among the recurring motifs of his work was a large clock, much like the one in the prison yard outside his window. Time hung heavy over Jones, who was denied parole repeatedly. Finally, parole was granted him in early February 1969. Almost immediately, his health began to fail and he was rushed into the prison hospital. On the verge of becoming a free man, Frank Jones died of liver disease on February 15, 1969. His body was sent to Clarksville for burial with the money he had earned from his artwork.

Today, some of his 500 drawings can be seen in such major museums as the National Museum of American Art in Washington, D.C.

Whether Frank Jones was an innocent man unjustly punished or a rapist and murderer has never been fully determined. What is certain is that he was a true artist.

Further Reading

Adele, Lynn. "Jones, Frank Albert." The Handbook of Texas Online. Available online. URL: http://www. tshaonline.org/handbook/online/articles/JJ/fjobn. html. Downloaded March 5, 2009.

Perry, Regenia A. *Free Within Ourselves: African-American Artists in the Collection of the National Museum of American Art.* San Francisco: Pomegranate Communications, 1992, pp. 114–119.

Steed, Dee. "The Devil in Contemporary Primitive Art." Cited in *History/Black Vision: The Visionary Image in Texas.* Austin: University of Texas at Austin, 1987.

Jones, Lois Mailou

(1905–1998) *painter, illustrator, textile designer, educator*

Lois Mailou Jones enjoyed one of the longest and most productive careers of any African-American artist. While most celebrated for her combining of cubist and African imagery, she worked in a wide range of styles and was one of the most influential black art teachers of the 20th century.

She was born in Boston, Massachusetts, on November 3, 1905. Her father was the first African American to graduate from Boston's Suffolk Law School, but he never took the bar exam to become a lawyer. He earned a living as the superintendent of an office building, where the family lived on the top floor. As a small child, Jones accompanied her mother, who was a beautician, to the homes of well-to-do white clients. While her mother worked, Jones would copy the paintings on the walls with crayons.

On a scholarship, she attended the Boston Museum School of Fine Art where she also worked part-time. "I made the museum my home," she later said, "drawing until it closed." She graduated in 1927 and earned a teacher's certificate, but when she applied for a graduate assistantship at the museum, she was rejected because of her color. Museum officials advised her to go to the South, where she could help "her people."

She did so and was hired to run the art department at Palmer Memorial Institute, a boarding school for black students in Sedalia, North Carolina. Jones did such an outstanding job at Palmer that in 1930 Howard University in Washington, D.C., one of the leading black institutions of higher learning, invited her to teach in their new art department. She remained at Howard for 47 years, teaching drawing, watercolor painting, and design to generations of future black artists, such as sculptor ELIZABETH CATLETT.

In 1937, Jones took her first sabbatical to study and paint in France. She fell in love with the city of Paris and even learned French so she could talk with the people. Her street scenes of Paris and African-inspired paintings were exhibited in Parisian art salons, making her the first African-American female artist to be celebrated abroad. Her fascination with African art and culture led to one of her most famous paintings, *Les Fétiches* (1938), a colorful montage of five African masks, each representing a different tribal group. Her incorporating of the cubist style with African subjects was revolutionary and much imitated. For more than two decades, Jones continued to live in Paris for part of each year, with the exception of the years of World War II (1939–45).

Jones took great satisfaction in her dual career as teacher and artist, and she encouraged other black art teachers at Howard and other schools to continue being artists. She transformed her studio into what she called "Little Paris" and invited them to work and display their paintings there. Among this group of artist/teachers was celebrated painter and printmaker ALMA W. THOMAS.

Jones's work was colorful and design-oriented but could also powerfully express the social injustice blacks experienced in the United States. In her well-known painting *Meditation* (1944), an elderly black man awaits his lynching with prayerful serenity. The artist based the painting on an eyewitness account of an actual lynching, but viewers were confused by the peacefulness of the work and she later retitled it *Mob Victim* to make

This picture of a very young Lois Mailou Jones was taken by famed African-American photographer Addison Scurlock. *(Photographs and Prints Division, Schomburg Center for Research in Black Culture, the New York Public Library, Astor, Lennox and Tilden Foundations)*

island of Haiti at the invitation of the government. Jones painted the countryside and people and taught drawing classes in the capital city of Port-au-Prince. The couple regularly returned to Haiti for many years. Jones was so popular there that the Haitian government made her a chevalier of the National Order of Honor and Merit. She even painted a portrait of Haitian president Paul Magloire and his wife.

At home in the United States, Jones became just as honored for her work. She won first prize in competitions at the National Museum in Washington, D.C., in 1940, 1947, 1960, and 1963. In 1955 she became the first African American admitted to the Washington Society of Artists. The Boston Museum of Fine Art, which had rejected her decades earlier, bought her collage *Ubi Girl from Tai Region, Nigeria* in 1974, the first work the museum ever acquired by an African-American artist. She also became the first African American to have a solo exhibition at the museum.

Jones retired from Howard University's art department in 1977. Her husband died in 1982. She continued to paint into her eighties and died in 1998 at age 93, one of the last African-American artists of her generation.

"She championed the black artist," wrote Edmund Barry Gaither, director of the Museum of the National Center of Afro-American Artists, "but not just through the model of her energy and her determination, but through the quality of her work and her teaching."

the situation clearer. Yet, as DAVID C. DRISKELL wrote, "The deep compassion that lies behind this harrowing portrait against the waste of black lives is made all the more effective because the artist has avoided the stylistic clichés of righteous indignation and moral fervor."

In 1953, Jones married Haitian artist Louis Vergniard Pierre-Noel, whom she had first met 20 years earlier at Columbia University in New York, where they were both graduate students. With her husband she traveled to the West Indian

Further Reading

Bearden, Romare, and Harry Henderson. *A History of African-American Artists: From 1792 to the Present.* New York: Pantheon Books, 1993, pp. 381–388.

Benjamin, Tritobia Hayes, and Lois Mailou Jones. *The Life and Art of Lois Mailou Jones.* San Francisco: Pomegranate Communications, 1994.

Gillespie, Fern. "The Life and Legacy of Lois Mailou Jones." *Howard Magazine,* Winter 1999, pp. 8–13, 19.

"Lois Mailou Jones 1905–1998." Available online. URL: http://www.howard.edu/library/Art@Howard/LMJ/page2.htm. Downloaded April 3, 2009.

Newsome, Effie Lee, Lois Mailou Jones, illustrator. *Wonders: The Best Children's Poems of Effie Lee Newsome.* Honesdale, Pa.: Boyds Mills Press, 1999.

Robinson-English, Tracey. "Celebrating Lois Mailou Jones: The Grande Dame of the Art World (1905–1998)." *Ebony,* December 1, 2005, pp. 124–128.

Further Viewing

Persistent Women Artists. Reading & O'Reilly, VHS, 1996.

L

Lawrence, Annette

(1965–   ) *installation artist, mixed-media artist, painter, educator*

The huge and unique installations of Annette Lawrence explore the boundaries of time and space and their uses. Born on January 28, 1965, in Rockville Centre, New York, Lawrence attended the University of Hartford in West Hartford, Connecticut, earning a Bachelor of Fine Arts degree in 1986. She went on to earn a Master of Fine Arts degree at the Maryland Institute's College of Arts Hoffberger School of Painting in 1990. In 1996, she began teaching at the School of Visual Arts at the University of North Texas in Denton as an assistant professor of painting and drawing. Since 2002, she has been an associate professor there.

The Dallas African American Museum mounted her solo show *Annette Lawrence: Installation* in 1998. Other shows followed in the Dallas Visual Arts Center (1999) and the Arthur Roger Gallery in New Orleans, Louisiana (2001).

Many of Lawrence's installations are environmental works that are set up in a particular location and then taken down and not transported to another museum. She often uses string, paper, and tape in her explorations of space. She is also concerned with time in her art. In the exhibition, *Edge* (2005), at Dunn and Brown Contemporary in Dallas, she explored the passing of time as seen through documents and records. The exhibit included mixed-media art and paintings on paper as well as installations. She has also been part of the group shows *Word Play* (2007) at the Nancy Wilson Scanlow Gallery in Austin and *Decoding Identity* (2009) at the Museum of the African Diaspora in San Francisco, California.

Concerned about the amount of junk mail she was receiving, Lawrence decided to collect 13 months of it, weighing 265 pounds. Then she cut the mail into two-inch-wide strips and stacked it on shelves in early 2009 at the Flatbed Press Gallery in Austin, Texas, under the title *Free Paper*. There was one stack for each month's worth of junk mail. The Dallas Museum of Art was so impressed by the exhibition that it bought Lawrence's pile for the month of December. Art reviewer Rachel Koper called the exhibit "good-looking art with heavy recycling mojo, but the primacy of the craftsmanship is what's paramount." Lawrence herself has called the exhibit "both a commentary on the disposability of consumer culture and an attempt to introduce order and meaning."

Annette Lawrence has served as artist-in-residence at the Tanera Mor International Artists Workshop in Tanera Mor, Scotland (2007), and the American University, Washington, D.C. (2008). She lives in Denton, Texas.

Further Reading

Annette Lawrence's Official Web site. Available online. URL: http://www.annettelawrence.net/main.html. Downloaded March 29, 2009.

Koper, Rachel. "Annette Lawrence: Free Paper." *Austin Chronicle*, January 30, 2009.

Lewis, Samella. *African American Art and Artists.* Berkeley: University of California Press, 2003, pp. 313–315.

Olsen, Valerie Loupe. *Annette Lawrence: Theory.* Houston, Tex.: Glassell School of Art of the Museum of Fine Art, 2003.

Willour, Clint. *Annette Lawrence and Sydney Yeager, Common Themes/Material Differences.* Arlington: University Gallery at University of Texas at Arlington, 2004.

Lawrence, Jacob
(1917–2000) *painter, illustrator, educator*

Perhaps the best-known and most popular African-American artist of the 20th century, Jacob Lawrence told the story of black people in series of narrative paintings that were filled with a primitive power that was also expressively modern.

He was born in Atlantic City, New Jersey, on September 17, 1917. The eldest child of a railroad cook, Lawrence and his family moved to Easton, Pennsylvania, where his father pursued work as a coal miner. When he was seven, his parents separated and he moved with his mother in 1924 to Philadelphia and then Harlem, the black community of New York City. Lawrence later credited his strong visual sense to the bright decor of the furnishings in the family's Harlem apartment.

He attended public schools and enrolled in the after-school art program at the Utopia Children's Center. The center's director, CHARLES H. ALSTON, quickly recognized Lawrence's talent and nurtured it. Through Alston, the young man met artist AARON DOUGLAS and writer Langston Hughes. Lawrence, even at this early stage of his career, showed a love of narrative art, creating diorama paintings of scenes out of corrugated cardboard.

The Great Depression (1929–39) caused Lawrence's mother to lose her job, and the family went on welfare. To help out, Lawrence dropped out of high school and got a job planting trees and draining swamps in upstate New York for the federally run Civilian Conservation Corps.

On his return to New York City in 1934, he studied art at the Harlem Community Art Center, headed by sculptor AUGUSTA SAVAGE. Encouraged by Savage, Lawrence began to paint the world around him, concentrating on Harlem's vibrant street life. He developed a highly stylized technique that was characterized by simplified shapes, bright colors, and a flattened perspective. Many of his paintings resembled poster art raised to the highest level.

A great reader, Lawrence became infatuated with the life of Toussaint Louverture, a black slave who became the founder of the republic of Haiti in the West Indies. Originally, Lawrence planned a single painting of Louverture but gradually realized he could not do justice to his life in one frame. When completed in 1937, *The Life of Toussaint L'Ouverture* consisted of no fewer than 41 separate paintings or, as Lawrence called them, panels.

This grand work established Lawrence's reputation as a leading black artist at age 21. Over the next decade he produced an astonishing number of similar historical series that told in pictures the lives of famous people. They included *The Life of Frederick Douglass* (1938, 40 panels); *The Life of Harriet Tubman* (1939, 31 panels); and *The Life of John Brown* (1941, 22 panels). Some of Lawrence's series were based on an event or group of people, such as his monumental *The Migration of the Negro* (1940–41, 60 panels). In this work, he drew on his own family's history to tell the sprawling story of black people from the rural South moving to the industrial cities of the North in the early decades of the 20th century. When *The Migration* was exhibited at New York's

The most acclaimed African-American artist of the 20th century, Jacob Lawrence had a long and productive career until his death in 2000 at the age of 82. *(Anthony Barboza)*

Downtown Gallery, Lawrence became the first African-American artist to be represented by a mainstream art gallery. In 1942, the Museum of Modern Art in New York City put together a traveling exhibition of his work.

By the late 1940s, Lawrence was the most respected and famous black artist in America, a title he was uncomfortable with. He felt guilty for receiving so much attention when many of his colleagues were struggling to sell their work. Such thoughts put Lawrence into a deep depression, and in July 1949 he entered a psychiatric hospital in Queens, New York, for treatment. Even while recovering from depression, the prolific artist could not stop painting. He created the *Hospital* series in 1950 after his release.

Lawrence enjoyed teaching, which he had done sporadically since the 1930s. He later taught art at Brandeis University in Waltham, Massachusetts, and the New School for Social Research and the Pratt Institute in New York City. In 1964 he lived for a year in Nigeria in Africa. On his return to the United States, he took a position at the University of Washington in Seattle. He remained there until his retirement in 1983.

Lawrence was elected to the American Academy of Arts and Letters in 1984 and the following year was recognized with a special citation by the Washington State Senate.

He was also an illustrator. Among his works are a collection of Aesop's fables and a book of verse about Underground Railroad activist Harriet Tubman, called *Harriet and the Promised Land* (1993).

After a long and productive career, Jacob Lawrence died on June 9, 2000, at age 82. He was survived by his wife, Gwen Knight, who died in 2005 and was also an artist. A major retrospective of his work, "Over The Line: The Art and Life of Jacob Lawrence," was mounted by the Whitney Museum of American Art in New York in late 2001. It has since traveled to several other museums.

During the last 30 years of his life, Lawrence worked on a series called *Builders*. It depicted men and women working together to erect what appeared to be a skyscraper. In these paintings, wrote Suzanne Ramljak in the *New York Times Book Review*, the artist developed a theme that "was also an image that mirrored Lawrence's own constructive endeavor: a figure striving to refashion the world through creative labor."

Further Reading

Duggleby, John. *Story Painter: The Life of Jacob Lawrence.* San Francisco, Calif.: Chronicle Books, 1998.

Hills, Patricia, and Jacob Lawrence. *Jacob Lawrence: Moving Forward.* New York: DC Moore Gallery, 2008.

Howard, Nancy Shroyer. *Jacob Lawrence: American Scenes, American Struggles* (Closer Look Activity Book). Worcester, Mass.: Davis Publications, 1996.

Lawrence, Jacob. *Harriet and the Promised Land.* New York: Aladdin Paperbacks, 1997.

Lawrence, Jacob, Peter T. Nesbett, and Michelle Dubois, eds. *The Complete Jacob Lawrence.* Seattle: University of Washington Press, 2001.

Nesbett, Peter T. *Jacob Lawrence: The Complete Prints (1963–2000), A Catalog Raisonne.* Seattle: University of Washington Press, 2005.

Nesbett, Peter T. and Michelle Dubois, eds. *Over the Line: The Art and Life of Jacob Lawrence.* Seattle: University of Washington Press, 2001.

Further Viewing

Jacob Lawrence: An Intimate Portrait (1993). Homevision Entertainment, VHS, 2000.

Jacob Lawrence: The Glory of Expression (1994). L & S Video, VHS, 1999.

Lee, Spike

(Shelton Jackson Lee)
(1957–) *filmmaker, screenwriter, film producer, actor, educator*

The leading contemporary African-American filmmaker working today, Spike Lee has created over the past 25 years a significant body of work that confronts and challenges both white and black America.

He was born Shelton Jackson Lee on March 20, 1957, in Atlanta, Georgia. His father, Bill Lee, is a jazz musician. His mother, Jacquelyn Lee, taught for years in a private school mainly for white students. She gave him the nickname "Spike" because he was a tough little guy as a child.

When he was in first grade, the family moved to Cobble Hill, which was then a predominantly white neighborhood in Brooklyn, New York. "We were the first black family to move in," Lee has said, "and this is amazing to me: no one moved out because the Lees moved in."

Given the opportunity to attend his mother's private school, Lee chose to go to public school, where he would be among black students like himself. After high school, he enrolled in all-black Morehouse College in Atlanta, where he majored in mass communications.

While Lee was in college, his mother died unexpectedly in 1977. To escape his grief, he saw as many movies as he could. One film, *The Deer Hunter*, about the war in Vietnam, convinced him he should be a filmmaker. After graduating from Morehouse, Lee was accepted into the graduate film program at New York University's (NYU) Tisch School of Arts. He was almost kicked out of the program for making a controversial short film about a black writer working on a new version of the silent film classic *Birth of a Nation* that portrayed blacks as inferior to whites. However, Lee's next student film, the 45-minute documentary *Joe's Bed-Stuy Barbershop: We Cut Heads* won widespread praise and received the Motion Picture Arts and Sciences' Student Academy Award in 1983.

Upon graduating, Lee plunged into his first feature film, *The Messenger*, the story of a bicycle messenger in New York City, based partly on his own experiences. The project fell apart when he could not raise the money necessary for the ambitious film. "We were devastated," he later recalled, and he decided to make a film on a more modest budget.

The result was the comedy *She's Gotta Have It* (1986), which Lee shot in 12 days for $175,000, using rented equipment. The film, about a black female artist and the three men in her life, was an unexpected hit that earned more than $7 million. Lee also won rave reviews for his acting as the comic Mars Blackmon, one of the three suitors. He would go on to appear in supporting roles in many of his future films.

Now a hot property as a director, Lee made his second feature, *School Daze* (1988), a musical based on his experiences at Morehouse, released by Columbia Pictures. His subsequent picture is considered by many to be his best to date, *Do the Right Thing* (1989). It dealt with a day in the life of a mostly black Brooklyn neighborhood and the tensions that develop at a local pizza shop owned by a white Italian-American and his two sons. The film's climatic race riot, which results in the pizzeria's destruction, was condemned by some people who thought Lee was endorsing violence as a reaction to racism. The film, however, was evenhanded in its criticism. It presented the white restaurant owner with great sympathy, while showing one of the instigators of the riot to be a bigmouthed fool.

"Spike Lee's undeniable power to infuse his images with energy and insight and his determination to structure and direct a film in a style all his own . . . made *Do the Right Thing* . . . one of the most distinct and invigorating movies of the decade," wrote film historian Donald Bogle.

Now considered one of the leading filmmakers of his generation, Lee produced on average a film a year through the 1990s, making him also one of the most prolific of American directors. These films were noted for their excellent casting of fine African-American actors, a bold and kinetic visual style, and challenging (and often controversial) subject matter. *Mo' Better Blues* (1990) was inspired by Lee's father, who wrote the film's score. *Jungle Fever* (1991) was about an interracial affair and featured a galvanizing performance by Samuel L. Jackson as the protagonist's drug addict brother.

Lee's next film was his most ambitious to date: the three-hour biographical film *Malcolm X* (1992), about the life and death of the celebrated black political leader. The film won Lee some of his best reviews to date and earned two Academy Award nominations, one for Denzel Washington in the title role. However, Lee was widely criticized by both whites and black for blatant merchandising of Malcolm's name and image. He responded by saying that this commercialization was totally in keeping with Malcolm X's own call for black enterprise and empowerment.

After several lightweight films, Lee returned to the central issue of race relations in *Get on the Bus* (1996), the fictionalized story of a group of black men riding from Los Angeles, California,

Prolific filmmaker Spike Lee is on location for *Summer of Sam*, his penetrating 1999 study of a New York neighborhood in the grip of a serial killer. *(Photofest)*

to Washington, D.C., for the Million Man March organized by Nation of Islam leader Louis Farrakhan in 1995. Next came the documentary *4 Little Girls* (1997), about the bombing of a Birmingham, Alabama, church in 1963 that killed four black girls. *He Got Game* (1998) was another gritty urban drama about a star high school basketball player and his convict father, played again by Denzel Washington. Another film based on real events was the ambitious *Summer of Sam* (1999), which followed fictional characters during the summer of 1977 when the serial killer David Berkowitz ("Son of Sam") was terrorizing New York City. It was Lee's first film that did not feature a single major black character.

Lee returned to racial issues with the savage satire *Bamboozled* (2000), about a black writer who creates a hit television show based on the traditionally racist minstrel shows of the past. The film generated much discussion but failed completely at the box office.

Lee returned to documentary filmmaking with *Jim Brown: All American* (2001), an ambitious film about the life of the celebrated football player and actor, who appeared in Lee's *He Got Game*. After a couple of films that were poorly received, Lee directed his most successful commercial film yet, the crime thriller *Inside Man* (2006) about a bank heist that starred Denzel Washington and British actor Clive Owen. The same year, he directed another moving television documentary for HBO, the two-part *When the Levees Broke: A Requiem in Four Acts* about Hurricane Katrina. The hard-hitting film accused the government and local officials of gross neglect in their handling of the disaster. It won three Emmys, including one for Lee for Outstanding Direction for Nonfiction Program. *The Miracle of St. Anna*, an epic war film about four black soldiers stationed in Italy during World War II, appeared in 2008. Lee's next two projects were a documentary on basketball great Kobe Bryant and the musical *Passing Strange*, both made for television in 2009. His documentary about New Orleans, *If God Is Willing and da Creek Don't Rise*, showed on HBO in 2010.

Controversial, fiercely independent, and always opinionated, Spike Lee continues to challenge himself and his audience with his highly personal films. His message to his audience is "that they have to think. In my opinion people don't think enough. Television and music have become narcotics."

Lee is a master teacher of film at his alma mater, NYU's Tisch School of the Arts, and Harvard University in Cambridge, Massachusetts. He lives in New York City with his wife, Tanya Lynette Lewis, and their two children.

Further Reading

Abrams, Dennis. *Spike Lee: Director* (Black American of Achievement). New York: Chelsea House, 2008.

Aftab, Kaleem, and Spike Lee. *Spike Lee: That's My Story and I'm Sticking to it.* New York: W. W. Norton, 2006.

Fuchs, Cynthia, ed. *Spike Lee: Interviews.* Jackson: University Press of Mississippi, 2002.

Haskins, James. *Spike Lee: By Any Means Necessary.* New York: Walker & Company, 1997.

Massood, Paula, ed. *The Spike Lee Reader.* Philadelphia, Pa.: Temple University Press, 2008.

Further Viewing

Bamboozled (2000). New Line Cinema, VHS/DVD, 2001.

4 Little Girls (1997). HBO Home Video, VHS/DVD, 1999/2001.

Malcolm X (1992). Warner Home Video, VHS/DVD, 2000.

Spike Lee Joint Collection (Clockers/Jungle Fever/Do The Right Thing/Mo' Better Blues/Crooklyn). Universal Home Entertainment, DVD box set, 2006.

When the Levees Broke: A Requiem in Four Acts (2006). HBO Home Video, DVD box set, 2006.

Lee-Smith, Hughie
(Hughie Lee Smith)
(1915–1999) *painter, educator*

A master painter of alienation of the individual in society, Hughie Lee-Smith evoked a universal loneliness through his lost and isolated characters adrift in a surreal world of crumbling urban landscapes.

He was born Hughie Lee Smith on September 20, 1915, in Eustis, Florida. His parents were Luther and Alice Williams Smith. Interested in art from an early age, he changed his name to Lee-Smith because he felt Smith was too commonplace a name for the celebrated artist he intended to become.

His parents separated when he was still a child, and he moved to Cleveland, Ohio, with his mother. Lee-Smith attended the Cleveland School of Art at 19 and won a *Scholastic* magazine scholarship to study at the Detroit Society of Arts and Crafts School for a year. He then attended the Cleveland Institute of Art. In Cleveland he also became seriously interested in acting and dance and appeared in plays and with dance companies regularly until the 1950s.

After graduating in 1938, Lee-Smith taught briefly at Claflin College, a black school in Orangeburg, North Carolina. While there, he met and married Mabel Eueridge, and the couple moved to Detroit the following year. During World War II (1939–45), he worked in an airplane engine factory and then joined the U.S. Navy, where he painted "morale-building" pictures at the Great Lakes naval base. After the war, Lee-Smith returned to Detroit and enrolled at Wayne State University on the G.I. Bill. His painting style then was realistic, and he won the prize for oil painting at the Michigan State Fair in 1951. Two years later he graduated from Wayne State with a Bachelor of Science degree in art education.

By the mid-1950s, Lee-Smith's style changed dramatically as he came under the influence of American painter Edward Hopper and Italian surrealist Giorgio De Chirico. Like Hopper, he used open, often desolate spaces to convey a sense of isolation for his solitary characters. Because many of his paintings depicted black people, as in *Boy on Roof*, the connection between their alienation and a racially hostile and deprived environment was powerfully made.

In 1955, Lee-Smith had his first major one-person exhibition at Howard University in Washington, D.C., and won the National Academy of Design Emily Lowe Award two years later. He moved to New York City, where his wife died in 1961, and became artist-in-residence at Howard from 1969 to 1971. In 1972, he became adjunct professor of history at Trenton State College (now The College of New Jersey). The same year, he became an instructor at the Art Students League in New York City, a position he retained until 1984. He married Patricia Ferry, a former student, in 1978.

While best known for his surreal landscapes and often-tormented characters, Lee-Smith was also a gifted portrait painter. The U.S. Navy commissioned him to paint a portrait of Admiral Samuel Gravely, the first African-American admiral. He also painted a series of portraits of famous blacks from Maryland for the Maryland State Commission on Afro-American History and Culture.

Relegated for decades to being an African-American artist, Lee-Smith achieved national prominence only in 1988 when a retrospective of his work opened at the New Jersey State Museum and traveled across the country. Another major retrospective of his more recent work was held at the Mint Museum in Charlotte, North Carolina, in 1995. In the 1980s, his work lost some of its hopelessness and there was more optimism in his paintings. Hughie Lee-Smith died on February 23, 1999 in Albuquerque, New Mexico at age 83.

Today he is seen as an important American painter whose sense of alienation transcends race to achieve a truly universal appeal.

"I am sincerely trying to get at something invisible and almost impossible to express," he once said. "I think my paintings have to do with an invisible life—a reality on a different level."

"Lee-Smith," wrote Gerrit Henry in his book *Art in America,* "is an elder statesman of the American imagination."

Further Reading

Bearden, Romare, and Harry Henderson. *A History of African-American Artists: From 1792 to the Present.* New York: Pantheon Books, 1993, pp. 328–336.

"Hughie Lee-Smith (1915–1999)." Available online. URL: http://www.mojoportfolio.com/artist_search/african_american/lee-smith.html. Downloaded March 6, 2009.

King-Hammond, Leslie. *Hughie Lee-Smith* (The David C. Driskell Series of African American Art). San Francisco, Calif.: Pomegranate Communications, 2010.

Riggs, Thomas, ed. *St. James Guide to Black Artists.* Detroit, Mich.: St. James Press, 1997, pp. 319–322.

Robinson, Jontyle Theresa, David Driskell, Elisavietta Ritchie, and Richard A. Long. *Three Masters: Eldzier Cortor, Hughie Lee-Smith, Archibald J. Motley, Jr.* New York: Kenkeleba Gallery, 1988.

Lemmons, Kasi

(Karen Lemmons)
(1961–) *filmmaker, screenwriter, actor*

Kasi (pronounced "Casey") Lemmons is one of the most promising of a new generation of black women filmmakers. Her first film, *Eve's Bayou,* was the most financially successful independent film of 1997.

She was born on February 24, 1961, in St. Louis, Missouri, into an interracial family. She studied acting and dance in school and at 18 landed her first film role as a hostage in the television movie *11th Victim* (1979). Through the 1980s Lemmons appeared on a number of television series, including *The Cosby Show* and *Walker, Texas Ranger.*

Interested in screenwriting and directing, she enrolled in film school in New York City in the late 1980s and made a short documentary, *Fall from Grace* (1987), about homeless people.

Soon Lemmons's film acting career took off, and she had solid roles in such films as *The Silence of the Lambs* (1991); *The Five Heartbeats* (1991), directed by ROBERT TOWNSEND; and *Drop Zone* (1992), costarring Wesley Snipes. Her husband, actor Vondie Curtis-Hall, directed her in the film *Gridlock'd* (1997) opposite the late rap singer Tupac Shakur. Curtis-Hall encouraged her to try to get her original screenplay, *Eve's Bayou,* produced. When actor Samuel L. Jackson agreed to coproduce the film and also play a leading role, *Eve's Bayou* became a reality. Lemmons decided to direct the project herself.

The sensitive story of a black woman in Louisiana and her relationship with her womanizing father (Jackson), *Eve's Bayou* (1997) won rave reviews and became the most successful independent film of the year. Her second film, *Dr. Hugo* (1998), featured her husband in the title role.

Lemmons spent several years on her much-anticipated third feature film, *The Caveman's Valentine* (2001). Written by George Dawes Green and based on his award-winning novel, *The Caveman's Valentine* is the intriguing story of a former musician and homeless man (again played by Samuel L. Jackson) who sets out to solve the murder of a man whose body he discovers. Filled with memorable images and beautifully filmed, *The Caveman's Valentine* featured a tour de force performance by Jackson. Nevertheless it was a commercial failure.

Her most recent film, *Talk to Me* (2007), is the biography of a real-life Washington, D.C., radio personality Petey Greene, starring Don Cheadle. Lemmons still occasionally acts in films and on television. "The longer I'm in the business, the longer I realize it's a miracle that any movie gets made," she said in an interview with the *New York Times.* "You have to put blinders on. You're swimming upstream, and you have to believe you can swim upstream. I keep a belief alive: I can do it."

Further Reading

Alexander, George. *Why We Make Movies: Black Filmmakers Talk About the Magic of Cinema.* New York: Harlem Moon, 2003, pp. 253–272.

"Kasi Lemmons (biography and interview)." The African American Literary Book Club. Available online. URL: http://aalbc.com/reviews/kasi_lemmons.htm. Downloaded March 6, 2009.

"Kasi Lemmons." Internet Movie Database. Available online. URL: http://www.imdb.com/name/nm05014351. Downloaded March 6, 2009.

"The Ready Return of a True Believer." *New York Times* (July 8, 2007): A & R, p. 14.

Further Viewing

The Caveman's Valentine. Universal Home Video, VHS/DVD, 2001.

Eve's Bayou (1997). Lionsgate Home Entertainment, DVD, 2003.

Talk to Me (2007). Universal Home Video, DVD and HD DVD, 2007.

Lewis, E. B.

(Earl Bradley Lewis)
(1956–   ) *illustrator, graphic designer, painter, educator*

A children's book illustrator for more than 15 years, E. B. Lewis has quickly established himself as a leader in the field with his soft, beguiling watercolors.

He was born in Philadelphia, Pennsylvania, on December 16, 1956. His father, formerly a boxer, was an art handler at the Philadelphia Museum of Art, and two of his uncles are professional artists. As a child, Lewis attended the Saturday morning Temple University School Art League run by one of his uncles. He later took formal art classes with Philadelphia painter Clarence Wood.

In 1975, Lewis enrolled in Temple's Tyler School of Art, majoring in graphic design, illustration, and art education. After graduating in 1979, he taught for a while, supplementing his income by freelancing as a graphic designer. Watercolor became his favorite medium, and in 1986 a Philadelphia gallery exhibited his watercolor paintings. The show was critically acclaimed and led to another exhibit two years later at Philadelphia's Rosenfeld Gallery.

Lewis's first two illustrated books for children, *Fire on the Mountain,* a retelling of an Ethiopian folktale, and *Big Boy,* about a boy growing up in Tanzania, East Africa, were published in 1994. According to *Booklist,* Lewis's use of color in *Fire on the Mountain* "achieve[s] intriguing contrast and articulates characters' faces with power and expression."

His bright, impressionistic watercolors have proved particularly enriching in stories set in the past, such as *The Times They Used to Be* (2002) and the Coretta Scott King Book Award–winning *The Bat Boy and His Violin* (1998), a story of a father-son relationship set against the Negro baseball league of the late 1940s. Another Coretta Scott King Award went to *My Rows and Piles of Coins* (1999), written by Tanzanian-born writer Tololwa M. Mollel, who earlier collaborated with Lewis on *Big Boy.*

Other recent works include *This Little Light of Mine* (2005), Lewis's visual interpretation of the famous Negro spiritual and *The Negro Speaks of Rivers* (2009), in which he illustrates the famous poem by black writer Langston Hughes.

Lewis teaches illustration at the University of the Arts in Philadelphia. He was a Distinguished Scholar in 2001–02 at Albany State University in Albany, Georgia. In November 2002, his newest watercolor paintings were exhibited at the Coleman Fine Art Galley in Charleston, South Carolina. Lewis is a member of the Society of Illustrators in New York City.

"I like the strong human interest stories," Lewis has written. "The kind that evoke emotion . . . stories that touch the heart."

Further Reading

Curtis, Gavin, and E. B. Lewis, illustrator. *The Bat Boy and His Violin.* New York: Aladdin Paperback, 2001.

Hughes, Langston, and E. B. Lewis, illustrator. *The Negro Speaks of Rivers.* New York: Hyperion, 2009.

Official Web site of E. B. Lewis. Available online. URL: http://www.eblewis.com/. Downloaded March 6, 2009.

Public Domain, and E. B. Lewis, illustrator. *The Little Light of Mine.* New York: Simon & Schuster, 2005.

Rockman, Connie C., ed. *The Eighth Book of Junior Authors and Illustrators.* New York: H. W. Wilson, 2000, pp. 317–319.

Lewis, Edmonia

(Mary Edmonia Wildfire Lewis)
(ca. 1843–ca. 1911) *sculptor*

The first African-American sculptor to achieve national and international fame, Edmonia Lewis helped revive the neoclassical style in stirring works that drew on both her African and Native American heritage.

The date and place of her birth is in question: she was probably born Wildfire Lewis between 1843 and 1846 either in Greenhigh, Ohio, or around Albany, New York, where her parents moved. Her father was a freed black and a servant. Her mother was a full-blooded Chippewa Indian. Both parents died when she was still a child, and she was raised for a time by her mother's tribe. Lewis supported herself by making and selling moccasins and baskets in upstate New York.

Lewis's brother, Sunrise, went to California to mine gold and struck it rich. He paid for her education in Albany schools and then Oberlin College, in Oberlin, Ohio. Although it was one of the first American colleges to admit blacks, Oberlin was not a bastion of liberalism. Lewis, who took the first name of Edmonia, suddenly found herself accused of attempting to poison her white roommates. She was beaten by the local townspeople,

arrested, and put on trial. She was finally released on insufficient evidence, but she remained a marked woman. The following year, she was again arrested, this time for allegedly stealing school supplies. While she was acquitted a second time, she was not allowed to graduate.

Two things Lewis took away from her years at Oberlin were a classical education and a burning desire to become an artist. She moved to Boston, Massachusetts, a center of the movement to end slavery, abolitionism. She opened a studio in a building where she shared space with black painter EDWARD MITCHELL BANNISTER and other artists. She was introduced to leading abolitionist and newspaper editor William Lloyd Garrison, who admired her determination and introduced her to well-known sculptor Edmund Brackett. Brackett gave her works to copy and provided her with her only professional training.

Lewis began to create her own original sculptures, including a medallion of abolitionist John Brown and busts of such abolitionists as Garrison and Charles Sumner. The work that made her reputation, however, was a bust of Colonel Robert Gould Shaw, the courageous white leader of the all-black Massachusetts 54th regiment in the Civil War. She made and sold one hundred plaster copies of Shaw's bust and used the money to travel to Europe in 1865. She settled in Rome, Italy, and opened a studio. A member of a small colony of American artists, some of them women, Lewis attracted attention both with her powerful sculptures and her colorful, masculine dress.

Lewis worked in a neoclassical style, the same anatomically realistic style pioneered by the ancient Greeks and Romans. Like them, she depicted the human figure heroically and dramatically. Lewis chiseled directly out of marble, without benefit of a model to work from.

Proud of her Native American background, Lewis made a trilogy of works based on the legendary warrior Hiawatha, the hero of Henry Wadsworth Longfellow's famous poem. It consisted of *Hiawatha, The Marriage of Hiawatha,* and *The*

Departure of Hiawatha. Another Indian-inspired work was *The Arrow Maker,* which depicted an Indian father teaching his daughter the craft of making arrows.

One of Lewis's most powerful works was *Forever Free* (1867). It depicted an African-American couple who had just received the news that slavery had ended. This work was exhibited in Chicago and then Rome and currently is on display at Harvard University in Cambridge, Massachusetts. Perhaps Lewis's most ambitious work was the two-ton *Death of Cleopatra* (1876), depicting the final moments of the ancient Egyptian queen. This great work was rediscovered in 1972 at a race-track outside of Chicago and was restored by the National Museum of American Art in Washington, D.C.

After many years in Europe, Lewis returned to the United States. She became the only African-American artist to have her work displayed at the Centennial Exposition in Philadelphia, Pennsylvania. Her last major commission was for a Baltimore church in 1883. After that, the neoclassical style she championed fell out of vogue, and her career quickly faded. She disappeared from view, and little is known of her last years. Even the year of her death is uncertain. Some art historians believe she was alive as late as 1911, because she was seen that year living in Italy.

While Lewis's last years are a mystery, enough of her sculptures remain to testify to her genius, her passion for justice, and her pride in her dual heritage. Her celebrated career provided a model for every female African-American artist who followed in her footsteps.

Further Reading

Bolden, Tonya. *Wake Up Our Souls: A Celebration of Black American Artists.* New York: Abrams Books for Young Readers, 2004, pp. 12–19.

Lewis, Jane Johnson. "Edmonia Lewis." About.com: Women's History. Available online. URL: http://womenshistory.about.com/od/edmonialewis/p/edmonia_lewis.htm. Downloaded March 6, 2009.

Lewis, Samella. *African American Art and Artists.* Berkeley: University of California Press, 2003, pp. 40–43.

Webb, Aliske. *Edmonia Lewis—The Sculptor They Called "Wildfire."* CD-ROM. Bookmice.com Inc., 2000.

Wolfe, Rinna Evelyn. *Edmonia Lewis: Wildfire in Marble.* Berkeley, Calif.: Muse Wood Press, 2001.

Lewis, Norman
(Norman Wilfred Lewis)
(1909–1979) *painter, printmaker, educator*

A social realist who later forsook figurative art for the purer aesthetics of abstract painting, Norman Lewis was also one of the founders of an influential black artists' group, Spiral.

He was born Norman Wilfred Lewis on July 23, 1909, in New York City. His parents were from the Caribbean Islands and as a youth he studied at the Harlem Art Center under the direction of sculptor AUGUSTA SAVAGE. Her influence can be seen in the sculptural look of some of his early paintings. In the early 1930s, Lewis attended New York's Columbia University. He became a member of the Artists Union in the 1930s and helped found the art center at Bennett College in Greensboro, North Carolina.

Some of Lewis's first paintings were of black urban life, such as *Washerwoman* (1936) and *Madonna* (1939). After World War II (1939–45), Lewis's work became steadily more abstract and nonfigurative, as in such paintings as *Untitled 5* (1945), *Fantasy* (1946), and *Harlem Turns White* (1955). He became associated with the Studio 35 artist group that included leading abstract expressionists Jackson Pollock and Robert Motherwell. Beginning in 1949 he had no fewer than seven solo exhibitions at the prestigious Marion Willard Gallery in New York.

Breaking with a long tradition of socially driven black art, Lewis spoke out boldly in favor of aesthetic ideas over political and social ones in art. In 1963,

Photographer Anthony Barboza captures painter Norman Lewis's love of abstract forms in this intriguing portrait. *(Anthony Barboza)*

he founded Spiral with fellow black artist ROMARE BEARDEN and 13 others. Although he eschewed realism, Lewis never abandoned the emotions and feelings that fueled his social consciousness in his earlier works, and he was fully committed to the Civil Rights movement. For example, *Processional* (1965), one of his finest abstract paintings, is suggestive of marching demonstrators.

Lewis was elected a member of the American Academy of Arts and Letters in 1970 and received a Guggenheim Memorial Foundation Fellowship in 1975. He later taught art at Columbia University in New York City. Norman Lewis died on August 27, 1979.

"A painting should always be doing something when it is being looked at," he once said, "but something of itself, not words or musical notes."

Further Reading

Craven, David, Ann Eden Gibson, Lowery S. Sims, and Jorge D. Vineciano. *Norman Lewis: Black Paintings, 1946–1977.* New York: Studio Museum in Harlem, 1998.
Gibson, Ann. "Recanting the Canon: Norman Lewis and Jackson Pollack." *Artforum,* March 1992.
"Norman Lewis." Answers.com. Available online. URL: http://www.answers.com./topic/norman-lewis. Downloaded March 6, 2009.
Riggs, Thomas, ed. *St. James Guide to Black Artists.* Detroit, Mich.: St. James Press, 1997, pp. 324–326.

Lewis, Samella
(Samella Sanders Lewis)
(1924–   ) *art historian, writer, educator, arts administrator, museum curator, painter, documentary filmmaker*

A leading contemporary African-American art historian, Samella Lewis has promoted black art and artists in her writing, films, and as an arts administrator and curator. She has also found time to produce her own art in a wide variety of forms and genres.

She was born Samella Sanders on February 27, 1924, in New Orleans, Louisiana. She painted her first portraits while still in high school. Her *Portrait of Warren Kenner* (1940), painted when she was only 16, shows a mastery of realism remarkable for her age. She graduated with honors and enrolled at Dillard University in New Orleans on a scholarship in 1941. She later switched to the Hampton Institute in Virginia from which she received her Bachelor of Science degree in art in 1945. The following year she returned to Hampton as an art instructor.

She left soon to attend Ohio State University in Columbus, Ohio, where she earned her Master of Arts degree in 1948 and a doctoral degree in 1951. Sanders married Paul Gad Lewis in 1948, and the couple moved to Los Angeles, California, in the early 1950s, where he taught computer programming. They have two children.

Lewis returned to teaching in 1953 when she was appointed to head the art department at Florida Agricultural and Mechanical (A & M) University. The art department was in poor shape when she arrived, and she worked tirelessly to build it up. At one point, she told A & M's president that she would paint his portrait in return for better funding for her department.

The Lewises were also active in the growing Civil Rights movement. To intimidate them, members of the Ku Klux Klan once shot out the rear windows of their house. Tired of the racism facing them in the South, the family moved north to Plattsburgh, New York, where Lewis taught art history and humanities at the local campus of the State University of New York. She remained there for 10 years and helped establish a local chapter of the National Association for the Advancement of Colored People.

In 1966, Lewis took on a second teaching assignment as associate professor at California State University at Long Beach. The same year she made her first documentary film, *The Black Artists* (1966), a historical survey of African-American art. In the next few years she made documentaries about several black artists, including her friend and colleague Bernie Casey and sculptor RICHMOND BARTHÉ.

Lewis was hired as coordinator of education at the L.A. County Museum of Art in 1968. She was amazed to find black and African art gathering dust in the museum's basement. Administrators ignored her suggestions to display this art in the museum. On the defensive, she hired black art teachers to conduct workshops for black students. The museum did not like her activism and attempted to discredit her in public. The scheme backfired, and the museum ended up apologizing to her.

Discouraged by her treatment at the museum, Lewis left to establish the Contemporary Crafts Gallery in an old building in Los Angeles with Bernie Casey. It remained a leading showcase for the work of African-American artists through the 1970s. In 1976, Lewis founded the Museum of African American Art in L.A., where she remained as senior curator until 1986. Also in 1976, she became editor-in-chief of the *International Review of African American Art.* Two years later she published *Art: African American,* which quickly became the standard college textbook on the subject. A revised and expanded edition entitled *African American Arts and Artists* was published in 2003.

Amid all these academic activities, Lewis found time to create her own art. In the late 1940s and 1950s, she produced genre paintings and portraits in watercolors, charcoal, and wax crayon. More recently, she has explored and created computer art, lithographs, mixed-media works, and serigraphs, prints made by a silkscreen process.

Samella Lewis taught at Scripps College in California from 1970 to 1984, where she was director of humanities and is currently professor emerita of art history there. She received a Doctor of Humane Letters degree from her alma mater, Hampton Institute, in 1990.

Further Reading

Lewis, Samella. *African American Art and Artists.* Berkeley: University of California Press, 2003.

———. *African American Art for Young People.* Los Angeles: Unity Works, 1991.

Riggs, Thomas, ed. *St. James Guide to Black Artists.* Detroit, Mich.: St. James Press, 1997, pp. 326–328.

"Samella Lewis." Answers.com. Available online. URL: www.answers.com/topic/samella-lewis. Downloaded March 6, 2009.

Loyd, Overton
*(1954–   ) illustrator, stage designer,
graphic designer, animator, painter*

An illustrator whose work ranges from record
album covers to television caricatures, Overton
Loyd is representative of a new breed of pop artist
who is equally at home with a pen, paintbrush,
and computer.

He was born on April 20, 1954, in Detroit,
Michigan. As a teenager, he got his start as an
artist drawing caricature portraits at state fairs.
Loyd was working as a magazine illustrator when
he went to work for George Clinton, leader of
Parliament/Funkadelic, a groundbreaking rhythm
and blues band. He not only designed and illustrated album covers and posters for the group
but also produced their multimedia shows and
designed their outrageous costumes.

Through this work he moved into animation
and the making of music videos in the 1980s.
His work on the music video *Atomic Dog* won
Billboard's Best Use of Computer Graphics
Award.

Loyd's love of caricature led him to work as
a featured caricaturist on the television game
show *Win, Lose or Draw* (1987–90). He continues to work in the music field, designing album
covers and other graphic materials for such record
companies as Capitol, Disney, Motown, and Rhino
Records. He also paints fine art in a unique style
he calls "urban expressionism." In 2006 and 2007,
Loyd had several exhibits of his artwork at the
Crewest Gallery in Los Angeles where he lives.

"My intention is to use art to transcend cultural barriers—generating a breakthrough in
communication, transforming the norm," Loyd
has said of his work.

Further Reading
The Official Overton Loyd Web site. Overvision.com.
    Available online. URL: http://www.overtonloyd.
    com. Downloaded March 6, 2009.
"Overton Loyd's Free Artist Portfolio." Available
    online. URL: http://www.absolutearts.com/
    portfolios/o/oloyd. Downloaded March 27, 2009.
Overvision. Available online. URL: http://www.
    overvision.com/. Downloaded March 6, 2009.

M

Marshall, Kerry James

(1955–) *painter, installation artist, sculptor, educator, graphic designer, printmaker, photographer*

A storyteller and artist who draws on the history of world art in his vivid paintings, Kerry James Marshall is one of the more successful African-American artists of his generation.

He was born on October 17, 1955, in Birmingham, Alabama, and moved to Los Angeles, California, with his family at age eight. As a young boy, he copied pictures from art history books that he found at the local library and copied his favorite superheroes from comic books. Both would have a profound influence on his mature work. Marshall attended the Otis Art Institute in Los Angeles, and earned a Bachelor of Fine Arts degree in 1978.

Like fellow artist JACOB LAWRENCE, Marshall tells stories in his stylized, narrative paintings, always depicting his black characters as black as possible to reflect the racism in American society. Much of his work resembles folk art raised to a new level of artistic sensibility. His social consciousness comes through clearly in such works as *Souvenir*, a series of sculptures and paintings celebrating the 1960s Civil Rights movement.

In *RYTHM MASTR*, perhaps his best-known work, Marshall recalls the comic strips of his youth in 20 panels of newspaper comic strips blocked against the glass window of a museum's display cases. The audacious work recalls the old newspapers used by inner-city dwellers as curtains to block prying eyes from seeing in. In Marshall's feverish narrative, age-old African sculptures are brought to life to battle a contemporary enemy in cyberspace. Marshall has been production designer on several films including JULIE DASH's *Daughters of the Dust* (1991).

He received a National Endowment for the Arts Visual Artists Fellowship in 1991 and an American Academy of Arts and Letters Award in 1996. Marshall received an honorary doctorate from his alma mater, the Otis Art Institute, in 1999. Marshall had been an assistant professor of art at the University of Illinois' School of Art and Design in Chicago, from 1993 to recently.

His work has been featured in group shows at the School of the Art Institute of Chicago (1995) and the Whitney Museum of American Art in New York City (1997). His 1994 traveling solo show, *Telling Stories, Selected Paintings,* was organized by the Cleveland Center for Contemporary Art in Ohio.

His show *Kerry James Marshall: One True Thing, Meditations on Black Aesthetics* (2004), which originated at the Miami Art Museum in Florida, was his first major solo exhibition in five years. It included painting, sculpture, video, and photography. Two murals, *Visible Means of Support,* that Marshall created with a group of local muralists, were unveiled in February 2009 at the San Francisco Museum of Modern Art. The murals depict the estates of George Washington and Thomas Jefferson, slyly showing the slaves who supported their plantations hidden among the bushes and trees. "The coloring book stuff," Marshall said referring to the simplistic style, "seduces people to become engaged and has them acknowledge the subtext of these places at the same time." Marshall lives in Chicago with his wife, actress Cheryl Lynn Bruce.

"An artist's responsibility is to manufacture surprise," Marshall has said. "I take the challenge to do so very seriously. What is art anyway, if not the construction of synthetic phenomena from the raw material of life."

Further Reading

Dembosky, April. "Street Art Comes in from the Cold." *New York Times,* March 8, 2009, Arts & Leisure, p. 23.

Donaldson, Jeff, Nathaniel McLin, Charles Mills, Helen Molesworth, Elizabeth A.T. Smith, and Robert Fitzpatrick. *Kerry James Marshall: One True Thing: Meditations on Black Aesthetics.* Chicago: Museum of Contemporary Art, 2003.

"Kerry James Marshall." Art:21. Available online. URL: http://www.pbs.org/art21/artists/marshall/index.html. Downloaded March 6, 2009.

Marshall, Kerry James. *Kerry James Marshall.* New York: Harry N. Abrams, 2000.

Sangster, Gary, and Terrie Susltan. *Kerry James Marshall: Telling Stories: Selected Paintings.* Cleveland, Ohio: Cleveland Center for Contemporary Art, 1994.

Martin, Darnell

(1964–) *filmmaker, screenwriter, television director, actress*

The first female African-American filmmaker to direct a film produced by a major Hollywood studio, Darnell Martin has proved over the last decade to be a gifted screenwriter and director who approaches her characters with fresh insight and humanity.

She was born in the Bronx, New York, on January 7, 1964. Unlike many black filmmakers who were originally actors and actresses, Martin started behind the camera and not in front of it. A graduate of Sarah Lawrence College in Bronxville, New York, she went on to New York University's graduate film program. To pay her tuition, Martin produced a number of music videos. After finishing school, she worked as second assistant camera-person on director SPIKE LEE's breakthrough film *Do the Right Thing* (1989) and the quirky, innovative black horror film *Def by Temptation* (1990).

Martin was now ready to direct her first film, the short *Suspect* (1992). It was acclaimed at the New York Public Theater's Young Black Cinema showcase and also won the Director's Choice Award at the Edison Black Maria Film Festival.

Based on this promising work, Martin was chosen as one of eight directing fellows at the Sundance Institute's Annual Filmmaker's Laboratory in Utah. This led to her first feature, produced by Columbia Pictures, *I Like It Like That* (1994), a comedy drama she wrote herself. The film was about a Latina woman from the Bronx with marital problems who ventures into Manhattan to take a job at a recording company. Lauren Velez was memorable in the leading role, with strong support from veteran actress Rita Moreno as her mother-in-law and Griffin Dunne as her manipulative boss. While the film was not a huge hit, discerning critics praised it for its insights into American Latino life rarely seen before on the big screen.

Through the rest of the decade, Martin built up her directorial résumé working on episodes of such top-notch television dramatic series as *Homicide: Life on the Streets, ER,* and the HBO prison series *Oz.* Her second feature film, *Prison Song,* which she cowrote with the film's star, rapper Q-Tip, was released in 2000.

Turning her talents to television, Martin directed a well-received adaptation of Zora Neal Hurston's classic novel *Their Eyes Were Watching God* (2005), starring Halle Berry. *Cadillac Records* (2008), her first feature film in eight years, was about the rise of Chicago's Chess Records and rock 'n' roll in the 1950s, focusing on the early careers of bluesman Muddy Waters, singer Etta James, and rock pioneer Chuck Berry. Amazon. com called the film "a worthy entry in the niche genre of movies about rock and roll roots."

"I have a very strong respect for the characters," Martin has said about her approach to filmmaking. "It starts with the writing. And in the directing the only people that I ever consider as my collaborators are the actors. I think character is so important because we're dealing with humanity and we're dealing with relationships, which to me is the most cathartic and important thing about fiction."

Further Reading

"Darnell Martin." Available online. URL: http://www. answers.com/topic/darnell-martin. Downloaded March 6, 2009.

"Darnell Martin," The Internet Movie Database. Available online. URL: http://www.imdb.com/ name/nm0552140/. Downloaded March 6, 2009.

Seymour, Gene. "Black Directors Look Beyond Their Nude." *New York Times* (January 11, 2009), Arts and Leisure, pp. 11–15.

Further Viewing

Cadillac Records (2008). Sony, DVD, 2009.
I Like It Like That (1994). SONY, DVD, 2004.

Mayhew, Richard
(1924–) *painter, educator*

A modern master of the neglected genre of landscape painting, Richard Mayhew's soft, impressionistic, often abstract depictions of nature seem to come from a world that is universal and timeless.

He was born in Amityville, New York, on Long Island, on April 3, 1924. His father, Alvin Mayhew, was a housepainter of Native American, African American, and Portuguese ancestry. His mother, Lillian Goldman, was part Cherokee Indian and part African American. When Mayhew was in his teens, the family briefly moved to New York City and then returned to Amityville.

Mayhew was drafted into the Marines during World War II (1939–45). He did not like the military, and on his discharge in 1945 he became an illustrator of medical texts. His other main interest was music, and he sang professionally with jazz bands into the early 1950s. About that time Mayhew attended the Brooklyn Museum Art School in Brooklyn, New York. His early paintings were still lifes and landscapes, the genre he would later make his life's work. In 1955 the Brooklyn Museum mounted his first solo exhibition.

Among Mayhew's teachers were abstract artists Reuben Tom and Hans Hofmann, who would strongly influence his work. While landscapes were considered old-fashioned in the 1950s, Mayhew's approach to the form was hardly traditional. He did not paint outdoors but indoors, relying on his memory, not on immediate observations or even photographs to re-create what he had seen in nature. While humans appear in his earlier paintings, he gradually eliminated them entirely. "Nature is the star of these paintings," Jacqueline Francis has observed, "and the dynamism of nature parallels the artist's fluid manner of painting."

Mayhew favors trees, meadows, bushes, and ponds over mountains and rivers in his landscapes. During the 1970s his work was often abstract in concept, but by the 1980s it became more realistic, while never losing its aura of a hazy, unspecific world not quite real. "I felt that by retaining elements of nature, such as bushes, trees, hills, ponds and grasses, you held onto this humanistic response," he has said. "So at the height of the abstract period, my paintings stayed with the landscape."

Mayhew joined the black artists group Spiral in 1963. As a member, he served as an important link between the older circle of black artists and the younger, post–World War II generation. Realizing that his art was less socially related to black life than that of other artists, he decided to get involved in the black community in other ways. Living in a multiracial community in the Ramapo Mountains in New Jersey, Mayhew helped establish a community arts center where creative people could come and share their work and ideas.

He taught art at the Brooklyn Museum Art School from 1963 to 1968. In 1977 he joined the faculty of Pennsylvania State University in University Park and remained there until his retirement in 1991. He now lives and works in Santa Cruz, California. Mayhew's paintings were part of the group show *Forms of Abstraction* (2007) at the G. R. N'Namdi Gallery in New York City. His recent solo show *Transcendental Landscapes* (2009) was held at the Avram Gallery, at Stony Brook Southampton, New York.

Richard Mayhew received the National Academy of Design Merit Award in 1977 and the Grumbacher Gold Medal in 1983.

Further Reading

Bearden, Romare, and Harry Henderson. *A History of African-American Artists: From 1792 to the Present.* New York: Pantheon Books, 1993, pp. 470–477.

LeFalle-Collins, Lizzetta. "The Spiritual Realm of Richard Mayhew—the Life and Works of Painter Richard Mayhew." BNET Business Network. Available online. URL: http://findarticles.com/p/articles/mi_m1546/is_2_15/ai_62024105. Downloaded March 6, 2009.

Schmidt-Campbell, Mary. *Richard Mayhew: An American Abstractionist.* New York: The Studio Museum in Harlem, 1978.

Welsh, Clarissa J. "Alchemist." *Artweek,* September 23, 1993, pp. 18–19.

Further Viewing

Richard Mayhew: Spiritual Landscapes. L & S Video, VHS, 2000.

McCullough, Geraldine
(Geraldine Hamilton McCullough)
(1922–2008) *sculptor, painter, educator*

One of the few women sculptors to tackle the challenge of welded sculpture, Geraldine McCullough burst onto the art scene in 1964, winning a major art competition as an almost complete unknown.

She was born Geraldine Hamilton McCullough on December 1, 1922, in Kingston, Arkansas. Her family moved to the Chicago area when she was three. She graduated from the School of the Art Institute of Chicago in 1948 with a master's degree in art education. McCullough began her career as a painter, winning two scholarships in a figurative painting contest at school.

After graduating, she got a position as an art teacher at Wendell Phillips High School in the Bronzeville section of Chicago and later became a professor of art at Rosary College in River Forest, Illinois. During this time, she was befriended by sculptor RICHARD H. HUNT, who urged her to try welded sculpture, his specialty. Taking his advice, McCullough got her husband, Lester McCullough, to teach her the demanding skill of welding. Soon this petite black woman was working with massive pieces of metal, welding one into the other. She displayed her new work for the first time at the Century of Negro Progress Exposition in Chicago in 1963.

The following year, McCullough entered, without an invitation, the 159th annual exhibition of the distinguished Pennsylvania Academy of Fine Arts. Her sculpture, the *Phoenix*, an impressive steel and copper abstract work weighing 250 pounds, won the George D. Widener Memorial Gold Medal for "most meritorious work" in sculpture. The 42-year-old McCullough became a public celebrity. She appeared in such magazines as *Ebony* and was seen on several national television programs, including the game show *To Tell the Truth*. She was even invited in 1966 to tour the Soviet Union as a guest artist, traveling to Moscow and Leningrad (St. Petersburg). Her first one-person show of her sculptures opened at the Ontario Gallery in 1967. The same year she was named chairperson of the art department at Rosary College (now Dominican University) in River Forest, Illinois. She retired from that position in 1989.

Her work continued to win praise and prizes. She was included in the 1996–97 exhibition *Three Generations of African-American Women Sculptors: A Study in Paradox* at New York's Equitable Gallery and *SANKOFA: Celebrating 25 Years of Black Dimensions in Art, Inc.* (2000) at the Albany, New York, International Airport Gallery. McCullough died on December 15, 2008, at age 86.

Further Reading

"Geraldine McCullough." Womanmade Gallery. Available online. URL: http://www.womanmade.org/biography.html?/. Downloaded March 29, 2009.

Rubinstein, Charlotte Streifer. *American Women Sculptors: A History of Women Working in Three Dimensions*. Boston: G. K. Hall, 1990.

Watson-Jones, Virginia. *Contemporary American Women Sculptors*. Phoenix, Ariz.: Oryx, 1986.

McGruder, Aaron
(1974–) *cartoonist*

The most challenging and controversial of contemporary black cartoonists, Aaron McGruder gleefully satirizes both black and white culture in his irreverent comic strip and subsequent animated television series *The Boondocks*.

He was born in May 29, 1974 in Chicago, Illinois, and later moved with his family to Columbia, Maryland. While attending the University of Maryland in College Park, McGruder got the idea for a black comic strip. "I was a big fan of *Bloom County* and *Calvin and Hobbes*," he recalled, "and I decided to try something like that—a social satire targeting racial politics and popular culture."

McGruder first displayed his comic, *The Boondocks,* on an Internet Web site called The Hitlist Online in February 1996. He met with enough encouragement from readers to move it to *The Diamondback,* the independent student newspaper at the University of Maryland, that December. The strip gained national attention and was picked up by *The Source,* an urban music

Aaron McGruder's controversial comic strip *Boondocks* debuted in 1999, when the artist was only 25 years old. *(AP Photo/Gail Burton)*

magazine. After graduating with a degree in African-American studies, McGruder was offered a syndicated deal for his comic strip by Universal Press Syndicate. It debuted in 1999 in 250 newspapers nationwide, one of the most impressive debuts of any syndicated strip.

The Boondocks is the story of Huey and Riley Freeman, two precocious black kids who move from their inner-city home on Chicago's South Side to live with their Grandpa in the middle-class, predominantly white suburb of Woodcrest. The strip deals with the adjustments the boys make to this strange, new environment.

Huey, the older brother, is a committed socialist, while Riley is just as committed to the capitalist system and its many material temptations. Among the friends they make in their neighborhood are the cute but confused Jazmine DuBois; the Japanese boy Hiro Otomo, who knows turntable bushido; and Caesar, a young rapper from Brooklyn. Jazmine's parents are the interracial couple Tom and Sarah DuBois. He is a buppie ("black upwardly mobile professional") and she is a white activist working for the NAACP.

The Freeman brothers and their friends bear little resemblance to the children in most other comic strips. They are street-smart, enjoy terrorizing their neighbors with ghetto talk, and question everything from the white establishment to contemporary black culture.

"Pop culture needs to be more creative," McGruder has said. "I've been [especially] critical of contemporary black music. I'd like to see more variety. Not everyone has to sound like Jay-Z or DMX."

One of the other targets of this merciless satirist is Robert Johnson, chief executive officer of Black Entertainment Television. Johnson, whom McGruder sees as a money mogul with little concern for the black community, has countered that the cartoonist is "irresponsible and simpleminded."

After several false starts, McGruder finally created an animated series based on his strip that debuted on Cartoon Network's spin-off network Adult Swim on November 6, 2005. The series was initially produced by REGINALD HUDLIN, who left three months later when he was hired by BET.

In March 2006, McGruder suspended *The Boondocks* comic strip to focus his energies on the successful television show. As of August 2010, he has not revived the strip. The series won a Peabody Award in 2007 for the episode "Return of the King," in which a disillusioned Martin Luther King, Jr., turns out to be still alive. McGruder collaborated with Hudlin and illustrator Kyle Baker on the graphic novel *Birth of a Nation* (2004).

Further Reading

"Aaron McGruder." Available online. URL: http://www.answers.com/topic/aaron-mcgruder. Downloaded March 8, 2009.

Duncan, Collum Danny. "Down with the Boondocks: Aaron McGruder rages against the machine." *Sojourners Magazine*, April 1, 2005, pp. 40–43.

McGruder, Aaron. *All the Rage: the Boondocks Past and Present*. New York: Three Rivers Press, 2007.

McGruder, Aaron, Reginald Huldin, and Kyle Baker. *Birth of a Nation: A Comic Novel*. New York: Three Rivers Press, 2005.

The Boondocks official Web site. Available online. URL: http://www.boondockstv.com Downloaded March 8, 2009.

Further Viewing

The Boondocks: The Complete First Season (2005). Sony, DVD box set, 2006.

Micheaux, Oscar

(Oscar Devereaux Micheaux, "The Father of Independent Black Filmmakers")
(1884–1951) *filmmaker, film producer, screenwriter, novelist*

One of the first and most prolific of independent black filmmakers, Oscar Micheaux dealt in his more than 30 films with the real problems and experiences of African Americans, blazing a trail for the black directors who came after him.

He was born Oscar Devereaux Micheaux on January 2, 1884, on a farm near Murphysboro, Illinois, the fifth of 13 children. Little is known about his family and childhood, but at the age of 17 he traveled to Chicago, where he earned a living as a shoeshine boy and a Pullman porter on the railroad. In 1904 Micheaux went west and with his savings bought a homestead in South Dakota. Although he was the only black homesteader in the region, he experienced little if any racism at the hands of his white neighbors. He worked hard and in five years he expanded his spread to 500 acres of plowed land.

The winters on the plains were cold and the nights long, and Micheaux found reading one of his favorite pleasures. He decided that he could write a novel as good as any he had read and began a novel based on his experiences as a black homesteader. The finished book, *The Conquest: The Story of a Negro Pioneer,* was turned down by every publisher he sent it to. Micheaux, who was nothing if not resourceful, published the book himself in 1913 with his meager savings. *The Conquest,* which dealt with an interracial romance based on Micheaux's own experiences, was not a very good novel, but his genius lay in his ability to market his material.

He loaded copies of his novel into the back of his car and drove across the countryside, selling his book door-to-door to neighboring farmers and local storeowners. Unlike other writers, Micheaux was one of their own and wrote about things that they themselves had experienced. While his writing career was beginning to flourish, his farm did not. He blamed the loss of the homestead on his father-in-law's financial incompetence. In 1915 he moved with his wife to Sioux City, Iowa, where he established the Western Book and Supply Company, which published his second novel, *The Homesteader,* with a plot similar to his first book.

NOBLE JOHNSON and his brother George had started the independent Lincoln Motion Picture Company with offices in Lincoln, Nebraska, and Los Angeles, California. The Johnsons read *The Homesteader* and approached Micheaux about adapting it to film. Micheaux agreed, but only on the condition that he would be allowed to direct the film himself. The Johnsons believed, rightly, that Micheaux knew nothing about filmmaking, and they turned him and his book down. Undaunted, Micheaux decided not only to direct his own film of the book but produce it as well.

He went back to the small farmers who had bought his book and offered them a chance to become stockholders in his Micheaux Film and Book Company at $75 to $100 a share. He soon had enough money to make a feature-length film of *The Homesteader* (1919), which he marketed the same way he sold his books. He drove from city to city with a print of the film and showed it to the owners of black audience movie houses. He not only told the owners about his film but the story of the next film he planned to make and the actors who would appear in it. Some theater owners were willing to pay in advance for exclusive rights to show the next film in their theaters.

From 1919 to 1948, Micheaux produced nearly 30 films, many of which have not survived. Because he shot most of his films on budgets of no more than $15,000, they were technically poor and featured many amateurish actors. To further confound the issue, Micheaux never reshot a scene. Anxious to get the film finished and distributed, he left poor lighting, flubbed lines, and similar errors in his finished product that other filmmakers would have edited out.

For all these flaws, Micheaux remains a giant in the independent black cinema. Other black filmmakers were content to copy popular genre films, such as westerns, gangster films, and musicals, using black actors. Micheaux, on the other hand, made films about subjects he felt black audiences would care about. His movies are about such serious topics as racial prejudice among blacks, passing the color line, white racism, and the role of religion in black life.

Among his most notable silent films were *Within Our Gates* (1920), which dealt in part with the lynching of a black man, and *Body and Soul* (1925), which starred black actor Paul Robeson in his first American film role, as a hypocritical black preacher with a criminal past.

In 1928, as silent films were giving way to sound films, Micheaux went bankrupt. He continued, however, to produce films, directing and producing the first black-made film of the sound era, *The Exile* (1931). For several years, Micheaux was the only black independent filmmaker to work in the sound era.

Despite his success, Micheaux was under constant attack from critics in the black community who complained about his depictions of black people drinking and gambling. They also criticized him for focusing on the black middle class in most of his films and not poor blacks. Yet within their limitations, Micheaux's films shed remarkable insight on the problems faced by black men, and especially black women, in the United States.

By the 1940s, Micheaux's output slowed down and he returned to writing novels, still drawing on his experiences as a homesteader. His final film, the three-hour-long *The Betrayal*, was a commercial flop on its release in 1948. A few years later, the independent black cinema disappeared, as movie houses became more integrated along with the rest of America. Oscar Micheaux died on March 25, 1951, in Charlotte, North Carolina, an obscure and forgotten figure.

In the 1970s, this pioneer filmmaker was rediscovered through a revival of his films and a documentary about his career. In 1987 a star was dedicated to "The Father of Independent Black Filmmakers" on Hollywood's Avenue of the Stars. A comprehensive retrospective of Michaeux's films and that of pioneering black directors SPENCER WILLIAMS and WILLIAM ALEXANDER was held in February 2009 by the Film Society of Lincoln Center in New York City. The U.S. Postal Service issued a stamp honoring Michaeaux in June 2010 as part of its Black Heritage Series.

Further Reading

Bowser, Pearl, Jane Gaines, and Charles Musser, eds. *Oscar Micheaux and His Circle: African-American Filmmaking and Race Cinema of the Silent Era.* Bloomington: Indiana University Press, 2001.

Green, J. Ronald. *With a Crooked Stick: The Films of Oscar Micheaux.* Bloomington: Indiana University Press, 2004.

Mcgilligan, Patrick. *Oscar Micheaux: The Great and Only: The Life of America's First Black Filmmaker,* New York: Harper Perennial, 2008.

Young, Earl James, Jr., and Dr. Beverly J. Robinson, eds. *The Life and Work of Oscar Micheaux: Pioneer Black Author and Filmmaker.* San Francisco, Calif.: Khafra K Omrazeti KMT Publications, 2003.

Further Viewing

Harlem Double Feature: Girl in Room 20 (1942)/*God's Step Children* (1938). Alpha Home Entertainment, DVD, 2006.

Veiled Aristrocrats (1932). Grapevine Video, DVD, 2007.

Within Our Gates (1919). Grapevine Video, DVD, 2007.

Morgan, Sister Gertrude
(1900–1980) *folk painter, singer, poet*

A true religious visionary, Sister Gertrude Morgan celebrated the good news of Christian salvation in her often cluttered, Scripture-filled paintings, whose childlike style disguised a surprisingly sophisticated sense of color and design.

She was born Gertrude Morgan on April 7, 1900, in Lafayette, Alabama. A member of Dr. J. B. Miller's Baptist church, Morgan claimed to have experienced a religious vision when she was 37 years old. The voice of God urged her to "go and preach, tell it to the world."

Two years later, she left her husband and moved to New Orleans, Louisiana, where she became

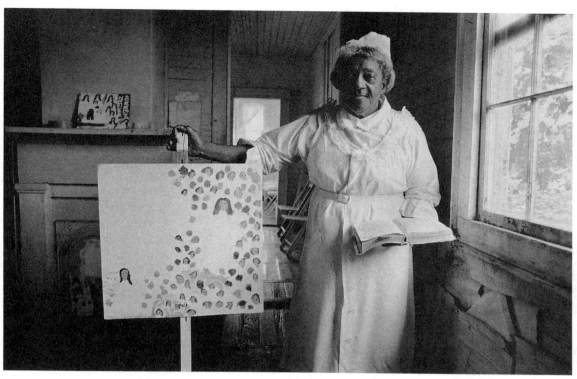

Sister Gertrude Morgan stands with one of her spirit-filled paintings in one hand and a Bible in the other. *(© Owen Murphy, Jr., 1974)*

a street preacher. She joined the Holiness and Sanctified Church, whose main form of worship was dancing and singing. Together with two other street missionaries, Mother Margaret Parker and Sister Cora Williams, Morgan raised the money from her ministry to build a chapel and a child care center in the suburb of Gentilly.

In 1956, Sister Gertrude, as she now called herself, began to paint in earnest. Her paintings were intensely religious, often including choirs of angels, biblical figures, and God and the devil. She painted and drew her works with acrylic paints, watercolors, ballpoint pens, and even wax crayons. Color tone was a major characteristic of her work. She used it to express psychological states and moods. Goodness and purity were expressed in bright primary colors, while evil

appeared in such non-primary colors as brown and violet.

As she grew older, Morgan's painting grew more apocalyptic, often focusing on scenes from the Book of Revelation in the New Testament, which deals with the Second Coming of Christ. One of her favorite chants and slogans was "Jesus Is My Airplane," which she literally pictured in several paintings with herself and Jesus flying through the air in a plane.

In 1965, the chapel and child care center was destroyed by Hurricane Betsy, and Morgan became a nurse and companion to an elderly woman. About this time she had a second vision and saw herself as God's chosen bride. After that she dressed all in white and surrounded herself with a white environment. She invited people to come to her all-white Prayer Room where she prayed, sang, and preached. Her painting became more and more obsessive. She painted everything around her in rainbow colors, from her guitar case to lampshades to even the back of a "For Sale" sign in her yard.

Her paintings were exhibited in 1972 at the Louisiana Arts and Science Center in Baton Rouge, Louisiana, and were including in the show "Louisiana Folk Paintings" at the Museum of American Folk Art in New York City the following year.

Sister Gertrude Morgan died in her sleep in the summer of 1980. The first comprehensive retrospective exhibition of her work, *Tools of Her Ministry: The Art of Sister Gertrude Morgan,* was held at the New Orleans Museum of Art from November 2004 to January 2005.

"[The] subtlety and variety of composition and technique make her among the most complex and sophisticated [of black folk] artists," wrote Jane Livingston and John Beardsley in their book *Black Folk Art in America 1930–1980.*

Further Reading

Fagaly, William A. *Sister Gertrude Morgan: Tools of Her Ministry,* New York: Rizzoli, International Publications, 2004.

Livingston, Jane, and John Beardsley. *Black Folk Art in America 1930–1980.* Jackson: University Press of Mississippi, 1989, pp. 96–103.

Perry, Regenia A. *Free Within Ourselves: African-American Artists in the Collection of the National Museum of American Art.* San Francisco: Pomegranate Communications, 1992, pp. 140–146.

"Tools of Her Ministry: The Art of Sister Gertrude Morgan." Resource Library. Available online. URL: http://www.tfaoi.com/aa/5aa/5aa94.htm. Downloaded March 30, 2009.

Further Listening

King Britt Presents: Sister Gertrude Morgan. Rope-A-Dope, CD, 2005.

Morrison, Keith
(Keith Anthony Morrison)
(1942–   ) *painter, printmaker, muralist, educator, writer, art curator, arts administrator*

A surrealist whose bizarre narrative paintings are both nightmarish and redemptive, Keith Morrison draws heavily on the folklore and superstitions of his native Jamaica.

He was born into a middle class family on May 20, 1942, in Linstead, Jamaica, in the West Indies. After graduating from high school, he immigrated to the United States. He enrolled in the School of the Art Institute of Chicago, Illinois, in 1959 and earned a Bachelor of Fine Arts degree and a Master of Fine Arts degree. After a two-year stint of teaching in public schools in Gary, Indiana, Morrison became a professor at Fisk University in Nashville, Tennessee.

His first paintings were large black-and-white abstract works. He continued to paint in an abstract style until 1975, when his work changed dramatically. He began to draw on his Caribbean and African roots in figurative paintings that had abstract designs but also recalled the folktales and voodoo religious rites of his childhood.

Zombie Jamboree (1988), one of the best-known of his works, is typical of this style. In the painting, three large, frightening-looking animals, resembling horses, are seated in a circle in front of a haunted pond, where ghosts and skeletons dance on the waters at twilight. A mummified figure hanging above them symbolizes death and resurrection. The painting draws on the legend Morrison heard in childhood about the magical moment at dusk when spirits enter the world. The unlucky human who witnesses this event is supposedly drawn into the pond waters. On an even more personal level, Morrison had a childhood friend who drowned in a pond at dusk. In this painting and many others, he struggles with the idea of death and resurrection.

Among his other best-known paintings are *Chariot* (1988) and *A Night in Tunisia* (1991), whose title and theme is taken from a famous composition by jazz musician and composer Dizzy Gillespie.

Morrison has taught at the University of Chicago; the Maryland Institute, College of Art; and the University of Michigan at Ann Arbor, among other schools. From 1988 to 1992 he taught at the University of Maryland in College Park, where he was the chairperson of the art department.

Morison was dean of academic affairs at the San Francisco Art Institute from 1993 to 1994 and dean of College of Creative Arts at San Francisco State University from 1994 to 1996. He continues to teach art at SFSU and was dean for the Tyler School of Arts at Temple University in Philadelphia until January 2008.

Morrison represented Jamaica at the 1994 Caribbean Biennial in Santo Domingo, Dominican Republic, in 1994 and also at the 2001 Venice Biennale. He is the author of numerous articles on art in newspapers and periodicals and wrote the book-length catalog *Art in Washington and Its Afro-American Presence: 1940–1970*. Morrison has curated a number of exhibits including *Metaphor/Commentaries: Contemporary Artists in Cuba* (1999) at the Fine Arts Gallery at San Francisco State.

"Comedy is a distinct part of my work," Morrison has said. "Sometimes I simply amuse myself; at other times the work is tragic-comic. In any case, I have a hard time taking the subject of my work very seriously. In my world there is a lot of misery, but people laugh bittersweet at adversity."

Further Reading

Ater, Renee. *Keith Morrison* (The David C. Driskell Series of American Art, Vol. 5). San Francisco, Calif.: Pomegranate Communications, 2005.

Driskell, David C. *Contemporary Visual Expressions: The Art of Sam Gilliam, Martha Jackson-Jarvis, Keith Morrison, William T. Williams: Inaugural Exhibit, Anacosti*. Washington, D.C.: Smithsonian Institution Press, 1987.

The Official Keith Morrison Web site. Available online. URL: http://www.keithmorrison.com. Downloaded March 8, 2009.

Perry, Regenia A. *Free Within Ourselves: African-American Artists in the Collection of the National Museum of American Art*. San Francisco: Pomegranate Communications, 1992, pp. 146–150.

Motley, Archibald J., Jr.
(1891–1981) *painter, muralist*

The first black artist to portray black social life in all its vigor and vitality, Archibald J. Motley, Jr., was one of the most celebrated figures of the Harlem Renaissance of the 1920s and 1930s.

He was born on October 7, 1891, in New Orleans, Louisiana. His father, Archibald Motley Sr., operated a general store and later became a Pullman porter on the railroad. Motley Sr. worked to organize the Pullman porter union with black labor leader A. Philip Randolph.

The family moved to St. Louis when Motley was two, then Buffalo, New York, and finally Chicago, Illinois. His family wanted him to study architecture, but Motley was determined to be an artist. He attended the School of the Art Institute of Chicago, paying for his tuition by working as a museum custodian. During summer vacation in 1917, he worked on the trains as a Pullman porter with his father. He sketched the people and places he saw crossing the country by train and made his first paintings on railroad laundry bags.

Motley graduated from the Art Institute the following year but was unable to support himself by his painting for a decade, taking jobs as a plumber and coal heaver to pay the bills. In 1924 he married Edith Granzo, who was white and had dated him secretly in high school. Their only child, Archibald J. Motley III, was born in 1933.

Motley's first painting to gain public and critical attention was *Mending Socks* (1924), a thoughtful and touching portrait of his grandmother. He considered it his finest portrait, and it won the popular prize at the Newark Museum in Newark, New Jersey, in 1927. Another painting, *Black Belt*, won the Harmon exhibition's gold medal in 1928. That same year he had his first solo exhibition at the New Galleries in New York City, where nearly every painting on display was sold. Motley was one of the first African-American artists to have a gallery show.

Motley's growing reputation earned him a Guggenheim Fellowship in 1929 that allowed him to travel to Europe. He fell in love with the nightlife of Paris, France, and created *Blues* (1929), a fascinating slice of Parisian nightlife at a jazz nightclub, where black men danced freely with French women. Only partly realistic, the painting melded the dancers' bodies with the band's instruments in intriguing abstract patterns. The work marked the beginning of Motley's fascination with black nightlife that would pervade his art for the next decade and beyond.

The artist showed blacks at play, as they were—fun-loving, laughing, sweaty, and unpretentious. Critics complained that he was creating stereotypes as damaging to black Americans as previous stereotypes created by white artists. But Motley did not see it that way. "It is my earnest desire and ambition to express the American Negro honestly and sincerely, neither to add nor detract," he said.

Motley's street scenes teemed with life and vitality. His famous *Bronzeville* series of paintings in the 1930s depicted black urban life in Chicago in such memorable canvases as *Barbecue*, *The Picnic*, and *Saturday Night*. He created murals with similar themes and historical ones for Chicago public buildings under the federally sponsored Works Progress Administration. One of his best-known murals is *U.S. Mail* (1936), which depicts a stagecoach, for a post office in Illinois.

His wife's death in 1945 plunged Motley into a deep depression. He gave up painting for eight years and worked in a studio factory designing plastic shower curtains. He found the work therapeutic and restful. In 1953, he visited his nephew Willard Motley, a best-selling novelist, in Cuernavaca, Mexico. The change of scenery invigorated the artist and he returned to work. After a brief fling with surrealism, Motley returned to his older style, which by now was viewed by many as old-fashioned and irrelevant. Other black artists in the 1960s criticized Motley's art for not reflecting the troubled times of the civil rights and Black Power era.

To prove them wrong, he began an ambitious painting in 1963 to commemorate the 100th anniversary of the Emancipation Proclamation of President Abraham Lincoln, which freed southern blacks from slavery. After 10 years of work, he felt the painting unfinished and abandoned it. An allegorical work of great power, it offered a sobering view of the 1960s, touching on the assassination of Martin Luther King, Jr.; the bombing of the Birmingham, Alabama, church that killed four black girls; and other events.

Motley's work was neglected, and many of his paintings were misplaced or lost at this time. His last years, however, saw him receive the honor due him as a pioneer artist of the 20th century. In 1980, he was one of 10 African-American artists honored at the White House by President Jimmy Carter. The visit concurred with a group show of the artists at the Corcoran Gallery of Art in Washington, D.C. Archibald J. Motley Jr. died on January 16, 1981, in Chicago.

Ten years later, his son, a curator at the Chicago Historical Society, mounted a centennial exhibit of his father's work that included more than 100 "lost" paintings that he had recovered. The exhibition toured the country and was displayed at four other major museums. It was accompanied by a string of lectures and symposia about the artist and his work that took place in New York City; Atlanta, Georgia; and Washington, D.C.

Further Reading

"Archibald Motley, Jr." Available online. URL: http://www.answers.com/topic/archibald-motley. Downloaded April 3, 2009.

Bearden, Romare, and Harry Henderson. *A History of African-American Artists: From 1792 to the Present.* New York: Pantheon Books, 1993, pp. 147–156.

Coleman, Floyd. "Down Home and Uptown: Archibald Motley, Jr., and the Evolution of African-American Art." *Legacy,* February/March 1995, pp. 18–24.

Hardy, P. Stephens, and Sheila Jackson Hardy. *Extraordinary People of the Harlem Renaissance.* New York: Children's Press, 2000, pp. 47, 208–212.

Mooney, Amy M. *Archibald J. Motley, Jr.,* (David C. Driskell Series of African American Art). San Francisco: Pomegranate Communications, 2004.

Robinson, Jontyle Theresa, and Wendy Greenhouse. *The Art of Archibald J. Motley, Jr.* Chicago: Chicago Historical Society, 1991.

Mr. Imagination

(Gregory Warmack)
(1948–   ) *folk sculptor, mixed-media artist, jewelry designer*

A master of taking found objects and turning them into intriguing folk art, Mr. Imagination started out as a street artist and, despite his subsequent fame, has kept the spirit of the street in his work.

He was born Gregory Warmack two months prematurely on March 30, 1948, in Chicago, Illinois. His family was poor and barely scraped by on Chicago's South Side. Warmack discovered his artistic abilities at a very young age.

"As a kid, I would cut up old boxes and paint on these or just use anything I could find," he has said. "By the time I was a teenager, my room was so full of art I slept under the kitchen table." Unlike other children who drew or painted, Warmack carved African masks from tree bark and created exotic jewelry from beads.

He soon took to the streets, calling himself Mr. Imagination, and supported himself by making signs and teaching art to neighborhood children. In 1978 he was shot twice in the stomach by a mugger in a botched robbery. While on the operating table, his life hanging in the balance, he had an out-of-body experience. "It was all very peaceful," he later recalled, "almost as if I was travelling through history and looking at ancient civilizations."

During his recuperation, he developed a deep interest in African art, especially the art and culture of ancient Egypt. His fascination with reincarnation, part of ancient Egyptian beliefs, grew. Using sandstone he found on the streets, one of his favorite materials, he created Egyptian sarcophagi. Another work, *Meditation,* is a sandstone temple inspired by Eastern African civilization.

Many of Mr. Imagination's works were fashioned out of more everyday objects, such as old nails and worn-out paintbrushes, which he transformed into human figures. A one-person show, *The World of Mr. Imagination,* appeared at the Carl Hammer Gallery in Chicago in 1986. "He reclaims something which is dead, and gives it new life," observed gallery owner Hammer.

More recently, the artist has become obsessed with beverage bottle caps. He has used them to cover multidimensional works and construct others. He even dressed in a denim jacket and hat covered with bottle caps and received visitors to his studio sitting on one of two bottle cap-covered thrones. Mr. Imagination created his largest commission, a bottle sculpture for the Coca-Cola Olympic Salute to Folk Art at the Atlanta Olympics, in 1992. He has created original artwork for the House of Blues clubs in Las Vegas, Nevada; Miami, Florida; and Chicago. In 2002 he moved to South Bethlehem, Pennsylvania, where he has been involved in art projects at Lehigh University. On January 20, 2008, his home was destroyed by fire, along with much of his artwork and his dog. Local residents have raised funds to help Mr. Imagination rebuild. "He has a level of intensity that a lot of people would never have," said Silagh White, director of Arts Lehigh and a leader in the relief effort. "[His] life balance was his work. Everything about his life is art."

A master of self-promotion, he has been called "the most visible self-taught artist of his generation" by art historian Regenia A. Perry.

"Imagination," says Mr. Imagination, "is something people use 24 hours a day . . . it's a universal thing."

Further Reading

Patterson, Tom. *Reclamation and Transformation—Three Self-Taught Chicago Artists—David Philpot,* *Mr. Imagination, Kevin Orth.* Evanston, Ill.: Terra Museum of American Art, 1994.

Riggs, Thomas, ed. *St. James Guide to Black Artists.* Detroit, Mich.: St. James Press, 1997, pp. 551–553.

Rozelle, Robert V., Alvia Wardlaw, and Maureen A. McKenna, eds. *Black Art, Ancestral Legacy: The African Impulse in African-American Art.* Dallas, Tex.: The Dallas Museum of Art, 1989, pp. 42–44, 166, 186, 225–227, 271.

Use Your Imagination: The Mr. Imagination Site and Weblog. Available online. URL: http://www.misterimagination.com/. Downloaded April 3, 2009.

Webster, Richard A. "Mr. Imagination." Available online. URL: http://www.outsiderfolkart.com/outsiderart/e-i/GregoryWarmackMr.ImaginationBiography.htm. Downloaded April 3, 2009.

N

Nance, Marilyn

(1953–) *photographer, mixed-media artist, storyteller, educator, curator*

A self-professed photographer-storyteller, Marilyn Nance has used her camera to capture the spiritual power of African Americans from a Baptist church service in Brooklyn, New York, to the funeral of an African Akan priest.

She was born in New York City on November 12, 1953. She earned a Bachelor of Fine Arts degree in communications graphic design from the Pratt Institute in Brooklyn, New York, in 1976.

Beginning in 1986, Nance made it her mission to record various black religious and cultural groups, capturing in their rites, festivals, and ceremonies what she calls "the dynamic relationship between American and African culture." Among her subjects are Appalachian folk musicians; black Indians in New Orleans, Louisiana; and the residents of an African-style village in South Carolina.

As an artist-in-residence at the Studio Museum in Harlem, New York, in 1993–94, Nance created ambitious art spaces or installations around her photographs, providing room for storytelling, one of her first loves. The 12-piece installation *Celebration and Mourning* even allows viewers the opportunity to create their own stories.

"Each individual photograph suggests a depth of meaning," she has said. "The strength of the work is in its collective ability to engage viewers in the synthesis of ideas."

Nance is a two-time finalist for the W. Eugene Smith Grant in Humanistic Photography and received three New York Foundation for the Arts fellowships (photography in 1989 and 2000; nonfiction literature in 1993).

In 1996, she earned a Master of Fine Arts degree in photography from the Maryland Institute College of Art in Baltimore. Three years later she earned a second master's degree in interactive telecommunications from New York University's Tisch School of the Arts and served as Curator of Photography for the Digital Schomburg Project. In this position she selected 500 illustrations and photographs of African Americans from the 19th century from the collections of the research libraries of the New York Public Library.

Nance's pictures have appeared in the *New York Times* and the *Village Voice* and such magazines as *Life* and *Essence*. Her work is part of the permanent collection of the Smithsonian Institution's National Museum of American Art and the Schomburg Center for Research in Black Culture's Preservation of the Black Religious Heritage Project. She currently serves as a multimedia technology specialist for New York City's Department of Education and is an instructor in

Photographer Marilyn Nance is seen here reviewing an African-American image in the digital collection of the Schomburg Center for Research in Black Culture, which she curated. *(© Marilyn Nance)*

the photography department at New York University's Tisch School of the Arts. Nance received a New York Foundation for the Arts Fellowship in Photography in 2000 and was included in a group show *The Black Photographer* at the Brooklyn Museum of Art in 2001. In July 2010, Nance sued the Broadway musical *Fela!* for using one of her photographs for a backdrop without her permission.

"In her work Nance discovers the survival and reclamation of African culture," Gina Murtagh has written. "Like the lyrics of a sermon or gospel song, the work is rich in metaphor, using

references to the divine to describe an earthly condition.

Further Reading

Nance Marilyn. *Religion: African-American Spiritual Expressions.* March 10–May 15, 1990. Syracuse, N.Y., 1990.

Soulsista Says . . . (Marilyn Nance's Home Page). Available online. URL: http://www.marilynnance. com/. Downloaded March 8, 2009.

Willis, Deborah. *Reflections in Black: A History of Black Photographers from 1840 to the Present.* New York: W. W. Norton, 2000, p. 174.

Ormes, Jackie
(Zelda Jackson Ormes)
(1911–1985) *cartoonist, painter*

The first African-American woman to have a nationally syndicated comic strip, Jackie Ormes created black female characters whose independence and determination in the face of racism were decades ahead of their time.

She was born Zelda Jackson on August 1, 1911, in Pittsburgh, Pennsylvania. Later, she moved to Chicago, Illinois, and at age 24 got a job as a sportswriter for the black weekly newspaper the *Pittsburgh Courier*. In 1937 she created a full-color narrative comic strip for the *Courier* entitled *Torchy Brown, From Dixie to Harlem*. Torchy Brown was an attractive black teenager growing up in poverty in the South who dreamed of being an entertainer and playing the legendary Apollo Theater in Harlem, the black section of New York City. Over the next three years, *Courier* readers avidly followed Torchy's romantic adventures as she used her beauty and intelligence to climb the ladder to show business success. She also took time out from her career to fight racism, male chauvinism, and environmental pollution, decades before it became a national issue. "I've never liked dreamy little women who can't hold their own," Ormes once said in defense of her cartoon character.

Torchy was not only the first independent black heroine in comics but predated *Brenda Starr*, her first white counterpart, by three years. Ormes made sure that while the strip had glamour and romance it also depicted some of the grim reality of black America in the 1930s. The strip was popular enough to be picked up in syndication by a dozen other black newspapers but was not profitable enough to prevent it from being discontinued three years later. Ormes then turned to the more lucrative world of magazine and advertising art.

In 1942, however, she returned to journalism, becoming a reporter for the *Chicago Defender*, another prominent black newspaper. She created the single panel comic *Candy*, about a black maid. A better and more popular strip was *Patty Jo 'N' Ginger*, which she created between 1946 and 1950. Another single panel cartoon, it featured a little black girl, Patty Jo, who lived with her adult sister Ginger. Patty Jo, although a cute tyke, had the same grit and determination as Torchy Brown. She regularly stood up to bigotry and in one panel even carried a picket sign to protest injustice. Patty Jo became so popular among black readers that a Patty Jo 'N' Ginger doll was manufactured.

Encouraged by her newfound success, Ormes resurrected Torchy Brown in 1950 in a new strip called *Torchy Brown's Heartbeats*. The strip ran for five years and led Ormes to design a line of cut-out fashions called *Torchy's Togs* for a paper doll version of her sexy character. In her revealing lingerie, Torchy was a popular pinup girl for young black servicemen in the armed forces.

Ormes again retired Torchy in 1955, although *Patty Jo 'N' Ginger* continued to appear until around 1962. Arthritis brought Ormes's cartooning career to an end in the 1970s, but she took up painting, creating murals and portraits of children in her last years. An enthusiastic doll collector, she had about 150 of them and was an active member of the Chicago Chapter of the United Federation of Doll Clubs.

Jackie Ormes died on Christmas Day, 1985 at age 74. If she had been born about 30 years later, she might have become a well-known American cartoonist, but throughout her career she was unable to break into the white establishment press. It would be more half a century before BAR-BARA BRANDON-CROFT became the second black female cartoonist to be syndicated, in 1991.

As comic historian Bill Crouch wrote, it was nearly that long "before mainstream soap-opera strips could even come close to the realism and passion that Ormes presented in these [social] themes."

The Ormes Society, an organization dedicated to supporting black females in the comics industry, was founded in 2007. Ormes's work was included in the exhibit *Out of Sequence: Underrepresented Voices in American Comics* at the Krannet Art Museum at the University of Illinois at Champaign in 2008–09.

Further Reading

Goldstein, Nancy. *Jackie Ormes: The First African American Woman Cartoonist.* Ann Arbor: University of Michigan Press, 2008.

Norris, Kyle. "Comic Crusader: Remembering Jackie Ormes." Available online. URL: http://www.npr.org/templates/story/story.php?storyId=93029000. Downloaded March 9, 2009.

The Ormes Society Web site. Available online. URL: http://theormessociety.com/. Downloaded March 9, 2009.

Robbins, Trina. *The Great Women Cartoonists.* New York: Watson Guptill, 2001.

Owens-Hart, Winnie
(1949–) *ceramist, educator, writer*

An artist who combines traditional African crafts with a modern sensibility, Winnie Owens-Hart is a leading African-American ceramist.

Born in Washington, D.C., in 1949, she attended the Philadelphia College of Art (now the University of the Arts) in Pennsylvania, graduating with a Bachelor of Arts degree in fine arts in 1971. She received her Masters of Fine Arts degree in ceramics and sculpture from Howard University in Washington, D.C., in 1974. Owens-Hart studied ceramics with Nigerian artist Abbas Ahuwan at the Haystack Mountain School of Crafts in Maine during the summer of 1974. Her fascination with African pottery led her to visit the pottery village of Ipetumadu in Nigeria three years later. She returned in 1979 to study with the Yoruba women potters as an apprentice for a year.

While only women can make pottery in the Yoruban culture, they are not permitted to play the traditional tribal drums in communal ceremonies. The women can, however, play the ceramic drums they make. This inspired Owens-Hart to create her *Drum with Reptile Motif* (1993), a clay fire earthenware with open holes in the side that a woman drummer would play by slapping with the palms of her hands. Another African-influenced work is *Twice* (1998–99), a glazed earthenware mask in traditional Ipetumadu pot form that is a memorable self-portrait of the artist. As one art center Web site explains, "her work examines the correlation between external forces and a person's psyche."

Owens-Hart has had numerous group and solo exhibitions. One of the most recent was *From This Earth: Ceramics by Winnie Owens-Hart and Her Followers* (2007–08) at the Winston-Salem Delta Fine Arts Center in Winston-Salem, North

Carolina. It included the work of 10 of her former students. In another collaborative project, she coordinated volunteers and high school students in the creation of 1,200 handmade decorative memory bricks of local heritage to line the Gateway oval walkway in Arlington, Virginia. Her work is in the permanent collection of the Smithsonian's Renwick Gallery in Washington, D.C.

Owens-Hart has taught art at Howard since 1976 and has written numerous articles on ceramics and fine art. She is the founder of the Ile Amo Research Center dedicated to aboriginal ceramics where she holds workshops in the creating of traditional ceramics. Owens-Hart is the recipient of a National Endowment for the Arts Grant and the Lifetime Achievement in the Craft Arts Award. She lives in Gainesville, Virginia. "Our individual life experiences determine how we are shaped, and, in turn, how we shape the clay," she has said.

Further Reading

"Artist Archives—Winnie Owens-Hart." Artist Residencies, McCall Center for Visual Art. Available online. URL: http://www.mccollcenter.org/site/nav.cfm?cat=14&subcat=67&subsub=0&action=bio&artist_id=160. Downloaded March 17, 2009.

Bolden, Tonya. *Wake Up Our Souls—A Celebration of Black American Artists.* New York: Abrams Books for Young Readers, 2004, pp. 108–110.

"Winnie Owens-Hart." Available online. URL: http://www.ackland.org/art/exhibitions/transatlantic/winnie.htm. Downloaded March 17, 2009.

P

Parks, Gordon

(Gordon Roger Alexander Buchanan Parks)
(1912–2006) *photographer, filmmaker, film producer, writer, composer, musician*

Gordon Parks crowded several lifetimes of achievement into his 90-plus years. Although he is best known for his riveting, documentary-style photographs for *Life* magazine, he has also left an indelible mark as a filmmaker, author, and composer of both serious and popular music.

He was born Gordon Roger Alexander Buchanan Parks on November 30, 1912, in Fort Scott, Kansas, the youngest of 15 children. His father, Andrew Jackson Parks, was a farmer, and his mother, Sarah Ross Parks, a cleaning woman. Although poor, Parks had a memorable Midwestern childhood, which he described in vivid detail decades later in his first book, the autobiographical novel *The Learning Tree* (1963). The title came from his mother, who encouraged him to rise above prejudice and economic difficulties. "Let this place be your learning tree," she told him. "Trees have good fruit and bad fruit, and that's the way it is here. Remember that."

She died when he was 15, but he carried her words with him when he later quit high school, left home, and moved in with a married sister in St. Paul, Minnesota. His brother-in-law did not get along with Parks and threw him out of their home.

Parks decided to go back to high school and slept nights in trolley cars as they traveled around the city. When the country entered the Great Depression (1929–39), the homeless teenager realized he needed to work to survive. He quit high school a second time and pursued a variety of jobs—floor mopper, bellboy in a hotel, and piano player in a bordello, where he would compose and play his own tunes. When a visiting bandleader heard his song "No Love" at the hotel where Parks worked, he played it there with his band and again on national radio. On the strength of this song, Parks was hired to go on tour as pianist with another band, but the tour broke up in New York, and he was once again broke and on his own.

Parks joined the Civilian Conservation Corps (CCC), which worked on cleaning up and beautifying national parks and other recreational areas with government sponsorship. In 1933, while working for the CCC, Parks met and married Sally Avis, the first of his three wives. The couple soon moved to Minneapolis, Minnesota, where he worked briefly as a semiprofessional basketball player, a sport in which he excelled in high school. While working as a dining car waiter on the railroad, he accidentally discovered the powerful photographs of Great Depression–era people in magazines of photographers working for the Farm Security Administration (FSA). Soon Parks decided to become a photographer himself and bought a secondhand camera for $7.50. Although a few of his photographs were bought by local newspapers, Parks realized he was likely to earn far more in commercial and fashion photography. He boldly walked into a leading Minneapolis department store and offered his services to the manager. He was assigned to a photo shoot but later discovered to his dismay that he had double exposed every picture but one. He enlarged that one and showed it to the manager, who was impressed enough to give him another chance.

There was not enough freelance work to support his growing family in Minneapolis, and the Parkses moved to Chicago, Illinois. There he was hired by the Southside Community Arts Center and given his own darkroom in which to develop his pictures. The Arts Center mounted an exhibition of his photographs, which earned him a Julius Rosenwald Fund Fellowship, the first ever given to a photographer. Recalling the vivid, social photos of the FSA, Parks used his fellowship to work for the organization. The group's director, Roy Stryker, took Parks under his wing and trained him to be a photojournalist. Parks discovered that photographs could tell a story as well as words, if not sometimes better. In 1942, he interviewed and photographed a Washington, D.C., government cleaning woman, Ella Watson. Although he took many pictures of her, one stands out from the others and has become Parks's most famous photograph. In it, Watson stands solemnly, broom and mop in hand, before a large American flag. The photo, *American Gothic*, is a stirring challenge to American ideals that have not been fulfilled for many Americans. It established Parks's commitment to the underdogs of society.

During World War II (1939–1945), Parks served as a photographer in the Office of War Information and was the only black employee. In 1944 he rejoined Stryker on assignment for the Standard Oil Company of New Jersey. Standard Oil would seem a strange choice for Parks, but his photographs of the oil company's workers reflected the pride and strength of the American working man and woman.

In another bold move, Parks applied for a job in 1949 at *Life* magazine, then the nation's leading photo magazine. When asked what he was interested in, Parks told the photo editor he wanted to do a story on a Harlem gang leader. Although he knew no gang leaders, Parks was able to make contact with one and followed him around for several days. The resulting photo essay was published in *Life* to great acclaim, and Parks was hired as the magazine's first black staff photographer. He remained there for 20 years, completing some 300 assignments. He was an amazingly versatile photographer, covering everything from society events to urban crime. His most celebrated work came in 1961 when he chronicled the story of Flavio, a Brazilian boy living in the slums of Rio de Janeiro, where he was dying of malnutrition and bronchial asthma. Parks's photo essay in *Life* was so powerful that money poured in to help Flavio. He was treated for free by an American hospital and returned happy and healthy to his family.

When he left *Life* in 1969, Parks had already embarked on his third career as a filmmaker. His film *Diary of a Harlem Family* won an Emmy for best television documentary in 1968. The following year Hollywood producers invited him to write, direct, and produce a film adaptation of his book *The Learning Tree*. It was the first time an African American directed a major Hollywood movie. The film was a critical success, and two years later Parks directed the crime-action film *Shaft* (1971), the first and probably best of the so-called blaxploitation films that featured tough, often amoral black heroes. He directed several more feature films, including the sequel *Shaft's Big Score* (1972) and *Leadbelly* (1975), a biographical drama about the black blues and folk singer. The commercial failure of this film soured Parks on Hollywood, and his only subsequent feature film was a recording of his ballet *Martin* (1989), a celebration of the life of civil rights leader Martin Luther King, Jr.

A multitalented artist, Gordon Parks is seen here during the making of his first feature film, *The Learning Tree.* *(Photofest)*

Calling himself a "weekend composer," Parks wrote a piano concerto, a symphony, three sonatas, and musical scores for several of his films. He was awarded the Spingarn Medal from the NAACP in 1972 and received the National Medal of Art from President Ronald Reagan in 1988.

On his 88th birthday in 2000, the cable television station Home Box Office aired a documentary *Half Past Autumn: The Life and Works of Gordon Parks.* This was also the title of a touring retrospective of his photographs that originated in 1998 at the Corcoran Gallery in Washington, D.C. Having published 12 books, Gordon Parks, at age 90, began working on a biography of one of his favorite painters, the Englishman J. M. W. Turner. Gordon Parks died on March 7, 2006, at age 93. His eldest son, Gordon Parks Jr., a filmmaker, died in a plane crash in 1979. His daughter Toni Parks is also a photographer.

Further Reading

Berry, Skip. *Gordon Parks* (Black Americans of Achievement). New York: Chelsea House, 1990.

Parks, Gordon. *A Hungry Heart: A Memoir.* New York: Washington Square Press, 2007.

———. *Voices in the Mirror: An Autobiography.* New York: Harlem Moon, 2005.

Parr, Ann. *Gordon Parks: No Excuses.* Gretna, La.: Pelican Publishing Company, 2006.

Stange, Maren. *Bare Witness: Photographs by Gordon Parks.* New York: Skira, 2007.

Further Viewing

Half Past Autumn: The Life and Works of Gordon Parks (2000). HBO Home Video, VHS/DVD, 2001/2006.

The Learning Tree (1969). Warner Home Video, VHS, 1994.

Shaft/Shaft's Big Score! (1971). Warner Home Video, DVD, 2006.

Perkins, Angela L.

(1948–   ) *computer graphic artist, graphic designer, educator*

A pioneer in the innovative world of computer art, Angela Perkins uses imagination and the latest technology to create exciting, original artworks.

She was born in 1948 in Chicago, Illinois, and earned her Bachelor of Arts degree from California State University, Los Angeles, School of Fine Arts. After graduating, she worked as a freelance graphic artist and designer, then attended Harvard University School of Design in Cambridge, Massachusetts, to earn a Master of Arts degree in design studies in 1990 and a doctorate in design in 1993.

Her interest in computer art began while she was a fellow at the Massachusetts Institute of Technology in 1988. A fascination with the rich colors and the incandescent light generated by the computer led her to think about the artistic possibilities from these sources.

As she experimented and explored, Perkins found that different techniques led her to different kinds of art using computers. In one of her first series, she focused on celebrated black women. She began with a photograph of the subject, then manipulated it to create abstract forms. Layers upon layers of images created a three-dimensional quality that transformed the photographs. In another series, *Interiors,* Perkins focused on the

interior of fruits and vegetables. She scanned the actual objects, illuminating them with light and making ink jet prints on paper. "The illuminated interiors suggest a spiritual presence, acting as metaphors for human emotions and enlightenment," writes Nicholas Capasso, associate director of the DeCordova Museum and Sculpture Garden in Boston, Massachusetts. "Perkins seeks to reveal the presence of the sacred in the mundane."

Perkins's computer art has been exhibited at several venues, including the group show *The Computer in the Studio* at the Computer Museum in the DeCordova Museum. She has taught at several institutes, including the Massachusetts College of Art, Boston, where she was an instructor of design, and the Boston Architectural Center, where she taught computer graphics. Perkins currently lives in San Francisco, California.

"The work of Angela Perkins represents the exhilarating and dynamic possibilities of the computer as art tool," the art historian SAMELLA LEWIS has written. "The process of making art using the computer . . . [was] as magical as using a brush, [or] crayon or . . . crafting," Perkins has said. "Whether I clicked keys, [or] used a mouse or stylus in front of a screen, the event became transporting. The computer and I were one."

Further Reading

Gaither, Edmund Barry. "Angela Perkins and the Computer as Palette." *International Review of African American Art* 10, no. 2 (1992): 40–47.

Lewis, Samella. *African American Art and Artists.* Berkeley: University of California Press, 2003, pp. 323–325.

Perry, Tyler

(Emmitt Perry. Jr.)

(1969–   ) *filmmaker, screenwriter, playwright, actor, film and television producer*

A multi-gifted artist whose message of family values and forgiveness has attracted an eager audience of millions of African-Americans, Tyler Perry has created a franchise built on a string of successful plays and films.

He was born Emmitt Perry, Jr., on September 14, 1969, in New Orleans, Louisiana. His father, a carpenter, physically and verbally abused his mother, himself, and his three siblings. "There were times when I felt I wasn't going to make it," he has said. "It was nothing but the grace of God that helped me make it through."

Watching the *Oprah Winfrey Show* one day, Perry was inspired to write himself letters, expressing his anger and frustration about the obstacles in his life and how he could extricate himself from them through love and forgiveness. From the letters he eventually fashioned a musical he called *I Know I've Been Changed*. In 1992, Perry took his life savings and moved to Atlanta, Georgia, where he hoped to stage a production of his play. He mounted a production, but few people came, and the experience was a disaster. Low on funds, Perry spent the next months living out of run-down motels and his car. But his faith in himself only grew stronger as he got involved in a local church. In 1998, a promoter booked his play into a theater that had previously been a church. *I Know I've Been Changed*, with its uplifting message and down-home humor, became a hit with local black audiences and set the pattern for Perry's future works. The play moved downtown to Atlanta's Fox Theater where it had a long run.

By now, Perry was busy writing nine new plays in the next nine years, two of them collaborations with popular Dallas, Texas, pastor T. D. Jakes. The major character that reoccurred in most of the plays was a formidable black grandmother with a big mouth and an aggressive attitude called Madea. Perry modeled her after his own mother Maxine and his Aunt Mayola. A recognizable character for many black families, full of good humor and love, Madea was played by Perry himself, first in his plays and then in his first feature film *Diary of a Mad Black Woman* (2005), produced and financed by the Lionsgate film studio and Black Entertainment Television. *Diary*, despite poor reviews, drew in a huge audience of primarily African Americans and was the number one grossing film in its first week of release. It was quickly followed by a string of other comedies about black family life starring Perry as Madea, including *Madea's Family Reunion* (2006), *Daddy's Little Girls* (2007), *The Family That Preys* (2008), and *Madea Goes to Jail* (2009). Another film *Meet the Browns* (2008) was adapted into a television series (2009–) produced by Perry, who also directed many episodes. Another Perry sitcom, *House of Payne* (2007–09) on TBS, was the highest-rated first-run syndicated cable television program in history. His film adaptation of Ntozake Shange's hit Broadway play *For Colored Girls Who Have Considered Suicide When the Rainbow Is Enuf* was released in November 2010.

A book Perry wrote, *Don't Make a Black Woman Take Off Her Earrings: Madea's Uninhibited Commentaries on Life and Love* (2006), was number one on the *New York Times'* Best Seller List for eight weeks. DVDs of Perry's plays and movies and sundry other merchandise sell briskly on his Web site. In fall 2008, he opened a 200,000 square-foot studio in Atlanta that has five sound stages and a 400-seat screening room.

For all his success, Perry has remained humble and has given back to the black community. Among his many benefactions is Perry Place, a 20-home community he built in New Orleans for the survivors of Hurricane Katrina in 2005.

In January 2009, Perry was the recipient of the Brandon Tartikoff Legacy Award from the National Association of Television Program Executives. Explaining his phenomenal success, Perry has said, "I know my audience, and they're not people that the studio knows anything about."

Further Reading

Johnson, Pamela K. "Diary of a Brilliant Black Man." *Essence.* Available online. URL: http://www.tylerperry.com/articles/essence.html. Downloaded March 16, 2009.

The New Tyler Perry.com Interactive. Available online. URL: http://www.tylerperry.com/. Downloaded March 16, 2009.

"Tyler Perry." Internet Movie Database. Available online. URL: http://www.imdb.cocm/name/nm13471531. Downloaded March 17, 2009.

Further Viewing

Diary of a Mad Black Woman (2005). Lionsgate Home Entertainment, DVD, 2005.

Tyler Perry's Meet the Browns (2008). Lionsgate Home Entertainment, DVD, 2008.

Tyler Perry—The Plays. Lionsgate Home Entertainment, DVD box set, 2007.

Pierce, Elijah
(1892–1984) *folk carver*

One of the most successful African-American folk artists of the 20th century, Elijah Pierce is remembered for colorful and complex woodcarvings that reflected both his deep religious faith and wide-ranging secular interests.

He was born near Baldwyn, Mississippi, on March 5, 1892. As a boy, he carved images on trees near his home. His father, an ex-slave, was a farmer, but Elijah disliked farming and at 16 went to work for a local white barber. When the man died, Pierce managed his barbershop for several years. In 1916 Pierce's first wife died, and he took to the open road. He worked for the railroad for a time and traveled by rail as far away as St. Louis, Missouri. He finally settled in Danville, Illinois, and returned to being a barber. He met his future second wife, Cornelia Hoeston, and married her in Columbus, Ohio, which became his home for the remaining 60 years of his life.

In Columbus, Pierce began to carve again. His first work was a small animal he made as an anniversary present for his wife. While continuing with his barbering, he worked zealously at his woodcarving. He carved countless alligators, horses, dinosaurs, and other animals, both real and imaginary. He used many of his carvings as a teaching tool in his second career as an itinerant Baptist preacher.

"Every piece of work I carve is a message, a sermon," he said in a 1979 interview. Many of his works depicted biblical stories—Noah's Ark, the Three Wise Men, Jonah and the Whale. His carvings were mostly in reliefs on panels or consisted of small figures later mounted on paper or cardboard. The two most elaborate examples of the latter style and Pierce's masterworks are *The Book of Wood* (1932) and *Crucifixion* (1933). The former included 33 individual scenes from the life of Christ, one for each year of his life, and took six months of intensive work. *Crucifixion* contained more than 30 individual figures, giving a panoramic view of Christ's death on the cross.

Pierce and his wife would load a selection of his religious carvings in their car and go on the road, using them to illustrate his sermons at fairs, schools, and churches throughout the Midwest.

Despite this exposure, Pierce's reputation as a gifted folk artist grew slowly. During the 1940s his carving became more sophisticated in design and focused more on secular subjects, including politicians, sports heroes, and popular entertainers. He stopped carving in the mid-1950s, after the death of his second wife, for reasons that remain unclear. In 1954, however, he built his own barbershop and filled a room in it with his carvings, calling it the Pierce Barbershop and Art Gallery. He remains one of the few black folk artists who have displayed and marketed their work.

By the early 1970s, people from all over the country and abroad were visiting Pierce's gallery to admire and buy his work. Then in his late seventies, he resumed carving and worked constantly to fill numerous commissions. Some of his carvings dealt with current social and political issues, such as the humorous *Nixon Being Chased by Inflation.* His first exhibition in a museum took place in 1971 at the Hopkins Hall Gallery at Ohio State University in Columbus. Other shows followed at the Pennsylvania Academy of the Fine Arts in

Philadelphia, Pennsylvania, and the Phyllis Kind Gallery in New York City. In 1973 Pierce won the first prize at the International Meeting of Naive Art in Zagreb, Yugoslavia.

In 1979, he took the unusual step of hiring Leroy Alman, a young black man, as his assistant. Alman closely collaborated with Pierce on a number of pieces and eventually became a recognized folk artist in his own right.

Elijah Pierce's last years were satisfying ones in which the world celebrated his achievements. He died on May 7, 1984. Enterprising, active, and prolific in his art, he remained humble to the end. "I didn't even know I was an artist 'til they told me," he said in 1976. More than 300 pieces of Pierce's work are owned by the Columbus Museum of Art in Columbus, Ohio. The Elijah Pierce Gallery at the Martin Luther King, Jr., Performance and Cultural Arts Center in Columbus was named in his honor.

Further Reading

"Elijah Pierce-Biography." A Columbus State Resource Guide. Available online. URL: http://www.CSCC. edu/ElijahPierce/bio.htm. Downloaded March 9, 2009.

Livingston, Jane, and John Beardsley. *Black Folk Art in America 1930–1980.* Jackson: University Press of Mississippi, 1989, pp. 116–121.

Moe, John F. *Amazing Grace: The Life and Work of Elijah Pierce.* Columbus, Ohio: Martin Luther King, Jr. Center for Performing and Cultural Arts, 1990.

Riggs, Thomas, ed. *St. James Guide to Black Artists.* Detroit, Mich.: St. James Press, 1997, pp. 416–417.

Roberts, Norma J., ed. *Elijah Pierce Woodcarver.* Seattle: University of Washington Press, 1993.

Pindell, Howardena

(Howardena Doreen Pindell)
(1943–   ) *mixed-media artist, painter, museum curator, educator*

A contemporary artist of bold vision, Howardena Pindell has challenged the art establishment with both her original mixed-media works and her outspoken opinions on black art and artists.

She was born on April 14, 1943, in Philadelphia, Pennsylvania. By the age of 12, she was resolved to become an artist and enrolled at Boston University's School of Fine Arts in 1961. Pindell graduated with a Bachelor of Fine Arts degree in 1965 and earned a Master of Fine Arts degree from Yale University in New Haven, Connecticut, in 1967. She earned a doctorate from the New School/Parsons School of Design in 1999.

Pindell took a different career path from that of many American artists who enter teaching. She took a job as exhibition assistant at the Museum of Modern Art (MOMA) in New York City. She worked her way up to associate curator at MOMA by 1979.

Pindell's first paintings were realistic city scenes, but she soon moved on to abstract art. Unlike many abstract artists such as ALMA W. THOMAS, who concentrate on color, Pindell was more interested in the texture of her works. To this purpose, she began applying heavily layered painted paper dots, fiber, and sequins to her canvases.

In 1979 Pindell was seriously injured in an auto accident and lost part of her memory. For therapy, she collected postcards of places she had been or visited in order to help bring back memories associated with these places. She incorporated the postcards into her paintings, cutting them into strips and gluing them onto a board or canvas. She would then paint between the strips.

Pindell's outspoken political views have gained her the criticism of both conservatives and radicals. She raised a storm of controversy in 1988 when she published a list of the few black artists whose work has been shown in major galleries and museums. Again, she appropriated her personal problems into her art. *Autobiography: Water/ Ancestors, Middle Passage/Family Ghosts* (1988) dealt with her African slave ancestors and the harsh treatment of slave women. *Autobiography:*

Air/C5560 (1988) superimposed her own words and famous quotations over painted silhouettes of her body that contained stains of her own blood. Her recent show, *One Artist's Journey Through Change: Works of Howardena Pindell,* was mounted at St. Joseph's College in Brooklyn, New York, in early 2009.

A professor of art at the State University of New York at Stony Brook since 1984, Howardena Pindell was a visiting professor at Yale University in New Haven, Connecticut, in 1995. Among the awards she has won are the Boston University Alumnus Award in 1983, the Studio Museum in Harlem Artist Award in 1994, and the IAM Pioneer Award in 2000.

Further Reading

"Howardena Pindell Biography-Selected Works." JRank. org. Available online. URL: http://biography.jrank. org/pages/2930/Pindell-Howardena.html. Downloaded March 9, 2009.

Pindell, Howardena. "Some Reminiscences." *Kaleidoscope,* winter/spring 1996, pp. 12–16.

Riggs, Thomas, ed. *St. James Guide to Black Artists.* Detroit, Mich.: St. James Press, 1997, pp. 418–420.

Sims, Lowery S., and Howardena Pindell. *The Heart of the Question: The Writings and Paintings of Howardena Pindell.* New York: Midmatch Arts Press, 1997.

Weber, Sandra. "Long Island Q & A: Howardena Pindell, The Subtle and Not-So-Subtle Politics Inside the Artworld." *New York Times,* October 21, 1990.

Further Viewing

Howardena Pindell: Atomizing Art (1998). L & S Video, VHS, 1999.

Pinderhughes, John

(1946–) *photographer, writer*

One of the few African-American photographers known for his landscapes, John Pinderhughes depicts the Atlantic coastline in pictures that are finely detailed and richly poetic.

He was born in Washington, D.C., on January 28, 1946. When he was still young, his family moved to Alabama and then to New Jersey. He attended Howard University in Washington, where he first became interested in photography. He graduated in 1968 and attended the Washington National Educational Television Film Production School. Finishing there in 1972, Pinderhughes had his first solo show the same year at the Metropolitan Applied Research Center in New York City.

He first became known for his insightful narrative portrait series of individuals seen in various settings, including reflections in mirrors. His more recent landscapes are just as intimate and personal as his portraits and powerfully evocative. "His photographs," wrote photography historian Deborah Willis, "reveal a tender and detailed intimacy with [both land and sea]. He explores a range of tonal variations, pattern and textural design, light, and delineated line."

Pinderhughes's photographs are part of the permanent collection of the Museum of Modern Art and the Studio Museum in Harlem, both in New York City. He has had one-person shows at the W. E. B. Dubois Institute at Harvard University in Cambridge, Massachusetts; the Museum of African American History in Detroit, Michigan; and the Bronx Museum of the Arts in New York City. One of his most recent exhibitions was *Majestic Vista: Landscapes of Eastern Long Island* at the June Kelly Gallery in New York in 2000. Pinderhughes was part of the group show *Reflections in Black: A History of Black Photographers from 1840 to the Present,* first exhibited in 2000 at the Arts and Industries Gallery of the Smithsonian Institution in Washington.

He is also a commercial photographer whose clients include McDonald's, Kodak, and the Ford Motor Company. Pinderhughes's commercial art earned him the Clio Award in 1988 for television commercials and the Catholic Education Business Administrators' Award of Excellence 10 times between 1982 and 1992. He is a member of the Kamoinge Workshop, a group of

African-American photographers formed in New York City in 1963. In 2005, Pinderhughes and nine other Kamoinge photographers went to the Gulf Coast to photograph communities devastated by Hurricane Katrina. He also serves on the board of the South Fork Shelter Island chapter of the Nature Conservancy.

Pinderhughes has written four children's books illustrated with his photographs. His cookbook, *Family of the Spirit Cookbook* (1990), was praised by *Newsweek* magazine as "more than a cookbook . . . an affectionate album of portraits from African-American kitchens."

Further Reading

Cole Harriet, and John Pinderhughes. *Coming Together: Celebrations' for African American Families.* New York: Hyperion, 2003.

"Fellow John Pinderhughes. Katrina: An Unnatural Disaster." Available online. URL: http://www. soros.org/resources/multimedia/katrina/fellows/ pinderhughes.php. Downloaded March 9, 2009.

Pinderhughes, John. *Family of the Spirit Cookbook: Recipes and Remembrances from African American Kitchens, Featuring Verta Mae Grosvenor and Leah Chase* (1990). New York: Amistad, 2001.

Willis, Deborah. *Reflections in Black: A History of Black Photographers from 1840 to the Present.* New York: W. W. Norton, 2000, pp. 193, 282, 320–332.

Pinkney, Brian

(Jerry Brian Pinkney, J. Brian Pinkney)
(1961–   ) *illustrator, writer, educator*

A master of the illustrative technique of scratch-board, Brian Pinkney has followed in the celebrated footsteps of his father to become a leading contemporary illustrator of children's books.

He was born in Boston, Massachusetts, on August 28, 1961. His father, Jerry Pinkney, is a children's book illustrator and writer. His mother, Gloria Jean Pinkney, is a children's book writer. From an early age, Pinkney watched his father in his studio at work and was inspired to emulate him. He set up his own studio as a child in a closet and used his father's discarded materials to draw and paint. He also served as a model for characters in his father's books.

Pinkney enrolled at the Philadelphia College of Art in Pennsylvania in 1979 and drew illustrations for the school newspaper. He earned a Bachelor of Fine Arts degree in 1983. He went on to earn a Master of Fine Arts degree from the School of Visual Arts in New York City.

The first book he illustrated, under the name J. Brian Pinkney, was *Shipwreck on Mystery Island* (1985). For his third book, *The Boy and the Ghost* (1990), written by Robert D. San Souci, he used his father as a model for the character of the ghost. He has since collaborated with San Souci on a number of popular books, including *Sukey and the Mermaid* (1992) and *Cendrillon: A Caribbean Cinderella* (2002).

Pinkney's illustrations for *Where Does This Trail Lead?* (1991) earned him a Coretta Scott King Honor Book Award. The same year he married Andrea R. Davis, a children's book author like his mother. Together they have collaborated on many works, including a series of biographies about famous black Americans that include *Alvin Ailey* (1993), *Bill Pickett: Rodeo-Ridin' Cowboy* (1996), *Ella Fitzgerald: The Tale of a Vocal Virtuosa* (2002), and *Boycott Blues: How Rosa Parks Inspired a Nation* (2008).

"When I illustrate stories," Pinkney has said, "I like to be personally involved." When he worked on the biography of modern dancer Alvin Ailey with his wife, they both took dance lessons. Other of his books are based on his own experiences. *Where Does This Trail Lead?,* written by Burton Albert, was inspired by Pinkney's experiences as a boy during summers spent on Cape Cod, Massachusetts. *Max Found Two Sticks* (1994), the first book he both wrote and illustrated, is based on his childhood experience of playing the drums, a hobby he still pursues with enthusiasm.

Among the other works he has both written and illustrated are *Cosmo and the Robot* (2000), *Benjamin and the Shrinking Book* (2003), and *Hush, Little Baby* (2005).

Pinkney's striking style of illustration is based on the technique of scratchboard, in which a white board is covered with black ink. The artist scratches off the ink with a sharp tool to create an image with the revealed white underneath. He then can add color to the scratched area with watercolors.

"I like working in scratchboard because it allows me to sculpt the image," explained Pinkney. "When I etch the drawing out of the board, I get a rhythm going with my line which feels like sculpture to me."

Brian Pinkney is a member of the Society of Illustrators and has shown his work in several of their original art shows. He has taught at the Children's Art Carnival in Harlem, New York City, and at his alma mater, the School of Visual Arts.

Further Reading

Cummings, Pat, ed. *Talking with Artists, Volume 2: Conversations with Thomas B. Allen, Mary Jane Begin, Floyd Cooper, Julie Downing, Denise Fleming, Sheila Hamanaka, Kevin Kenkes, William Joyce, Maira Kalman, Deborah Nourse Lattimore, Brian Pinkney, Vera B. Williams and David Wisniewski.* New York: Simon & Schuster, 1995.

Pinkney, Andrea Davis, and Brian Pinkney, illustrator. *Boycott Blues: How Rosa Parks Inspired a Nation.* New York: Amistad, 2008.

Pinkney, Brian. *Hush, Little Baby.* New York: Amistad, 2005.

———. *Max Found Two Sticks* (1994). New York: Aladdin Paperbacks, 1997.

San Souci, Robert D., and Brian Pinkney, illustrator. *Cut from the Same Cloth: American Women of Myth, Legend and Tall Tale.* New York: Puffin, 2000.

Telgen, Diane, ed. *Something About the Author, Volume 74.* Detroit, Mich.: Gale Research, 1993, pp. 191–193.

Pinkney, Jerry
(1939–) *illustrator, writer, educator*

Arguably the most celebrated of African-American book illustrators, Jerry Pinkney has brought dozens of children's books to life with his vibrant, colorful, realistic pictures. His signature style has also graced everything from postage stamps to table settings.

He was born on December 22, 1939, in Philadelphia, Pennsylvania, one of six children. The Pinkney household was so hectic that as a child Jerry could only find solitude for his drawing underneath an old grand piano that his handyman father had painted pink.

Although no one in his family had ever been involved in the arts, Pinkney's parents encouraged his gift, and he earned a scholarship to the Philadelphia Museum College of Art in 1957. Advertising design was his major, but out of curiosity he took courses in painting, drawing, and printmaking. "Had it not been for those three courses," he later said, "I might have gone in another, more commercial direction."

After working for a year in a flower shop while freelancing as a typographer, Pinkney went to work for the Rustcraft Greeting Card Company in Denham, Massachusetts. Gradually he started to freelance illustrations, first for textbooks and then children's books, beginning with *The Adventures of Spider: West African Folk Tales* (1964), with text by Joyce Cooper Arkhurst. Folktales and fairy tales would become some of his specialties as an illustrator.

By the late 1960s, black illustrators were finally coming into their own in children's book publishing, due to the increased awareness of African-American literature and culture. "It was exciting," recalled Pinkney, "and gave me an opportunity which might have taken much longer had it not been for that movement."

In 1971, he moved to Croton-on-Hudson, New York, where he established a studio he still works in today. Through the 1970s and 1980s, Pinkney illustrated books by such outstanding black children's writers as M. D. Taylor, Adjai Robinson, Virginia Hamilton, and Julius Lester.

He and Lester have collaborated on numerous books, including the best-selling folk tale *John Henry* and four volumes of *Uncle Remus Tales,* witty retellings of the classic animal tales first written by white author Joel Chandler Harris in the late 1800s and early 1900s.

In 1996, Lester and Pinkney took on their greatest challenge. They adapted one of the most controversial of children's stories, *Little Black Sambo,* which had been banned by many libraries in the 1960s for its demeaning stereotypes of blacks. They retitled the story *Sam and the Tigers* and gave it a more positive spin. To date, it has sold more than 100,000 copies. The model for Sam in the story was Pinkney's eight-year-old grandson. He usually works from models and does extensive research on all his books to capture the reality of his characters.

For all his preparation, once Pinkney starts to draw he relies on his instincts. "I don't see things until I draw them," he has explained. "When I put a line down, the only thing I know is how it should feel and I know when it doesn't feel right."

In the 1980s, Pinkney designed the first nine postal stamps for the U.S. Postal Service's Black Heritage Series. They included such important historical figures as Underground Railroad leader Harriet Tubman, civil rights leader Martin Luther King, Jr., and black scientist Benjamin Banneker. He has called the stamp designing "one of the most difficult projects I've ever worked on." One of the problems he faced was working on such a small scale. Another was working with a committee that had to approve his designs and concepts.

Pinkney's wife, Gloria Jean, is a writer, silversmith, and his closest collaborator. Together they have four children. One son, BRIAN PINKNEY, is also a well-known children's book illustrator. Another son, Myles, is a photographer. Together they collaborated on the book *In the Forest of Your Remembrance* (2001), a short story collection. The stories were written by Gloria and illustrated by Jerry, Brian, and Myles.

Among the numerous prizes and awards Jerry Pinkney has won are three Coretta Scott King Honor Book Awards and five Coretta Scott King Awards, most recently for his illustrations for *Goin' Someplace Special* (2002), with text by Patricia McKissack. He has also won three Caldecott Honor Book Awards. In 2010, Pinkney won the coveted Caldecott Medal for *The Lion & the Mouse,* his first book without a written narrative. Having illustrated several of Hans Christian Andersen's most beloved tales, Pinkney was the U.S. nominee for the Hans Christian Andersen Award in 1997. He was a visiting critic and then adjunct professor at the Rhode Island School of Design in Providence, Rhode Island, from 1969 to 1971.

Pinkney's watercolor paintings were exhibited, along with his son Brian's artwork, at the inaugural opening of the new headquarters of the National Center for Children's Illustrative Literature in Abilene, Texas.

"Books are my first love because of the union of design and illustration," says Jerry Pinkney. "The most exciting thing for me is to get a fresh book in the mail and open it for the first time."

Further Reading

Carvajal, Doreen. "Authentic Vision for Storybooks." *New York Times,* August 21, 2001, pp. E1, E3.

Hedblad, Alan, ed. *Something About the Author, Volume 107.* Detroit, Mich.: Gale Research, 1999, pp. 159–162.

"Jerry Pinkney." Available online. URL: http://www.harpercollins.com/authors/12598/Jerry-Pinkney/index.aspx?authorID=12598. Downloaded March 9, 2009.

Lester, Julius, and Jerry Pinkney, illustrator. *The Old African.* New York: Dial Books, 2005.

Pinkney, Gloria, and Jerry, Brian, and Myles Pinkney, illustrators. *In the Forest of Your Remembrance: Thirty-Three Goodly News Tellings for the Whole Family.* New York: Phyllis Fogelman Books, 2001.

Pinkney, Jerry. *The Nightingale*. New York: Phyllis Fogelman Books, 2002.

Pinkney, Jerry, and Brian Pinkney. *Illuminated Literature: The Art of Jerry and Brian Pinkney*. Augustus, Calif.: Morris Museum of Art, 2005.

Piper, Adrian

(Adrian Margaret Smith Piper)
(1948–) *performance and video artist, installation artist, writer, educator*

One of the most controversial and uncompromising of contemporary black performance artists, Adrian Piper has been confronting the public with ugly truths of racism and sexism for four decades.

She was born Adrian Margaret Smith Piper on September 20, 1948, in Harlem, the black section of New York City. An only child, she learned to draw at the age of three from her maternal grandmother, a former high school teacher. By five, she was writing and illustrating her own stories. She attended the New Lincoln School in Manhattan on a scholarship and took art classes in the afternoon at New York's Museum of Modern Art.

Piper left home in 1965 and worked for a time as a discotheque dancer at two New York nightclubs. The following year she enrolled in the School of Visual Arts in New York and began to study yoga, a lifelong interest. Piper was the first African-American artist to become part of the conceptual art movement, in which the focus is placed less on art objects themselves and more on the means and processes by which they are produced. Conceptual art also involves the use of video and photographs within a total art environment. Piper began performing conceptual pieces in small clubs and theaters in New York and elsewhere. Her first art works were published in Vito Acconci's *0 to 9 Magazine* in 1968.

She majored in philosophy at the City College of New York and graduated in 1974 summa cum laude. She then earned a Master of Arts degree from Harvard University in Cambridge, Massachusetts, in 1976 and received a fellowship to study philosophy in Germany the following year.

Through the 1980s, Piper developed and performed such personal performance pieces as *Four Intruders Plus Alarm Systems*, *It's Just Art*, *Funk Lessons*, and *A Tale of Avarice and Poverty*.

Uncompromising in her political and social beliefs, Piper withdrew her conceptual work *1965–1975: Reconsidering the Object of Art* from the Los Angeles Museum of Contemporary Art in 1995 when she learned that cigarette manufacturer Philip Morris was a sponsor.

Having taught at several universities, in 1990 she became a professor of philosophy at Wellesley College in Wellesley, Massachusetts. After 10 years there, Piper sued the college in 2000 for fraud and breach of contract. Shortly afterward, she suffered a ruptured appendix and nearly died. She has since recuperated and settled her differences with Wellesley, where she continues to teach. She was visiting guest professor at the Royal Danish Academy of Art from 2005 to 2007.

In an article in O, the Oprah Winfrey magazine, she had this to say about the experience: "In that moment [of crisis] my will to live and create surged up with uncontrollable force. I became a live electrical current, awake to the reality that I am a warrior; and that I believed in myself and my work enough to fight to the death for them."

Adrian Piper: A Retrospective 1965–2000 opened at the University of Maryland's Fine Arts Gallery in 2000. *Everything*, Piper's first New York solo show in eight years, opened at the Elizabeth Dee Gallery in 2008. A combination of video news footage, text, installation, and photographs, the exhibit addressed such issues as racial violence and the natural disaster of Hurricane Katrina. In a review in the *New York Times*, Karen Rosenberg wrote that these new works were "less confrontational than the body-oriented conceptual art which she's best known for, [but] her voice remains poignant and philosophical."

Further Reading

Adrian Piper Research Archive. Available online. URL: http://www.adrianpiper.com. Downloaded May 7, 2002.

Berger, Maurice, ed., and Adrian Piper. *Adrian Piper: A Retrospective.* Baltimore: University of Maryland Baltimore County Center for Art and Visual Culture, 2000.

Piper, Adrian. *Out of Order, Out of Sight: Selected Writing in Meta-Art, 1968–1992 (2 Volumes).* Cambridge, Mass.: MIT Press, 1999.

Piper, Adrian, and Houston Conwill. *Colored People: A Collaborative Book Project.* Distributed Art Publishers, 1992.

Piper, Adrian, Kara Walker, and others. *Witness to Her Art.* Annandale-on-Hudson, N.Y.: Bard College, 2007.

Pippin, Horace
(1888–1946) *folk painter*

Considered one of the finest American folk painters of the 20th century, Horace Pippin captured the black experience in a wide range of deceptively simple paintings that exhibited a mastery of color, composition, and design.

He was born on February 22, 1888, in West Chester, Pennsylvania, in extreme poverty. His father abandoned the family when Horace was very young, and his mother moved to Goshen, New York, where she found work as a domestic.

As a boy, he was punished by his teachers for drawing illustrations of his spelling words. On weekends, Pippin visited local racetracks to draw the horses and their riders. His mother became ill when he was 15, and he left school to work at various times as a junk dealer, a molder, and a hotel porter to support the family. When his mother died in 1911, Pippin moved to New Jersey, where he found work in a foundry. He regained his interest in art and worked other jobs in warehouses where paintings were stored. On the job, he would study the paintings to determine the different style of each artist.

When the United States entered World War I (1914–18) in 1917, Pippin enlisted in the army. He was sent to France, where he took part in several major battles and was seriously wounded in the right shoulder. He was the recipient of the Croix de Guerre and the Purple Heart. The war proved to be the defining experience of his life and his art.

Discharged in 1918, Pippin returned home to West Chester and married Jennie, a young widow. Unable to work because he could not lift his right arm, he lived on his army pension and a job riding a laundry wagon with his wife. Now 40 years old, Pippin began to paint, although he had never had an art lesson. Unable to lift a paintbrush, he took a hot poker and burned an outline of a painting into an oak table leaf and then applied house paint to the outline. The process was painstaking, but within a year, he was able to hold a brush and started to paint in earnest.

His first major painting, *The End of the War: Starting Home* (1931), took him three years to complete. It is meticulous in detail, right down to the picture frame, on which he hand-carved hand grenades, bombs, and other war paraphernalia. The painting, which does not celebrate but condemns war, established universal peace as a central theme in his work.

As obsessed as he was with war, Pippin soon was painting a wide range of subjects, from black life in the South to biblical scenes to scenes from American history. Unlike other black folk artists, Pippin rarely repeated himself, although his direct and elemental style was instantly recognizable.

Completely untaught, Pippin was an artist of great intuitive powers. "The pictures which I have already painted come to me in my mind," he once said, "and if to me it is a worthwhile picture, I paint it. I go over the picture in my mind several times and when I am ready to paint it I have all the details that I need."

In 1937, one of Pippin's paintings was seen by chance by the local critic and historian Christian Brinton in the window of a shoe repair shop. Brinton was stunned by Pippin's artistry and helped him get a one-person show of 10 of his paintings at the West Chester Community Art Center. The following year four of his paintings were displayed in the show *Masters of Modern Painting* at the prestigious Museum of Modern Art (MOMA) in New York City. Not long after, Robert Carlen, a Philadelphia gallery owner, began to exhibit and sell Pippin's work.

More exhibits and honors quickly followed, including an honorable mention for his painting *Cabin in the Cotton* in a competition held by the Philadelphia Academy of Fine Arts.

His most celebrated work was a narrative series of three paintings about the trial of the 19th-century abolitionist John Brown. Pippin felt particularly drawn to the subject because his grandmother was present at Brown's hanging by federal troops at Harpers Ferry, Virginia, in 1859. She told him about the event when he was a child. The climactic painting, *John Brown Goes to His Hanging* (1942), shows the composed Brown being taken down the road to the gallows in a horse-drawn cart while a crowd of spectators look on. In the lower right corner of the painting Pippin's grandmother stands, looking directly at the viewer.

Pippin's last years were riddled with tragedy. His wife was declared mentally ill and was committed to a state hospital in 1944, leaving Pippin alone and heartbroken. His last completed painting, *Man on Bench* (1946), is a painful self-portrait. He died on July 6, 1946, of a stroke. His wife passed away 10 days later. That same year Pippin's painting *Milkman of Goshen* won the J. Henry Scheidt Memorial Prize of the Philadelphia Academy.

Pippin's paintings, filled with life, power, and a quiet dignity, continue to be admired. "My opinion of art," he once said, "is that a man should have a love of it, because it is my idea that he paints from his heart and his mind."

Further Reading

Lyons, Mary E. *Starting Home: The Story of Horace Pippin, Painter* (African-American Artists and Artisans). New York: Atheneum, 1993.
Pippin, Horace. *Horace Pippin: The Phillips Collection . . . with an Essay by R. Bearden.* Seattle: University of Washington Press, 1981.
Stein, Judith E. *I Tell My Heart: The Art of Horace Pippin.* North Hollywood, Calif.: Universe Publishing, 1993.
Venezia, Mike. *Horace Pippin* (Getting to Know the World's Greatest Artists). Danbury, Conn.: Children's Press, 2008.

Further Viewing

Horace Pippin: There Will Be Peace. L & S Video, VHS, 1999.

Polk, P. H.
(Prentice Herman Polk)
(1898–1984) *photographer*

A pioneering African-American photographer, P. H. Polk is best remembered for his powerful portraits of the poor but proud black people of the rural South.

He was born Prentice Herman Polk in Bessemer, Alabama, on November 25, 1898, one of five children. Surrounded by poverty, Polk managed to get into the Tuskegee Institute in Tuskegee, Alabama, then called Tuskegee Normal Sand Industrial Institute. He studied photography with C. M. BATTEY, head of the photography department. While Polk learned the basics of portrait photography from his gifted teacher, the two did not get along, and Polk left Tuskegee, learning the rest of the photographer's art from a correspondence course.

Unlike many early photographers, who did their best to remove all shadows from their work, Polk became obsessed with the interplay of light and shadow in his photographs. He greatly admired the shadowy masterpieces of Dutch painter Rembrandt, whose work Polk said always went "to the shadow side."

Polk returned to Tuskegee in 1927, the same year Battey died, and opened his own photography studio. The institute noticed Polk's innovative

Photographer P. H. Polk was a master of the use of light and shadow to illuminate his powerful portraits. *(Anthony Barboza)*

work and in 1928 hired him as an instructor in the photography department. He was named the head of the department in 1933. Although he gained fame for his sensitive portraits of such famous visitors to Tuskegee as writer Langston Hughes and Tuskegee's celebrated teacher and research scientist George Washington Carver, he was equally attracted to the poor black farm people of surrounding Macon County.

Around 1930, Polk began his celebrated series of portraits, which he called simply *Old Characters.* These unadorned pictures of poor blacks posed in or just outside their crude, dirt-floored cabins captured the spirit and individuality of each subject. The most famous is *The Boss* (1932), a striking portrait of a defiant black woman. "Wearing

a tattered sweater, an apron, and a scarf," wrote photography historian Deborah Willis, "her body language and facial expression represent a woman in control of her identity."

In 1938, Polk moved to Atlanta, Georgia, where he opened a studio. But it failed, and within a year he was back at Tuskegee as official photographer, a position he retained until his retirement. He was a faithful chronicler of Tuskegee campus life, and during World War II (1939–45) he made an invaluable visual record of the training and progress of the famed Tuskegee Airmen, a band of students who flew bombing raids over Nazi Germany.

Polk won the Black Photographers Annual Testimonial Award in 1980 and received a National Endowment for the Arts Fellowship in 1981. He died on December 29, 1984, at age 86.

Further Reading

Higgins Chester, Jr., P. H. Polk and Meredith Soles. *Through These Eyes: The Photographs of P. H. Polk.* Newark: University Gallery/University of Delaware, 1998.

Riggs, Thomas, ed. *St. James Guide to Black Artists.* Detroit, Mich.: St. James Press, 1997, pp. 430–431.

Shaw, Louise E. *P. H. Polk: Southern Photographer.* Atlanta, Ga.: Nexus Press, 1986.

"Through These Eyes: The Photography of P. H. Polk." University of Delaware Web site. Available online. URL: http://www.udel.edu/museums/past/polk/index.html. Downloaded March 10, 2009.

Willis, Deborah. *Black Photographers: 1840–1940: An Illustrated Bibliography.* New York: Garland Publishing, 1985, pp. 37, 45–46, 70–71, 118, 173.

Porter, James A.
(James Amos Porter)
(1905–1970) *art historian, painter, educator, museum curator*

The first African-American art historian, James A. Porter may have done more to promote and advance the cause of black American art than any other individual in the 20th century.

He was born James Amos Porter on December 22, 1905, in Baltimore, Maryland, and grew up in Washington, D.C. Drawn to art at an early age, he enrolled at Howard University in Washington in 1923 and earned a Bachelor of Arts degree in 1927. Drawn to both teaching and painting, Porter was appointed an assistant professor at Howard the year he graduated. He later did graduate work at Columbia University and the Art Students League in New York City. In 1935 Porter traveled to Paris, France, on a fellowship from the Institute of International Education. He studied medieval archaeology at the Sorbonne, a world-famous university in Paris. He also visited Belgium, Germany, Holland, and Italy, studying African arts in numerous museums.

On his return to the United States, Porter earned a Master of Arts degree in art history from New York University's Institute of Fine Arts in 1937. He returned to Howard to teach. A remarkable teacher, Porter focused on African-American art and its history, a subject largely ignored by the art establishment and the public. In 1943, he published *Modern Negro Art*, which remains a standard work on the subject. It was reprinted with a new preface in 1969.

Porter traveled to the Caribbean islands in 1945, where he was entranced by the local people, many of them of African descent. He took many photographs of local people and painted portraits of them. In 1953, he was appointed head of the art department at Howard and director of its art gallery. Over the years, Porter mounted many one-person shows of African-American artists. While he was overall an excellent critic, he used his influence against those black artists of whom he did not approve. One of these was PALMER C. HAYDEN, whose exaggerated black subjects Porter branded as racist. Today Hayden is considered one of the finest of 20th-century African-American painters.

Porter was a painter of considerable gifts himself. His paintings are mostly realistic, three-dimensional, full of warm colors, and show careful attention to detail. He remains best known for his still lifes and portraits. His *Woman Holding a Jug* won first prize at the Arthur A. Schomburg Portrait Contest in 1933. His *Self Portrait 1957* and *Portrait of Dorothy* are both in the permanent collection of the National Portrait Gallery in Washington. A series of 25 West African paintings completed during a 1963 trip to West Africa were later exhibited at the Howard Gallery of Art. Other visits to Haiti and Cuba in the Caribbean inspired more paintings of local places and people.

In 1966, President Lyndon B. Johnson awarded Porter and 26 other American teachers the first National Gallery of Art Medal and Honorarium for Distinguished Achievement in Art Education. James A. Porter died on February 28, 1970, in Washington. In 1990, Howard honored him with the first James A. Porter Colloquium of African American Art Study, which has since become an annual event. A memorial exhibition of his work was held at Howard in 1972.

"As long as I am alive and able to give expression to my experiences and ideas," Porter once wrote, "I shall deem it a privilege as well as an obligation to show the concrete results of my efforts with all others."

Further Reading

"James Amos Porter 1905–1970." Available online. URL: http://www.artnoir.com/index.porter.html. Downloaded March 10, 2009.

Perry, Regenia A. *Free Within Ourselves: African-American Artists in the Collection of the National Museum of American Art.* San Francisco: Pomegranate Communications, 1992, pp. 150–154.

Porter, James A. *Modern Negro Art* (Moorland-Springarn Series). Reprint, Washington, D.C.: Howard University Press, 1992.

———. *James Amos Porter (1905–1970): Spotlight on his works on paper: drawings, sketches, vignettes, portraits, bookplates, illustrations, murals.* Dundee, Scotland: Westport Foundation and Gallery, 1998.

Powers, Harriet
(1837–1910) *folk quilter*

A simple Georgia farm wife, Harriet Powers raised the craft of quiltmaking to something approaching a fine art by skillfully combining African traditions with European ones.

Little is known of her early life. She was born a slave in the vicinity of Athens, Georgia, on October 28, 1837. She married a farmer and sometime after slavery ended in 1865 she took up quilting as a hobby. How many quilts Powers made over the next 35 years is unknown. Only two have survived; both are spectacular. Unlike most handmade quilts of the time that were merely decorative, Powers's two are narrative works that tell a story in numerous scenes.

Her so-called *Harriet Quilt* was completed before 1890 and contains 11 scenes from the Old and New Testaments of the Bible. It started with the story of the Garden of Eden and ended with the crucifixion of Jesus Christ. The human figures on the quilt were cut out of material and applied to the quilt in a traditional African appliqué process. The narrative form of the biblical stories is an adopted European tradition. Powers probably did not invent this style of quiltmaking, but her two surviving quilts are considered the best examples existing today.

Her work probably would have been lost if not for Jennie Smith, a persistent Southern white artist. Smith saw Powers's story quilt at the country fair in Athens in 1890 and offered to buy it. In her diary, Smith described Powers in these words: "She is about sixty-five years old, of a clear ginger cake color, and is a very clean and interesting woman who loves to talk of her 'old miss' and life 'before de wah.'"

Although friendly toward Smith, Powers refused to sell her the quilt. She later changed her mind, possibly under pressure from her husband. She asked for $10, but when Smith offered her $5, she accepted.

"After giving me a full description of each scene with great earnestness," wrote Smith, "she

departed but has been back several times to visit the darling offspring of her brain."

Today the *Harriet Quilt* resides in the Smithsonian Institution in Washington, D.C., something that surely would have surprised Harriet Powers, who died on January 1, 1910. Her other surviving quilt, the *Bible Quilt* (ca. 1895), is at the Boston Museum of Fine Art. It consists of 15 scenes from the Bible intermingled with strange, astronomical symbols that remain something of a mystery.

"The imagination of the designer, the composition of the scenes, the attractive color combination, and the method of execution elevate the designs above the status of mere quilts to paintings in fabric," wrote art historian Regenia A. Perry. Harriet Powers's grave was rediscovered in the Gospel Pilgrim Cemetery in Athens in 2005.

Further Reading
Adams, Jeanne Marie. "The Harriet Powers Pictorial Quilts." *Black Arts 3, Number 4,* 1979, pp. 12–28.
"Harriet Powers," Southern Quilters website. Available online. URL: http://xroads.virginia.edu/~ug97/ quilt/harriet.html. Downloaded March 10, 2009.
Lyons, Mary E. *Stitching Stars: The Story Quilts of Harriet Powers.* New York: Aladdin Paperbacks, 1997.
Rizzoli Art Series. *Harriet Powers's Bible Quilts.* New York: Rizzoli, 1994.

Prince-Blythewood, Gina
(Gina Maria Prince)
(1969–   ) *filmmaker, television director, screenwriter, film and television producer*

One of the most promising black women filmmakers of her generation, Gina Prince-Blythewood had to wait eight years after her spectacular big screen debut before directing another feature movie.

She was born Gina Maria Prince on June 10, 1969, and was adopted six months later. After high school, Prince entered UCLA Film School and was the recipient of both the Gene Reynold's Scholarship for Directing and the Ray Stark Memorial Scholarship for Outstanding Undergraduate. She also loved sports and ran competitive track, an interest that would later emerge in her first feature film.

Prince graduated in 1991 and almost immediately wrote three scripts for the black sitcom *A Different World* (1987–93). Next, she was hired as story editor for the short-lived Fox TV series *South Central* (1994) and then became executive story editor of the NBC courtroom drama *Sweet Justice* (1994–95), for which she also wrote two episodes. She became coproducer and writer for another courtroom drama, *Courthouse* (1996). In 1995, Prince got the opportunity to direct for the first time for a CBS Schoolbreak Special, *What About Your Friends?* The script, which she also wrote, was a sensitive story of three black teen girls and their lives after high school. It earned Prince two Emmy nominations for writing and directing and an Image Award from the NAACP for best children's special.

In May 1998, Prince married actor Reggie Rock Bythewood. She worked as consulting producer for another series, the college drama *Felicity* (1998–99), writing one of the show's outstanding episodes about an adopted girl looking for her birth mother, a subject that had autobiographical overtones. Prince's next project would make her famous. She wrote and directed the feature film *Love and Basketball* (2000), an urban romance between two young athletes, played by Omar Epps and Sanaa Lathan, and co-produced by SPIKE LEE. The film, which debuted at the Sundance Film Festival, was realistic and moving and earned Bythewood an Independent Spirit Award for Best First Feature.

That same year, Bythewood adapted the Terry McMillan novel *Disappearing Acts* and directed it for HBO. It again starred Sanaa Lathan as a music teacher seeking a career as a singer who becomes romantically involved with a construction worker played by Wesley Snipes. Another eight years would pass before Bythewood would have the opportunity to direct another feature film. She continued to work in television and produced the film *Biker Boyz* (2003), written and directed by her husband.

Finally, Bythewood was given the chance to direct another movie, her own adaptation of the popular Sue Monk Kidd novel *The Secret Lives of Bees* (2008). It is the story of a 14-year-old white girl, played by Dakota Fanning, in South Carolina in 1964 who is adopted into a black family. The film earned nearly $40 million at the box office, making it the second most successful film directed by a black for the year. ". . . I know now that I can get my script read by everybody and the doors will be opened wider," she has said.

Further Reading

Alexander, George. *Why We Make Movies: Black Filmmakers Talk About the Magic of Cinema.* New York: Harlem Moon, 2003, pp. 381–396.

"Biography." Available online. URL: http://www.variety.com/profiles/people/Biography/31266/Gina+Prince_Bythwood.html?dataS. Downloaded March 16, 2009.

"Gina Prince-Blythewood." Available online. URL: http://www.imdb.com/name/nm0697656/. Downloaded March 16, 2009.

Seymour, Gene. "Black Directors Look Beyond Their Niche." *New York Times,* January 11, 2009, Arts and Leisure, pp. 11, 15.

Further Viewing

Disappearing Acts (2000). HBO Home Video, DVD, 2001.

Love & Basketball (2000). New Line Home Video, DVD, 2008.

The Secret Life of Bees (2008). Fox Home Video, DVD, 2009.

Prophet, Nancy Elizabeth
(1890–1960) *sculptor, educator*

A pioneering African-American sculptor of bold and expressive heads, Nancy Elizabeth Prophet became an artist against overwhelming odds that eventually brought her promising career to a tragic end.

She was born on March 19, 1890, in Warwick, Rhode Island, and was half black and half Narragansett Indian. Prophet decided as a young woman she wanted to be an artist, a career path her family strongly advised against, but she would not be dissuaded. At age 24, she enrolled at the prestigious Rhode Island School of Design in Providence, Rhode Island, where she was the only black student at that time. After graduating in 1918, she married Francis Ford, a black man originally from Maryland, and began to market her artwork. Racism and prejudice made it difficult for her to sell her work, however. One gallery only agreed to mount an exhibit of her sculptures if she promised not to attend the opening!

In 1922, Prophet made the fateful decision to move to Paris, France, where she hoped to develop as an artist without the fear of racism. She arrived alone in Paris with $350 in her purse. She was accepted as a student at the Ecole des Beaux-Arts in Paris but lived in unspeakable squalor. The little money she had left she spent on a shared apartment. One day she was reduced to stealing a piece of meat from the plate of her roommate's dog.

"I work away on my first piece with a dogged determination to conquer," she wrote in her journal in August 1922. "I remember how sure I was that it was going to be a living thing, a master stroke, how my arms felt as I swung them up to put on a piece of clay."

Lonely, she invited her husband to join her in Paris. This was a grave mistake: Ford was an unambitious man who drank heavily, and they soon divorced. But all these hardships were forgotten when her sculptures were accepted for exhibition at two prominent Parisian salons in 1924.

The following year, black activist and writer W. E. B. DuBois, one of Prophet's most ardent supporters, paid for her to return to the United States to stimulate interest for her work at art museums and among collectors. Another admirer was black painter HENRY O. TANNER, who lived in Paris. He nominated her sculpture *Head of a Woman* for the Harmon Foundation Prize in 1929. She won the prize and returned to the United States permanently in 1932. That year was the high point of Prophet's career. She won the Greenough Prize from the Newport, Rhode Island, Art Association, and her sculpture *Congolaise*, a cherrywood head of a Masai warrior of Africa, was bought by Gertrude Payne Whitney. It was later displayed in the Whitney Museum of American Art in New York City.

The following year, Prophet joined the faculty at Atlanta University in Atlanta, Georgia, at the recommendation of DuBois. Soon afterward she began teaching at Spelman College, a black school for women in Atlanta. She remained there until 1944.

Disillusioned by the difficulty of selling her work, Prophet left Spelman and returned to Providence. She hoped to regain the momentum of her career but found little interest in her work there. Unable to support herself as a sculptor, she took a job as a domestic servant, the career her family had advised her to pursue years earlier. One of the most gifted women sculptors in America found herself trapped in a menial job while her sculptures sat outdoors, exposed to the elements and rotting because she could not afford to store them. She deliberately destroyed other works out of frustration. Sadly, few of her sculptures survive today.

Prophet did not sell another work in her lifetime and died in obscure poverty in December 1960. Her funeral was paid for by her last employer.

A gifted and determined artist whose career peaked early and then fell apart, Nancy Elizabeth Prophet dramatically illustrates the difficulties of the black artist in the early decades of the 20th century. If she had enjoyed the middle-class advantages and the financial security of her more fortunate contemporary META VAUX WARRICK FULLER, her life and career might have turned out very differently.

Further Reading

Barnwell Andrea D., ed. *Hale Woodruff, Nancy Elizabeth Prophet, and the Academy.* Atlanta Ga.: Spelman College Museum of Fine Arts, 2007.

"Nancy Elizabeth Prophet." Available online. URL: http://www.answers.com/topic/nancy-elizabeth-prophet. Downloaded March 10, 2009.

Rozelle, Robert V., Alvia Wardlaw, and Maureen A. McKenna, eds. *Black Art, Ancestral Legacy: The African Impulse in African-American Art.* Dallas, Tex.: The Dallas Museum of Art, 1989, pp. 145, 286.

Puryear, Martin
(1941–   ) *sculptor, educator*

A sculptor of exacting craftsmanship and meticulous design, Martin Puryear draws on the great tradition of worldwide craftspeople as well as his own protean imagination.

He was born on May 23, 1941, in Washington, D.C., the eldest of seven children. His father, Reginald Puryear, was a postal worker, and his mother, Martina, was an elementary teacher. He enrolled at the Catholic University of America in Washington in 1959 and graduated with a Bachelor of Arts degree in 1963. In 1964, Puryear joined the Peace Corps and was sent to the West African nation of Sierra Leone. For two years he taught biology, French, English, and art at a mission school. He also worked with native craftsmen and carpenters and learned from them traditional methods of wood joinery using hand tools.

Puryear's strong interest in the craft of woodworking next led him to Sweden, where he studied etching and sculpture at the Swedish Royal Academy of Art in Stockholm from 1966 to 1968. During this time he met master woodcraftsman James Krenov who was living in Stockholm at that time. Meeting Krenov had a profound effect on his sculpture.

On his return to the United States, Puryear enrolled in graduate school at Yale University in New Haven, Connecticut, and received a Master of Fine Arts degree in 1971.

His earliest paintings and prints were realistic. During his years in Africa his work became increasingly abstract, and since his return from Sweden he has devoted himself almost entirely to work in three dimensions. Wood continues to be the primary medium for Puryear, although he has worked with bronze, granite, and steel, as well as less conventional sculptural materials such as thatch, stone masonry, molded rawhide, and tarred wire mesh.

In his work, Puryear aims to distill complex shapes into a kind of essential form. Unlike minimalists, his works can be replete with myriad associations, and they almost always bear the evidence of their making—the wooden surfaces, especially, alive with the marks of the hard tools he uses to finish them. His works in public places are often quite large and are usually generated by the nature of the site.

Puryear moved to a studio in Brooklyn, New York, in the early 1970s. The studio was destroyed in a fire in 1977, and the following year he moved to Chicago, Illinois.

He is the recipient of numerous awards and fellowships, including a Louis Comfort Tiffany grant in 1982, a John S. Guggenheim Memorial Foundation Grant in 1982–83, and a John D. and Catherine T. MacArthur Foundation Fellowship in 1989. That same year he won the grand prize at the São Paulo Biennial in Brazil, where he was the only artist from the United States represented. Puryear was a visiting artist at the American Academy of Rome in 1986. In 2003, Puryear served on the Jury for the World Trade Center Site Memorial Competition. The Museum of Modern Art (MOMA) in New York City mounted a 30-year retrospective of his work in 2007–08. His works are part of the permanent collections of such prestigious museums as the Guggenheim, MOMA, and the Whitney Museum of American Art in New York City; the National Gallery of Art in Washington, D.C.; and the Art Institute of Chicago.

"Puryear's work intersects at the crossroads of the fine art and craft tradition," wrote Crystal Britton. "It celebrates an ancestral tradition that in his hands—whether creating a functional chair or an architectural abstraction of a teepee—becomes modern art."

Considered by some to be one of the most influential and innovative American sculptors alive today, Martin Puryear lives in upstate New York.

Further Reading

Benezra, Neal. *Martin Puryear.* London: Thames & Hudson, 1993.

Crutchfield, Margo. *Martin Puryear: Exhibition Venues, the Virginia Museum of Fine Arts, Richmond, March 6–May 27, 2001.* Charlottesville: University of Virginia Press, 2001, pp. 163.

Desai, Wishakha, and Kathy Halbreich. *Connections: Martin Puryear.* Boston: Boston Museum of Fine Art, 1990.

Elderfield, John, Elizabeth Reede, Richard Powell, Michael Auping, and Martin Puryear. *Martin Puryear.* New York: Museum of Modern Art, 2007.

Gibson, Eric. "Visionary Sculpture." *Washington (D.C.) Times,* February 9, 1992.

Randall, Herbert
(Herbert Eugene Randall, Jr.)
(1936–) *photographer, educator*

Photographer Herbert Randall's remarkable chronicle of the "freedom summer" of 1964 in a Mississippi town waited 35 years before it finally saw the light of day and made him famous.

He was born on December 16, 1936, in the Bronx, New York, of African-American and Native American heritage. He was the second of three children of Herbert Randall Sr., a factory worker, and Jane Hunter Randall, a homemaker. Randall attended junior college and studied photography with Harold Feinstein in 1957. The following year he went to work as a freelance photographer for the Associated Press (AP) and other publications.

In 1964, Randall received a John Hay Whitney Fellowship for Creative Photography and used it to finance a trip to Hattiesburg, Mississippi, to document the Civil Rights movement there. He made the trip hidden under a blanket in the back seat of a car for his own safety. Once in Hattiesburg, Randall took more than 1,800 photographs of the turmoil and excitement as civil rights activists came under attack by white racists in that small southern city. He took pictures of community centers, voter registration campaigns, and outbursts of violent reaction from local whites. His photograph

of Rabbi Arthur Lelyveld, bloodied after being attacked by a racist with a tire iron, appeared in newspapers and magazines around the world. Surprisingly, only four more of Randall's pictures from that time were published.

After returning to New York, Randall spent the next 15 years teaching photography in city high schools. He moved to the Shinnecock Indian reservation in Southampton, New York, in 1981, where he worked as a school bus driver and a custodian.

In 1998, Randall donated his entire collection of negatives from Freedom Summer to the University of South Mississippi in Hattiesburg. About a hundred of them were first exhibited the following year on the Hattiesburg campus to commemorate the 35th anniversary of that summer.

The interest generated by this show resulted in the publication of the photographs in the book *Faces of Freedom Summer: The Photographs of Herbert Randall* (2000). "This is," according to one reviewer, "the only record of a single town in the midst of the Civil Rights revolution in America." The book was accompanied by another major exhibition of Randall's work at the Parrish Art Museum in Southampton.

Randall's photographs reside in the permanent collections of the Museum of Modern Art in New York City; the George Eastman House in Rochester, New York; and the Library of Congress in Washington, D.C.

Herbert Randall waited 35 years for his insightful collection of civil rights photographs to be appreciated by the public. *(Anthony Barboza)*

"When asked to make a statement regarding my work I'm sometimes amused," Randall has said, "for my sincerest hope is that the work has made the statement." Now retired, Randall continues to live on the Shinnecock reservation.

Further Reading

"Mississippi Summer Photograph by Herbert Randall." Special Collection, the University of Southern Mississippi Libraries. Available online. URL: http://www.lib.usm.edu/spcol/exhibitions/item_of_the_month/iotm_feb_09.html. Downloaded March 31, 2009.

Randall, Herbert, and Bobs M. Tusa. *Faces of Freedom Summer: The Photographs of Herbert Randall.* Tuscaloosa: University of Alabama Press, 2001.

"Southern Discomfort: Photographer Herbert Randall Recalls the Freedom Summer of 1964." Available online. URL: http://sagharborexpress. sagharborpublishing.com/shexpress/arts/southern-discomfort-photographer-herbert-randall-recalls-the-freedom-summer-of-1964-2124. Downloaded March 31, 2009.

Ransome, James E.
(1961–   ) *illustrator, educator, muralist*

The illustrator of more than two dozen children's books, James E. Ransome is a powerful storyteller with a strong, dramatic drawing style.

He was born on September 25, 1961, in Rich Square, North Carolina, where his grandmother raised him. As a child, he read the Bible to her and was inspired by the beautiful illustrations that accompanied the biblical stories. Some of his first drawings were copies of these Bible pictures, along with the art from comic books. Ransome's introduction to art was a correspondence course in cartooning that he read about in a comic book advertisement.

This situation changed when he moved to Bergenfield, New Jersey, in his early teens. He attended Bergenfield High School, where he took courses in filmmaking and photography. "Through filmmaking," he has written, "I discovered the many ways to pace a story with the aid of camera angles and framed images." His film teacher encouraged him to take a drawing class, which reintroduced Ransome to illustration.

After high school, he enrolled in the Pratt Institute in Brooklyn, New York. There he met JERRY PINKNEY while sitting in on a senior class in illustration. Pinkney was the first African-American illustrator Ransome knew, and he encouraged the student to pursue illustration. Pinkney later became his friend and mentor. While at Pratt, Ransome was one of 12 finalists out of 2,000 artists to illustrate the annual Citibank calendar. He graduated from Pratt with a Bachelor of Fine Arts degree.

The first children's book he illustrated was *Aunt Flossie's Hats (and Crab Cakes Later)* (1990) by Elizabeth Fitzgerald Howard, which immediately established him as a sensitive illustrator of African-American families. Other books about rich, warm characters in black families followed, including *Do Like Kyla* (1990), *Does Your Grandpa Say Galoshes?* (1991), and *Uncle Jed's Barbershop* (1993). In a review in *Booklist*, critic Deborah Abbott said Ransome's paintings for this last book "capture memorable characters and family life in the rural South with a warmth and depth that is truly moving."

Ransome's magnificent painterly illustrations for *The Creation* (1994), a poetic retelling of the biblical creation story by black writer James Weldon Johnson, helped the book win a Coretta Scott King Award. Two of Ransome's best-known books deal with slavery and its effects on black children. *Sweet Clara and the Freedom Quilt* (1999), written by Deborah Hopkinson, is about a slave girl who creates a map of the Underground Railroad on a patchwork quilt. *The Wagon* (1999), written by Tony Johnston, was awarded the Simon Wiesenthal Memorial of Tolerance Award. It is a 12-year-old boy's account of plantation life before and during the Civil War.

More recently, Ransome has turned his hand to African-American folklore in such works as *How Animals Save the People: Animal Tales from the South* by J. J. Reneaux and *The Secret of the Stones* by Robert D. San Souci, both published in 2000. He has also collaborated with his wife, children's author Lesa Cline-Ransome, on several books, including a biography of legendary black baseball player Leroy "Satchel" Paige. Another recent biography, *Pele* (2009), is about the famous soccer player.

Ransome received the NAACP Image Award in 1999 for his book *Let My People Go*. Two years later he received the Rip Van Winkle Award given by the School Library Media Specialists of Southeast New York for his body of work. Ransome's traveling exhibition, *Visual Stories*, has been touring the nation since 2003. He has created murals for several institutions including the National Underground Railroad Freedom Center in Cincinnati, Ohio, and the Children's Museum in Indianapolis, Indiana.

James E. Ransome currently teaches illustration at the Pratt Institute and lives in Rhinebeck, New York, with his wife and their four children.

"What makes illustrating so exciting is that each book has a special voice, and my approach to each is different," Ransome has said. "Whether it be through my choice of palette, design or perspective, there is always a desire to experiment and explore."

Further Reading

Cline-Ransome, Lesa, and James E. Ransome, illustrator. *Satchel Paige*. New York: Aladdin Paperbacks, 2003.

Hopkinson, Deborah, and James E. Ransome, illustrator. *Sky Boys: How They Built the Empire State Building*. New York: Schwartz & Wade, 2006.

Johnson, James Weldon, and James E. Ransome, illustrator. *The Creation*. New York: Holiday House, 1995.

Johnston, Tony, and James E. Ransome, illustrator. *The Wagon*. New York: Mulberry Books, 1999.

Official James Ransome Web site. Available online. URL: http://www.jamesransome.com. Downloaded March 10, 2009.

Peacock, Scot, ed. *Something About the Author, Volume 123*. Detroit, Mich.: Gale Research, 2001, pp. 128–132.

Thomson, Sarah L., and James E. Ransome, illustrator. *What Lincoln Said*. New York: Collins, 2008.

Rembert, Winfred
(1945–   ) *folk leather painter*

A unique artist who creates vivid scenes from his eventful life on large pieces of leather, Winfred Rembert rose to artistic success after serving seven years in prison and working for decades as a heavy equipment operator and longshoreman.

He was born out of wedlock on November 22, 1945, in Americus, Georgia. Abandoned by his parents, he was raised by his great-aunt Lillian,

Folk artist Winfred Rembert paints his powerful scenes from the rural South of his youth on large pieces of leather. *(Sharon McBlain)*

whom he lovingly called "Mama." As a child, he worked in the cotton fields and was never able to attend school more than part-time. The Remberts were poor but felt a part of the black community. All that changed during a race riot in Americus in 1965. In an effort to flee the riot, 20-year-old Rembert stole a car and was later captured by police. In jail, a deputy sheriff entered his cell to beat him. Rembert eventually defended himself, overpowered the deputy, and fled with his gun. When he was caught this time, vigilantes took turns beating him and finally drove him to a remote spot at dawn. They strung him up by his feet to a tree. Rembert was certain he was going to be lynched.

"All I could see were feet," he recalled. "And I saw a pair of wingtip shoes walk into the crowd."

Whoever the man wearing the shoes was, he saved Rembert's life. However, Rembert was beaten again and brought back to jail. He was later convicted and sentenced to 27 years.

Rembert was sent to Reedsville State Prison. He was later assigned to a prison work camp in Ashburn, Georgia. While at that camp he met his future wife Patsy, who lived near the camp, and learned the craft of tooling leather at Bainbridge Public Work Camp from an older prisoner who made decorative billfolds. Rembert's sentence was commuted to seven years, and he was released in 1974. He and Patsy married and moved to Rochester, New York, where they lived briefly. While living in Rochester he made billfolds and purses but abandoned those efforts as unprofitable. After a brief return to Georgia, the Remberts moved to

Bridgeport, Connecticut. There he worked as a heavy equipment operator and longshoreman.

The Remberts, who had eight children, moved to nearby New Haven, Connecticut, in 1986. Rembert eventually had to stop working because of injuries sustained on the job. His wife suggested he pick up leatherwork again, this time to re-create moments from his past. He finished his first leather painting in 1997 and gave it as a gift to a friend who ran an antiquarian bookstore. When a customer admired the work, the storeowner sold it to him and gave Rembert the money. Encouraged by the sale, the artist set up a small studio in his New Haven home and began tooling pictures on leather pieces, some as large as five feet by three feet. Then he dyed them, completing perhaps one work a month. The work was painstaking and unforgiving, since one mistake could ruin an entire picture. There is no erasing on leather.

In 1999, Rembert met Jock Reynolds, the director of the Yale University Art Gallery, at a meeting of local members of the artistic community. Reynolds was deeply impressed by Rembert's work and the following year mounted an exhibit of his paintings at the Yale Gallery along with that of HALE WOODRUFF under the title *Southern Exposure*. Yale has since purchased for its permanent collection three of Rembert's pieces depicting lynchings.

Rembert's unique leather paintings vividly recount scenes and experiences from his early life in Georgia. In *Labor Pains*, a woman gives birth to her baby in a cotton field. In *Chain Gang III*, part of a series, Rembert is seen at work in a field with other prisoners. He is the only worker with his head down, not wanting to be identified by the viewer.

"Winfred is entirely self-taught," Reynolds has said. "But he has this remarkably sophisticated sense of imagery and color and composition."

Rembert's work was exhibited at the Kresge Gallery at Ramapo College of New Jersey in Mahwah in 2002 and at the Hand Workshop in Richmond, Virginia, in 2003. The same year his autobiography for children, *Don't Hold Me Back: My Life and Art*, was published. More recently his first solo show, "Memories of My Youth" appeared at New York's Adelson Galleries from April to June, 2010.

Further Reading

Doherty, Donna. "Call Him 'Artist' Winfred Rembert's First Solo Show Confirms What Many Already Knew about His Leather Paintings." *New Haven Register*, May 13, 2010.

King, Chris. "A Lifetime Patiently Etched into Leather." *New York Times*, December 23, 2000, Connecticut section, p. 1.

Oppenhimer, William and Ann. "The Indelible Images of Winfred Rembert." *The Folk Art Messenger*, Summer/Fall, 2003.

Rembert, Winfred. *Don't Hold Me Back: My Life and Art*. Chicago: Cricket Books, 2003.

Southern Exposures: Works by Winfred Rembert and Hale Woodruff. New Haven, Conn.: Yale University Art Gallery, 2000 [brochure].

Winfred Rembert's Official Web site. Available online URL: http://www.winfredrembert.com/. Downloaded March 10, 2009.

Ringgold, Faith

(1930–   ) *painter, quilter, sculptor, illustrator, writer, educator, performance artist*

One of the most multitalented African-American female artists of her generation, Faith Ringgold has expressed her thoughts about feminism, race, and politics through sculpture, multimedia works, paintings, illustrations, and most strikingly in about 100 painted story quilts.

She was born on October 8, 1930, in New York City. Her father drove a sanitation truck and her mother studied fashion design and taught her how to sew. At the age of two Ringgold came down with asthma, an allergic disorder of the respiratory system. Confined to bed by her ailment, she first discovered the joy of creating art. "The days when

I lay in bed were the foundation of my life as an artist," she has said. "There I was, making things in my bed: drawings, watercolors. . . . Art was fun. It was something I could do alone."

After graduating from high school, Ringgold enrolled at the City College of New York in 1948.

Two years later she married a jazz musician. They had two daughters, but the marriage soon broke apart. She earned a Bachelor of Arts degree in 1952 and began teaching art at the School of Education at City College a few years later. When she earned her Master of Arts degree from City

Faith Ringgold sits before one of her more than 100 story quilts, some of which she has adapted into children's books. *(© Grace Matthews, 1993)*

College in 1959, Ringgold decided she wanted to become a professional artist. She was further inspired to do so after a trip to France and Italy with her mother and daughters to view the great masters of European art. When she returned home, Ringgold set up a small studio in her dinette and began to paint. She married Burdette Ringgold in the early 1960s, and he encouraged her to take her work to galleries.

She gradually evolved from imitating the work of white artists to creating her own African-American style. One of her first mature works was *Die,* a 12-foot-wide mural that depicted an urban race riot in graphic detail. By the early 1970s, Ringgold was an activist in the women's liberation and Black Power movements that swept the nation. Her strong feminist beliefs were expressed fully in *For the Women's House,* another large mural created for the Women's House of Detention on Rikers Island in New York. In 1971 she helped found Where We at Black Women, with Kay Brown and Dindga McCannon, a women artists' group that sought more opportunities for black women artists.

In 1973, Rutgers University in New Brunswick, New Jersey, mounted a 10-year retrospective of Ringgold's paintings. One of her students questioned why she did not display works using the techniques she was teaching her. These included such crafts as beading, quilting, figure making, and tie-dyeing. This caused Ringgold to ponder her development as an artist of African heritage, and she began to focus on these neglected styles.

The most celebrated of her new works were her painted story quilts, which combined her love of craft and painting with her love of storytelling. To date, she has made more than 100 quilts. Ringgold thinks up her story and characters and then breaks the story down into scenes or chapters. After much work, she makes her quilt and writes the text of the story on it with black felt markers.

Tar Beach, a partly autobiographical quilt story about a girl who flies above the rooftop of her Harlem home in 1939, became her first children's book. It won the Coretta Scott King Award for Illustration and was also named a Caldecott Honor Book. Since then, Ringgold has written and illustrated more than 10 children's books, including *If a Bus Could Talk: The Story of Rosa Parks* (1999) and *O Holy Night* (2004). She has also created new illustrations for Zora Neale Hurston's story *The Three Witches* (2005) and Gwendolyn Brooks's poetry collection *Bronzeville Boys and Girls* (2006). Ringgold is the recipient of the 2005 President's Award from the Amistad Center for Art and Culture and the 2006 Harlem Arts Alliance Gold Legacy Visual Arts Award. A gala "Faith Ringgold: A Celebration," was held in her honor at Rutgers on May 17, 2009.

Recently Ringgold has turned to performance art. Her *The Wake and Resurrection of the Bicentennial Negro* combines dance, art, and music, and it has been performed in churches and colleges across the country.

Faith Ringgold is a professor of art at the University of California in San Diego. Her daughter Michele Wallace is a writer and author of the book *Black Macho and the Myth of the Superwoman* (1979).

Further Reading

Cameron, Don. *Dancing at the Louvre: Faith Ringgold's French Collection and Other Story Quilts.* Berkeley: University of California Press, 1998.

Farrington, Lisa E. *Faith Ringgold* (The David C. Driskell Series of African American Art, Vol. 3.) San Francisco, Calif.: Pomegranate Communications, 2004.

Gouma-Peterson, Thalia, and Kathleen McManus Zurke. *Faith Ringgold: Paintings, Sculptures, Performance.* Wooster, Ohio: The College of Wooster Art Museum, 1985.

Holton, Curlee Raven, and Faith Ringgold. *Faith Ringgold: A View from the Studio.* Piermont, N.H.: Bunker Hill Publishing, 2005.

Ringgold, Faith. *Tar Beach.* Cleveland Heights, Ohio: Dragonfly Books, 1996.

————. *We Flew Over the Bridge: The Memoirs of Faith Ringgold*. Durham N.C.: Duke University Press, 2005.

Venezia, Mike. *Faith Ringgold* (Getting to Know the World's Greatest Artists). Danbury, Conn.: Children's Press, 2008.

Further Viewing

Faith Ringgold: The Last Story Quilt (1992). Home Vision, VHS, 1999.

I Can Fly, Part 5: Kids & Women Artists in Their Studies. L & S Video, DVD.

Rowe, Nellie Mae
(Nellie Mae Williams)
(1900–1982) *folk installation artist, painter, dollmaker*

A remarkable artist who transformed her home environment into the ultimate work of art, Nellie Mae Rowe incorporated painting, drawing, collage, sculpture made of chewing gum, and dolls into what she called her "playhouse."

She was born Nellie Mae Williams on July 4, 1900, in Fayette, Georgia, 20 miles south of the city of Atlanta. She was one of 10 children born to Sam Williams, an ex-slave blacksmith and basketmaker, and Luella Swanson Williams, a quilter, who taught her the craft as a child. Growing up, Williams displayed an early aptitude for art. She twisted pieces of laundry into the shape of dolls and drew pictures on scraps of paper.

Williams married Ben Wheat when she was 16. They farmed for a living, then moved to Vinings, a suburb of Atlanta in 1930, where she worked as a domestic.

Wheat died six years later, and Nellie Mae married Henry Rowe in 1937. He built her a one-story cottage by the Chattahoochee River, where she lived for the remaining 40 years of her life. Henry Rowe died in 1948. Alone and lonely, his widow began to decorate her home and yard with her highly eccentric artwork. She hung bottles, chimes, paintings, and photographs from trees and on her house. She placed homemade dolls around the place to greet passersby and created fantastic sculptured heads out of chewing gum that she collected in a coffee can. A sign on her door read "My Home Is Clean Enough to Be Healthy and Dirty Enough to Be Happy."

What made Rowe happy did not please many of her neighbors. Some of them thought she was practicing hoodoo magic and vandalized her playhouse. Rowe's response was to invite them to tour her property and sign a guest book. The attitudes of the naysayers changed, and from 1973 to 1975 more than 800 visitors signed her guest book. Her playhouse soon attracted regional attention and became a tourist attraction.

In the decade from 1972 to 1982, Rowe concentrated on drawings made with ballpoint pens and felt-tip markers. Dense, complex works, they were noted for their linear design and warm colors. Many drawings contained messages of her strong religious faith.

While a number of the art objects in her playhouse were personal and autobiographical, Rowe also created pieces that reflected the life around her. During the series of child murders in Atlanta in 1979–81, she created *Atlanta's Missing Children*, a painting that centered on a mysterious conjurer woman of healing power. She hung the work on her screen door to comfort people who were distraught over the crimes.

Rowe's drawings were exhibited in a public building for the first time in 1976 as part of a group exhibit sponsored by the Atlanta Historical Society. Two years later art dealer Judith Alexander began to represent and sell her work.

Nellie Mae Rowe died of cancer among her beloved artworks on October 18, 1982. In 1998, a retrospective of her work, *The Art of Nellie Mae Rowe: Ninety-Nine and a Half Won't Do*, was held at the Museum of American Folk Art in New York City.

"Her work is not only a declaration of her innate sense of design and color and the skillful variation of a selected vocabulary of form," wrote Lee Kogan, "it is also a testament to the force of her personality, innate wisdom, and creative vision." Rowe put it more simply: "I would take nothin' and make somethin' out of it."

Further Reading

Cook, Sterling. *Two Black Folk Artists: Clementine Hunter and Nellie Mae Rowe.* Oxford, Ohio: Miami University Art Museum, 1986.

Kogan, Lee, and Nellie Mae Rowe. *The Art of Nellie Mae Rowe: Ninety-Nine and a Half Won't Do.* Jackson: University Press of Mississippi, 1998.

Livingston, Jane, and John Beardsley. *Black Folk Art in America 1930–1980.* Jackson: University Press of Mississippi, 1989, pp. 122–127.

"Nellie Mae Rowe (1900–1982)." New Georgia Encyclopedia. Available online. URL: http://www.newgeorgiaencyclopedia.org/nge/Article.jsp?id=h-1037. Downloaded March 10, 2009.

S

Saar, Alison
(1956–) *sculptor, printmaker, illustrator*

One of the few contemporary sculptors who works primarily in wood, Alison Saar captures both the terrible burden of slavery and the mystical power of a still-remembered African past in her remarkable sculptures.

She was born on February 5, 1956, in Los Angeles, (L.A.) California, one of three daughters. Her father, Richard W. Saar, is a white art conservator and writer. Her mother, BETYE SAAR, is a sculptor and collagist, and was an important role model for both Alison and her sister Lezley, who is also a professional artist.

Saar enrolled at Scripps College in Claremont, California, in 1974. She graduated four years later with a dual degree in art history and studio art, a rare accomplishment for an African-American artist. She received a Master of Fine Arts degree from the Otis Art Institute in L.A. in 1981. The following year, at age 26, Saar had her first solo exhibition at L.A.'s Jan Baum Gallery.

Since the 1990s, Saar has sculpted mostly in woods, adding metals and found objects over the wooden surface. One of her first and best-known wood sculptures is *Terra Firma* (1991), a sleeping figure of a black man resting on the earth. It is composed of wood, tin, tar, and found objects. The man seems weary from the physical and psy-chological weight of slavery. This profound work was part of the Whitney Museum of American Art's 1994 group exhibit *Black Male Representations of Masculinity in Contemporary American Art.*

In *Clean House* (1993), the figure of a black woman is covered in tin and aluminum paint with tree limbs literally growing out of her. The tree imagery in this and other works may refer to the fact that escaping slaves often hid in the roots of trees while making their way north.

"Saar is perhaps revealing the sanctity of nature," writes art critic Ajontyle Theresa Robinson, "and the creatures that dwell in and within natural objects."

The powerful appeal of Saar's work has resulted in many exhibitions. In 1992 alone, she had five solo shows at the Museum of Contemporary Art in Baltimore, Maryland; the Cleveland Center for Contemporary Art in Ohio; and other museums. *Alison Saar: Whither* opened at the Phyllis Kind Gallery in New York City in 2007. In 2008, *Alison Saar: Thither* was mounted at LA Louver in Venice, California. Saar's 13-foot tall sculpture of abolitionist Harriet Tubman, commissioned by the City of New York, was unveiled in Harlem at 123rd Street in September 2007.

Further Reading
"Alison Saar LA Louver." Available online. URL: http://www.lalouver.com/html/saar_bio.html. Downloaded April 1, 2009.

Hunt, Erica, and Alison Saar, illustrator. *Arcade.* Berkeley, Calif.: Kelsey Street Press, 1996.

Roberts, Mary Nooker, and Alison Saar. *Body Politics: The Female Image in Luba Art and the Sculpture of Alison Saar.* Berkeley: The Museum of the University of California, 2000.

Saar, Alison. *Duped: Prints by Alison Saar.* Delaware Center for the Contemporary Arts, 2007.

Saar, Betye, Lezley Saar, Alison Saar, and Tracye Saar-Cavanaugh. *Family Legacies: The Art at Betye, Lezley, and Alison Saar.* Seattle: University of Washington Press, 2005.

Shepherd, Elizabeth, ed. *Secrets, Dialogues, Revelations: The Art of Betye and Alison Saar.* Seattle: University of Washington Press, 1997.

Further Viewing

Betye and Alison Saar: Conjure Women of the Arts (1994). L & S Video, VHS, 1999.

Similar Differences: Betye and Alison Saar. Fellows of Contemporary Art, VHS, 1990.

Saar, Betye
(Betye Irene Maze)
(1926–   ) *sculptor, collagist, mixed-media artist, educator, illustrator*

A leading contemporary female artist, Betye Saar uses discarded objects from the collective and personal past to create intriguing collages and other works that speak about a racist past and a turbulent present.

She was born Betye Irene Maze in Los Angeles, California, on July 30, 1926, the eldest of three children. Her father died when she was six, and the family moved to Pasadena, where her mother worked as a seamstress and domestic. She enrolled at UCLA and earned a Bachelor of Arts degree in 1949. She married artist Richard W. Saar in 1951, and they had three daughters. Saar became a costume designer for the Napa Valley Theater Company in 1968, the same year that she divorced her husband. She pursued painting until she was inspired by an exhibit of the box assemblages of Joseph Cornell. In 1966, she created her first "window assemblage," *Mystic Window for Leo* (1966).

"The window is a way of traveling from one level of consciousness to another, like the physical looking into the spiritual," she has said.

The Civil Rights movement of the 1960s and 1970s led to one of Saar's most celebrated works, *The Liberation of Aunt Jemima* (1972). This humorous but challenging assemblage depicts the stereotyped mammy from a pancake-mix box transformed into a revolutionary. She wields a broomstick in one hand and a rifle in the other. Another assemblage, *Spirit Catcher* (1976), focuses on African mysticism in spiritual objects. Saar finds the objects she uses in her collages and assemblages at swap meets, junkyards, and secondhand stores.

In 1975, the Whitney Museum of American Art in New York City mounted a one-person show of Saar's work. In recent years, her art has gotten more personal and autobiographical. In *Watching* (1995), a self-portrait of the artist stares out from behind an old furnace grate on which sits a figure of the stereotyped black Jim Crow. An abstract series called *Letters from Home* was inspired by the discovery of her great-aunt's letters.

Saar was twice awarded National Endowment of the Arts (NEA) Fellowships, in 1974 and 1984. She received a Guggenheim Memorial Foundation Grant in 1991, the James Van DerZee Grant in 1992, the Distinguished Art Award from the Fresno Art Museum in 1993, and an honorary doctorate degree from the California Institute of the Arts in 1995. She taught art at the Otis Art Institute in Los Angeles from 1976 to 1983. Saar has also illustrated *A Secretary to the Spirits*, a book by black author and poet Ishmael Reed.

Recent solo exhibitions of her work have been held at the Anderson Ranch Art Center, Snowmass, Colorado (1999); the Savannah College of Art and Design, Savannah, Georgia (2000); and the Crocker Art Museum, Sacramento, California (2006).

Betye Saar is at work on one of her fascinating assemblages in her California studio. *(Photofest)*

Her daughter ALISON SAAR is a well-known sculptor. Mother and daughter collaborated on the work *The House of Gris Gris* (1988) for the Wright Art Gallery of UCLA. Another daughter, Lezley, is also an artist.

"I am intrigued with combining the remnants of memories, fragments of relics, and ordinary objects with the components of technology," Betye Saar has said. "It's a way of delving into the past and reaching into the future simultaneously. The art itself becomes the bridge."

Further Reading

Betye Saar's official Web site. Available online. URL: http://betyesaar.net/. Downloaded March 10, 2009.

Carpenter, Jane H., David C. Driskell, and Betye Saar. *Betye Saar* (The David C. Driskell Series of African American Art, vol. 2). San Francisco, Calif.: Pomegranate Communications, 2003.

Riggs, Thomas, ed. *St. James Guide to Black Artists.* Detroit, Mich.: St. James Press, 1997, pp. 464–465.

Shepherd, Elizabeth, ed. *Secrets, Dialogues, Revelations: The Art of Betye and Alison Saar.* Seattle: University of Washington Press, 1997.

Steward, James Christen, Deborah Willis, Kellie Jones, Richard Candida Smith, and Lowery Stokes Sims. *Betye Saar: Extending the Frozen Moment.* Berkeley: University of California Press, 2005.

Further Viewing

Betye and Alison Saar: Conjure Women of the Arts (1994). L & S Video, VHS, 1999.

Similar Differences: Betye and Alison Saar. Fellows of Contemporary Art, VHS, 1990.

Saunders, Raymond

(1934–) *painter, mixed-media artist, educator*

An abstract artist with an unusually expressive personal vision, Raymond Saunders incorporates his experiences and that of the black urban landscape into his bright-colored paintings through numbers, letters, and a bewildering array of found objects, from tin cans to ticket stubs.

He was born in Pittsburgh, Pennsylvania, on October 28, 1934. He attended the Carnegie

Raymond Saunders is known for his eccentric and highly personal paintings and assemblages. *(Anthony Barboza)*

Institute of Technology in Pittsburgh from 1950 to 1953 and then studied at the Pennsylvania Academy of the Fine Arts in Philadelphia from 1953 to 1957. Saunders earned a Bachelor of Fine Arts degree in 1960 from the Carnegie Institute and a Master of Fine Arts degree in 1961 from the California College of Arts & Crafts in Oakland, California.

His first paintings were exercises in pop art, featuring bold colors and such recurring figures as the cartoon character Mickey Mouse and sidewalk hopscotch boxes. Saunders's work has become more fragmented and ambitious over the years. His later paintings are mixed-media assemblages including everything from the names of his favorite jazz musicians to odds and ends he has picked up in his many travels to Mexico and Europe. The objects include parking signs, discarded gum wrappers and soda bottles, and plaster figurines. These things vie for attention with chalked letters and stenciled numbers, usually all set against a black background.

Although his works appear to be random views of a disjointed reality, there is nothing casual about Saunders's approach to his art. He is one of the few contemporary artists who never considers his work quite finished. He has been known to enter galleries where his paintings are on display to add touches here and there to improve a canvas. In reviewing a 1998 exhibit of his paintings at Hunter College in New York City, Eleanor Heartney wrote, "Saunders operates between exuberance and poignancy, rude energy and elegance, muted outrage and gentle humor. This vibrant show provided a chronicle of pleasure, pain, and inescapable contradictions."

An eccentric and expressive artist whose work often defies description, Raymond Saunders lives in Oakland, where he is professor of painting at California College of the Arts. He maintains studios in Paris, France, and Venice, Italy. His work is sold through the Stephen Wirtz Gallery in San Francisco, California, where he had solo exhibitions in 1999, 2001, 2003, 2005, and 2007.

Further Reading

Heartney, Eleanor. "Raymond Saunders at Hunter College," *Art in America.* Find Articles website. Available online. URL: http://www.findarticles.com/m1248/n9_v86/21268588/pl/article.jhtml. Downloaded July 11, 2002.
"Raymond Saunders Biography." Stephen Wirtz Gallery. Available online. URL: http://www.wirtzgallery.com/bios/bio_saunders.html. Downloaded March 10, 2009.
Riggs, Thomas, ed. *St. James Guide to Black Artists.* Detroit, Mich.: St. James Press, 1997, pp. 467–470.
Stephen Wirtz Gallery. *Raymond Saunders.* San Francisco: Stephen Wirtz Gallery, 2003.

Savage, Augusta
(Augusta Christine Fells)
(1892–1962) *sculptor, educator*

One of the most influential African-American art teachers of the 20th century and a bold spokeswoman for black artists, Augusta Savage tragically never fulfilled her own promise as a leading sculptor.

She was born Augusta Christine Fells on February 29, 1892, in Green Cove Springs, Florida, the seventh of 14 children. Her father, Reverend Edward Fells, was a Methodist minister who beat her when he found her making animals out of clay. "My father," she said years later, "almost whipped all the art out of me."

To get away from her family, she married John T. Moore when she was 15. They had a daughter a year later, and soon thereafter Moore died. Augusta moved back with her parents. By now, her father had accepted her artistic gifts, and she sold sculpted heads of local people. In 1915 she married carpenter James Savage, whom she later divorced, but she kept his name.

On her own, Savage traveled to New York City to pursue her career as a sculptor, leaving her daughter behind with her parents. She was befriended by sculptor Solon Borglum, father of Gutzon Borglum, the man who created the heads of the presidents on Mount Rushmore. Borglum helped her enter the art program at Cooper Union. Although she ran out of money to pay for her expenses, her teachers persuaded the school's board of trustees to give her a scholarship. In 1923 Savage applied for a summer art school at the Palace of Fontainebleau outside of Paris, France, but was rejected because she was black. Incensed by this blatant act of racism, the 31-year-old Savage challenged the decision, bringing her national attention. This bold act hurt her career, as she was unable to promote her art and found herself spending more and more time being a political activist.

She did, however, gain some fame as a portrait sculptor. She made a bust of black leader and NAACP cofounder W. E. B. DuBois for the Harlem branch of the New York Public Library at West 135th Street. Today it is considered the best likeness of DuBois in existence. She also sculpted a bust of black leader Marcus Garvey. While working with Garvey, Savage met his associate in the "Back to Africa" movement, Robert L. Poston, whom she married in 1923. Poston died a short time later on a ship returning from the African nation of Liberia, where Garvey planned to establish a colony of African Americans. It was Savage's last marriage.

Perhaps Savage's best-known bust was of her nephew. Entitled *Gamin,* it captured the humanity and liveliness of black youth. Savage spent the years 1929 to 1932 in Europe on two Rosenwald Fellowships and set up the Savage Studio of Arts and Crafts in Harlem on her return. She was a charismatic and demanding teacher who inspired her students to do their best. They included such

Sculptor and teacher Augusta Savage communicated the joy she found in creating art to her many students. *(Photofest)*

future artists as sculptor WILLIAM E. ARTIS and painter NORMAN LEWIS. In 1937, Savage was appointed the first director of the Harlem City Arts Center. She also helped to establish the Harlem Artists Guild.

That same year, Savage was commissioned to create a work for the upcoming New York World's Fair that would reflect "the American Negro's contribution to music." The resulting work, *The Harp* (1939), took her two years to complete and was her largest sculpture. The 16-foot harp was made up of a line of singing black children who were its strings. A black adult male in the front of the harp offered the viewer a bar of musical notes. While critics considered it one of her lesser works, *The Harp* became one of the most celebrated artworks of the World's Fair. Unfortunately, there was not money to cast the plaster sculpture in bronze, and it was bulldozed and destroyed along with the Fair's buildings when the event ended.

In 1939, Savage returned to the Harlem City Arts Center only to find that she had been replaced as director. It closed a few years later. Undaunted, Savage opened her own Salon of Contemporary Negro Art in Harlem, where she exhibited the work of such future luminaries as RICHMOND BARTHÉ, BEAUFORD DELANEY, and JAMES LESESNE WELLS. It quickly closed due to a lack of money.

Disillusioned and bitter, Savage moved to Saugerties, New York, in 1945, where she worked for a commercial mushroom grower. She taught children art in local summer camps and wrote stories and murder mysteries that would never be published. In early 1962, she moved back to New York City to live with her daughter. She died there of cancer on March 26, 1962, all but forgotten in the art world.

Augusta Savage's life would have been a tragic one if not for the great legacy she left behind as both a teacher and an artist. "I have created nothing really beautiful, really lasting," she once said, "but if I can inspire one of these youngsters to develop the talent I know they possess, then my monument will be in their work." And so it is.

Further Reading

Bearden, Romare, and Harry Henderson. *A History of African-American Artists: From 1792 to the Present.* New York: Pantheon Books, 1993, pp. 114, 168–180.

Bolden, Tonya. *Wake Up Our Souls: A Celebration of Black American Artists.* New York: Abrams Books for Young Readers, 2009, pp. 38–44.

Perry, Regenia A. *Free Within Ourselves: African-American Artists in the Collection of the National Museum of American Art.* San Francisco: Pomegranate Communications, 1992, pp. 154–158.

Schultz, Michael

(1938–) *filmmaker, television director*

The most commercially successful black filmmaker of the 1970s, Michael Schultz has directed more hours of film and television programming than any black director with the exception of OSCAR MICHEAUX.

He was born on November 10, 1938, in Milwaukee, Wisconsin. As a young man, he was drawn to the theater and entered the theater arts program at Marquette University in his home state. He moved to New York City in 1964, after earning a degree, and worked as an actor at the American Place Theater in Manhattan. He got his first directorial assignment in 1966 at Princeton University in New Jersey. The following year, Schultz was hired as a staff director at the newly founded Negro Ensemble Company in New York. He was nominated for a Tony award for best director for the drama *Does a Tiger Wear a Necktie?,* the Broadway debut of actor Al Pacino.

Schultz's first film was *Together for Days* (1973), followed by *Honeybaby, Honeybaby* (1974), which starred black actress Diana Sands in her last screen role. Neither film was a hit, but *Cooley High* (1975), his third film, a low-budget comedy about black teens in the 1960s, was a surprise smash that grossed more than $13 million.

Over the next few years, Schultz directed three films with comedian/actor Richard Pryor that are generally considered among his best— *Car Wash* (1976), which also starred IVAN DIXON; *Greased Lightning* (1977), based on the life of the first black racing driver, Wendell Scott, with a script by MELVIN VAN PEEBLES; and *Which Way Is Up?* (1977), in which Pryor played multiple roles.

Now a leading Hollywood director, Schultz was hired to direct the extravagant rock musical *Sgt. Pepper's Lonely Hearts Club Band* (1978), featuring the music of the Beatles. The film, the most expensive ever directed up to that time by a black, was an embarrassing flop, and Schultz never regained his momentum as a filmmaker. Subsequent films such as *Carbon Copy* (1981) and the rap musical *Kush Groove* (1985) are of interest solely for having introduced leading black actors Denzel Washington and Blair Underwood.

Since the mid-1980s Schultz has worked primarily in television, directing many made-for-television movies and series episodes. His first TV movie, *For Us, the Living: The Story of Medgar Evers* (1983), based on the life and tragic death of civil rights leader Medgar Evers, is one of his best. Among the numerous television series he has worked on are *Diagnosis Murder*, *Chicago Hope*, *Ally McBeal*, *Boston Public*, *Everwood*, and *Dirty Sexy Money*. In 2010, he directed his first feature film in more than two decades, the comedy *Pool Boy*. Schultz is married to actress/producer Lauren Jones. Their son Brandon is an actor.

Further Reading

Alexander, George. *Why We Make Movies: Black Filmmakers Talk About the Magic of Cinema.* New York: Harlem Moon, 2003, pp. 71–86.

Bogle, Donald. *Toms, Coons, Mulattoes, Mammies, & Bucks: An Interpretative History of Blacks in American Films.* New York: Continuum, 1997, pp. 258, 259, 288, 345.

"Michael Schultz." Internet Movie Database. Available online. URL: http://www.imdb.com/name/nm0776317/. Downloaded April 1, 2009.

Moon, Spencer. *Reel Black Talk: A Sourcebook of 50 American Filmmakers.* Westport, Conn.: Greenwood Press, 1997, pp. 299–306.

Further Viewing

Car Wash (1976). Universal Home Video, VHS/DVD, 2001/2003.

Cooley High (1975). MGM Home Entertainment, DVD, 2000.

For Us, the Living: The Story of Medgar Evers (1983). Anchor Bay Entertainment, VHS, 1999.

Scott, Joyce J.

(Joyce Jane Scott)
(1948–) *jewelry designer, quilter, sculptor, installation artist, performance artist, printmaker, educator*

An artist of protean variety, Joyce J. Scott is acclaimed for work that ranges from delicate miniature jewelry to huge installation art that fills a museum room.

She was born Joyce Jane Scott in Baltimore, Maryland, on November 15, 1948. Both her grandmothers and her mother, Elizabeth Caldwell Scott, were quilters. Her paternal grandfather carved canoes and her maternal grandfather was a blacksmith and basketmaker. It is no surprise that with such a family heritage Scott showed an early interest in crafts of all kinds.

She attended the Maryland Institute's College of Art and earned a Bachelor of Fine Arts degree in 1970. She earned a Master of Fine Arts degree the following year at the Instituto Allende, in San Miguel de Allende, Guanajuato, Mexico. In 1976, she studied at the Haystack Mountain School of Crafts on Deer Isle, Maine.

Scott's work, in whatever form, draws on African, Latin American, Native American, and African-American cultural heritage. Scott likes to draw on an equally wide array of material in her works. For example, the ambitious installation piece *Images Concealed* (1995) is composed of beads, glass rice, coal, thread, wire, and aluminum foil. Her *P-Melon #1* is a head made out of blown glass, beads, and thread.

Things That Go Bump in the Night III was shown at Franklin & Marshall College in Lancaster, Pennsylvania, in 2002. It consisted of beaded sculpture, jewelry, and monoprints. An updated version of the retrospective *Kickin' it with Joyce J. Scott* toured 10 museums through 2007.

Scott is also a prolific performance artist. Among her many pieces are *The Body Politic*, *Bite and Smile*, and *Women of Substance*. One of her most popular pieces is the both humorous and serious *Thunder Thigh Revue* (1982), which deals with the problems faced by full-figured black females in American society.

A popular artist who enjoys meeting her public at lectures and workshops, Scott was the recipient of the Maryland State Arts Commission fellowships and a National Endowment for the Arts fellowship in crafts.

"Scott's work," writes art historian Crystal A. Britton, "constantly challenges the viewer to consider and reconsider reality. Her works, informed by West African influences, are almost always narrative in nature."

Scott has said "that the function of art is to effect change."

Further Reading

"Joyce J. Scott (1948–)" Maryland Art Source. Available online. URL: http://www.marylandart source.org/artists/detail_000000136.html. Downloaded March 11, 2009.

Riggs, Thomas, ed. *St. James Guide to Black Artists.* Detroit, Mich.: St. James Press, 1997, pp. 475–476.

Scott, Joyce, George Ciscle, and Leslie King-Hammond. *Joyce J. Scott Kickin' It With the Old Masters.* Baltimore, Md.: Baltimore Museum of Art, 2000.

Wilson, Judith. *Joyce J. Scott: Images Concealed.* San Francisco: San Francisco Art Institute, 1995.

Scurlock, Addison

(1883–1964) *photographer*

One of the most successful and influential photographers in Washington, D.C., for more than five decades, Addison Scurlock was a master of clarity and the panoramic photograph as well as a pioneer in African-American news photography and newsreels.

He was born on June 18, 1883, in Fayetteville, South Carolina. His father was a politician who moved the family to Washington, D.C., in 1900, where he eventually became a lawyer. After high school, young Addison was drawn to the still-new craft of photography and learned the business from Washington photographer Mores P. Rice, for whom he worked as an apprentice.

In 1904, Scurlock went into business for himself as a portrait photographer, working out of his parents' home. He saved enough money to open his own studio on U Street in Washington in 1911, where he would remain for more than half a century. Scurlock became the leading chronicler of Washington's large African-American community and was named the official photographer for all-black Howard University.

He became a master of what came to be called the "Scurlock look." His photographs were idealized pictures of his subjects—both ordinary

Photographer Addison Scurlock stands by his camera bag at the beginning of an illustrious career. *(The Anthony Barboza Collection)*

blacks and celebrities such as physician Charles Drew, educator Mary McLeod Bethune, and poet Paul Laurence Dunbar. His photographs showed no shadows; each face was bathed in a clear, even light, and the photographer later retouched features if necessary to show the subject to best advantage.

Scurlock's panoramic shots of large groups of people were unparalleled for capturing every face and detail with crystal clarity. Perhaps his most celebrated photograph is of Marian Anderson performing her historic concert at the Lincoln Memorial in June 1939 to a sea of spectators. This is just one of many newsworthy moments that Scurlock and his sons, Robert and George, captured for their news photo service that provided pictures for a number of leading black newspapers. The younger Scurlocks were also attracted to the medium of film and made weekly newsreels of Washington events that were shown in local theaters.

As the years went on, Robert and George assumed more of the responsibilities of the Scurlock Studios while their father pursued his first love—portraiture. In 1948 they established the Capital School of Photography, at which many people, including returning veterans of World War II, learned the techniques of news photography. Among their students was Jacqueline Bouvier, a reporter for the *Washington Times-Herald,* who would later marry Senator John F. Kennedy and still later become first lady when he was elected president in 1960.

Addison Scurlock died on December 16, 1964 at age 81. Robert Scurlock died in 1994.

The Scurlock look, according to historian Jane Freundel Levy, captured "dignity, the uplifting quality of the demeanor of every subject . . . [Scurlock] clearly saw each one as above the ordinary."

Further Reading

Fearing, Jeffrey John. "Addison Scurlock and the Scurlock Studies of Washington, D.C." HU Archives Net. Available online. URL: http://www.hu archivesnet.howard.edu/0011huarnet/fearing1. htm. Downloaded March 11, 2009.

Sullivan, George. *Black Artists in Photography, 1840–1940.* New York: Cobblehill Books, 1996, pp. 83–97.

Willis, Deborah. *Reflections in Black: A History of Black Photographers from 1840 to the Present.* New York: W. W. Norton, 2000, pp. 37, 38, 41–42.

Simmons, Alex

(1952–   ) *comic book creator, writer, educator*

In comic book history, there have been few black superheroes or characters and even fewer black comic book artists and writers. Alex Simmons is one of the first black comic book creators to achieve mainstream status with two original characters—one human and the other superhuman.

A freelance writer and editor, Simmons was born in June 1, 1952, in New York City. He started out writing juvenile mysteries and other young adult books for various publishers. He got a job writing for Eclipse Comics in the early 1980s and created the comic book *The Demon Chronicles.* Soon afterward he came up with the idea for a comic about a black soldier of fortune in the 1930s named Arron Day. Better known as Blackjack, Day tangled with German Nazis and fascist Japanese before and during World War II (1939–1945). Simmons's character is partially inspired by Indiana Jones of the Steven Spielberg films and real-life African-American adventurer Eugene Jacques Bullard.

"I wanted a book about a hero who is black," Simmons has said, "and whose exploits could shine a revealing light on the present. After all, it's from our past that we project our future."

Simmons took his idea to DC Comics, home of Superman and Batman, which turned it down. Then he tried Eclipse Comics; that company liked the idea but unfortunately went out of business before a deal could be struck. Other comic book companies passed on *Blackjack.*

"Over a period of 10 years," Simmons recalled, "I'd written and rewritten the concept and the stories, and I'd test-marketed the results with friends, strangers, and comic books peers alike. The overwhelming favorable results helped me determine that there was a market and a need for this series. I just had to make it happen myself."

Simmons formed his own company, Dark Angel Productions, and put out the first issue of *Blackjack* with art by Joe Bennett. It was a hit, leading to several other comics as well as a graphic novel, *Blackjack: Blood and Honor.* An anthology, *Blackjack: Buried Secrets,* contained five illustrated short stories and a novella. While Simmons has written all the Blackjack stories mentioned, different artists have illustrated each separate work.

Blackjack's success led Simmons back to DC Comics, where editors asked him to create a new African-American superhero for their *Batman* series. He came up with the masked hero Orpheus, who is the star of the five-issue miniseries *Batman: Orpheus Rising.* The first issue, with artwork by Dwayne Turner, came out in August 2001.

"I didn't want yet another angry young black man trying to get back at the man, or get a piece of the action," Simmons explained. "I wanted him fun, exciting, motivated, brave and scared and fresh and more."

Simmons also wrote the *Tarzan* Sunday comic strip with artist Eric Battle for United Features Syndicate and has written radio drama episodes of *Blackjack* for a series at the Museum of Broadcasting in New York City. He has written a two-part Superman story for DC and has created a series of young adult novels about the Raven League, a group of kids who help famed detective Sherlock Holmes. In addition, Simmons teaches an art-in-education program in schools, libraries, and museums called the Art of Making Comics. He is the recipient of an Uncommon Spirit Award for excellence in exploring the art form of comics.

Further Reading

"Alex Simmons." East Coast Black Age of Comics Convention '09." Available online. URL: http://ecbacc.com/wordpress/2009/03/10/a;ex=simmons-at-ecbace-2009/. Downloaded March 12, 2009.

Simmons, Alex. Blackjack: *Blood and Honor, The Graphic Novel.* Bronx, N.Y.: Dark Angels Productions, 2000.
Simmons Alex, and Bill McCay. *Buffalo Bill Wanted!* (The Raven League). New York: Razorbill, 2007.
The Official Alex Simmons Web site. Available online. URL: http://www.simmonshereandnow.com/. Downloaded March 12, 2009.

Simms, Carroll H.

(Carroll Harris Simms)
(1924–   ) *sculptor, painter, jewelry designer, ceramist, educator*

Inspired by the Bible, southern folk art, and African art, Carroll H. Simms brings a profound spirituality to all his work from huge sculptures to small ceramic pots.

He was born on April 29, 1924, in Bald Knob, Arkansas. His father, Tommie Sims, was a mechanic who abandoned the family before Carroll was born. His mother, Rosa Hazel Harris Sims, brought up her children in her parents' home. Simms's maternal great-grandfather was a freed slave and the first teacher of a school for Negroes. As a boy, Simms drew pictures of trains and learned quilting from his grandmother. The family moved to Toledo, Ohio, in 1938. Six years later he entered Hampton Institute in Virginia on a scholarship. Here Simms discovered sculpture and ceramics and met black artist JOHN BIGGERS, who painted murals at Hampton.

Simms went on to study art at the Toledo Museum School of Fine Arts in 1945, the first African American to be accepted there on a scholarship. But college life was not free of racism. Because he was black, he could not live on campus but boarded above a black funeral home six miles away. The proximity of the dead bodies below him was so disturbing that many nights he slept in the nearby woods.

Simms persevered, however, and won first prize in sculpture at the Toledo Museum's exhibitions in 1948 and 1949. The following year he took a job as a teacher of ceramics and sculpture in the new art department at Texas Southern University (TSU), created by John Biggers.

Simms continued to produce original art while he taught, making his first forays into jewelry and textile design. In 1954 he received a Fulbright grant to study in England and became an apprentice to the famous British abstract sculpture Jacob Epstein. His other mentor there was William Fogg, a leading authority on African art. Under these two influences, Simms's work moved from the realistic to the symbolic. Perhaps the most striking work he created in England was *Christ and the Lambs* for St. Oswald's Church in Coventry. The nine-foot-tall crucified Christ is a distorted figure with elongated arms outstretched but no cross.

In 1968, Simms traveled to Nigeria in Africa and made a thorough study of African folk literature and art, particularly focusing on religious shrines and relics. The trip inspired his largest sculpture to date—*The African Queen Mother* (1968), a 12-foot-tall abstract work that Simms states "depicts sacred traditional life in Africa and aspects of African religious tradition in the New World." The work sits before a reflecting pool he designed in front of TSU's Martin Luther King Center of Communications. An experimenter who likes to try different materials, Simms created his *Water Angels* (1960) in Plexiglas and his soaring *Man the Universe* (1975–76) in cast aluminum.

Simms's work, including sculptures and fountains, can be found all over the city of Houston. Along with Biggers, he has helped train several generations of African-American artists and art curators at TSU. Art, according to Simms, is "the universal spiritual force that makes the dignity, the heritage, and origin of black culture inseparable from all existence."

Simms retired as professor of art from TSU in 1987. The Carroll H. Simms Sculpture Garden in the campus center is named in his honor. In 1999, the African American Museum in Dallas renamed the Biennial Southwest Black Art Competition and Exhibition the Carroll Harris Simms National Black Art Competition and Exhibition after him.

Further Reading

Bearden, Romare, and Harry Henderson. *A History of African-American Artists: From 1792 to the Present.* New York: Pantheon Books, 1993, pp. 437–446.

"Interview with Caroll Harris Simms," Connexions. Available online. URL: http://cnx.org/content/m16135/latest. Downloaded March 12, 2009.

Riggs, Thomas, ed. *St. James Guide to Black Artists.* Detroit, Mich.: St. James Press, 1997, pp. 485–487.

Simpson, Lorna

(1960–   ) *photographer, installation artist, video artist, filmmaker*

Lorna Simpson is one of the most prominent and challenging African-American photographers of her generation. Her photo installations use photographs and text to acknowledge and challenge the many problems faced by black women in American society.

She was born on August 13, 1960, in Brooklyn, New York. She entered the School of Visual Arts in New York City in 1978 and earned a Bachelor of Fine Arts degree in 1982. She earned a Master of Fine Arts degree from the University of California, San Diego, in 1985. The same year, Simpson had the first exhibition of her photographs at the Alternative Gallery in San Diego.

Her work continued to be displayed in both group shows and individual exhibits through the late 1980s. She became the first African-American female artist to represent the United States at the celebrated Venice Biennials show in Venice, Italy, in 1990.

Simpson's work, like that of her contemporaries RENEE COX and LYLE ASHTON HARRIS, is often politically and socially challenging. Her photographs are less accessible than Cox's and the text that accompanies many of them is often cryptic and difficult to decode. Many of Simpson's works are a series of pictures of parts of the black female body, often clothed, or bodily adornments.

Wigs (1994) consists of 21 lithographic images of different women's wigs. "By focusing on wigs as hair unattached to a body," writes one critic, "Simpson exposes hairstyle as an alterable or removable embellishment in probable conflict with its absent owner."

"Simpson acknowledges in her art the invisibility, devaluation, and marginalization of black women," writes Jontyle Theresa Robinson. "She confronts gender-defining institutions, the tradition of male prerogative, and the male hegemonic [dominating] worldview that presumes its own view of the universe constitutes reality."

Some of Simpson's most outstanding works include 9 *Props,* a stirring tribute to pioneer African-American photographer JAMES VAN DER ZEE, and *Places with a Past,* a profound work about the slave trade in South Carolina, a collaboration with actress Alva Rogers that included relics and audiotapes.

More recently, Simpson has turned from photography to video and film. Her work in this medium includes the video projection *Call Waiting* (1997) and *Corridors* (2003). She has had solo exhibits in New York City at the Studio Museum in Harlem (2002) and at the Whitney Museum of American Art, which mounted a 20-year retrospective of her work in 2007.

"It's all about being able to revisit things differently," she said in an interview, "so the films are another version of constructed or contrived scenarios. . . They're about actors who are playing specific roles in the same way that I would have someone pose for me in the earlier work."

Simpson is the author of the book *Art on My Mind: Visual Politics.* She lives in Brooklyn with her husband photographer Jim Casebere and their daughter.

Further Reading

Cotton, Holland. "Exploring Identify as Problematic Condition." *New York Times,* March 2, 2007, p. E27.

Enwezor, Okwui, Helanie Posner, Hilton Als, Isaac Julien, Thelma Golden, and Shamim M. Mamim. *Lorna Simpson.* New York: Harry N. Abrams, 2006.

Jones, Kellis. *Lorna Simpson* (Contemporary Artists). London: Phaidon Press, 2002.

Riggs, Thomas, ed. *St. James Guide to Black Artists.* Detroit, Mich.: St. James Press, 1997, pp. 488–490.

Simpson, Lorna, and Sarah J. Rogers. *Lorna Simpson: Interior/Exterior, Full/Empty.* Columbus: Ohio State University Press, 1998.

Willis, Deborah, and Andy Grundberg. *Lorna Simpson.* San Francisco: Friends of Photography, 1993.

Wolf, Sylvia, and Abby Levine, eds. *Focus: Five Women Photographers: Julia Margaret Cameron/Margaret Bourke-White/Flor Garduno/Sandy Skoglund/Lorna Simpson.* Morton Grove, Ill.: Albert Whitman, 1994.

Singleton, John
(John Daniel Singleton)
(1968–) *filmmaker, screenwriter, film producer*

The youngest person and first African American to be nominated for an Academy Award as best director, John Singleton burst onto the scene with one of the most thoughtful and powerful films about black urban youth yet made.

He was born in Los Angeles (L.A.), California, on January 6, 1968. His father, Danny Singleton, is a mortgage broker, and his mother, Sheila Ward, a sales executive for a pharmaceutical company. Although they never married, the couple raised their only child responsibly in separate households.

A movie addict, Singleton decided he wanted to be a filmmaker when he was nine. Soon he was creating little animated movies with numerous drawings that he would flip through. By the time he entered the Filmic Writing Program at the University of California at Los Angeles (UCLA) in 1986, he had already written a number of screenplays. Twice at UCLA, he won the Jack Nicholson Writing Award for best feature-length screenplay.

Within a month of his graduation, Columbia Pictures agreed to buy his screenplay *Boyz N the Hood,* about three black youths growing up on the streets of South Central L.A. Singleton would only agree to the sale if Columbia allowed him to direct his own screenplay. Impressed by his confidence and initiative, the studio agreed and gave him, at age 23, a budget of $7 million to make the picture.

The finished film, released in 1991, was a tremendous critical and commercial success. Largely autobiographical, *Boyz* focused on the young Tre Styles, who comes to live with his father Furious. It is this strong father figure that saves Tre from the sad fate of his two friends, a pair of brothers raised by their mother.

The film introduced Cuba Gooding Jr. as Tre and rapper Ice Cube, in his first film role, as his drug-dealing friend. It also helped propel Laurence Fishburne, who played the father, into the front rank of black film actors.

Made with the careful attention to detail of a good novel, *Boyz* rises to a shuddering climax when Ricky, Doughboy's athletic brother, with a promising future ahead of him, is senselessly shot down by rival gang members. His death scene is one of the most disturbing and intense in contemporary films.

"Mr. Singleton may not be saying anything new about the combined effects of poverty, drugs, and aimlessness on black teenagers," wrote Janet Maslin in the *New York Times.* "But he is saying something familiar with new dramatic force, and in ways that a wide and varied audience will understand."

The film ended up grossing about $100 million and earned Singleton a nomination for best director and one for best original screenplay. Deemed one of the golden boys of Hollywood, Singleton made his second movie about black girls whose boyfriends die on the streets. *Poetic Justice* (1993) was about Justice, a hairdresser, played by singer Janet Jackson, who deals with her grief by writing poetry. The poetry she reads in the film was written by real-life poet Maya Angelou. Justice falls in

Filmmaker John Singleton is on location for his first and most celebrated film, *Boyz n the Hood. (Photofest)*

love with a postal worker played by Tupac Shakur, another rapper from whom Singleton drew a topnotch performance. The film, however, was criticized for lacking the focus and dramatic impact of *Boyz,* and it flopped at the box office.

A similar fate was met by Singleton's third feature, *Higher Learning* (1995), that reunited him with Fishburne and Ice Cube. Critics panned the film, which dealt with racial and sexual politics on a college campus, even more harshly than *Poetic Justice.* They especially disliked its moralizing and stereotyped characters.

Singleton considered his next film, *Rosewood* (1997), his most mature to date. It was also his first film for which he did not write the screenplay. Based on true events, *Rosewood* was about the destruction of a black community in rural Florida in 1923 by white racists. Praised by many critics, it did not find an audience.

"On an epic scale," wrote black critic Stanley Crouch, "it moved the Afro-American experience into the kinds of mythic arenas . . . where the real and the mythological stood together, where authenticity and poetic exaggeration reinforced each other, where real characters and archetypes spoke to one another and worked together."

After making *Shaft* (2000), a remake of the 1970s classic blaxploitation film about a black detective, Singleton directed *Baby Boy* (2001). The film marked his return to the familiar landscape of black urban L.A. Originally meant to be a vehicle for Tupac Shakur, who died in a drive-by shooting in the interim, *Baby Boy* starred pop singer and model Tyrese Gibson as Jody, an aimless young man who has two children by different women but still prefers to live at home with his mother.

The film recaptured much of the dramatic weight and power of *Boyz*, especially in the scenes between Jody and his mother's boyfriend, played by Ving Rhames. Jody's decision to commit himself to the mother of his son gave the movie a positive, upbeat ending, although it did not gloss over the problems of young black men and their relationships. Unfortunately, *Baby Boy* also failed at the box office, making some observers wonder if any serious drama about black people can succeed in the movie marketplace. Gibson starred in Singleton's next two films, *2 Fast 2 Furious* (2003), a sequel to the action film *The Fast and the Furious*, and *Four Brothers* (2005), a family crime drama for which he won a NAACP Image Award for Outstanding Directing in a Feature Film. His latest film, the thriller *Abduction*, is scheduled to be released in 2011. Singleton has also produced a number of films through his production company New Deal Entertainment.

Despite the unevenness of his work and his difficulties with the Hollywood system, John Singleton continues to be, along with SPIKE LEE, one of the few black filmmakers who strives to say something meaningful about the contemporary black experience. He looks forward to the future with optimism. "I'm a veteran," he has said, "but I still have some growing to do, becoming a better filmmaker and a better storyteller."

Singleton was married to Akousa Busia, a Ghanaian princess, in 1996. The couple divorced the following year. He has a daughter, Hadar, from the marriage.

Further Reading

Alexander, George. *Why We Make Movies: Black Filmmakers Talk About the Magic of Cinema*. New York: Harlem Moon, 2003, pp. 460–474.

Barboza Craigh, ed. *John Singleton: Interviews* (Conversations with Filmmakers Series). Jackson: University Press of Mississippi, 2009.

Moon, Spencer. *Reel Black Talk: A Sourcebook of 50 American Filmmakers*. Eastport, Conn.: Greenwood Press, 1997, pp. 315–322.

Singleton, John, and Veronica Chambers. *Poetic Justice: Filmmaking South Central Style*. New York: Delta, 1993.

"The Films of John Singleton." Available online. URL: http://www.johnsingletonfilms.com/. Downloaded March 12, 2009.

Further Viewing

Baby Boy (2001). Sony, VHS/DVD, 2002/2001.

John Singleton Collection (*Boyz n the Hood, Poetic Justice, Higher Learning*). Sony, DVD box set, 2001.

Rosewood (1997). Warner Home Video, VHS/DVD, 2000/1997.

Sklarek, Norma
(Norma Merrick Sklarek)
(1928–) *architect, educator*

The first African-American woman to become a licensed architect in the United States, Norma Sklarek distinguished herself as a meticulous designer, a talented teacher, and an architect of flair and imagination.

She was born Norma Merrick on April 15, 1928, in New York City. Her father, Dr. Walter Ernest

Merrick, was a physician who was originally from the Caribbean island of St. Vincent. Her mother, Amy Willoughby, was from the island of Barbados.

An only child, Merrick was close to her father, who encouraged her to pursue architecture. After a year of studying liberal arts at Barnard College in New York, she entered the School of Architecture at Columbia University. "I had never seen a T-square or a triangle," she later said when she began to study architecture. The program was difficult, but Merrick worked hard, graduated, and then passed a grueling, 36-hour, four-day licensing exam on her first try, a remarkable feat in 1950.

She was turned down for some 20 positions before being hired by the New York Department of Public Works. Finding the work unfulfilling, Merrick got another job with the architectural firm of Skidmore, Owings, and Merrill, one of the largest firms in the country. She gained invaluable experience at Skidmore, working on intensely detailed assignments.

In 1960, Merrick moved to California and took a position with Gruen and Associates. She became the first woman to be a director of other architects and managed up to 50 architects at one time. Two years later, she became the first black woman to become a licensed architect in the state of California. Twenty years would pass before another black woman achieved this distinction. In 1967, she married Rolf Sklarek and they had two sons.

Among the many buildings to which Sklarek has contributed are the American Embassy in Tokyo, Japan; the California Mart, the largest fashion center in the world at 2.5 million square feet; and the San Bernardino City Hall, selected as one of the Outstanding City Halls in the United States by the Library of Congress and the American Institute of Architects (AIA).

Sklarek taught at UCLA from 1972 to 1978. She joined Weldon, Becket, and Associates in Santa Monica in 1980 as a vice president. Then she worked on the Passenger Terminal One at the Los Angeles International Airport, completed in time for the 1984 Summer Olympics.

Her husband died in 1984, and the following year she married physician Cornelius Welch. The same year, Sklarek established the first and largest architectural firm completely run by a woman, Siegel-Sklarek-Diamond. Discouraged by the small jobs the firm received, she left in 1989 and joined the Jude Partnership in Venice, California, where she remained until 1992. Today she is semiretired.

Sklarek has served as director of the L.A. chapter of the AIA and currently is chairperson of the AIA's National Ethical Council. She has also served as commissioner of the California State Board of Architectural Examiners and was director of the University of California's Architects Guild from 1984 to 1987.

Howard University in Washington, D.C., created the Norma Merrick Sklarek Architectural Scholarship Award in her honor.

"Architecture should be working on improving the environment of people in their homes, in their places of work, and their places of recreation," Sklarek has said. "It should be functional and pleasant, not just in the image of the ego of the architect."

Further Reading

"Architect Norma Sklarek." Available online. URL: http://www.greatbuildings.com/architects/Norma-Sklarek.html. Downloaded March 13, 2009.

"Norma Sklarek," Essortment.com. Available online. URL: http://www.essortment.com/normasklarek_rqbo.htm. Downloaded March 13, 2009.

Smith, Jessie Carney, ed. *Notable Black American Women*. Detroit, Mich.: Gale Research, Inc., 1992, pp. 27–28.

Statom, Therman

(1953–) *glass sculptor, installion artist, mixed-media artist, educator*

One of the few American artists who works primarily in the medium of glass, Therman Statom brings a sublime lyricism and sharp wit to this neglected art form.

He was born in Florida on April 30, 1953. He studied glassblowing at the Pilchuck Glass School in Stanwood, Washington, and earned a Bachelor of Fine Arts degree from the Rhode Island School of Design in Providence in 1974. Statom earned a Master of Fine Arts degree from the Pratt Institute of Art and Design in Brooklyn, New York, in 1980. Through the 1980s, he combined a teaching career at UCLA and other schools with his career as an artist.

Statom's approach to glass is unique and exhilarating. There is nothing delicate or fragile about such works as *Green Ladder* (1988), a glass ladder painted in green and yellow paint with red accents. His series of glass houses from that decade are covered with pastel crayons and decorated with shards of colored glass. The series gives a new twist to the old adage, "People who live in glass houses shouldn't throw stones." Another work, *Map Room* (1994), is a fantastical arrangement of maps of the earth and the heavens sealed into glass boxes to imply a social message.

One of Statom's most ambitious projects is the trio of mammoth chandeliers he created for the Los Angeles Public Library. Each glass arm of this collagelike chandelier is 18 feet in diameter, weighs 1,750 pounds, and contains glass jars, animals, and figures. For Statom the chandeliers represent the worlds of human endeavor, natural phenomena, and spirituality.

Statom was the recipient of a National Fellowship Fund Award in 1978 and was awarded three NEA fellowships, in 1980, 1982, and 1988. His works reside in the permanent collections of the High Museum of Art in Atlanta, Georgia; the Los Angeles County Museum of Art and the Detroit Institute of Arts in Michigan. Recent solo exhibitions include *Through the Looking Glass* (2006) at the California Center for the Arts, Escondido; *Nascita* (2008) at the Bemis Center for Contemporary Art, Omaha, Nebraska; and *Therman Statom: Stories of the New World* (2009) at the Orlando Museum of Art, Florida. In this last show,

Statom used a mirrored maze and video projections and the theme of Spanish explorer Ponce de Leon's quest for the Fountain of Youth in order "to explore both historic and contemporary themes of hope, discovery, ambition and destiny."

In the words of artist and writer SAMELLA LEWIS, Therman Statom is "one of the least predictable and unique artists in the field [of glass]."

Further Reading

Lewis, Samella. *African-American Art and Artists.* Berkeley: University of California Press, 2003, p. 243.

Riggs, Thomas, ed. *St. James Guide to Black Artists.* Detroit, Mich.: St. James Press, 1997, pp. 508–509.

Statom, Therman. *River Myths. An Installation.* Tampa, Fla.: Tampa Museum of Art, 2002.

Therman Statom's official Web site. Available online. URL: http://www.thermanstatom.com/. Downloaded March 13, 2009.

Steptoe, Javaka
(1971–) *illustrator, writer, educator*

The son of a pioneering African-American children's book illustrator, Javaka Steptoe has proved himself in just a few short years a worthy successor to his father.

He was born in Brooklyn, New York, on April 19, 1971, the second of four children. His father was illustrator and author JOHN STEPTOE and his mother is artist Stephanie Douglas. His parents separated when he was quite young and he spent time living with one parent and then the other. He and his sister and brother were models for his father's illustrations. John Steptoe died of AIDS in 1989 when Javaka was 18.

Like both his parents, he attended the New York High School of Art and Design and then studied at the art school of the Cooper Union. His first book as an illustrator was published when he was 26 years old.

In Daddy's Arms I Am Tall: African Americans Celebrating Fathers (1997) was a compilation of 13 poems by various black authors, including Angela Johnson, E. Ethelbert Miller, and Leonard D. Moore. Besides illustrating the book, Steptoe wrote one of the poems, "Seeds," a tribute to his late father. "I was able to think about my father and how he affected me, and how I affected him, and give something to him by honoring his memory," he wrote.

The complex but stunning collages of cut paper and found objects that make up the illustrations took Steptoe four years to complete. The effort was well worth it, however, for *Daddy's Arms* won the Coretta Scott King Award for Illustration and was named an American Library Association (ALA) Notable Children's Book. Steptoe was also nominated for NAACP Image Award for Outstanding Children's Literary Work.

Javaka went on to illustrate *Do You Know What I'll Do?* (2000), a classic book by Charlotte Zolotow originally published in 1958 and *A Pocketful of Poems* (2001) by Nikki Grimes.

He has also followed in his father's steps of writing and illustrating his own works. These include *The Scream* (2002), *Block Party* (2003), and *The Jones Family Express* (2005). *Hot Day on Abbott Avenue* (2004), with story by Karen English, was a Jane Addam's Honor Book.

When not illustrating and writing, Javaka Steptoe teaches art to children.

"He [my father] taught me I should do something I love for a living or I will never be happy," Steptoe has said. "And that I should never let other people compromise my artwork."

Further Reading

Cotton, Cynthia, and Jakava Steptoe, illustrator. *Rain Play*. New York: Henry Hott, 2008.

Grimes, Nikki, and Javaka Steptoe, illustrator. *A Pocketful of Poems*. Boston: Clarion Books, 2001.

Meyers, Walter Dean, and Javaka Steptoe. *Amiri and Odette: A Love Story*. New York: Scholastic, 2009.

Rockman, Connie C., ed. *Eighth Book of Junior Authors and Illustrators*. New York: H. W. Wilson, 2000, pp. 500–502.

Steptoe, Javaka, illustrator. *In Daddy's Arms I Am Tall: African Americans Celebrating Fathers*. New York: Scholastic, 2002.

Steptoe, John
(John Lewis Steptoe)
(1950–1989) *illustrator, writer*

A precocious artist who burst onto the children's book scene with his first published work at age 19, John Steptoe was one of the first children's authors to explore the lives of urban black children.

He was born John Lewis Steptoe on September 14, 1950, in the Bedford-Stuyvesant section of Brooklyn, New York, to John Oliver, a transit worker, and Elesteen Hill Steptoe.

A natural artist, Steptoe attended the New York High School of Art and Design, graduating in 1967. There he met his future wife, artist Stephanie Douglas. The couple had two children and later separated. Black artist John Torres spotted Steptoe's talent and recruited him into the eight-week summer art program at the Vermont Academy in Saxtons River, Vermont, which was funded by the Ford Foundation.

Steptoe's talent blossomed at the Academy, and soon the 16-year-old was serving as a mentor to other students who would watch him at work in an attic studio. When asked by one of his instructors what he wanted to do, Steptoe replied: "I want to create books for black children."

That fall, staying in an apartment offered him by the same teacher, he completed his first children's book, *Stevie*, which was accepted and published by Harper & Row in 1969. The book, one of the first written specifically for and about black children, created a sensation and made Steptoe a national celebrity. The book was so popular that it was reprinted in *Life* magazine.

Although set in a black inner-city neighborhood and written in the vivid language of urban street talk, *Stevie* had a universal theme. It was about a child who resents his younger foster brother, a situation that many children—black and white—could relate to. Steptoe's heavy-lined, dark-colored pictures were compared by some critics to the religious paintings of French artist Georges Rouault.

Through the 1970s and early 1980s, Steptoe continued to write and illustrate books about the world of black children in such popular titles as *Uptown* (1970), *Train Ride* (1971), and *Daddy Is a Monster . . . Sometimes* (1980).

He also occasionally illustrated books by other writers, such as *She Came Bringing Me That Little Baby* by Eloise Greenfield and *OUTside/Inside: Poems* and *All the Colors of the Race: Poems* by Arnold Adoff.

In 1984, he turned to the world of Native Americans, producing *The Story of Jumping Mouse: A Native American Legend* (1984). A Caldecott Honor Book, it was the tale of a brave mouse who journeys to a far-off land and is magically transformed into a mighty eagle.

He followed this with perhaps his most beloved book, *Mufaro's Beautiful Daughters: An African Tale* (1987), which took him two and a half years to complete. This beautiful variation on the Cinderella story earned Steptoe the Coretta Scott King Award and was named an ALA Notable Book and a Caldecott Honor Book.

"*Mufaro* was healing for me," Steptoe wrote. "Working on the book was a way for me to learn more about loving myself. One of the marvels of the book experience is that when it is finished others can join in the experience, too."

Sadly, Steptoe would share the book experience only once more in *Baby Says* (1988). He died of complications from AIDS on August 28, 1989, about two weeks before his 39th birthday. He was survived by a son, JAVAKA STEPTOE, who is also a children's book illustrator, and a daughter, Bweela.

A gifted and sensitive illustrator and author who pioneered African-American children's books, John Steptoe has a library in Brooklyn named in his honor. The Coretta Scott King/John Steptoe Award for New Talent was established in 1995 to yearly recognize an outstanding new black author or black illustrator.

Further Reading

Adoff, Arnold, and John Steptoe, illustrator (1984). *All the Colors of the Race: Poems.* New York: Sag Harbor, N.Y.: Beech Tree Books, 1992.

Berg, Julie. *John Steptoe (Young at Heart).* Edina, Minn.: Abdo & Daughters, 1994.

Commire, Anne, ed. *Something About the Author, Volume 63.* Detroit, Mich.: Gale Research, 1991, pp. 157–167.

Primm, E. Russell. *Favorite Children's Authors and Illustrators: John Steptoe to Charlotte Zolotow.* Mankato, Minn.: Child's World, 2007.

Steptoe, John. *Daddy Is a Monster . . . Sometimes* (1980). Reprint, New York: HarperTrophy, 1983.

———. *Mufaro's Beautiful Daughters: An African Tale.* New York: Live Oak Media, 2003.

———. *Stevie* (1969). Reprint, New York: HarperTrophy, 1986.

Stout, Renee

(Renee L. Stout)
(1958–) *mixed media artist, sculptor, painter*

An intriguing artist whose strange sculptures and other works contain the tools of the conjurer and spiritualist, Renee Stout has focused her art on the healing rites and rituals of her African ancestors and their descendants.

She was born on February 13, 1958, in Junction City, Kansas, where her father was stationed in the U.S. Army. When she was a year old, the family moved to Pittsburgh, Pennsylvania, their hometown. She enrolled at Carnegie-Mellon University in Pittsburgh in 1976 and earned a Bachelor of Fine Arts degree. Stout started her career as a realistic painter but turned to mixed-media sculpture by the time she moved to Washington, D.C., in 1985. She began to explore her African heritage, trying to find personal comfort and confirmation in its peoples and cultures.

Much of Renee Stout's art is inspired by the ceremonial and religious rites of her ancestral Africa. *(Photo by Greg Staley)*

"I'm attracted to spiritual societies," she has said. "[Spirituality] seems like a means of survival in a world that you can't always understand."

The connections she makes between the African past and the African-American present are often imaginative and personal. In *Fetish #2* (1988), a plaster body cast of an African tribal woman is embedded with a boxed photograph of an infant. *Traveling Root Store #2* (1995) is an open suitcase contained various root and herbal remedies used by spiritualists and root workers. This last work is part of a project entitled *"Dear Robert, I'll See You at the Crossroads,"* referring to the legendary blues musician Robert Johnson and the supposed pact he made with the devil at the crossroads. Most of the pieces in this project are replete with Voudon, or voodoo, artifacts, fortune-teller cards, and love potions.

"Stout's work evokes the mysteries and possibilities of human experience, and the strategies employed to make life better," writes Marla C. Berns, director of the University Art Museum at the University of California at Santa Barbara, where Stout's work has been exhibited. Other solo exhibitions of her work include *Fatima's Dreams* (2004) at Barrister's Gallery, New Orleans, Louisiana; *Church of the Crossroads* (2006) at the Arts Center, St. Petersburg, Florida; and *Journal: Book One* (2007) at Hemphill Fine Arts, Washington, D.C. Stout was artist-in-residence at the College of Visual and Performing Arts, George Mason University, Fairfax, Virginia, in 2006.

In a society where violence and chaos all too often rule, Renee Stout seeks answers in the wisdom of past civilization and peoples.

"I am trying to create art that helps me put together what are only fragments," she has said, "to try to create a whole, so that I can gain a better understanding of my own existence."

Further Reading

Berns, Marla, and George Lipsitz. *Dear Robert, I'll See You at the Crossroads: A Project by Renee Stout.* Santa Barbara: University of California, Santa Barbara, 1996.

Owen-Workman, Michelle A., Renee Stout, and Stephen Bennett Phillips. *Readers, Advisors, and Storefront Churches: Renee Stout, a Mid-Career Retrospective.* Kansas City, Mo.: Belger Arts Center, 2003.

Renee Stout's official Web site. Available online. URL: http://www.reneestout.com/. Downloaded March 13, 2009.

Wyatt, MacGaffey, Michael D. Harris, Sylvia H. Williams, and David C. Driskell. *Astonishment Power: The Eyes of Understanding: Kongo Minkisi/ The Art of Renee Stout.* Washington, D.C.: Smithsonian, 1993.

T

Tanner, Henry O.
(Henry Ossawa Tanner)
(1859–1937) *painter*

The first African-American artist to achieve international fame, Henry O. Tanner created brilliantly colored genre and biblical paintings that radiate warmth and a deep religiosity. No black painter before the 20th century is as highly regarded or better known.

He was born Henry Ossawa Tanner on June 21, 1859, in Pittsburgh, Pennsylvania, the eldest of nine children. His father, Benjamin Tucker Tanner, was a deacon and later a bishop in the African Methodist Episcopal Church. His mother, Sarah Miller Tanner, was a private school teacher who escaped slavery on the Underground Railroad. His unusual middle name, Ossawa, came from the Kansas town of Osawatomie, where abolitionist John Brown began his personal war against slaveholders.

The family moved to Philadelphia when Tanner was still a boy, and at age 13 he decided he would become an artist after watching a painter work on a landscape in a nearby park. His parents were initially opposed to their son's choice, and his father had him apprenticed to a friend who owned a flour mill. The scheme backfired: Tanner's delicate health was ruined by the hard work in the mill, and he recuperated at home for several years. Realizing how much his art meant to him, his parents finally encouraged him to paint to regain his health. He took several trips to the Adirondack Mountains in Upstate New York and to Florida for health reasons and brought along his easel to use in creating beautiful landscapes.

In 1880, with his parents' blessing, Tanner became only the second African American to enroll in the Pennsylvania Academy of the Fine Arts in Philadelphia, the oldest art school in the nation. He studied under the American realist painter Thomas Eakins. Eakins's emphasis on the human anatomy made a deep impression on Tanner's later work. Impatient to make his way in the world, Tanner left the Academy after several years. He moved to Atlanta, Georgia, where he opened a photography studio. The studio failed and he got a job teaching drawing at Atlanta's Clark University. But nothing he did could support the young man financially.

In 1890, he had an exhibition of his paintings, mostly landscapes, in Cincinnati, Ohio, arranged by two white patrons, Bishop Joseph Hartzell and his wife. When not a single painting sold, Bishop Hartzell bought them all, providing Tanner with the money he needed to travel to Europe. In January 1891, he started for Rome, Italy, where he planned to stay, but when he arrived in Paris, France, he fell in love with the city and remained there. He studied at the Académie Julien, where he learned the academic style of European painting that was realistic in technique but took its subject matter from history and the Bible.

It was in Paris that Tanner first began the biblical paintings he is best known for today. His *Daniel in the Lion's Den* (1893) won honorable mention in the Paris Salon Exhibition of 1896. A few years later the painting won silver medals in Paris and the Pan American exhibition in Buffalo, New York. Another biblical painting, *Resurrection of Lazarus* (1897), was the first of a number of Tanner paintings bought by the French government.

But Tanner did not forget America, where he continued to visit. Among his black genre paintings of this period is the outstanding *The Banjo Lesson* (1893), in which an old black man patiently teaches the instrument to a youth.

While he returned to the United States several times, Tanner found too much racial prejudice there, and Paris became his permanent residence until his death. In 1899 he married Jessie Macauley Olssen, a white opera singer from San Francisco, California. They had one son, Jesse Ossawa, who later attended England's Cambridge University.

Tanner's reputation as a painter of impressionistic power grew not only in his adopted land but at home, too. His work won numerous awards in America, and numerous young African-American artists made pilgrimages to his home in Paris when arriving in France to study and work. The older artist was an inspiration to many of them. However, when civil rights leaders asked him to get involved in the movement, he refused. He felt it was enough to make his contribution to equality through his art.

When World War I broke out in Europe in 1914, most American artists went home, but Tanner and his wife stayed. He worked for a time with the American Red Cross's Department of Public Information and was given permission to sketch and paint in the French war zone. His paintings of African-American soldiers stationed in France are a unique record of their participation.

Henry O. Tanner, a giant in African-American painting, spent most of his career in Paris, France. *(Photographs and Prints Division, Schomburg Center for Research in Black Culture, the New York Public Library, Astor, Lenox and Tilden Foundations)*

After the war ended in 1918, Tanner felt increasingly isolated as fewer and fewer Americans came to Paris. The French, however, had accepted him as a national treasure by then and he received numerous honors. In 1923 he was elected a chevalier of the French Legion of Honor. Four years later, he was elected a full member of the National Academy of Design in New York, the first African American to become a member.

But during these years Tanner also experienced great personal loss. In 1925, his beloved wife died, and soon his son suffered a breakdown in health that required years of recuperation. Although his own health declined, Tanner continued to paint until 1936. He died in Paris on May 25, 1937, his passing mourned by many on both sides of the Atlantic.

In 1973, Tanner was commemorated on a U.S. postal stamp in the American Arts series. In 1996, his painting *Sand Dunes at Sunset, Atlantic City,* was purchased for the permanent art collection of the White House in Washington, D.C. It was the first work by an African-American painter to receive such an honor.

Further Reading

Bearden, Romare, and Harry Henderson. *A History of African-American Artists: From 1792 to the Present.* New York: Pantheon Books, 1993, pp. 78–109.

Bruce, Marcus C. *Henry Ossawa Tanner: A Spiritual Biography.* New York: The Crossroad Publishing Company, Herder & Herder, 2002.

"Henry O. Tanner: A Mystical Painter." Smithsonian American Art Museum. Available online. URL: http://www.americanart.si.edu/exhibitions/online/tanner/tanner_main.html. Downloaded March 13, 2009.

Mathews, Marcia M. *Henry Ossawa Tanner: American Artist* (Negro American Biographies and Autobiographies). Chicago: University of Chicago Press, 1995.

Mosby, Dewey F. *Across Continents and Cultures: The Art and Life of Henry Ossawa Tanner.* Kansas City, Mo.: Nelson-Atkins Museum of Art, 1995.

Perry, Regenia A. *Free Within Ourselves: African-American Artists in the Collection of the National Museum of American Art.* San Francisco: Pomegranate Communications, 1992, pp. 158–166.

Further Viewing

Henry Ossawa Tanner. The Tanner Film Group, VHS, 1991.

Thomas, Alma W.

(Alma Woodsey Thomas)
(1891–1978) *painter, educator*

One of the most original and appealing American abstract painters of her time, Alma W. Thomas only fulfilled the promise of her abilities after retiring from a lifetime of teaching at age 70.

She was born Alma Woodsey Thomas on September 22, 1891, in Columbus, Georgia, the eldest of four daughters. Her father, John Harris Thomas, was a businessman, and her mother, Amelia Contey, a seamstress. Thomas was born with impaired hearing, which her mother claimed resulted from the fright she experienced when a white lynch mob trespassed on their land during her pregnancy.

The family moved to Washington, D.C., when Thomas was 15 and lived in a house on 15th Street, where Thomas would remain for the rest of her long life. Her first ambition was to become an architect, but she later decided to pursue teaching. She taught arts and crafts at a settlement house in Wilmington, Delaware, where her specialty was making puppets and staging plays with them.

She entered Washington's Howard University in 1921 to study costume design. Professor James V. Herring convinced her to enter the school's new art department. She graduated in 1924 with the first art degree given from Howard. Thomas was hired to teach art at Washington's Shaw Junior High School, where she would remain for the next 35 years.

She continued to paint while teaching, working mostly in watercolors. In 1943 she helped Herring found the Barnett-Aden Gallery, the first private art gallery in Washington to exhibit the work of African-American artists. Three years later she became a member of artist LOIS MAILOU JONES's "Little Paris" group made up of teachers who were also artists.

Thomas's still lifes and other realistic paintings were deemed competent but did not win her a large following in the art world. Then in 1950 she began taking art classes at American University in Washington and became interested in abstract art. She retired from teaching in 1960 and hoped to devote the rest of her life to painting. However, her arthritis was so serious that she wondered if she would ever paint again. With time, however, she adjusted and continued to paint. When JAMES A. PORTER of Howard University offered to mount a retrospective of her work in 1966, Thomas decided to add some new paintings to the exhibit.

"I began to think about what I would see if I were in an airplane," she later said. "You see only streaks of color. And so I began to paint as if I were in that plane." The tiny dots of color that created circular mosaics in Thomas's new work were like atomic particles that energized the canvases. In such paintings as *Elysian Fields* and *Red Azaleas Singing and Dancing* she re-created the world of nature that she loved so dearly.

She called her new series "Earth Paintings." The public reception to her revitalized style encouraged Thomas to attempt more experiments with color. In 1969, she began to produce her "Space Paintings," inspired by the space program's moon landing that year. The large canvases sparkled with patterns of colors set against a white background. In 1972, at age 80, Thomas had her first one-person exhibition in a museum, the Whitney Museum of American Art in New York City, where she was the first black woman artist to be so honored. She was further honored the same year when the Metropolitan Museum of Art in New York bought one of her paintings for its permanent collection.

"The use of color in my paintings is of paramount importance to me," she once said. "Through color I have sought to concentrate on beauty and happiness, rather than on man's inhumanity to man."

Thomas continued to paint, struggling against the ravages of age and arthritis. When too weak to sit in her studio, she would paint in her living room, turning the large canvas in her lap as she painted. In 1977, President Jimmy Carter received her with honor at the White House. She died on February 24, 1978, during heart surgery at Howard University Hospital. She was 86 years old.

Never married, Thomas devoted her life to her students and her art. "If the paintings have a greatness of spirit," wrote Adolphus Ealey, "and if their delightful and exuberant color and pattern convey a sparkling vitality and a *joie de vivre,* they also testify to the integrity of the artist's commitment to the vision of art that sustained her all her life."

In 2009, Thomas was one of a small group of select artists whose work was borrowed from Washington museums to be displayed at the White House by President Barack Obama.

Further Reading

"Alma Woodsey Thomas (1891–1978)." AskArt.com. Available online. URL: http://www.askart.com/ASKART/artists/biography.aspx?artist=30109. Downloaded March 13, 2009.

Bolden, Tonya. *Wake Up Our Souls: A Celebration of Black American Artists.* New York: Abrams Books for Young Readers, 2004, pp. 96–99.

Cotter, Holland. "Colors from a World of Black and White." *New York Times,* October 11, 2009, *Week in Review,* p. 3.

Sims, Lowry Stokes. *Stroke! Beauford Delaney, Norman Lewis and Alma Thomas.* New York: Michael Rosenfeld Galleries, 2005.

Thomas, Alma. *Alma Thomas Phantasmagoria, Major Paintings from the 1970s.* New York: Michael Rosenfeld Galleries, 2001.

———. *Alma W. Thomas: A Retrospective of the Paintings.* San Francisco: Pomegranate Communications, 1998.

Thompson, Bob
(Robert Thompson)
(1937–1966) *painter*

In a career that spanned only nine years, Bob Thompson created a substantial body of work that teemed with soaring angels and colorful demons. It was both strikingly original and squarely in the grand traditional of the European masters.

He was born Robert Thompson on June 26, 1937, in Louisville, Kentucky. When he was 13, his father was killed in an auto accident, an event that sent him into a deep depression. To help him, his mother, a schoolteacher, sent him to live with her sister in Boston. In 1955 Thompson entered the premedical program at Boston University (BU) to please his mother, who wanted him to become a doctor.

Still depressed, he dropped out of BU and returned to Louisville, where he enrolled as an art major at the University of Louisville. At first Thompson pursued art as therapy for his depression, but he soon found his calling as an artist. In the summer of his junior year he went to the art colony at Provincetown, Massachusetts, where he met the unorthodox artist Red Grooms, whose three-dimensional works were both pointed and playful. He returned to Louisville in the fall of 1958 but dropped out before graduating and moved to New York City in 1959. Here he joined Grooms and two other artists who had opened a gallery for their work. Thompson had his first solo show at the Delancey Street Museum in 1960. The same year he married Carol Penda, whom he had first met in Provincetown.

Thompson's large figurative paintings were inspired by the great artists of the Renaissance in Europe, whose work he admired above all others. This obsession set him apart from most contemporary American artists, who were still creating abstract paintings. The art world began to take notice of his talent, and in 1961 Wall Street stockbroker and arts patron Walter Gutman gave Thompson a grant to travel to Europe. The Thompsons lived in London, England, then Paris, France, and finally settled on the Spanish island of Ibiza. Thompson soaked up the great art of the European masters like a sponge. He was particularly attracted to the works of the Dutch artist Hieronymus Bosch and the Spanish artist Francisco Goya, with their grotesque creatures and frightening, phantasmagoric visions of heaven and hell. Thompson adapted their vision

to his paintings, adding the bright, garish colors of the 20th century French painter Henri Matisse.

The demons that filled his canvases drove Thompson's work. He painted incessantly, living extravagantly when he was not painting with the money from his many sales. In late 1963 the Thompsons returned to the United States, where the critics and public were overwhelmed by the new work the artist brought back with him. The paintings were exhibited at the Martha Jackson Gallery in New York, and the show broke records for gallery attendance. Critics praised his bold, contemporary take on the Renaissance style, and major museums bought his paintings.

While many of his works reflected medieval and Renaissance themes, such as *St. George and the Dragon* (1961–62), other were autobiographical, and still others reflected his love of music, such as *Homage to Nina Simone* (1965), with its vibrant lines and collagelike figures that seemed to pulsate with the raw energy of the black singer's music.

In November 1965, Thompson traveled to Rome, Italy, where he was again inspired by the great Italian artists of the past. Overworked, exhausted, and taking heroin, he underwent gall bladder surgery in March 1966. After the operation his doctors cautioned him to recuperate and take a rest from work. But Thompson found this impossible and quickly returned to a full schedule of painting. He became seriously ill and died in Rome on May 30, 1966, of lung complications. He was less than a month away from his 29th birthday.

Bob Thompson left behind more than 1,000 paintings, a remarkable oeuvre for so short a career. Today, his paintings are in the collections of the Hirshhorn Museum in Washington, D.C., the Metropolitan Museum of Art in New York City, and the School of the Art Institute of Chicago. A major retrospective of Thompson's work consisting of more than 100 paintings was held at the Whitney Museum of American Art in New York in 1998–99.

Further Reading

Diawara, Manthia. "Bob Thompson." Art Forum, December 1998. Available online. URL: http://findarticles.com/p/articles/mi_m0268/is_4_37/ai_53479692. Downloaded March 13, 2009.

Golden, Thelma. *Bob Thompson.* Berkeley: University of California Press, 1998.

Lewis, Samella. *African American Art and Artists.* Berkeley: University of California Press, 2003, pp. 172–173.

Perry, Regenia A. *Free Within Ourselves: African-American Artists in the Collection of the National Museum of American Art.* San Francisco: Pomegranate Communications, 1992, pp. 172–178.

Thrash, Dox

(1892–1965) *printmaker*

A masterful printmaker who invented a bold, new technique, Dox Thrash brought a shadowy, expressive power to his graphic images that is unique.

He was born on March 22, 1892, in Griffin, Georgia. His formal education ended in the fourth grade and about that time he took an art correspondence course. He left Georgia at age 16 and moved to Illinois, where he worked as an elevator operator while taking art classes at the School of the Art Institute of Chicago.

During World War I (1914–18), he joined the U.S. Army and fought in France as part of the American Expeditionary Force. He was wounded in combat and with his disability pension returned to the Art Institute where he continued to study until 1923. Then he went on the road, living the hobo life in New York, Massachusetts, and Connecticut, sketching people and places wherever he went.

Thrash finally settled in Philadelphia, Pennsylvania, in the early 1930s and got a job with the federally funded national Works Progress Administration's Graphic Arts Workshop. While there he made an unusual discovery about carborundum crystals commonly used by printmakers to remove images from lithograph stones. Thrash discovered that he could use these coarse grains to roughen the surface of copper plates and create unique etchings. The resulting images were shadowy, with soft colors and dynamic tonal variation. Thrash called the prints he made from this technique Opheliagraphs, in honor of his mother. Other workshop members adapted the technique and contributed to it, but Thrash's prints remain the most artistic and distinctive.

He created his brooding prints in many genres—including rural landscapes (*Georgia Cotton Crop, Deserted Cabin*), urban landscapes (*Freight Yard*), and simple studies of people (*Morning Paper*). One of his best known prints is *Defense Worker,* a stunning study of an African-American industrial worker as modern-day hero.

Thrash's most productive period ended in the 1940s, but he continued to produce prints until his death in 1965. His bold work has had a major influence on such African-American printmakers as BOB BLACKBURN, CHARLES WHITE, and CLAUDE CLARK. Today, only 188 of his prints are known to exist.

In 2001, the Philadelphia Museum of Art, one of the first museums to obtain his prints back in 1941, mounted a major retrospective of his work. *Dox Thrash: An African American Master Printmaker Rediscovered* was part of the museum's 125th anniversary.

Further Reading

"Dox Thrash (1892–1965)." Available online. URL: http://www.regallery.com/thrash_dox/thrash-biography.html. Downloaded March 13, 2009.

Ittmann, John. *Dox Thrash: An African-American Master Printmaker Rediscovered* (The Jacob Lawrence Series on American Artists). Seattle: University of Washington Press, 2002.

Riggs, Thomas, ed. *St. James Guide to Black Artists.* Detroit, Mich.: St. James Press, 1997, pp. 527–528.

Tolliver, Mose
(Mose T)
(1915–2006) *folk painter, illustrator*

Mose Tolliver was a folk artist of arresting imagination. His demons, animals, and naked women inhabit a universe that is alternately terrifying and whimsical.

He was born on July 4, in 1915, in Pike Road, Alabama, near the town of Pintala. His parents, poor tenant farmers, moved their family of 12 children to Macedonia, Alabama, when he was still a child. Leaving school at an early age, Tolliver worked as a farm laborer and gardener. As an adult he moved to Montgomery, where he got a job in the shipping department of a furniture factory. He married in 1941 and with his wife, Willie Mae, raised 14 children.

Tolliver served briefly as a laborer on a Georgia army base during World War II (1939–45). After the war, he returned to his job in the furniture factory. One day in 1965 a load of marble fell on him and crushed both feet. He went on disability and could walk only with the aid of crutches.

Tolliver's interest in art developed after a friend took him to an art exhibit. He began to paint using house paint on masonite plywood. He was limited to a painting surface that would fit in his lap because he only painted when seated on his bed. His dogs, mice, turtles, bigheaded people, and other fanciful creatures are often humorous and lyrical, linking his work to such other black folk artists as BILL TRAYLOR. What makes Tolliver's work unique is his strange choice of color and the erotic energy of some of his recurring images. His curious but sophisticated color combinations include gray and turquoise, mauve and lavender, and aqua and orange.

One recurring motif is his "Ladies on Scooters," which consist of naked women atop huge, disembodied penises. The images, while outrageous, are more fantastic than erotic.

Tolliver had his first one-person show at the Montgomery Museum of Fine Arts in 1981. He was one of the first black folk artists of his time to have a solo exhibition at a major museum. He continued to paint into his late 80s, sometimes producing as many as 10 paintings a day. "I just want to paint my pictures!" the prolific artist said.

In 1993, a major retrospective of his work was mounted at the Museum of American Folk Art in New York City. He illustrated the poems of a friend, Alabamian Robert Ely, in *Mose T's Slapout Family Album: Poems* (1996).

"His work speaks to those who love it," wrote Julian Bond in the introduction to that book. "Like Tolliver himself, it is accessible—immediately striking a responsive chord." Mose Tolliver died of pneumonia on October 30, 2006, at age 91. His daughter Annie is also a folk artist.

Further Reading
Ely, Robert, and Mose Tolliver, illustrator. *Mose T's Slapout Family Album: Poems.* Montgomery, Ala.: Black Belt Press, 1996.

Haardt, Anton. *Mose T A to Z: The Folk Art of Mose Tolliver.* Montgomery, Al.: Saturno Press, 2007.

Livingston, Jane, and John Beardsley. *Black Folk Art in America 1930–1980.* Jackson: University Press of Mississippi, 1989, pp. 132–137.

Riggs, Thomas, ed. *St. James Guide to Black Artists.* Detroit, Mich.: St. James Press, 1997, pp. 528–529.

Townsend, Robert
(1957–) *filmmaker, television director, screenwriter, actor, film producer, comedian*

A talented comic and actor before he turned to filmmaking, Robert Townsend is one of the most upbeat of black directors. His spirit and enthusiasm have often compensated for the uneven quality of his work.

He was born on February 6, 1957, in Chicago, Illinois. He studied acting and theater at Illinois

State University in Normal. On graduating, he joined Chicago's celebrated Second City improvisational comedy troupe. He went on to perform stand-up comedy with some success before landing his first screen role in the comedy-drama *Willie and Phil* (1980). Other supporting roles followed in *Streets of Fire* (1983) and *A Soldier's Story* (1984), in which he gave one of his best dramatic performances.

Frustrated by the few good roles offered to black actors in films, Townsend decided to make his own film on the subject. Borrowing heavily on all his credit cards, he raised about $100,000 and shot *Hollywood Shuffle* (1987), which he produced, wrote, directed, and starred in. Episodic and satirical, *Hollywood Shuffle* was about a black actor (Townsend) struggling to make it in Hollywood. The actor held down demeaning jobs while auditioning for equally demeaning roles in films. Townsend's winning performance and the film's combination of sharp satire and gentle comedy made it an unexpected hit.

The success of *Hollywood Shuffle* led Townsend to meet actor Eddie Murphy, who asked him to direct *Raw* (1987), a filmed version of his stand-up act. Townsend's next film was the ambitious saga of a 1960s rhythm and blues singing group, *The Five Heartbeats* (1991), which he again acted in. The film tried to cover too much ground in the lives of the leading characters, and while the musical numbers were energizing and memorable, the drama was unfocused and predictable, with a sentimental ending that seemed forced.

The same problems plagued his next feature film, *The Meteor Man* (1993), in which Townsend played a meek schoolteacher who becomes an offbeat superhero cleaning up crime in his ghetto neighborhood. Although the film was a greater box office flop than *The Five Heartbeats*, one has to admire the director's bold attempt to deal with the contemporary black experience without resorting to sex, excessive violence, and foul language.

Since then, Townsend has concentrated his energies on directing for television. A short-lived variety show series, *Townsend Television*, appeared briefly on the Fox network in 1993. He was executive producer, writer, director, and star of *The Parent 'Hood* (1995–99), which aired on the Warner Brothers network. In this genial situation comedy, Townsend played a college professor raising four kids in New York City. More recently he has directed several television movies, including *Little Richard* (2000) and *Carmen: A Hip Hopera* (2001). *10,000 Black Men Named George* (2002) another TV movie, was about black union activist Asa Philip Randolph and his efforts to organize the black Pullman porters on railroads in the 1920s. In 2005, Townsend was executive producer and director of the HBO comedy series *Partners in Crime*, which won an Ace Cable award. His long-anticipated feature film, *Phantom Punch* (2008), starred Ving Rhames as heavyweight boxer Sonny Liston. He has directed 16 episodes of the TV dramatic series *Diary of a Single Mom* (2009–10).

Further Reading

Alexander, George. *Why We Make Movies: Black Filmmakers Talk About the Magic of Cinema.* New York: Harlem Moon, 2003, pp. 118–132.

Moon, Spencer. *Reel Black Talk: A Sourcebook of 50 American Filmmakers.* Westport, Conn.: Greenwood Press, 1997, pp. 329–334.

"Robert Townsend," The Internet Movie Database. Available online. URL: http://www.imdb.com/name/nm0870186/. Downloaded March 13, 2009.

Further Viewing

The Five Heartbeats (1991). Fox Home Video, 15th anniversary special edition DVDs, 2006.

Hollywood Shuffle (1987). MGM/Home Entertainment, VHS/DVD, 2000/2001.

A Soldier's Story (1984). Sony, VHS/DVD, 1998/1999.

10,000 Black Men Named George (2002). Paramount Home Video, DVD, 2003.

Traylor, Bill
(ca. 1856–ca. 1949) *folk painter*

A folk artist of lively wit and rich imagination, whose animals and people seem to dance off the page, Bill Traylor did not begin his artistic journey until the astonishing age of 85.

He was born a slave probably on April 12, 1856, on a plantation near Benton, Alabama. The exact date of his birth is unknown. His master's name was George Traylor, hence his surname. Still a boy when slavery ended, Traylor remained on the plantation as a sharecropper. He married and had 20 children. When his wife died in 1938, the 84-year-old Traylor moved to Montgomery, Alabama, where he worked for a short time in a shoe factory. Crippled by rheumatism, he retired on government assistance and led a nomadic life, sleeping at night in the back room of a funeral parlor and sitting on the sidewalk in the daytime, talking freely with the passersby.

At this unlikely juncture of his life, Bill Traylor began to draw. "It just come to me," he explained about the fanciful barnyard animals and country folk who populated his drawings. He drew them with astonishing speed with pencil on crumpled paper, shirt cardboard, and whatever else he could lay his hands on. The drawings began as simple geometric shapes, which he then developed into figures with color crayons.

Traylor's work appeared fully developed, as if he had been saving up his creative energies for all those years only to have them burst forth like flooding waters through a dam. His characters were by turn lyrical, humorous, and wonderfully grotesque. Many told narratives about experiences he recalled from his rural Southern childhood.

Traylor's folk drawings might have never gotten beyond the streets of Montgomery if not for a young local artist, Charles Shannon. Shannon befriended Traylor and immediately recognized the simple genius of his artwork. He collected his drawings and gave him the tools he needed to keep producing them. Realizing that people liked his work, Traylor hung them from a string on a fence and sold them to curious passersby. In 1940, a number of his drawings were exhibited at New South, an art center in Montgomery. The only other public display of his work in his lifetime occurred a year later at the Fieldston School in New York City.

After four years of constant productivity, Traylor's muse was interrupted by the entrance of the United States into World War II (1939–45). Amid the disruption of wartime, Traylor moved north to visit his various children in several different cities, including Chicago, Illinois, and Washington, D.C. If he produced any art during this time, it has not survived.

In 1946, Traylor returned to Montgomery, but he seemed to have lost the impetus for his art. He became ill within the year and died in a nursing home, probably on October 23, 1949 at age 93.

Today, Traylor's folk drawings and paintings are among the most sought-after in the folk art world. Unlike other black folk artists such as WILLIAM EDMONDSON and ELIJAH PIERCE, Traylor left few utterances about his art and how he came to create it. His delightful drawings remain another mystery of that unfathomable subject— the human creative spirit.

Further Reading

Helferstein, Josef, and Roman Kurzmeyer, eds. *Deep Blues: Bill Traylor 1854–1949*. New Haven, Conn.: Yale University Press, 1999.

Livingston, Jane, and John Beardsley. *Black Folk Art in America 1930–1980*. Jackson: University Press of Mississippi, 1989, pp. 138–145.

Lyons, Mary E., and Bill Traylor, illustrator. *Deep Blues: Bill Traylor, Self-Taught Artist* (African-American Artist and Artisans). New York: Scribner, 1995.

Maresca, Frank. *Bill Traylor: His Art, His Life*. New York: Knopf, 1991.

Sobel, Mechal. *Painting a Hidden Life: The Art of Bill Traylor*. Baton Rouge: Louisiana State University Press, 2009.

Turner, Morrie

(1923–) *cartoonist*

The first African-American cartoonist to reach a mainstream audience, Morrie Turner has brought a message of understanding, peace, and brotherhood to millions of readers through his landmark comic strip, *Wee Pals.*

He was born on December 11, 1923, in Oakland, California. He started drawing cartoons in the fifth grade and after high school served in the U.S. Army during World War II (1939–45). Turner created a comic soldier called Rail Head for his base newspaper in Kentucky. When he was discharged in 1946 he started sending his cartoons to various magazines. His first published cartoon appeared in a baking institution journal in 1947 and earned him $5.

To support himself, Turner got a job in the Oakland police department as a clerk. He tried out as a police artist but failed to make the grade. "I did some sketches," he recalled. "They'd say it looked like the suspect, but then the artist in me would refine the drawing until it no longer looked like the suspect."

In 1964, he left the Oakland police and devoted all his energies to cartooning. A strong advocate of integration and racial harmony, Turner created a comic strip about a group of kids from various ethnic backgrounds. He called it *Dinky Fellas,* and it was picked up by the *Chicago Daily Defender,* a black newspaper, for $40 a month. Wanting to reach a national audience, Turner took his idea to a cartoonists' meeting in 1964 and presented it to Charles Schulz, the creator of the popular *Peanuts* comic strip. Schulz loved the idea, and with his encouragement and support, Turner was able to sell the strip, now retitled *Wee Pals,* to the Lew Little Syndicate in 1965. Only five newspapers, however, picked up the strip from syndication.

Sadly, it took a national tragedy to make *Wee Pals* a hit. Within three months of the assassination of civil rights leader Martin Luther King, Jr., in 1968, *Wee Pals* was appearing in more than 100 U.S. newspapers. Its message of bringing people together was suddenly very important to all Americans in the face of growing racial tensions.

The strip's original cast of characters included Nipper, a black boy whose eyes are forever hidden beneath an oversized Confederate cap, and Sybil, a black girl with plenty of spunk. The white characters were the impish Wellington, the overweight Oliver, and tomboy Connie. Over time, Turner added Pablo, a Mexican-American; Trinh, a Vietnamese girl; Jerry, a brainy Jewish kid; and Charlotte, who is confined to a wheelchair.

Wee Pals is set in suburbia, far from the mean streets of urban America. While the kids' adventures are usually amusing, the social message of getting along is never far from the fore. While the Black Power advocates of the 1960s and 1970s rejected Turner's message of integration, it was embraced by millions of other Americans of all colors. In the Sunday color strip, Turner includes the Soul Circle, a feature celebrating real Americans of all ethnic backgrounds who have made important contributions to society.

The popularity of *Wee Pals* led to a network television show based on the strip called *Kid Power* that ran from 1973 to 1976. There was even a stage musical based on Turner's characters. The cartoonist has used his *Wee Pals* characters in campaigns involving a host of social issues, including antidrugs, human immunodeficiency virus (HIV) awareness, personal esteem, literacy, and personal hygiene and safety. Among the many awards Turner has received are the Brotherhood Award of the B'nai B'rith Anti-Defamation League, the National Cartoonist Society's Brotherhood Award, and the Milton Caniff Lifetime Achievement Award (2003). A 30-minute documentary of Turner's life, *Keeping the Faith with Morrie,* won best documentary at the Hollywood Black Film Festival in 2002. He continues to publish cartoon books with his Wee Pals characters that salute historical African-American groups, including celebrated African-American women and African Americans in the military.

Currently distributed by Creators Syndicate, *Wee Pals* has been surpassed in popularity by newer, more contemporary black comic strips, but it was Turner and his merry band of youngsters who paved the way for every other African-American cartoonist working today.

"When Morrie draws about children trying to find their way in an integrated community," said the late Charles Schulz, "the results show that Morrie has been more than a mere observer. Of course, the best part of it all is that *Wee Pals* is a lot of fun."

Further Reading

Ericsson, Mary K. *Morrie Turner: Creator of Wee Pals (People of Distinction)*. Danbury, Conn.: Children's Press, 1986.

Turner, Morrie. *Explore Black History with Wee Pals*. East Orange, N.J.: Just Us Books, 1998.

———. *Super Sistahs: Featuring the Accomplishments of African-American Women Past and Present*. Oakland, Calif.: Bye Publishing Services, 2005.

"Wee Pals by Morrie Turner." Creators.com. Available online. http://www.creators.com/comics/wee-pals-about.html. Downloaded March 13, 2009.

Van Der Zee, James
(James Augustus Joseph Van DerZee,
James Vanderzee)
(1886–1983) *photographer*

One of the most important and prolific African-American photographers of the 20th century, James Van Der Zee captured the spirit and promise of black culture in the 1920s and 1930s in his pristine and beautifully executed pictures.

He was born James Augustus Joseph Van Der Zee on June 29, 1886, in Lenox, Massachusetts. His parents, John and Susan Van Der Zee, were butler and maid to former president Ulysses S. Grant when the Grants lived in New York City. Later John worked as a sexton in a church in Lenox. James and his two brothers helped keep the church and its grounds clean for their father.

Van Der Zee bought his first camera when barely in his teens and took pictures of his schoolmates and family. He turned his bedroom closet into a darkroom where he could develop his pictures. Despite this early start in photography, it would be many years before Van Der Zee would make his living as a photographer.

About 1905, he moved to New York City with his brother Walter. He worked as a waiter and a part-time musician, playing the violin and the piano. After marrying Kate Brown in 1907, he moved back to Lenox but soon returned to New York. His wife disapproved of his photography and wanted him to find a more secure profession. They divorced after eight years of marriage.

Van Der Zee finally had enough savings to open a photographic studio on West 135th Street in Harlem in 1915. He ran it with his new love, Gaynella, a telephone operator he had met in an office where he worked for a time. The studio was called James's and Gaynella's Guarantee Photo Studio. The couple married the following year. Van Der Zee became known as "the picture-takin' man" in his neighborhood, and he photographed countless family portraits, weddings, funerals, and other special occasions. What set him apart from other studio photographers of the day was the painstaking care he took with each picture. He composed each photograph artistically, posing his subjects and even providing backgrounds and props to tell a story in the picture. His use of lighting was ingenious, and he would often retouch the final photograph with an etching knife or a retouching pencil to improve the appearance of his subject.

Another unusual technique Van Der Zee used was multiple-imaging, by which he superimposed one photograph over another. He often used this process in funeral pictures to show the departed person as he or she had looked in life. "I guess it was just a matter of not being satisfied with what the camera was doing," Van Der Zee told writer

After a lifetime of taking photographs, James Van Der Zee was suddenly rediscovered at age 83 when his work appeared in an exhibition at the Metropolitan Museum of Art in New York. *(Anthony Barboza)*

James Haskins. "I wanted to make the camera take what I thought should be there, too."

Although these superimposed pictures were admittedly sentimental, many of his other photographs accurately and memorably recorded the life of Harlem and its people honestly and straightforwardly.

Van Der Zee's career flourished during the years of the Harlem Renaissance (1920–35), a flowering of African-American culture in New York and other large cities. He photographed both the ordinary people of Harlem and the famous, including singer Florence Mills, dancer Bill Robinson, and boxer Joe Louis. Van Der Zee was the official photographer for black leader Marcus Garvey, whose "Back to Africa" movement was a defining moment for African Americans in the 1920s.

In 1942, Van Der Zee moved to his last studio on Lenox Avenue in Harlem, where he remained for 26 years. After World War II ended in 1945,

his business suffered as more and more people began taking their own pictures with new, inexpensive cameras. By the 1960s, Van Der Zee was a forgotten figure of an earlier era, but a researcher from the Metropolitan Museum of Art in New York rediscovered him. The museum was putting together a major photographic exhibit in 1968 called *Harlem on My Mind.* Museum curators were so impressed by Van Der Zee's work that they displayed more of his photographs in the show than anyone else's.

At age 83, this modest man was suddenly one of the most famous photographers in America. Books of his photographs were published, he was interviewed for magazines and newspapers, and the Metropolitan Museum bought 66 of his photographs for their permanent collection. Van Der Zee was given the Award of Merit from the Photographers Forum and lectured at the International Center of Photography in New York City. In 1969, the James Van Der Zee Institute opened on West 125th Street in New York to house his impressive collection of photographs spanning more than 50 years.

Gaynella died in 1976, but Van Der Zee lived another seven years, finally dying at age 96 in 1983. "I'd like to live to be a hundred," he said, five years before his death. "There's still a lot to learn. You never stop learning and you never stop trying to figure out what life is all about."

In 2002, James Van Der Zee was one of 15 American photographers honored in a series of stamps issued by the U.S. Postal Service.

Further Reading

Haskins, James. *James Van Der Zee: The Picture-Takin' Man.* New York: African World Press, 1991.

"James Van Der Zee (1886–1983)." Drop Me off in Harlem. Available online. URL: http://artsedge. Kennedy-center.org/exploring/harlem/faces/ vanderzee_text.html. Downloaded April 2, 2009.

Van Der Zee, James. *James Van Der Zee: Harlem Photographs 1928–1960.* New York: Delano Greenidge Editions, 2003.

Westerbeck Colin, ed. *The James Vanderzee Studio.* Chicago: The Art Institute of Chicago, 2004.

Willis, Deborah. *Reflections in Black: A History of Black Photographers from 1840 to the Present.* New York: W. W. Norton, 2000, pp. 3, 37, 38, 42–43, 64–66, 118.

Willis, Deborah and Rodger C. Birt. *Vanderzee: Photographer 1886–1983.* New York: Harry N. Abrams, 1993.

Van Peebles, Mario

(1957–) *filmmaker, television director, actor, screenwriter*

Twenty years after his father began the "blaxploitation" era of black cinema, Mario Van Peebles started a new wave of black films with his electrifying gangster drama *New Jack City* (1991).

He was born on January 15, 1957, in Mexico City. His father, filmmaker MELVIN VAN PEEBLES, cast him in his classic *Sweet Sweetback's Baadasssss Song* (1971) as the young Sweetback when he was 14. Although he enjoyed his first taste of film acting, Van Peebles decided to get an education and studied economics at Columbia University in New York City, earning a degree in 1978. The following year he got a job as an analyst for the Mayor's Office of Management and Budget. But he was drawn back to show business and turned to modeling and acting.

His first noticeable roles were in the 1984 films *The Cotton Club* and *Exterminator II.* He won critical praise for his role as a young soldier in *Heartbreak Ridge* (1986) and received a NAACP Image Award for his performance.

Two years later, Van Peebles starred in the television series *Sonny Spoon* (1988). During the show's brief run, he had his first experience directing several episodes. This led to directing assignments on such dramatic series as *21 Jump Street* and *Wiseguy.* In 1990, Van Peebles wrote the screenplay for the comedy *Identity Crisis,* which was directed by his father. The film was poorly received, but soon his first solo-directing job would make him famous.

New Jack City was the lurid story of the rise and fall of a drug kingpin, played memorably by black actor Wesley Snipes. It also featured Vanessa Williams and rap singer Ice-T. The film was shot for $8.5 million and grossed over $44 million in just a few weeks. It made a star of Snipes and made Van Peebles one of the hottest new directors in Hollywood.

Unfortunately, he was not able to repeat his success with his next film, the black western *Posse* (1993), which he also starred in. Since then, Van Peebles has directed *Panther* (1995), a film about the Black Panther movement of the 1960s and 1970s, written by his father. The two also codirected another gang film, *Gang of Blue* (1996).

Since then, Van Peebles has directed primarily for television and made a part documentary/part tribute to his father's struggle to get *Sweet Sweetback's Baadasssss Song* made. In this film, *Baadasssss!* (2004), he portrays his father. Van Peebles's most recent film is *Black, White and Blues* (2010) in which his father appears.

Van Peebles has continued to act in films, and he was especially impressive playing black political leader Malcolm X in the biographical film *Ali* (2001) about the life of boxer Muhammad Ali.

Further Reading

Bogle, Donald. *Toms, Coons, Mulattoes, Mammies, & Bucks: An Interpretative History of Blacks in American Films.* New York: Continuum, 1997, pp. 238, 288, 324, 341–342.

"Mario Van Peebles." Internet Movie Database. Available online. URL: http://www.imdb.com/name/namoo05522/. Downloaded March 14, 2009

Moon, Spencer. *Reel Black Talk: A Sourcebook of 50 American Filmmakers.* Westport, Conn.: Greenwood Press, 1997, pp. 341–350.

Samuels, Allison. "In the Name of the Father." *Newsweek,* May 24, 2004, pp. 58–59.

Van Peebles, Mario, Melvin Van Peebles, Ula Y. Taylor, and J. Tarika Lewis. *Panther: The Illustrated History of the Black Panthers and the Story Behind the Film.* New York: Newmarket Press, 1995.

Further Viewing
Ali (2001). Sony, The Director's Cut, DVD, 2004.
New Jack City (1991). Warner Home Video, Special Edition, 2 DVDs, 2005.

Van Peebles, Melvin
(Melvin Peebles)
(1932–) *filmmaker, actor, screenwriter, film producer, composer*

An iconoclastic figure in the American cinema, Melvin Van Peebles is a pioneer of the contemporary black cinema, whose key work set off an explosion of black-oriented films in the early 1970s.

He was born Melvin Peebles on August 21, 1932, in Chicago, Illinois. He moved with his father, a tailor, to Phoenix, Illinois, as a child. After high school, he attended Ohio Wesleyan University in Delaware, Ohio, and graduated in 1953. He then joined the U.S. Air Force and served as a flight navigator for three and a half years. On his discharge, Van Peebles moved briefly to Mexico, then San Francisco, California, where he married. The couple settled in Europe, where Peebles studied acting at the Dutch National Theatre in the Netherlands. They next moved to Paris, France, where they lived for close to a decade.

In France, Van Peebles wrote five novels, one of which, *La Permission,* he adapted into a film, *The Story of a Three-Day Pass* (1968). He wrote, directed, and produced *Pass,* which was about a black U.S. serviceman who has a romance with a French girl. The modest, low-budget film was well received by American critics and led Columbia Pictures to hire Van Peebles to direct the big-budget comedy *Watermelon Man* (1970), starring black comic and actor Godfrey Cambridge. It was the story of a bigoted, white insurance salesman who wakes up one morning to find that he has

Melvin Van Peebles began the cycle of blaxploitation films in the 1970s with an uncompromising film that he wrote, directed, produced, and starred in. *(Photofest)*

turned black. The film was a commercial flop, but Van Peebles took the money he was paid and used it to make an independent film that showed race relations in the 1960s in a very different light.

Van Peebles shot his new film—which he wrote, directed, produced, starred in, and wrote the musical score for—in 19 days on a shoestring budget of $500,000. This sum included a $50,000 loan from comedian-actor Bill Cosby. Called *Sweet Sweetback's Baadasssss Song* (1971), the film was the story of a pimp, played by Van Peebles, who finds new direction in his life when he witnesses two white police officers beating a young black revolutionary. Sweetback kills the two cops and flees from the law, finding time along the way to have sex with several willing women. The movie ends with its antihero escaping justice across the border and a superimposed message that promises A BAADASSSS NIGGER IS COMING BACK TO COLLECT SOME DUES.

Extremely graphic in its violence and sex even by today's standards, *Sweet Sweetback* was turned down by nearly every film distributor in Hollywood. Finally Cinemation agreed to take a chance on it, and they were glad they did. The film became a surprise hit and grossed $10 million in just a few weeks.

Black audiences were exhilarated by Van Peebles's unapologetic black hero, who struck back at white racism without a second thought. The film's success led to a string of similar films that featured amoral black heroes and heroines who fought racism, white villains, and occasionally black ones. The genre came to be called "blaxploitation" and it thrived for half a decade.

Ironically, Van Peebles himself never made another successful blaxploitation film. He soon drifted into the theater, an early love, and wrote two Broadway musicals, *Ain't Supposed to Die a Natural Death* and *Don't Play Us Cheap*. He adapted the second show into a film, which was a commercial disaster.

In the late 1970s and early 1980s, Van Peebles wrote several television dramas, including *Just an Old Sweet Song* (1976) and *Sophisticated Gents* (1981). By the 1980s the revolutionary filmmaker had tried his hand on Wall Street and became the only black trader on the American Stock Exchange.

More recently, Van Peebles has collaborated with his son MARIO VAN PEEBLES on several films as actor, director, and writer. They include the comedy *Identity Crisis* (1989) and a gangster film, *Gang of Blue* (1996). In 2004, his son directed a film about his efforts to get *Sweet Sweetback* made, *Baadasssss!* Van Peebles recently directed and starred in his first feature film in eight years,

Confessions of a Ex-Doofus—Itchy-Footed Mutha (2008), based on his 1982 Broadway musical *Waltz of the Stork*.

Although Melvin Van Peebles is a rebellious spirit who has turned his hand to nearly every kind of artistic endeavor, his greatest achievement to date remains his breakthrough film *Sweet Sweetback*, which not only started a new genre of black cinema but opened the doors for many talented black directors, actors, film editors, and cameramen.

Further Reading

Alexander, George. *Why We Make Movies: Black Filmmakers Talk About the Magic of Cinema.* New York: Harlem Moon, 2003, pp. 16–27.

Bogle, Donald. *Toms, Coons, Mulattoes, Mammies, & Bucks: An Interpretative History of Blacks in American Films.* New York: Continuum, 1997, pp. 16–17, 234–238.

"Melvin Van Peebles." Internet Movie Database. Available online. URL: http://www.imdb.com/name/nm0887708/. Downloaded April 2, 2009.

Sisario, Ben. "He's got It Bad or 'Baad' for His Art," *New York Times*, January 24, 2010, Arts and Leisure, p. 4.

Van Peebles, Melvin. *Sweet Sweetback's Baadasssss Song: A Guerilla Filmmaking Manifesto.* New York: Da Capo Press, 2004.

Van Peebles, Melvin, and Mario Van Peebles. *No Identity Crisis: A Father and Son's Own Story of Working Together.* New York: Simon & Schuster, 1990.

Further Viewing

How to Eat Your Watermelon in White Company (And Enjoy It) (2005). Homevision, DVD, 2007.

The Story of a Three Day Pass (1968). Xenon Studios, VHS, 1996.

Sweet Sweetback's Baadasssss Song (1971). Cinemation Industries, DVD, 2003.

Walker, Kara

(1969–) *silhouette artist, installation artist, printmaker, video artist, animator, educator*

One of the most popular African-American artists in contemporary America, Kara Walker is also one of the most controversial for her nearly life-size black, cut-paper silhouettes of slaves and their masters.

She was born in Stockton, California, on November 26, 1969. Her father, Larry Walker, is a respected painter. He moved the family to Atlanta, Georgia, where Kara attended high school. Already questioning the racial barriers that separate people, she dated white classmates. After high school, she enrolled in the Atlanta College of Art and graduated with a Bachelor of Arts degree in 1991. The same year the first exhibition of her artwork took place in Atlanta. Walker continued her education at the Rhode Island School of Design in Providence, earning a Master of Fine Arts degree in 1994. While at the Rhode Island School, Walker began to develop the silhouette technique that has made her famous. "My thing eventually came out in these silhouettes," she said in a 1998 interview. "Whereas before I used to avoid the race issue by just kind of mashing up different colors."

Her "thing" was creating large elaborate profiles of antebellum southern blacks and whites engaged in graphic acts of sex and violence. These narratives, framed in an elegant medium last seen in the neoclassicist revivalism of the late 18th and early 19th century, are meant to satirize race relations of the past and today.

"The elegant and lyrical line of Walker's cut edges, embellished with curling, ribbonlike flourishes and touches of whimsy, is a foil to the jolt that overtakes the viewer as her narrative is slowly revealed," wrote one art critic.

Not everyone has appreciated Walker's biting humor. She has been criticized for perpetuating old stereotypes of blacks by the International Review of African American Art and other organizations. Black artist BETYE SAAR waged a campaign of protest when Walker received a John D. and Catherine T. MacArthur Foundation "genius" grant in 1997, urging that the money be rescinded.

But the contemporary art world has embraced her work since her breakthrough exhibition at the Musée d'Art Moderne de la Ville de Paris in France in 1995. Since then she has had her work included in group shows at the Institute for Contemporary Art in Boston in 1996 and at the Whitney Biennal in New York City in 1997. Her first New York solo exhibition was held the following year at Wooster Gardens. Other solo shows have been held at the Renaissance Society in Chicago, Illinois, and the San Francisco Museum of

Modern Art in California. Walker was the U.S. representative to the São Paulo Biennale in Brazil in 2002.

Her first full-scale retrospective—*My Complement, My Enemy, My Oppressor, My Love*—opened at the Walker Art Center in Minneapolis, Minnesota, in February 2007 and traveled to several other museums, including the Whitney Museum of American Art in New York City. It included not only her signature cut-paper silhouettes, but collages, shadow-puppets, light projections, and video animations.

"It's interesting that as soon as you start telling the story of racism, you start reliving the story," Walker is quoted as saying in the Whitney guide to this exhibition. "You keep creating a monster that swallows you. But as long as there's a Darfur, as long as there are people saying, 'Hey, you don't belong here' to others, it only seems realistic to continue investigating the terrain of racism."

Kara Walker lives in New York City with her husband, jewelry designer Klaus Burgel and their daughter Octavia. She is a professor of visual arts at Columbia University.

Further Reading

DuBois Shaw, Gwendolyn. *Seeing the Unspeakable: The Art of Kara Walker.* Durham, N.C.: Duke University Press, 2004.

"Kara Walker." Art:21. Available online. URL: http://www.pbs.org/art21/artists/walker/index.html. Downloaded March 14, 2009.

Vergne, Philippe, Sander Gilman, Thomas McEvilley, Robert Storr, Kevin Young, Yasmil Raymond, and Kara Walker. *Kara Walker: My Complement, My Enemy, My Oppressor, My Love.* Minneapolis, Minn.: Walker Art Center, 2007.

Walker, Kara. *Kara Walker: Bureau of Refugees.* New York: Charta/Sikkema Jenkins & Company, 2008.

Walker, Kara, Thelma Golden, Annette Dixon, and Robert Reid-Phair. *Kara Walker: Pictures from Another Time.* New York: Distributed Art Publishers, 2002.

Walker, Shawn
(1940–) *photographer, educator*

A photographer of intense power, Shawn Walker is best known for his evocative portraits of the Harlem community he grew up in and for his surreal studies of his own shadow.

He was born in Harlem, the black section of New York City, on November 26, 1940. His first introduction to photography was through his uncle, a professional photographer. He began taking pictures of his family and friends with a camera at age five.

In 1962, he joined such other black photographers as ROY DeCARAVA, Al Fennar, Ray Francis, Lou Draper, and Herb Robinson to form the Kamoinge Workshop. The group's purpose was to provide American society with positive images of black Americans. They organized exhibitions of their work in New York City galleries and libraries and put out annual publications of their photographs.

Through the 1960s, Walker made a memorable series of photographs of Harlem and its streets and people. In the 1970s, he traveled abroad to photograph people and places in Africa, South America, and Cuba.

Walker's renowned shadow studies were inspired by the novel *Invisible Man* (1952) by black author Ralph Ellison. The intriguing ambiguities of these pictures of Walker's own shadow are the perfect visual equivalent of Ellison's central character, a young black man in search of his identity.

In the late 1980s, Walker began a new series of Harlem photographs that focused on religious rites and celebrations, such as baptisms and funerals. In 1987, he earned a Bachelor of Fine Arts degree from Empire State College in New York City. He continues to exhibit and work with the Kamoinge Workshop. His photographs have also have been exhibited at the Rockland Center for the Arts in West Nyack, New York; the Brooklyn Museum, the Schomburg Center for Research in Black Culture, and the International Center of

Photography, all in New York City. In the aftermath of Hurricane Katrina in 2005, Walker and other members of Kamoinge traveled to the Gulf Coast to photograph images of places and people devastated by the disaster.

Shawn Walker has been the recipient of grants from the New York Foundation for the Arts in 1991 and 1992 and Light Work, from which he also received the artist-in-residence award in 1989. He currently teaches photography at City College of the City University of New York and the Borough of Manhattan Community College.

Further Reading

Millstein, Barbara Head, ed. *Committed to the Image: Contemporary Black Photographers.* London, U.K.: Rizzoli International, 2001.

"Photographs by Shawn Walker." Katrina: An Unnatural Disaster. Available online. URL: http://www.soros.org/resources/multimedia/katrina/projects/HurricaneRace/story_WalkerShawn.php. Downloaded March 14, 2009.

Willis, Deborah. *Reflections in Black: A History of Black Photographers from 1840 to the Present.* New York: W. W. Norton, 2000, pp. 173–174, 245, 246.

Waring, Laura Wheeler
(1887–1948) *painter, illustrator, educator*

Noted for her richly textured portraits of celebrated African Americans, Laura Wheeler Waring is also remembered for her whimsical illustrations for children.

She was born Laura Wheeler on May 27, 1887, in Hartford, Connecticut, the second daughter of six children. Her father, Robert Foster Wheeler, was a minister and pastor of the Talcott Street Congregational Church in Hartford. Her mother, Mary Freeman Wheeler, was a public school teacher and an amateur artist.

Painting watercolors from her teens, Waring was hired as an art instructor at Cheyney State Teachers College near Philadelphia when she was 19.

A year later, she enrolled at the Pennsylvania Academy of the Fine Arts in Philadelphia. She taught at Cheyney nearly two decades before being appointed director of the school's art department in 1925. She remained in that position until her death.

In 1914, Waring was awarded the Cresson Travel Scholarship that allowed her to travel and study throughout western Europe. On her second trip abroad, in 1924, she studied at the Académie de la Grande Chaumière in Paris, France. While she was there, the well-known African-American painter HENRY O. TANNER introduced her to a number of leading black artists working in France, including PALMER C. HAYDEN, NANCY ELIZABETH PROPHET, and HALE WOODRUFF.

On her return to the United States, Waring's reputation as a portrait painter of warmth and great understanding grew. In 1926, she served as director of the Negro Art section at the Sesquicentennial Exposition in Philadelphia. The following year she won the gold medal in the annual Harmon Foundation Salon for her portrait *Anne Washington Derry.* Her portraits of famous blacks of the day included those of political leader and thinker W. E. B. DuBois, writer James Weldon Johnson, and singer Marian Anderson. Today many of these portraits reside in the permanent collection of the National Portrait Gallery in Washington, D.C.

In the 1920s, Waring also became a well-known illustrator of children's periodicals, including *The Brownie Book* and others. She also illustrated a number of covers for the NAACP journal *The Crisis.*

In the 1940s, Waring created a series of paintings in which she sensitively interpreted Negro spirituals. Included among her most experimental works are *Jacob's Ladder; Heaven, Heaven;* and *The Coming of the Lord.*

Laura Wheeler Waring died after a long illness on February 3, 1948. She "painted with a realism revealing not only her scrupulous objectivity, but the serene affection with which she regarded his subjects," wrote art historian DAVID C. DRISKELL.

Further Reading

Riggs, Thomas, ed. *St. James Guide to Black Artists.* Detroit, Mich.: St. James Press, 1997, pp. 550–551.

Smith, Jessie Carney, ed. *Notable Black American Women.* Detroit, Mich.: Gale Research, Inc., 1992, pp. 1,205–1,206.

"Waring, Laura Wheeler (1887–1948)." Available online. URL: http://www.blackpast.org/?q=aah/waring-laura-wheeler-1887-1948. Downloaded March 14, 2009.

Washington, James W., Jr.
(1909–2000) *sculptor*

The most celebrated sculptor of the northwestern United States, James W. Washington Jr. created primordial sculptures that seem to emerge from the stone as if nature itself and not the artist brought them forth.

He was born on November 10, 1909, in Gloster, Mississippi, near the city of Natchez. He was the third of five children of the Reverend James N. Washington, a preacher, and Lizzie Washington, a homemaker who played the accordion.

Washington's schooling ended at an early age, and he was apprenticed to a shoemaker. He eventually became an electrician, servicing the homes of black people because racism prevented him from getting a regular job with a utility company.

In 1943, he moved to Seattle, Washington, to work as a marine electrician at the Bremerton Naval Shipyard. The city would become his permanent home. Interested in painting since his teens, Washington studied in Seattle with local artist Mark Tobey.

The turning point in his life occurred on a visit to Mexico in 1951. He was introduced to some of Mexico's greatest mural artists, such as Diego Rivera, who inspired him. Then, while touring Aztec pyramids at the ancient city of Teotihuacan, he came upon a small volcanic stone that for some strange reason appealed to him. He picked it up and took it home with him.

Five years later, Washington felt moved to carve the stone and created his first sculpture, *Young Boy of Athens* (1956). He was so pleased with the results that he decided to give up painting and become a sculptor.

Young Boy of Athens was sparse and organic and looked like an ancient artifact. Washington's subsequent work had this same powerful, primitive look. Critics have compared his work to the folk sculpture of WILLIAM EDMONDSON. Both artists are known for their primitivism and fondness for sculpting animals. Washington's work, however, is more the deliberate work of a trained artist rather than a naive one. Nevertheless, his sculptures are no less expressive than Edmondson's, such as the huge rabbit and other creatures that emerge from his massive *Three Wonders of Nature* (1973). This sculpture sits in front of the Washington State Capitol in Olympia.

James W. Washington, Jr. became the best-known sculptor in Washington, a unique honor for a black artist in a state that is predominantly white. Many of his large works dot the cities of Seattle and Tacoma. The mayor of Seattle proclaimed May 20, 1973, the day he received the Governor's Art Award, as "James W. Washington, Jr., Day." In 1989, the Bellevue Art Museum held a major retrospective of Washington's sculptures and his early paintings. James W. Washington, Jr., died on June 7, 2000, in Seattle, at age 90. After his death, the city of Seattle declared his studio and home a historic landmark. The Washington State History Museum mounted the exhibit *Kindling the Flame of Creativity: The Life and Art of James W. Washington, Jr.,* in 2002.

"What I am trying to say with my sculpture," he once wrote, "is that each one of us has something within us waiting to be released and that something is spiritual, the spirit being the universality of life itself."

Further Reading

Ament, Deloris Tarzan, and Mary Randlett, photographer. *Iridescent Light: The Emergence of Northwestern*

Art. Seattle: University of Washington Press, 2002, pp. 152–164.

Bearden, Romare, and Harry Henderson. *A History of African-American Artists: From 1792 to the Present.* New York: Pantheon Books, 1993, pp. 462–469.

Karlstorm, J. Paul, and James W. Washington, Jr. *Spirit in the Stone: The Visionary Art of James W. Washington, Jr.* Seattle: University of Washington Press, 1989.

"Oral history interview with James W. Washington, Jr., 1987, June 29." Smithsonian Archives of American Art. Available online. URL: http://www.aaa.si.edu/corrections/oralhistories/transcripts/washin87.htm. Downloaded March 14, 2009.

Wayans, Keenen Ivory

(1958–   ) *filmmaker, television director, film producer, screenwriter, actor, comedian*

A keen satirist of black and white relations, Keenen Ivory Wayans came to prominence on television and has since become a successful commercial filmmaker.

He was born on June 8, 1958, in New York City. His father, Howell, was a supermarket manager and a devout Jehovah's Witness. His mother, Elvira, was a social worker. Wayans attended Tuskegee Institute in Alabama, where he majored in engineering. He dropped out of college in his senior year to pursue a career as a stand-up comic.

In 1988, the 30-year-old Wayans got the opportunity to direct his first film, *I'm Gonna Git You Sucka!,* a satire of the blaxploitation films popular in the 1970s. The film gained critical notice and gave him the opportunity to create a comedy skit show for the fledging Fox TV network, *In Living Color,* in 1990. The series bore a strong resemblance to the irreverent comedy of NBC's *Saturday Night Live,* but it focused on black stereotypes and interracial relations, something rarely seen on network television up to that time. The writing was sharp and funny, and the fine cast was headed by Wayans himself, his brother Damon, and a young Canadian comic, Jim Carrey.

"We take an exaggerated stereotype and really have fun with it," Wayans said in an interview with the *New York Times.* "If I take something and ridicule it to such a degree that people could never look at it as anything real, then it really helps destroy a preconceived notion."

In Living Color won an Emmy in its first year for outstanding variety, musical, or comedy program, and Wayans was named most promising producer in television by NOVA in 1991. When the show left the air in 1992, Wayans concentrated on acting and screenwriting. He cowrote the script for *The Five Heartbeats* (1991) with director ROBERT TOWNSEND. He wrote and directed the action films *Low Down Dirty Shame* (1994) and *Most Wanted* (1997), neither of which were box office hits. In 1997, Wayans also hosted a short-lived late night television talk show, *The Keenen Ivory Wayans Show,* on the UPN network.

Wayans has had his greatest success as a filmmaker to date with *Scary Movie* (2000), a no-holds-barred spoof of teen horror films, and its sequel, *Scary Movie 2* (2001). While often funny, these films exhibited a crudity in matters of sex and violence for which Wayans has been widely criticized. His most recent films are *White Chicks* (2004) and *Little Man* (2006).

Wayans married actress Daphne Polk in 2001. They have five children. The couple divorced in 2009. Besides his brother Damon, he has three other siblings who are actors—Marlon, Shawn, and Kim—as well as his nephew Damon Wayans, Jr.

Further Reading

Alexander, George. *Why We Make Movies: Black Filmmakers Talk About the Magic of Cinema.* New York: Harlem Moon, 2003, pp. 133–153

George, Nelson, and Keenen Ivory Wayans, designer. *In Living Color: The Authorized Companion to the Fox TV Series.* New York: Warner Books, 1991.

"Keenen Ivory Wayans," Internet Movie Database. Available online. URL: http://www.imdb.com/name/nm0005540. Downloaded March 14, 2009.

White, Katherine. *The Wayans Brothers* (Famous Families). New York: Rosen Publishing Group, 2005.

Further Viewing

I'm Gonna Git You Sucka! (1988). MGM/Home Entertainment, VHS/DVD, 2001.

In Living Color–Season 1 (1990). Fox Home Video, DVD box set, 2004.

Scary Movie 1 & 2 (2000). Buena Vista Home Video, DVD, 2004.

Weems, Carrie Mae

(1953–) *photographer, installation artist, educator*

An insightful and incisive artist who uses her camera to tell stories of racial prejudice and identity, Carrie Mae Weems is one of the most celebrated of African-American female photographers working today.

She was born on April 20, 1953, in Portland, Oregon. A gifted student, she did not go to college but worked as a dancer and waitress after high school. When she was 23, a friend asked her to take photographs of a political demonstration. The experience piqued Weems's interest in photography. She was further inspired by flipping through *The Black Photographers Annual.* "It was the first time that I saw images of black people that seemed to describe something that was truer about them more than anything else I'd seen."

She began taking photographs of everything and everyone around her and took her camera on trips to Mexico, the Pacific island of Fiji, and southern California. In 1979, she enrolled at the California Institute of the Arts in Valencia and earned a Bachelor of Arts degree in 1981. Weems earned two master's degrees, one in fine arts from the University of California at San Diego in 1984 and a second in folklore from the University of California at Berkeley.

Her use of narrative structure in her photograph series is clearly seen in the title of her first solo exhibition, *Family Pictures and Stories,* held at the Multi-Cultural Gallery in San Diego in 1984. Many of Weems's works focus on the problems facing blacks, especially black women, when they are forced to measure themselves against the standards of European beauty and identity. One of her most celebrated pictures is *Mirror, Mirror.* In it, a young black woman looks into a mirror in which she sees a white witch. The accompanying text reads "Mirror, mirror on the wall, who's the fairest of them all?" Mirror: "Snow White you black bitch, and don't you forget it!"

A strange, surreal feeling envelops her series *American Icons* (1988–89), which showcases ordinary household objects featuring African Americans in servile positions. At once humorous and disturbing, the images point up how thoroughly racism has been entrenched in American pop culture.

Another ambitious series *Untitled (Kitchen Table Series)* (1990) explores the relationships of a mother, father, and daughter as they gather at different times around a kitchen table. A lamp above the table illuminates the setting as if it were a stage. Weems's own text accompanies the photographs. In the narrative, the mother and father eventually separate, but the woman finds her identity as a result.

Her ambitious installation work "The Hampton Project" (2001) is built around the historic photographs of black and Indian students at the Hampton Institute of Virginia (now Hampton University) taken by photographer Frances Benjamin Johnston in 1900. Weems juxtaposes these images with those of Ku Klux Klan members on parade and other images imprinted on strips of cloth. The images are accompanied by an audiotape of Weems reading poetry.

More recent projects include *The Louisiana Project,* which commemorates the bicentennial of the Louisiana Purchase, and *Constructing History: A Requirement to Mark the Moment,* a multimedia installation that explores the human rights movement in the United States.

A teaching assistant at Berkeley in 1987, Weems has been an artist-in-residence and visiting professor at numerous schools, including the Visual Studies Workshop in Rochester, New York; the Art Institute of Chicago; and Hunter

College in New York City. She lives in Brooklyn and Syracuse, New York, with her husband artist Jeffery Hoone. Weems is the recipient of the 2005 Distinguished Photographers Award from Woman in Photography International. "My responsibility as an artist is to work, to sing for my supper, to make art, beautiful and powerful, that adds and reveals," she has said.

Further Reading

Cahan, Susan. *Carrie Mae Weems: The Louisiana Project.* New Orleans, La.: Newcomb Art Gallery, 2005.

Farrell, Laurie Ann, Stephanie Hughley, and Carrie Mae Weems. *Carrie Mae Weems: Constructing History.* Savannah, Ga.: Savannah College of Art and Design, 2009

Kirsh, Andrea, and Susan Fisher Sterling. *Carrie Mae Weems.* Washington, D.C.: National Museum of Women in the Arts, 1993.

Sills, Leslie. *In Real Life: Six Women Photographers.* New York: Holiday House, 2002, pp. 40–50.

Willis Deborah, Jeanne Zeidler, and Carrie Mae Weems. *Carrie Mae Weems: The Hampton Project.* New York: Aperture, 2001.

Further Viewing

Behind the Scenes with Julie Taymor, Nancy Graves, and Carrie Mae Weems. First Run Features, VHS/DVD, 1992/2002.

Welbon, Yvonne

(1969–　) *documentary filmmaker, screenwriter, film producer*

One of the most interesting and prolific of black independent filmmakers, Yvonne Welbon explores a range of subjects, including black female filmmakers, racism, and lesbians, in her experimental documentaries.

She was born in Chicago, Illinois, on May 24, 1969. She enrolled at Vassar College in Poughkeepsie, New York, in 1987 and graduated four years later. Welbon's first film, *Monique* (1991), was released the same year. It dealt with her first traumatic experience with racism and was named best documentary at the Festival of Illinois Film and Video Artists.

Welbon then decided to travel to Taipei, Taiwan, then Nationalist China, to teach English to Chinese students. She remained there for six years, during which time she learned Mandarin Chinese, founded and published an arts magazine, and directed four more films. Among them was *The Cinematic Jazz of Julie Dash* (1992–93), a perceptive interview with JULIE DASH, the black female director of the acclaimed film *Daughters of the Dust* (1991). The last of this group of films was the autobiographical *Remembering Wei Yi Fang, Remembering Myself . . .* (1995), which dealt with her experiences in Taiwan. The film was shown on the Public Broadcasting Service (PBS) series *P.O.V.* in 1996 and won two film festival awards.

On her return to the United States in 1991, Welbon enrolled at the School of the Art Institute of Chicago where she earned a Master of Fine Arts degree in film and video in 1994. She has since gone on to Northwestern University in Evanston, Illinois, to earn a doctoral degree.

Welbon's lesbianism led her to make what is probably her most celebrated film to date, *Living With Pride: Ruth Ellis @ 100* (1998). She met Ellis, a photographer, painter, and businesswoman, at a women's music festival and was astonished at her energy. The oldest African-American declared lesbian, Ellis died at age 101 in 2000. *Living with Pride* has won 10 awards for best documentary.

Welbon's latest project is the ambitious *Sisters in Cinema: Case Studies of Three First-Time Achievements by African American Women Directors in the 1990s* (2003). This documentary tells the little-known story of black female directors. Still unfinished, *Sisters in Cinema* is Welbon's doctoral thesis and has been transformed into a comprehensive website on the subject. Parts of *Sisters in Cinema* have been shown on the series *Split Screen* on the Independent Feature Channel on cable television. Welbon has also helped produce a number of independent films. Among them are the fictional feature *Stranger Inside* (2001) and the documentaries *The Waterfront* and *Garbage! The Revolution Starts at Home* (both 2007).

"I am particularly interested in personal history," Welbon says on her Web site. "I think it is important to know where one comes from to understand the path one is on. I believe the diversity of African American women's lives make both entertaining and educational storytelling."

Further Reading

"Yvonne Welbon." Sisters in Cinema Web site. Available online. URL: http://www.sistersincinema. com/filmmakers/ywelbon/bio.html. Downloaded March 14, 2009.

"Yvonne Welbon." Women Make Movies. Available online. URL: http://www.wmm.com/film catalog/makes/fm375.shtml. Downloaded March 14, 2009.

Further Viewing

The Cinematic Jazz Of Julie Dash (1992). VHS, Women Make Movies.

Living With Pride: Ruth Ellis @ 100 (1998). VHS, 1999.

Wells, James Lesesne

(1902–1993) *printmaker, painter, educator*

A modern master of printmaking, James Lesesne Wells expressed his deep religious faith in his powerfully evocative paintings and prints.

He was born on November 2, 1902, in Atlanta, Georgia. His father, Reverend Frederick W. Wells, was a Baptist minister, and his mother, Hortensia Ruth Lesesne Wells, a teacher.

When his father died, Wells's mother opened a private kindergarten, and he helped by teaching the students art. At age 13, Wells won first prize in painting at the Florida State Fair. He entered Teachers College at Columbia University in New York City in 1921 and earned a degree in art education. As a student, Wells was attracted to African sculpture, the woodcuts of German artist Albert Dürer, and the modern German expres-

sionist painters, all of whom would help to shape his own style. Among his earliest works were block print illustrations that appeared in the black journal *Opportunity* and other periodicals. In 1929 Wells became a member of the art department of Howard University in Washington, D.C. He remained there for nearly 40 years, teaching printmaking, ceramics, sculpture, and clay modeling.

A devout Christian, Wells often used biblical scenes in his work. His *The Flight into Egypt* (1929) was a striking interpretation of the flight of Jesus, Mary, and Joseph from Israel to escape the wrath of King Herod. Highly stylized, the painting is rich in color. Wells applied the paint in thick layers, giving the painting a sense of depth. Like all of Wells's religious paintings and prints, the work is devoid of sentimentality but spiritually expressive. *The Flight into Egypt* won the Harmon gold medal in 1931. Two years later, another biblical scene, *Escape of the Spies from Canaan*, a vivid woodcut, won the Harmon George E. Haynes prize for best work in black and white.

By then, Wells had largely abandoned painting to concentrate on printmaking. He felt prints, which could be reproduced cheaply, were a way for his art to reach the hands of black people who could not afford to buy an original painting. He became a bold innovator in graphic arts, especially in his use of color in printmaking, which had traditionally been limited to black and white. As director of the 135th Street Branch of the New York Public Library's (NYPL) summer art workshops, Wells taught and inspired such future black artists as JACOB LAWRENCE and CHARLES H. ALSTON.

Wells put his faith in action in the 1950s and 1960s, participating vigorously in the Civil Rights movement. His brother-in-law, Eugene Davidson, was president of the Washington chapter of the NAACP.

Wells retired from Howard in 1968 and had a one-person exhibition at Fisk University in Nashville, Tennessee, in 1973. As he grew older, Wells's prints became more daring in style. Some of the most impressive of his late prints were cut in color linoleum.

James Lesesne Wells received the Living Legend Award at the National Black Arts Festival in Atlanta, Georgia, in 1991. He died of heart failure on January 20, 1993, at Howard University Hospital.

Further Reading

Bearden, Romare, and Harry Henderson. *A History of African-American Artists: From 1792 to the Present.* New York: Pantheon Books, 1993, pp. 389–395.

"James Lesesne Wells." Available online. URL: http://www.answers.com/topic/james-lesesne-wells. Downloaded March 14, 2009.

Lewis, Samella. *African-American Art and Artists.* Berkeley: University of California Press, 2003, pp. 96–97.

Powell, Richard J. *James Lesesne Wells: Sixty Years in Art.* Washington, D.C.: Washington Project for the Arts, 1986.

Riggs, Thomas, ed. *St. James Guide to Black Artists.* Detroit, Mich.: St. James Press, 1997, pp. 558–560.

White, Charles
(Charles Wilbert White, Charles W. White)
(1918–1979) *painter, printmaker, educator*

A master of line drawing, Charles White almost single-handedly kept realism and social consciousness alive in a time when most artists were pursuing new trends. Ignored for years by critics, he is today considered one of the dominant African-American artists of his time.

He was born Charles Wilbert White on April 2, 1918, in Chicago, Illinois. His parents were not married, and they separated when he was three. His mother married a postal worker, Clifton Marsh, whose heavy drinking later ended the marriage. White then lived alone with his mother.

Because White was interested in art from an early age, his mother bought him his first oil painting set when he was seven. He used it to paint a landscape on a window blind, which upset his mother. She later came to cherish it and never had it removed. By age 15, White was displaying his drawings and paintings in churches and vacant lots to attract the attention of passersby.

White attended art classes at the School of the Art Institute of Chicago on Saturdays. His fellow students included MARGARET TAYLOR BURROUGHS and Charles Sebree. While in high school, he earned money by lettering signs. He also was drawn to the theater and designed sets for school productions.

White earned a scholarship to the Art Institute School after high school graduation. He finished a two-year course in one year and got a job as a mural painter with the federally funded Works Progress Administration (WPA) in 1939. There he created a mural of five "great Negroes," including Sojourner Truth, Booker T. Washington, and Marian Anderson. The work was exhibited at the Library of Congress to commemorate the 75th anniversary of the 13th amendment to the Constitution, which abolished slavery. Only 21 years old, Charles White was already an established artist.

While working for the WPA, White met sculptor ELIZABETH CATLETT, and they married in 1941. The couple moved to New Orleans, Louisiana, where Catlett got a job teaching at Dillard University. Once, when entering a segregated New Orleans restaurant, White was beaten by white racists. The incident strengthened his resolve to use his artistic gifts to fight prejudice and injustice in society.

"Painting is the only weapon I have with which to fight what I resent," he said in a 1940 interview. "Since I paint, I must paint about it."

White and Catlett moved to New York City in 1942, and the following year he was drafted into the army to serve in World War II (1939–45). White was creating camouflage painting in the engineers' regiment when he was diagnosed with tuberculosis (TB). He spent the next three years recuperating in a veterans' hospital in upstate New York.

Charles White strikes a pensive pose before a typically expressive portrait. *(Photographs and Prints Division, Schomburg Center for Research in Black Culture, the New York Public Library, Astor, Lenox and Tilden Foundations)*

On his discharge, he returned to New York City and had his first solo exhibition at the American Contemporary Artists Gallery in 1947. That fall, White and Catlett traveled to Mexico to meet and study with the famous Mexican muralists whose social realism they aspired to.

Both artists found inspiration in Mexico, but not with each other. Their marriage fell apart: Catlett remained in Mexico, and White returned to the United States. There, his TB flared up again and he spent another year in the hospital recovering from lung surgery. In 1950, White married Frances Barrett, a social worker, and traveled to Europe on his honeymoon. A few years later, he returned to a hostile America where demagogues such as Senator Joseph McCarthy were hunting down suspected Communists in government and the arts.

White continued to fight these evils, but his art became less epic and more human and realistic. Instead of finding inspiration in the great African Americans of the past, he turned his artist's eye to the everyday, ordinary heroes on the streets of America's crumbling urban landscape. His meticulous draftsmanship and photorealism was decidedly out of step with the American art world of the 1960s and 1970s, which was heavily into abstract styles.

He moved to California and became an activist in the Civil Rights movement, supporting the nonviolence protests of Martin Luther King, Jr. In 1965, White brought his ideas on art and society to the classroom, teaching at the Otis Institute of Art in Los Angeles. He remained there until his death.

He published *Images of Dignity* (1967), a remarkable collection of drawings that often used wintry landscapes as a powerful metaphor for racial oppression. The lone people in these pictures are often poor and beaten down by life, but they continue to survive.

Traditionalist though he might be, White was still capable of innovation in his art. In the late 1960s, he discovered some pre–Civil War posters that advertised slave auctions and offered rewards for runaway slaves. He used these artifacts as graphic backgrounds for his series of lithographs, *Wanted Posters*, that featured portraits of contemporary blacks.

Although his spirit remained strong, White's body continued to fail him. By the 1970s, he was forced to work with an oxygen tank. He died of respiratory illness on October 3, 1979. The next year he was posthumously honored at the White House for his life and work, along with nine other leading black artists.

"Art," White once wrote, "should take its place as one of the necessities of life, like food, clothing, and shelter."

Further Reading

Barnwell, Andrea D. *Charles White* (David C. Driskell Series of African American Artists, Volume 1). San Francisco: Pomegranate Communications, 2002.

Bearden, Romare, and Harry Henderson. *A History of African-American Artists: From 1792 to the Present.* New York: Pantheon Books, 1993, pp. 404–417.

"Charles Wilbert White (1918–1979)." Available online. URL: http://www.heritagegallery.com/ charles-white.html. Downloaded March 14, 2009.

White, Frances Barrett with Anne Scott. *Reaches of the Heart: A Loving Look at the Artist Charles White.* New York: Barricade Books, 1994.

Whitten, Jack
(1939–   ) *painter, mixed-media artist, educator*

An abstract artist of great depth and complexity, Jack Whitten raises profound philosophical questions and social concerns in his bold paintings.

He was born on December 5, 1939, in Bessemer, Alabama. His father, a coal miner, died when he was still a child. His mother was a seamstress. Whitten studied at the Tuskegee Institute in Tuskegee, Alabama, from 1957 to 1959; spent a year at Southern University in Baton Rouge,

Louisiana; and graduated from the School of Art of The Cooper Union in New York City with a Bachelor of Fine Arts degree in 1964.

Whitten made New York his permanent home and taught at Manhattan Community College from 1970 to 1975. During this time he developed a unique technique of abstract art in which he screened paints through fibers and then removed the excess paint to create images. While he never exhibited these paintings, he became well known for such experimental works as *Look Mom, Look, See the Funny People,* a composition consisting of strange beasts, symbolizing the polarized attitudes of different peoples in the United States and other countries.

Other works created strange optical illusions through thick buildups of paint, which he cut into, and the spraying of paint into bands of pure color. Whitten's more recent work has focused on mixed-media collages, such as *28 Black Holes* (1994), which includes such diverse materials as tinfoil, coffee, and a chair. In another work he juxtaposed acrylic paint pools with Afro-picks, homemade rakes, and other found objects. His painting *Black Monolith III: For Barbara Jordan,* a tribute to the late black U.S. congresswoman, hangs in the U.S. Embassy Mission Residence in Dakar, Senegal, Africa.

Jack Whitten has been an adjunct professor at Cooper Union since 1971 and also teaches at the School of Visual Arts in New York. His work was included in the group exhibition *Free Expressions: Contemporary Voice and Contemporary African American Artists from the Collection* (2002) at the Newark Museum in Newark, New Jersey. He was a recipient of the Painting and Sculpture Grant Program Award from the Joan Mitchell Foundation in 1995.

Whitten was working in his studio in lower Manhattan when he saw the first airplane, commandeered by terrorists, strike the World Trade Center on September 11, 2001. As a memorial, he created a huge panel embedded with ashes that took two years to complete. In 2008, the painting

was exhibited at the Atlanta Contemporary Arts Center in Atlanta, Georgia.

Art historian and writer Richard J. Powell has called Whitten "one of the leading virtuoso abstract artists in the United States."

Further Reading

"Jack Whitten." Alexander Gray Associates. Available online. URL:http://www.alexandergray.com/Artist-detail.cfm?ArtistsID=673&Collection=<i> Jack Whitten%Fi%. Downloaded March 14, 2009.

Riggs, Thomas, ed. *St. James Guide to Black Artists.* Detroit, Mich.: St. James Press, 1997, pp. 566–568.

Wright, Beryl J. *Jack Whitten.* Newark, N.J.: Newark Museum Association, 1990.

Williams, Michael Kelly

(1950–) *printmaker, sculptor, mixed-media artist, muralist, educator*

A leading contemporary African-American printmaker with a uniquely lyrical abstract style, Michael Kelly Williams has created luminous works that reflect both traditional African art and his own modern sensibility.

He was born in Neuilly-sur-Seine, France, on March 8, 1950. His family later moved back to the United States. He grew up in Detroit, Michigan, where his father ran a community art school. Inspired by his father's example, Williams attended the University of Michigan in Ann Arbor, where he graduated cum laude in 1975 with a Bachelor of Fine Arts degree in printmaking.

He later moved to New York City, where he joined the BOB BLACKBURN Printing Workshop. Blackburn became his mentor and teacher. Williams worked his way up from shop monitor to assistant to the director at the Workshop by 1983. He continued to work and teach there until 1994.

Williams's signature style is highly individualistic and reflects his rejection of the black nationalist political movement of the 1960s. While some other black artists shunned abstract art as "white," he embraced it, but in his own unique way. Williams's prints, while abstract, capture the rhythms and vibrancy of urban black culture, especially in its love of music. *Around Bout Midnight* (1984), one of his best-known prints, "has a singing energy suggestive of jazz," observed writer Joanne Harris.

A sculptor early in his career, Williams returned to the form in the 1990s, earning a Master of Fine Arts degree in sculpture at Brooklyn College, part of the City University of New York, in 1996. His sculptures combine traditional African folk art with more modern techniques, using a wide array of materials from rubber, clay, wood, and plastic telephone parts and bottle caps. His *Reach for a Star* (1995) consists of two semiabstract glass mosaic murals and eight panels he created in the lobby outside a public school cafeteria in Queens, New York. The ambitious work is a unique collaboration between the artist and third-grade students. He incorporated many of the stars they made into the background of the mural.

In 1992, Williams created two mosaics, *The El #2*, and *The El #5*, at the Intervale Avenue elevated trains station at 163rd Street in New York City. The works' abstract shapes vividly capture the sights and sounds of a ride on the elevated train.

"I have challenged myself by changing my method of working, my means, scale, and material . . ." Williams has written. "I find the retention of African traits and techniques within the tradition of African folk artists compelling, instructive, and profound. I have attempted to create new art from out of these meditations."

Further Reading

"El 2/El 5," Michael Kelly Williams (1992). NYC Subway.org. Available online. URL: http://www.nycsubway.org/perl/artwork_show?13. Downloaded March 14, 2009.

Eye, Soho. "Michael Kelly Williams Has a Gift." *Art World*, December 21, 1988.

Lewis, Samella. *African-American Art and Artists.* Berkeley: University of California Press, 2003, pp. 272–273.

Riggs, Thomas, ed. *St. James Guide to Black Artists.* Detroit, Mich.: St. James Press, 1997, pp. 571–572.

Williams, Paul R.
(Paul Revere Williams)
(1894–1980) *architect*

The first important African-American architect, Paul R. Williams left his distinctive mark in literally thousands of buildings and homes across Southern California in a career that spanned 60 years.

He was born Paul Revere Williams on February 18, 1894, in Los Angeles, the son of Chester Stanley and Lila Wright Williams. He attended Polytechnical High School in Los Angeles, where one of his teachers responded to his career goal by saying, "Who ever heard of a Negro architect?" This negative response only made Williams more determined to succeed. "I wanted to acquire new abilities," he later said. "I wanted to prove that I, *as an individual,* deserved a place in the world."

He studied at UCLA and then attended the Beaux Arts Institute of Design, where he won the Beaux Arts Medal. But becoming an architect would not be easy, even with a fine education. After graduating, Williams worked his way through the city phone book, calling every architectural firm he could find and asking for a job. The only job he was able to find was as a draftsman. He gradually worked his way up to chief draftsman. Having proven his ability to design buildings, Williams was finally given membership in the Society of Architects of Los Angeles.

He married Della Givens in 1917 and opened his own architectural office in 1923. Few jobs came his way at first, but he persevered. When an auto manufacturer asked him for primary drawings of a proposed $100,000 home, Williams said he could have them completed by 4 p.m. the following day. The client was astonished. Another

Architect Paul R. Williams holds the plans for one of his innovative buildings in this Betsy Grave Reyneau portrait. *(National Portrait Gallery, Smithsonian Institution/Art Resource, NY)*

architectural firm needed several weeks to complete the drawings. The man was so impressed when Williams brought the drawings by on the deadline that he gave him the job. He did not know that Williams worked for 22 hours straight without eating or sleeping to finish the drawings.

Soon Williams was in demand to build the homes of many Hollywood celebrities. They included silent screen stars Lon Chaney and Zazu Pitts, dancer Bill Robinson, and CBS network founder William Paley. The secret of Williams's success was tailoring each residence to the taste and personality of the client.

By the 1940s, Williams had become one of the most successful and well-known architects

in Southern California. Among the many buildings he designed completely or in part was the Hollywood Young Men's Christian Association building, the MCA Building in Beverly Hills, the Los Angeles International Airport, and the Los Angeles County Court House. He also designed the United Nations Building in Paris, France.

Over a career of 60 years, he designed more than 400 private residences and 2,600 other buildings. Williams was the first African-American member and Fellow of the American Institute of Architects. He was awarded the NAACP Spingarn Medal in 1953 for outstanding achievement. He also held honorary degrees from many colleges and universities, including Atlanta University in Georgia, the Tuskegee Institute in Alabama, and Howard University in Washington, D.C.

Paul R. Williams died on January 23, 1980, in Los Angeles. His daughter Norma Harvey was a design artist who often worked with her father as a color consultant. His granddaughter, Karen E. Hudson, is an author and the director of his archives.

Further Reading

Bogle Donald. *Bright Boulevard, Bold Dreams: The Story of Black Hollywood.* New York: One World Ballantine Books, 2005, pp. 64–66, 255–259, 263, 335.

Hudson, Karen E. *Paul R. Williams, Architect: A Legacy of Style.* New York: Rizzoli, 2000.

———. *The Will and the Way: Paul R. Williams, Architect.* New York: Rizzoli, 1994.

Williams, Paul R. *Paul R. Williams: A Collection of House Plans* (California Architecture & Architects). Los Angeles: Hennessey & Ingalls, 2006.

Williams, Spencer
(Spencer Williams, Jr.)
(1893–1969) *filmmaker, actor, screenwriter, film producer*

Best known as the bumbling, cigar-chomping Andy Brown of television's classic black situation comedy *Amos 'n' Andy*, Spencer Williams might be better remembered as the leading independent black filmmaker of the 1940s, who captured the black experience as few other directors ever have.

He was born on July 14, 1893, in Vidalia, Louisiana. The facts of his family and upbringing are sketchy. It is known that he moved to New York City as a teenager in 1910 and went to work for the theater impresario Oscar Hammerstein I as a "call boy," running errands and doing odd jobs backstage. During this time, Williams met the great black stage comedian and singer Bert Williams (no relation). Williams taught the young man the secrets of comic acting, which decades later would hold him in good stead when he played Andy Brown.

The recording studio interested Williams as much as the theater, however, and after a stint in the army during World War I, he made his first and only record, "It Feels So Good," with Lonnie Jackson on Okeh Race Records. Williams became an expert in the craft of recording and received an offer to come to Hollywood, California, and work for Christie Studios, which was trying to make the difficult transition from silent films to sound films.

Williams's job as sound technician led him to be hired to help with the dialogue on a series of black-cast comedies based on the stories of Jewish writer Octavius Roy Cohen. Soon Williams was appearing in a number of these films as an actor. These shorts, with such Shakespearean titles as *The Melancholy Dame* and *The Framing of the Shrew* (both 1929), may also have been directed by Williams, although white directors were given title credit. Today these movies are considered the first black talking films. Although featuring all black actors, the Christie films were aimed at primarily white audiences and employed the same unsavory black stereotypes that would continue in Hollywood films for two decades.

Independent black films made strictly for black movie audiences had been highly successful in the silent era, but they almost disappeared in the early 1930s due to the economic depression and

Spencer Williams is seen here in his signature role as Andy Brown on television's *Amos 'n' Andy*, a part he played after retiring from a memorable career as an independent black filmmaker. *(Photofest)*

the added expense of sound equipment. Black cinema experienced a revival by the mid-1930s, largely thanks to the success of George Randol's *Dark Manhattan* (1936). Williams acted in and wrote a number of these films. He usually played the villain in a celebrated series of black westerns that included *Harlem Rides the Range* (1938), *Two Gun Man from Harlem*, and *Bronze Buckaroo* (both 1939). In 1940 he wrote and acted in *Son of Ingogi* (1940), the first all-black sound horror film.

That same year Williams, who was living in Texas at the time, had a fateful meeting with Jewish film entrepreneur Alfred Sack, who agreed to finance a black film Williams wrote, directed, and acted in. *Blood of Jesus* (1941), filmed on a shoestring budget, was melodramatic and technically primitive for its day, but it was an honest, original study of the black religious experience. Some of its scenes, such as the documentary-like opening revival meeting and baptism in the river, were strikingly powerful.

Blood of Jesus was a surprise smash in segregated black movie houses in the South and North. Sacks immediately signed a long-term contract with Williams, who produced eight more films for him over the next six years. They included other religious dramas (*Go Down, Death*); comedies (*Dirty Gertie from Harlem, U.S.A.*); and straight dramas (*Of One Blood*). Sacks gave Williams complete artistic control, a rarity in independent black cinema. The films, especially the comedies, hold up well, despite their poverty-row budgets, as genuine artifacts of contemporary black life in the 1940s.

Williams retired after making his last film with Sack, *Beal Street Mama*, in 1947. He was living in quiet retirement in Tulsa, Oklahoma, in 1951 when he was invited to join the cast of television's first all-black comedy series, *Amos 'n' Andy*, based on the long-running radio show created by the white team of Charles Correll and Freeman Gosden. Although criticized for perpetuating stereotypes of black males as stupid bunglers or fast-talking schemers, *Amos 'n' Andy* had a cast of extraordinary black comic actors and ran successfully for two seasons. Its network, CBS, kept the program running in reruns until 1966, when increasing pressure from the NAACP and other groups forced its withdrawal from the air.

Spencer Williams died of kidney disease on December 13, 1969 in Los Angeles. *The Blood of Jesus* was selected by the U.S. Congress for the honor of being in the National Registry of Films in 1991.

Further Reading

Bogle, Donald. *Bright Boulevard, Bold Dreams: The Story of Black Hollywood.* New York: One World/Ballantine Books, 2005, pp. 86–87, 172, 310.

Jones, G. Williams. *Black Cinema Treasures: Lost and Found.* Denton: University of North Texas Press, 1997, pp. 31–35, 44–84.

Moon, Spencer. *Reel Black Talk: A Sourcebook of 50 American Filmmakers.* Westport, Conn.: Greenwood Press, 1997, pp. 367–372.

"Williams, Spencer," The Handbook of Texas Online. Available online. URL: http://www.tsha.online.org/handbook/online/articles/WW/fwiah.html. Downloaded March 16, 2009.

Further Viewing

The Amos & Andy Show—Vol. 1 (1951). Education 2000, DVD box set, 2005.

Spencer Williams Collection—4 Movies: Juke Joint, Go Down Death, Bronze Buckaroo, Blood of Jesus (1941–1947). Echo Bridge Home Entertainment, DVD, 2004.

Wilson, Ed
(Edward N. Wilson Jr.)
(1925–1996) *sculptor, illustrator, educator*

A sculptor of massive pieces that both celebrate the American experience and sometimes sharply criticize it, Ed Wilson was as committed to political change as he was to his art.

He was born Edward N. Wilson Jr. in Baltimore, Maryland, on March 28, 1925. His grandfather was a boat builder, store owner, and lay preacher. His mother encouraged his art ability. At the age of seven, Wilson came down with rheumatic fever and was confined to bed for a year. During this time he drew and painted watercolors. In high school, having regained his health, he excelled in football, basketball, track, and wrestling and had little time for art. He joined the U.S. Air Force after high school and served for three years during World War II (1939–45). After leaving the service, Wilson enrolled at the University of Iowa in Iowa City and earned a Bachelor of Arts degree in 1950.

He moved to North Carolina in 1951 and taught art at a black college there for the next 13 years. Frustrated by the lack of money in his department and the inherent racism he felt kept his school inferior to white ones, he became an activist in the growing Civil Rights movement. Wilson participated in marches and protests in the Durham–Chapel Hill area. He also began to create art.

"I started as a carver because I could beat that damned stone and it felt good," Wilson admitted in an interview. "I could take out my aggression, my feelings, physically, and yet at the same time, make forms that deal with [the] content of my experiences."

In 1961, he received his Master of Arts degree from the University of North Carolina in Greensboro and moved to Binghamton, New York, three years later. He became head of the art department at SUNY Binghamton. There he began to turn out an impressive array of large sculptures for public spaces in many cities. Among them were *JFK Memorial and Park* (1969), a massive granite and bronze sculpture that honored the late president John F. Kennedy, in Binghamton; and *Jazz Musicians* (1982–84), a bronze bas-relief in Baltimore, Maryland.

One of his most intriguing pieces is *Board of Directors*, which features 10 bronze dehumanized figures conspiring around a table. The sculpture is attached to a box covered with chrome plates that exposes the figures from every angle as they plot. It is a stinging if witty indictment of America's corporate leadership.

In another innovative work, *Middle Passage* (1977), at New Boys High School in Brooklyn, New York, Wilson created an environmental sculpture. Those that enter its narrow passageways can experience the claustrophobic feelings that African slaves must have had on the crowded slave ships bound for America.

Wilson also executed a trio of rugged bronze portraits of three famous African Americans— writer Ralph Ellison (1974–75), labor leader Whitney Young Jr. (1983–84), and slain civil rights leader Medgar Evers (1989–90).

Wilson's later sculptures tended to be more abstract than his earlier ones. He died of conges-

tive heart failure on November 26, 1996, at his home in Vestal, New York.

"There is a profound sense of humanism contained in these works that provide, for me, an identity, a spiritual focus, sustenance, and will to productively counter the otherwise dehumanizing impact of the republic at large," Wilson once wrote.

Further Reading

Riggs, Thomas, ed. *St. James Guide to Black Artists.* Detroit, Mich.: St. James Press, 1997, pp. 576–578.

Mshana, Fadhili. "A Conversation with Ed Wilson," *Ijele: Art eJournal of the African World.* Available online. URL: http://www.ijele.com/vol1/mshana. html. Downloaded April 2, 2009.

Thomas, Robert M., Jr. "Ed Wilson 71, a Sculptor and Art Teacher." *New York Times,* January 27, 1997, [obituary].

Wilson, Ellis
(1899–1977) *painter*

Known for his highly stylized, elongated figures without faces, Ellis Wilson found inspiration for his delightful paintings in the American South and the islands of the sun-drenched, brightly colored Caribbean.

He was born on April 30, 1899, in Mayfield, Kentucky. His father, Frank Ellis, was a barber and cabinetmaker. As a youth, Wilson was working as a window washer when he drew a picture out of soap on a dress shop window. The owner was so impressed by the crowd that came to see it that he asked Wilson to create a new picture every week.

Wilson attended a state school that later became Kentucky State College and took his first art course one summer at the School of the Art Institute of Chicago. He later studied commercial art at the Art Institute School and met such leading Chicago artists as illustrator Charles C. Dawson and sculptor RICHMOND BARTHÉ. Wilson worked for four years in a Young Men's Christian

Association cafeteria to support himself while continuing his art studies.

In 1928, he moved to New York City and gradually established himself as a painter, winning honorable mention for a painting in the 1933 Harmon exhibition of black artists. He was hired by the Works Progress Administration, a government program, to make a large three-dimensional model of New York City's five boroughs.

Wilson moved to a studio on East 18th Street, where he would work and live for the remaining 40 years of his life. He developed a distinctive style, depicting tall, elongated bodies of black people after the style of the 16th-century Spanish artist El Greco. He was also greatly influenced by the work of black artists AARON DOUGLAS and HORACE PIPPIN.

Wilson returned to Mayfield in 1947 and had an exhibit of his painting at the local library. Local press stories about his art led to a one-person show at the Speed Museum in Louisville, Kentucky. A second solo show in 1951 at the Contemporary Art Gallery in New York City won him praise in an *Art News* review for his "imaginative race of tall, regal Africans. . ."

Wilson's palette became brighter after his first visit to the West Indian island of Haiti in the early 1950s. "It came to me that at a distance, you see these people coming and going—and you don't see their features," he wrote. "They're black—they're a mass of darkness—so I started painting the faces flat."

Wilson's accessible paintings made him a popular artist in his later years. One of his paintings even appeared on the set of television's *The Cosby Show*. He died on January 1, 1977, in New York City.

Further Reading

Bearden, Romare, and Harry Henderson. *A History of African-American Artists: From 1792 to the Present.* New York: Pantheon Books, 1993, pp. 337–343.

"Ellis Wilson: So Much to Paint." Kentucky Educational Television website. Available online. URL: http://www.ket.org/elliswilson/. Downloaded March 16, 2009.

Riggs, Thomas ed. *St. James Guide to Black Artists.* Detroit, Mich.: St. James Press, 1997, pp. 578–579.

Sperath, Albert F., Margaret R. Vendryes, Steven H. Jones, and Eva F. King. *The Art of Ellis Wilson.* Lexington: University Press of Kentucky, 2000.

Wilson, Fred
(1954–) *sculptor, installation artist*

An artist whose work probes and challenges the very fabric of American society and its many prejudices, Fred Wilson has created artwork that questions the institution of the museum itself as an arbitrator of culture and taste.

He was born on August 25, 1954, in the Bronx, New York. He attended SUNY Purchase and graduated in 1976 with a Bachelor of Fine Arts degree. To support himself while pursuing his career as an artist, Wilson worked in museums as a guard, then as a curator and an arts educator. He began during this time to question the concept of museums and what they revealed about American society. What he found most fascinating was not what museums included in their collections but what they left out, especially the works and achievements of African Americans, Native Americans, and other indigenous peoples from around the world.

In his early works, he often used satire and his own experiences to criticize white America. A good example is *Guarded Men*, which consisted of four headless, uniformed, mannequin-like black museum guards. Wilson's work suggested that the invisible black men who wandered through museums were equally invisible in the world outside the museum.

Another work, *No Noa Noa, Portrait of a History of Tahiti* (1987), showed how Western societies turn Third World peoples into exotic sideshow creatures to entertain and titillate but who are not to be taken seriously.

With time, Wilson's work grew larger and more ambitious as he struggled with the idea of the museum as an illusionary and misleading institution. His *Rooms with a View: The Struggle Between Culture, Content and the Context of Art* encompassed numerous museum rooms, each satirizing a particular era of art and design. On the positive side, wrote A. M. Weaver, such works make Wilson "a promoter of museumology from a multicultural perspective."

In 1993, Wilson got the rare opportunity to put his aesthetics to the ultimate test. The Contemporary Museum of Art in Chicago invited him to complete a project of his choosing using the facilities of any museum in the city of Baltimore, Maryland. The artist picked the Maryland Historical Society, finding that it had completely overlooked the achievement of the state's African Americans and Native Americans.

His conceptual piece, *Mining the Museum*, literally reconstructed the museum, adding historical artifacts collecting dust in storage and juxtapositioning them with traditional pieces from the permanent collection. The point of all this was to force people to think about the nature of art and museums. For example, slave shackles were displayed alongside European-style antiques and crafts. In his "mining," Wilson even discovered the long-forgotten fact that the Historical Society was active in the efforts to create an African colony in Liberia for freed slaves in the early 1800s. "Anyone who sees 'Mining the Museum' is unlikely to look at museum exhibits in quite the same way," wrote the *Philadelphia Inquirer*.

In 2002, Wilson was artist-in-residence at the Pilchuck Glass School in Washington State, where he began to seriously work in this medium. He represented the United States at the 2003 Venice Biennale with his installation *Speak of Me as I Am*, which examined the role of black Africans in Renaissance Venice and focused in part on the Moor Othello, the tragic hero of Shakespeare's play. Wilson's 2006 exhibition *Black Like Me* at the Aldrich Contemporary Art Museum in Ridgefield, Connecticut, took its title from the 1961 book by John Howard Griffins, who dyed his skin black to experience racism in the American South.

Further Reading

Berger, Maurice, and Judy Gonzalez. *Fred Wilson: Objects and Installations, 1979–2000.* Baltimore: University of Maryland Baltimore Center for Art and Visual Culture, 2002.

Klein, Richard, and Fred Wilson. *Fred Wilson: Black Like Me.* Ridgefield, Conn.: Aldrich Contemporary Art Museum, 2006.

Whitfield, Tony. "Fred Wilson: Mining the Memory." *Sphere*, spring 1996, pp. 17–18.

Wilson, Fred. *Mining the Museum: An Installation Institution.* New York: New Press, 1994.

Wilson, Fred, Barbara Thompson, Mary Coffey, and Jessica Hegedorn. *So Much Trouble in the World: Believe It or Not!* Hanover, N.H.: Hood Museum of Art, 2006.

Withers, Ernest C.
(1922–2007) *photographer*

A lifelong resident of Memphis, Tennessee, Ernest C. Withers powerfully documented the diverse life of the city's black community for more than 50 years. Recent discoveries, however, show the photographer may also have been informing government authorities on the civil rights events he was documenting.

He was born in Memphis on August 7, 1922, and took his first pictures at the age of 14. He later became a freelance photographer and for more than 25 years kept a studio on Memphis's famed Beale Street in the heart of the blues district. He became well known for his memorable portraits of such famed blues and rhythm and blues musicians as B. B. King, Aretha Franklin, and Isaac Hayes. Perhaps his best-known photograph is of B. B. King and rock idol Elvis Presley side by side in oversized tuxedoes.

Also an enthusiastic baseball fan, Withers captured the grace and athletic prowess of such Negro League players as Jackie Robinson and

Willie Mays before they broke the color line into the major leagues.

His greatest contribution as a photographer, however, is his documentation of the Civil Rights movement of the 1950s and 1960s. When two white men were acquitted by an all-white jury of the murder of black youth Emmett Till in Mississippi in 1955, Withers published, at his own expense, a booklet entitled the *Complete Photo Story of Till Murder Case* that helped focus national attention on this gross miscarriage of justice. It indirectly helped spur the birth of the modern Civil Rights movement in the South.

When Martin Luther King, Jr., rose to prominence as a civil rights leader, Withers traveled with him and was present to photograph his assassination in May 1968 at Memphis's Lorraine Motel. He was also on the scene taking pictures at the forced integration of Central High School in Little Rock, Arkansas, in 1957.

Because he was black, Withers did not receive the recognition he deserved for many years. Knowing he would not get his pictures placed in many magazines and newspapers, he sometimes sold undeveloped rolls of film to white photographers. "There are a lot of Ernest Withers photos out there that no one knows are Ernest Withers," said William J. Hennessey, director of the Chrysler Museum of Art in Norfolk, Virginia.

In 1992, the Massachusetts College of Art in Boston organized the first public exhibition of Withers's civil rights photographs entitled *Let Us March On! Southern Civil Rights Photographs of Ernest C. Withers 1955–1968.* He was inducted into the Black Press Hall of Fame in 1988 and was the recipient of the Gordon Parks Legend Award from the Exposure Group in 2000. His pictures have appeared in numerous national periodicals including *Time, Newsweek, Ebony,* and *Jet.* Ernest C. Withers died of complications of a stroke on October 14, 2007, in Memphis. He was 85 years old.

In 2010, evidence surfaced that Withers had served as a paid informant for the FBI from 1968 to 1970, reporting on the activities of Martin Luther King and other civil rights leaders.

Further Reading

Hurley, Jack F., Brooks Johnson, Daniel J. Wolff, and Ernest Withers. *Pictures Tell the Story: Ernest C. Withers Reflects in History.* Norfolk, Va.: Chrysler Museum of Art, 2000.

Peterson, Alison J. "Ernest Withers, 85, Civil Rights photographer." *New York Times,* October 17, 2007, p. C12, [obituary].

Willis, Deborah. *Reflections in Black: A History of Black Photographers from 1840 to the Present.* New York: W.W. Norton, 2002, pp. 117, 137–138.

Withers, Ernest C. *Negro League Baseball.* New York: Harry N. Abrams, 2005.

Wolff, Daniel J., and Ernest Withers. *Ernest C. Withers: The Memphis Blues Again: Six Decades of the Memphis Music Photographs.* New York: Viking Penguin, 2001.

Woodruff, Hale
(Hale Aspacio Woodruff)
(1900–1980) *muralist, painter, printmaker, educator*

One of the most important figures in 20th-century African-American art, Hale Woodruff pioneered the black experience in art as a painter, muralist, and teacher, while always striving for innovation.

He was born Hale Aspacio Woodruff in Cairo, Illinois, on August 26, 1900, the only child of George and Augusta Woodruff. His father died soon after his birth, and his mother moved with him to Nashville, Tennessee, where she worked as a domestic. She nurtured his natural gift for drawing, and by high school Woodruff was cartoonist for the school paper.

After graduation in 1918, he attended John Herron Art Institute in Indianapolis, Indiana. Unable to fund his education, Woodruff left school but continued to paint and make a serious study of African art. His realistic painting *The*

Old Women won him second prize in a Harmon competition in 1926. The following year, local residents, impressed by his talent, raised enough money for Woodruff to go to Paris, France, to study and paint. He remained in France for four years and studied with HENRY O. TANNER, the expatriate black artist. At one time, to earn a living, Woodruff disguised himself as a Moroccan French citizen to obtain work on a road gang.

He returned to the United States in 1931 and was hired to teach art at Atlanta University in Georgia. Woodruff's reputation as a teacher is legendary. He encouraged black students to become artists, put on exhibitions of black artists in the college library, introduced printmaking into the curriculum, and brought students on visits to Atlanta's High Museum. Before these field trips, few blacks had seen the inside of an art museum in the South.

In 1934, Woodruff received a grant to travel to Mexico and study there. In Mexico, he met master muralist Diego Rivera, who put him to work grinding colors for a mural he was creating at a hotel in Mexico City. Heavily influenced by Rivera's epochal style, Woodruff returned to Atlanta and was commissioned to create two murals for the government-funded Works Progress Administration. The second of these, the two-paneled *Shantytown* and *Mudhill* at the Atlanta School of Social Work, is an eloquent cry against poverty.

Woodruff's next project is considered by many to be his greatest. Talladega College in Alabama asked him to create a series of murals for its library to commemorate the 100th anniversary of the *Amistad* trial in New Haven, Connecticut. In this trial a group of African slaves were charged with murder in a mutiny aboard a Spanish slave ship. Defended by former president John Quincy Adams, the defendants were found innocent and freed.

Knowing little about this historical event, Woodruff plunged into his research, managing to locate portraits of all the participants in the trial. The *Amistad Murals*, completed in 1940, are rightly celebrated for their meticulous historical accuracy, dramatic composition, and beautiful colors. Woodruff even painted himself into the work as one of the slaves on trial.

Other major murals followed, including two for the Golden State Mutual Life Insurance Company in Los Angeles, California, which depicted the history of African Americans in California. Completed in 1949, the murals were a rare collaboration with fellow muralist CHARLES H. ALSTON, created for a building designed by black architect PAUL R. WILLIAMS.

Woodruff continued to champion the work of other black artists who had long been ignored by the white establishment. In 1942, he began the Atlanta University art exhibition, which featured 107 paintings by 62 African-American artists in its first year. This annual event continued until 1970.

In 1945, Woodruff resigned from the Atlanta University art department and moved with his wife, Theresa Ada Baker, to New York City in 1946. He began teaching at New York University the following year and remained there until his retirement in 1968. Woodruff was so beloved by his students that in 1966 they elected him "Great Teacher."

But many people would call him a great artist as well, one who continually sought out new avenues of artistic expression. By the 1950s, Woodruff had turned his restless talent to abstract art but wove it together with African design and imagery. In 1963, he and ROMARE BEARDEN founded Spiral, a group of black artists who met weekly to discuss their work and problems. Spiral became a cooperative whose members helped each other get their work into museums and galleries.

In 1979, the Studio Museum in Harlem held a major retrospective of Woodruff's work. He died the following year on September 26, 1980. His son Roy Woodruff is also an artist.

"I have never taught how to do something," Woodruff once said about his teaching. "I have tried to recognize what the students are trying to do—and let them do it. I just try to light a fire under their coattails."

Further Reading

Barnwell, Andrea D., ed. *Hale Woodruff, Nancy Elizabeth Prophet and the Academy.* Atlanta, Ga.: Spelman College Museum of Fine Arts, 2007.

Bey, Sharif. *Aaron Douglas and Hale Woodruff: The Social Responsibility and Expanded Pedagogy of the Black Artist.* Saarbrücken, Germany: VDM Verlag Dr. Müller, 2008.

Lewis, Samella. *African-American Art and Artists.* Berkeley: University of California Press, 2003, pp. 65–68, 118.

Murray, Al. "Oral History Interview with Hale Woodruff, November 18, 1963," Smithsonian Archives of American Art Web site. URL: http://www.aaa.si.edu/collections/oralhistories/transcripts/woodru68.htm. Downloaded March 16, 2009.

Perry, Regenia A. *Free Within Ourselves: African-American Artists in the Collection of the National Museum of American Art.* San Francisco: Pomegranate Communications, 1992, pp. 182–186.

Shannon, Helen, ed. *Hale Woodruff: 50 Years of His Art.* New York: Studio Museum in Harlem, 1994.

Yarde, Richard
(1939–) *painter, illustrator, educator*

One of the most celebrated of contemporary watercolorists, Richard Yarde has brought a new energy and sensibility to this traditional genre of painting.

He was born on October 29, 1939, in Boston, Massachusetts. He earned his Bachelor of Fine Arts degree at Boston University in 1962 and went on to get a Masters of Fine Arts degree in 1964. He started his career as an artist painting images from African-American history, particularly celebrated people. In his second solo show at the Studio Museum in Harlem in 1977, however, he displayed his gift for watercolors, with a boldness and vision rarely seen before in this genre that has tended to the soft, romantic, and delicate.

In 1990, Yarde began a successful teaching career at the University of Massachusetts at Amherst. The following year, he was stricken with a serious illness that led to kidney failure. Confined to bed, unable to speak or even move, Yarde thought he would die. "My illness forced me to confront another aspect of my humanity: my need [for] and dependence on other people and on my spirituality."

Making a partial recovery, Yarde began to change his style. New works, such as the series *Self*, focused on body parts, covered or accompanied by mysterious series of dots. "[V]isually I liked the patterns," Yarde has said of these dots. "I feel for me, they represent also the mystery of basic building blocks of life that hold us together." A new spirituality was also present in such new works as *Mojo Hand* (1995–96) and *Ringshout* (2000).

Among Yarde's recent solo shows are *Visionary Anatomies* (2005–06) at the National Academy of Sciences, Washington, D.C., and *Kismet: New Work by Richard Yarde* (2006) at the St. Joseph College Art Gallery in New York. He illustrated his first children's book *Stompin' at the Savoy* in 2006. The Savoy Ballroom in Harlem was a mecca for jazz musicians and has been an inspiration for Yarde in his work. "Music and dance have always been a source of joy and inspiration for me," he has written. "When I saw photographs of dancers and musicians at the Savoy Ballroom I was struck with the drama of loving courtship in dance, the risk taking of the dancers, and the roots in African dance. . . . The Savoy became a source of creativity, joy, and strength to me which I want to share and honor."

Yarde is the recipient of the Academy Award in Art from the American Academy of Arts and Letters (1995) and the Commonwealth Award for Fine Art (2002). He lives in Northampton, Massachusetts, and continues to teach at the University of Massachusetts as a professor of fine art.

According to the R. Michelson Galleries, in Northampton, which represents him, Yarde "tackles the traditional intimate art of watercolor with unchanging bravado . . . on a heroic scale with dazzling color, rich symbols and deeply evocative imagery."

Further Reading

Callender, Courtney. *Richard Yarde: Recent Works.* New York: The Studio Museum in Harlem, 1971.

Campbell, Bebe Moore, and Richard Yarde, illustrator. *Stompin' at the Savoy.* New York: Philomel, 2006.

Lewis, Samella. *African-American Art and Artists.* Berkeley: University of California, 2003, pp. 295–299.

Richard Yarde's official Web site. Available online. URL: www.richardyarde.com/. Downloaded March 29, 2009.

Yoakum, Joseph E.
(1886–1972) *folk painter*

Among the most subtle and refined of American folk artists, Joseph E. Yoakum created haunting landscapes of mountains, rivers, and forests that are a curious blend of the real and the unreal.

He was born, according to his own account, on the Navajo Reservation in Window Rock, Arizona, in 1886, one of 13 children. His father was a farmer and, so Yoakum claimed, a full-blooded Cherokee. His mother was part Cherokee, part French, and part African American. She was a doctor or medicine woman, skilled in the art of herbal medicine. When Yoakum was still a child, the family moved to Kansas City, Missouri, where his father worked briefly in the railroad yards. Then they settled on a farm near Walnut Grove, Missouri. Yoakum's story after that, as he tells it, is as skillful a blend of fact and fancy as one of his colorful landscapes.

He ran away from home in his early teens and joined a traveling circus as a handyman. He claimed to have worked with both Buffalo Bill's Wild West show and the Ringling Brothers' circus, serving as John Ringling's personal valet. From about 1905 to 1910, he said he traveled the globe either with the circus or as a hobo. About 1910 he married and settled down, raising five children. He served in the army in France during World War I (1914–18). The next several decades of his life are vague. It is believed he married a second time in 1929 and ran an ice cream parlor with his wife on the South Side of Chicago. His second wife died in the late 1950s, and Yoakum retired on a government pension and moved into a senior housing project in Chicago. Starting in 1962, he began to create his odd paintings, claiming that they first appeared to him in a dream. From 1965 to 1970, he averaged a drawing a day, working first in pen or pencil and then filling in the images with watercolors. Most of his paintings are composed of a mixture of mountains, rivers, and tree groves, laid out with the skilled precision of a mapmaker. Yoakum's landscapes (people rarely appear in his work) are a strange combination of the real and the fantastic. The closer one examines them, the more mysterious they become. His mountains are like no other mountains; the winding roads lead nowhere. The documentary nature of his work is further enhanced by his careful signature and date of completion that appear neatly in the upper left corner of many works.

A key to Yoakum's work may lie in his strong religious beliefs. For him, God and nature were one, and he referred to his creative process as "spiritual enfoldment."

There were several public exhibitions of Yoakum's work in his lifetime, the first at the Sherbeyn Gallery in Chicago in 1968. Two years earlier, he had moved from his apartment to a storefront on Chicago's South Side. His health soon began to fail and in 1971 he entered a nursing home, where he died on Christmas Day 1972. That same year, his work was displayed by the Whitney Museum of American Art in New York City.

An expert draftsman with a sure sense of color, Joseph E. Yoakum created dreamscapes of America that continue to haunt our consciousness.

Further Reading

DePasse, Derrel B. *Traveling the Rainbow: The Life and Art of Joseph E. Yoakum.* Jackson: University Press of Mississippi, 2001.

"Joseph Yoakum." Foundation for Self-Taught American Artists. Available online. URL: http://www. foundationstaart.org/artist_single.aspx?artist=11. Downloaded March 16, 2009.

Perry, Regenia A. *Free Within Ourselves: African-American Artists in the Collection of the National Museum of American Art.* San Francisco, Calif.: Pomegranate Communications, 1992, pp. 186–191.

Yoakum, Joseph. *Animistic Landscapes: Joseph Yoakum Drawings.* Philadelphia, Penn.: Janet Fleisher Gallery, 1989.

Young, Purvis

(1943–2010) *folk painter, muralist*

One of the best-known and most celebrated of black folk artists, Purvis Young spent his adult life recreating in his vivid paintings his beloved but downtrodden hometown, one of the worst ghettos in an eastern U.S. city.

He was born on February 4, 1943, in Liberty City, a section of Miami, Florida. He later moved with his family to Overtown, an all-black neighborhood of Miami. Overtown was a model black community in Young's childhood, and proudly billed itself as the "Harlem of the South." When Interstate 95 was constructed through the city in the late 1950s, Overtown was torn apart and decimated. The community became rundown and seedy, the perfect breeding ground for poverty and crime. Young became part of its problems. He dropped out of school at 16 and pursued a life of petty crime. At age 18, he was arrested for breaking and entering and sentenced to three years in Raiford State Penitentiary in northern Florida. He could have left prison a hardened criminal, but one night in his cell he experienced a vision. "I woke up and the angels came to me," he said, "and I told 'em, you know, hey man this is not my life—and they said they were gonna make a way for me."

On his release in 1964, Young began to pursue a career as an artist. He went to the Overtown library and pored over books of art, falling in love with the masters. He began to draw, using discarded library books as sketchpads. Next he started to paint; setting up his studio in an abandoned warehouse, using house paint and old plywood, cardboard, and anything else he could get his hands on, as his canvases.

He created a large public mural in Overtown's Good Bread Alley. It was later taken apart and destroyed, but Young continued to paint with passion. His talent became known throughout the community and beyond. *Magic realism* was the term critics used to describe his deeply personal style, filled with angels hovering over blighted urban streets filled with people and violence. The contemporary world and the past melded in his idiosyncratic work. "A deep-seated sense of place and of history suffuses Young's ecstatic, rhythmic surfaces; his style is likewise the story of his longtime community," a critic wrote on the Web site of the Foundation for Self-Taught American Artists.

In 1999, prominent art collectors Mera and Don Rubell bought all of Young's warehouse paintings and donated many of them to museums. Celebrities such as Jane Fonda bought Young's work and praised it. "[T]he first thing that struck me was the hopefulness of the work," Fonda said. The year 2006 was a banner one for Young. A major retrospective of his work was mounted at the Boca Raton Museum of Art in Florida and a documentary of his life, *Purvis of Overtown*, was released. As his career was blossoming, however, Young was losing hope. His decade-long struggle with diabetes was intensifying, and he wondered if he would live long enough to enjoy his newfound fame. Then, a kidney transplant in January 2007 saved his life and restored his health. The same month he was named the Director's Choice during the art festival known as Art Miami. Sadly,

Purvis Young died in April 2010 of cardiac arrest and pulmonary edema. He was 67.

Today his work is in the collections of more than 50 museums and he is represented by the prestigious David Audry Gallery in New York City.

For all his celebrity, Young always remained humble and stayed in Overtown. "I paint what I see," he said. "I paint the problems of the world."

Further Reading

PurvisYoungNY.com. Available online. URL: http://www.purvisyoungny.com/Artist-Info. cfm?ArtistsID=603&Object=. Downloaded March 18, 2009.

Purvis Young's official Web site. Available online. URL: http://www.purvisyoung.com/index.cfm. Downloaded March 20, 2009.

Weber, Bruce. "Purvis Young, Folk Artist Who Peppered Miami with Image, Dies at 67." *New York Times,* April 24, 2010, p. A20 [obituary].

Young, Purvis. *Purvis Young: Painting the Blues.* Springfield, Ohio: Springfield Museum of Art, 1998.

———. *Purvis Young: Paintings From the Street.* Boca Raton, Fla.: Boca Raton Museum of Art, 2006.

BIBLIOGRAPHY AND RECOMMENDED SOURCES

Alexander, George. *Why We Make Movies: Black Film-makers Talk About the Magic of Cinema.* New York: Harlem Moon, 2003.

Barnwell, Andrea D. *The Walter O. Evans Collection of African-American Art.* Seattle: University of Washington Press, 2000.

Bearden, Romare, and Harry Henderson. *A History of African-American Artists: From 1792 to the Present.* New York: Pantheon Books, 1993.

Bernier, Celeste-Marie. *African American Visual Artists.* Edinburgh, Scotland: Edinburgh University Press, 2008.

Bogle, Donald. *Bright Boulevard, Bold Dreams: The Story of Black Hollywood.* New York: OneWorld/Ballantine Books, 2005.

———. *Primetime Blues: African Americans on Network Television.* New York: Farrar, Straus and Giroux, 2001.

———. *Toms, Coons, Mulattoes, Mammies, & Bucks: An Interpretative History of Blacks in American Films.* New York: Continuum, 2003.

Bolden, Tonya. *Wake Up Our Souls: A Celebration of Black American Artists.* New York: Abrams Books for Young Readers, 2004.

Britton, Crystal A. *African American Art: The Long Struggle.* New York: New Line Books, 2006.

Buckley, Caroline, ed. *Who's Who in American Art 1997–1998.* New Providence, N.J.: Marquis Who's Who, 1997.

Driskell, David C. *Two Centuries of Black American Art.* New York: Knopf, 1976.

Driskell, David, David Levering Lewis, and Deborah Willis Ryan. *Harlem Renaissance Art of Black America.* New York: Harry N. Abrams, 1994.

Falk, Peter Hastings, ed. *Who Was Who in American Art: 1564–1975.* Madison, Conn.: Sound View Press, 1999, 3 vols.

Hardy, P. Stephens, and Sheila Jackson Hardy. *Extraordinary People of the Harlem Renaissance.* Danbury, Conn.: Children's Press, 2000.

Jones, G. William. *Black Cinema Treasures: Lost and Found.* Denton: University of North Texas Press, 1997.

Katz, Ephraim, and Ronald Dean Nolen. *The Film Encyclopedia.* New York: Harper Resource, 2008.

Krantz, Les. *American Photographers.* New York: Facts On File, 1989.

Lewis, Samella. *African-American Art and Artists.* Berkeley: University of California Press, 2003.

Livingston, Jane, and John Beardsley. *Black Folk Art in America 1930–1980.* Jackson: University Press of Mississippi, 1989.

McDarrah, Fred W., and Gloria S. McDarrah. *The Photography Encyclopedia.* New York: Schirmer Books, 1999.

McNeil, Alex. *Total Television.* New York: Penguin Books, 1997.

Moon, Spencer. *Reel Black Talk: A Sourcebook of 50 American Filmmakers.* Westport, Conn.: Greenwood Press, 1997.

Munro, Eleanor C. *Originals—American Women Artists.* New York: Da Capo Press, 2000.

Perry, Regenia A. *Free Within Ourselves: African-American Artists in the Collection of the National Museum of American Art.* San Francisco: Pomegranate Communications, 1992.

Powell, Richard J. *Black Art and Culture in the 20th Century.* New York: Thames & Hudson, 1997.

Riggs, Thomas, ed. *St. James Guide to Black Artists.* Detroit, Mich.: St. James Press, 1997.

Rollock, Barbara. *Black Authors and Illustrators of Children's Books: A Biographical Dictionary.* New York: Garland, 1999.

Smith, Jessie Carney, ed. *Notable Black American Men.* Detroit, Mich.: Gale Research, Inc., 1999.

———. *Notable Black American Men, Book II.* Detroit, Mich.: Gale Research, Inc., 2006.

———. *Notable Black American Women.* Detroit, Mich.: Gale Research, Inc., 1992.

———. *Notable Black American Women, Book II.* Detroit, Mich.: Gale Research, Inc., 1996.

Sullivan, George. *Black Artists in Photography, 1840–1940.* New York: Cobblehill Books, 1996.

Wardlaw, Alvia. *Black Art, Ancestral Legacy: The African Impulse in African-American Art.* New York: Harry N. Abrams, 1990.

Willis, Deborah. *Reflections in Black: A History of Black Photographers from 1840 to the Present.* New York: W. W. Norton, 2002.

ENTRIES BY MEDIUM/AREA OF ACTIVITY

ANIMATOR
Loyd, Overton
Walker, Kara

ARCHITECT
Bond, J. Max, Jr.
Sklarek, Norma
Williams, Paul R.

ART HISTORIAN
Amaki, Amalia
Bearden, Romare
Driskell, David C.
Lewis, Samella
Porter, James A.

ARTS ADMINISTRATOR
Blackburn, Bob
DePillars, Murry N.
Donaldson, Jeff
Lewis, Samella
Morrison, Keith

CARTOONIST
Armstrong, Robb
Billingsley, Ray
Brandon-Croft, Barbara
Campbell, E. Simms
Commodore, Chester
Craft, Jerry

Harrington, Ollie
McGruder, Aaron
Ormes, Jackie
Turner, Morrie

CARVER
Pierce, Elijah

CERAMIST
Artis, William E.
Dave the Potter
Hathaway, Isaac Scott
Johnson, Sargent
Owens-Hart, Winnie
Simms, Carroll H.

CLOTHES DESIGNER
Bailey, Xenobia

COLLAGIST
Amaki, Amalia
Andrews, Benny
Bailey, Radcliffe
Bearden, Romare
Honeywood, Varnette
Saar, Betye

COMIC BOOK CREATOR
Simmons, Alex

COMPUTER ARTIST
Perkins, Angela

DECORATIVE ARTIST
Bailey, Xenobia

DOCUMENTARY FILMMAKER
Greaves, William
Lewis, Samella
Welbon, Yvonne

DOLL MAKER
Bailey, Xenobia
Holloway, Charnelle
Rowe, Nellie Mae

EDITORIAL CARTOONIST
Commodore, Chester
Harrington, Ollie

EDUCATOR
Alston, Charles H.
Amos, Emma
Andrews, Benny
Artis, William E.
Bey, Dawoud
Bibbs, Garry
Biggers, John
Blackburn, Bob
Bond, J. Max, Jr.

Browne, Vivian E.
Bryan, Ashley
Buchanan, Yvonne E.
Burke, Selma
Burroughs, Margaret Taylor
Catlett, Elizabeth
Clark, Claude
Colescott, Robert
Cowans, Adger
Crichlow, Ernest
Crite, Allan Rohan
DeCarava, Roy
Delaney, Joseph
DePillars, Murry N.
Donaldson, Jeff
Douglas, Aaron
Driskell, David C.
Edwards, Melvin
Feelings, Tom
Gilchrist, Jan Spivey
Gilliam, Sam
Harris, Lyle Ashton
Hathaway, Isaac Scott
Hendricks, Barkley L.
Holloway, Charnelle
Honeywood, Varnette
Humphrey, Margo
Hunt, Richard H.
Jones, Lois Mailou
Lawrence, Annette
Lawrence, Jacob
Lee, Spike
Lee-Smith, Hughie
Lewis, E. B.
Lewis, Norman
Lewis, Samella
Marshall, Kerry James
Mayhew, Richard
McCullough, Geraldine
Morrison, Keith
Nance, Marilyn
Owens-Hart, Winnie
Perkins, Angela

Pindell, Howardena
Pinkney, Brian
Pinkney, Jerry
Piper, Adrian
Porter, James A.
Prophet, Nancy Elizabeth
Puryear, Martin
Randall, Herbert
Ransome, James E.
Ringgold, Faith
Saar, Betye
Saunders, Raymond
Savage, Augusta
Scott, Joyce J.
Simmons, Alex
Simms, Carroll H.
Sklarek, Norma
Statom, Therman
Steptoe, Javaka
Thomas, Alma W.
Walker, Kara
Walker, Shawn
Waring, Laura Wheeler
Weems, Carrie Mae
Wells, James Lesesne
White, Charles
Whitten, Jack
Williams, Michael Kelly
Wilson, Ed
Woodruff, Hale
Yarde, Richard

FILMMAKER
Alexander, William
Burnett, Charles
Dash, Julie
Dixon, Ivan
Franklin, Carl
Gunn, Bill
Hooks, Kevin
Hudlin, Reginald
Lee, Spike
Lemmons, Kasi

Martin, Darnell
Micheaux, Oscar
Parks, Gordon
Perry, Tyler
Prince-Blythewood, Gina
Schultz, Michael
Simpson, Lorna
Singleton, John
Townsend, Robert
Van Peebles, Mario
Van Peebles, Melvin
Wayans, Keenen Ivory
Williams, Spencer

FILM PRODUCER
Alexander, William
Burnett, Charles
Dash, Julie
Greaves, William
Hudlin, Reginald
Johnson, Noble
Lee, Spike
Micheaux, Oscar
Parks, Gordon
Perry, Tyler
Prince-Blythewood, Gina
Singleton, John
Townsend, Robert
Van Peebles, Melvin
Wayans, Keenen Ivory
Welbon, Yvonne
Williams, Spencer

FURNITURE MAKER
Day, Thomas

GLASS SCULPTOR
Statom, Therman

GRAFFITI ARTIST
Basquiat, Jean-Michel

GRAPHIC ARTIST
Jones, Frank
Perkins, Angela

GRAPHIC DESIGNER
Lewis, E. B.
Loyd, Overton
Marshall, Kerry James
Perkins, Angela

ILLUSTRATOR
Alston, Charles H.
Andrews, Benny
Armstrong, Robb
Biggers, John
Brandon-Croft, Barbara
Bryan, Ashley
Buchanan, Yvonne E.
Burroughs, Margaret Taylor
Byard, Carole
Craft, Jerry
Crews, Donald
Crichlow, Ernest
Crite, Allan Rohan
Cummings, Pat
DePillars, Murry N.
Dillon, Leo
Donaldson, Jeff
Douglas, Aaron
Feelings, Tom
Gilchrist, Jan Spivey
Hathaway, Isaac Scott
Honeywood, Varnette
Humphrey, Margo
Jones, Lois Mailou
Lawrence, Jacob
Lewis, E. B.
Loyd, Overton
Pinkney, Brian
Pinkney, Jerry
Ransome, James E.
Ringgold, Faith
Saar, Alison
Saar, Betye

Steptoe, Javaka
Steptoe, John
Tolliver, Mose
Waring, Laura Wheeler
Wilson, Ed
Yarde, Richard

INSTALLATION ARTIST
Bailey, Xenobia
Conwill, Houston
Hammons, David
Hampton, James
Humphrey, Margo
Lawrence, Annette
Marshall, Kerry James
Piper, Adrian
Rowe, Nellie Mae
Scott, Joyce J.
Simpson, Lorna
Statom, Therman
Walker, Kara
Weems, Carrie Mae
Wilson, Fred

JEWELRY DESIGNER
Holloway, Charnelle
Mr. Imagination
Scott, Joyce J.
Simms, Carroll H.

METALSMITH
Holloway, Charnelle

MIXED-MEDIA ARTIST
Amaki, Amalia
Amos, Emma
Bailey, Radcliffe
Bailey, Xenobia
Birch, Willie
Buchanan, Beverly
Byard, Carole
Conwill, Houston
Cox, Renee
Hammons, David

Harris, Lyle Ashton
Holloway, Charnelle
Lawrence, Annette
Mr. Imagination
Nance, Marilyn
Pindell, Howardena
Saar, Betye
Saunders, Raymond
Statom, Therman
Stout, Renee
Whitten, Jack
Williams, Michael Kelly

MURALIST
Alston, Charles H.
Amos, Emma
Biggers, John
Birch, Willie
Crichlow, Ernest
Donaldson, Jeff
Douglas, Aaron
Morrison, Keith
Motley, Archibald J., Jr.
Ransome, James E.
Williams, Michael Kelly
Woodruff, Hale
Young, Purvis

**MUSEUM DIRECTOR
OR CURATOR**
Amaki, Amalia
Burroughs, Margaret Taylor
Driskell, David C.
Lewis, Samella
Morrison, Keith
Nance, Marilyn
Pindell, Howardena
Porter, James A.

PAINTER
Alston, Charles H.
Amos, Emma
Andrews, Benny
Bailey, Radcliffe

Bankston, John
Bannister, Edward Mitchell
Basquiat, Jean-Michel
Bearden, Romare
Biggers, John
Bowser, David Bustill
Brown, Frederick J.
Browne, Vivian E.
Bryan, Ashley
Buchanan, Beverly
Burroughs, Margaret Taylor
Clark, Claude
Colescott, Robert
Conwill, Houston
Cortor, Eldzier
Cowans, Adger
Crichlow, Ernest
Crite, Allan Rohan
Delaney, Beauford
Delaney, Joseph
DePillars, Murry N.
Donaldson, Jeff
Douglas, Aaron
Driskell, David C.
Duncanson, Robert Scott
Evans, Minnie
Gilchrist, Jan Spivey
Gilliam, Sam
Hammons, David
Harper, William A.
Hayden, Palmer C.
Hendricks, Barkley L.
Honeywood, Varnette
Hunter, Clementine
Johnson, Joshua
Johnson, Malvin Gray
Johnson, William H.
Jones, Lois Mailou
Lawrence, Annette
Lawrence, Jacob
Lee-Smith, Hughie
Lewis, E. B.
Lewis, Norman
Lewis, Samella

Loyd, Overton
Marshall, Kerry James
Mayhew, Richard
McCullough, Geraldine
Morgan, Sister Gertrude
Morrison, Keith
Motley, Archibald J., Jr.
Ormes, Jackie
Pindell, Howardena
Pippin, Horace
Porter, James A.
Rembert, Winfred
Ringgold, Faith
Rowe, Nellie Mae
Saunders, Raymond
Simms, Carroll H.
Stout, Renee
Tanner, Henry O.
Thomas, Alma W.
Thompson, Bob
Tolliver, Mose
Traylor, Bill
Waring, Laura Wheeler
Wells, James Lesesne
White, Charles
Whitten, Jack
Wilson, Ellis
Woodruff, Hale
Yarde, Richard
Yoakum, Joseph E.
Young, Purvis

PERFORMANCE ARTIST

Piper, Adrian
Ringgold, Faith
Scott, Joyce J.

PHOTOGRAPHER

Amaki, Amalia
Ball, James P.
Barboza, Anthony
Battey, C. M.
Bey, Dawoud
Buchanan, Beverly

Cowans, Adger
Cox, Renee
DeCarava, Roy
Harris, Charles
Harris, Lyle Ashton
Hendricks, Barkley L.
Higgins, Chester, Jr.
Marshall, Kerry James
Nance, Marilyn
Parks, Gordon
Pinderhughes, John
Polk, P. H.
Randall, Herbert
Scurlock, Addison
Simpson, Lorna
Van Der Zee, James
Walker, Shawn
Weems, Carrie Mae
Withers, Ernest C.

PRINTMAKER

Amos, Emma
Bearden, Romare
Bibbs, Garry
Blackburn, Bob
Burroughs, Margaret Taylor
Catlett, Elizabeth
Clark, Claude
Cortor, Eldzier
Crichlow, Ernest
Crite, Allan Rohan
DePillars, Murry N.
Donaldson, Jeff
Driskell, David C.
Hammons, David
Honeywood, Varnette
Humphrey, Margo
Hunt, Richard H.
Johnson, Sargent
Lewis, Norman
Marshall, Kerry James
Morrison, Keith
Saar, Alison
Scott, Joyce J.

Thrash, Dox
Walker, Kara
Wells, James Lesesne
White, Charles
Williams, Michael Kelly
Woodruff, Hale

QUILTER
Amaki, Amalia
Powers, Harriet
Ringgold, Faith
Scott, Joyce J.

SCREENWRITER
Burnett, Charles
Dash, Julie
Franklin, Carl
Greaves, William
Gunn, Bill
Hudlin, Reginald
Lee, Spike
Lemmons, Kasi
Martin, Darnell
Micheaux, Oscar
Perry, Tyler
Prince-Blythewood, Gina
Singleton, John
Townsend, Robert
Van Peebles, Mario
Van Peebles, Melvin
Wayans, Keenen Ivory
Welbon, Yvonne
Williams, Spencer

SCULPTOR
Alston, Charles H.
Artis, William E.
Bailey, Radcliffe

Barthé, Richmond
Bibbs, Garry
Biggers, John
Booker, Chakaia
Buchanan, Beverly
Burke, Selma
Byard, Carole
Catlett, Elizabeth
Chase-Riboud, Barbara
Conwill, Houston
Cuffie, Curtis
Edmondson, William
Edwards, Melvin
Fuller, Meta Vaux Warrick
Harper, William A.
Hathaway, Isaac Scott
Humphrey, Margo
Hunt, Richard H.
Johnson, Sargent
Lewis, Edmonia
Marshall, Kerry James
McCullough, Geraldine
Mr. Imagination
Prophet, Nancy Elizabeth
Puryear, Martin
Ringgold, Faith
Saar, Alison
Saar, Betye
Savage, Augusta
Scott, Joyce J.
Simms, Carroll H.
Stout, Renee
Washington, James W., Jr.
William A. Harper
Williams, Michael Kelly
Wilson, Ed
Wilson, Fred

SILHOUETTE ARTIST
Walker, Kara

STAGE DESIGNER
Loyd, Overton

STORYTELLER
Bailey, Xenobia
Nance, Marilyn

TELEVISION DIRECTOR
Dixon, Ivan
Hooks, Kevin
Martin, Darnell
Perry, Tyler
Prince-Blythewood, Gina
Schultz, Michael
Townsend, Robert
Van Peebles, Mario
Wayans, Keenen Ivory

TELEVISION PRODUCER
Hudlin, Reginald
Perry, Tyler
Prince-Blythewood, Gina

TEXTILE DESIGNER
Jones, Lois Mailou

VIDEO ARTIST
Buchanan, Yvonne
Hammons, David
Piper, Adrian
Simpson, Lorna
Walker, Kara

WEAVER
Amos, Emma

Entries by Artistic Style

Abstract Art
Chase-Riboud, Barbara
Driskell, David C.
Johnson, Malvin Gray
Lewis, Norman
Saunders, Raymond
Thomas, Alma W.
Whitten, Jack
Williams, Michael Kelly
Woodruff, Hale

Abstract Expressionism
Bearden, Romare
Brown, Frederick
Delaney, Beauford
Donaldson, Jeff

Collagism
Amaki, Amalia
Andrews, Benny
Bailey, Radcliffe
Bearden, Romare
Honeywood, Varnette
Saar, Betye

Color-Field School
Driskell, David C.
Gilliam, Sam

Cubism
Jones, Lois Mailou

Decorative Art
Bailey, Xenobia
Holloway, Charnelle
Ringgold, Faith

Expressionism and Post-Expressionism
Brown, Frederick J.
Browne, Vivian E.
Douglas, Aaron
Johnson, William H.
Lee-Smith, Hughie
Marshall, Kerry James
Ringgold, Faith
Thrash, Dox
Wilson, Ellis

Figurative Art
Alston, Charles H.
Catlett, Elizabeth
Cortor, Eldzier

Folk Art
Cuffie, Curtis
Dave the Potter
Edmondson, William
Evans, Minnie
Hampton, James
Hunter, Clementine
Jones, Frank
Morgan, Sister Gertrude
Mr. Imagination
Pierce, Elijah
Pippin, Horace
Powers, Harriet
Rembert, Winfred
Rowe, Nellie Mae
Tolliver, Mose
Traylor, Bill
Yoakum, Joseph E.
Young, Purvis

Genre Art
Crite, Allan Rohan
Delaney, Joseph
Hayden, Palmer C.
Lewis, Samella
Motley, Archibald, J., Jr.

Impressionism
Harper, William A.
Johnson, William H.
Tanner, Henry O.

Installation Art
Bailey, Xenobia
Conwill, Houston

Hammons, David
Humphrey, Margo
Lawrence, Annette
Marshall, Kerry James
Piper, Adrian
Scott, Joyce J.
Simpson, Lorna
Walker, Kara
Weems, Carrie Mae
Wilson, Fred

LANDSCAPE ART
Bannister, Edward Mitchell
Duncanson, Robert Scott
Mayhew, Richard
Yoakum, Joseph E.

MINIMALISM (REDUCTIONISM)
Johnson, Malvin Gray

MIXED-MEDIA ART
Amaki, Amalia
Bailey, Radcliffe
Bailey, Xenobia
Birch, Willie
Buchanan, Beverly
Byard, Carole
Conwill, Houston
Cox, Renee
Hammons, David
Harris, Lyle Ashton
Holloway, Charnelle
Lawrence, Annette
Mr. Imagination
Nance, Marilyn
Pindell, Howardena
Saar, Betye
Saunders, Raymond
Statom, Therman
Stout, Renee
Whitten, Jack
Williams, Michael Kelly

NEOCLASSICISM
Fuller, Meta Vaux Warrick
Lewis, Edmonia

NEOEXPRESSIONISM
Basquiat, Jean-Michel

NEOREALISM
Hendricks, Barkley L.

ORGANIC DESIGN
Puryear, Martin

PORTRAIT ART
Artis, William E.
Bey, Dawoud
Bowser, David Bustill
Burke, Selma
Burroughs, Margaret Taylor
Hathaway, Isaac Scott
Johnson, Joshua
Prophet, Nancy Elizabeth
Savage, Augusta
Waring, Laura Wheeler

PRIMITIVISM
Douglas, Aaron
Johnson, Sargent
Johnson, William H.
Lawrence, Jacob
Owens-Hart, Winnie
Saar, Alison
Washington, James W., Jr.
Yarde, Richard

PUBLIC ART
Amos, Emma
Biggers, John
Bowser, David Bustill
Douglas, Aaron
Edwards, Melvin
Honeywood, Varnette
Puryear, Martin
Statom, Therman

Washington, James W., Jr.
Wilson, Ed
Young, Purvis

REALISM
Barthé, Richmond
Blackburn, Bob
Porter, James A.

RELIGIOUS ART
Crite, Allan Rohan
Hampton, James
Morgan, Sister Gertrude
Simms, Carroll H.
Tanner, Henry O.
Wells, James Lesesne

SATIRICAL ART
Colescott, Robert
Cox, Renee
DePillars, Murry N.
Humphrey, Margo
McGruder, Aaron
Walker, Kara
Wilson, Fred

SOCIAL REALISM
Bearden, Romare
Catlett, Elizabeth
Clark, Claude
Crichlow, Ernest
Lewis, Norman
Thrash, Dox
White, Charles

**SURREALISM AND
    POSTSURREALISM**
Bankston, John
Bibbs, Garry
Morrison, Keith
Thompson, Bob

WELDED METAL ART
Hunt, Richard H.
McCullough, Geraldine

ENTRIES BY YEAR OF BIRTH

1750–1799
Johnson, Joshua

1800–1849
Ball, James P.
Bannister, Edward Mitchell
Bowser, David Bustill
Dave the Potter
Day, Thomas
Duncanson, Robert Scott
Lewis, Edmonia
Powers, Harriet

1850–1869
Tanner, Henry O.
Traylor, Bill

1870–1889
Battey, C. M.
Edmondson, William
Fuller, Meta Vaux Warrick
Harper, William A.
Hathaway, Isaac Scott
Hunter, Clementine
Johnson, Noble
Johnson, Sargent
Micheaux, Oscar
Pippin, Horace
Scurlock, Addison

Van Der Zee, James
Waring, Laura Wheeler
Yoakum, Joseph E.

1890–1899
Douglas, Aaron
Evans, Minnie
Hayden, Palmer C.
Johnson, Malvin Gray
Motley, Archibald J., Jr.
Pierce, Elijah
Polk. P. H.
Prophet, Nancy Elizabeth
Savage, Augusta
Thomas, Alma W.
Thrash, Dox
Williams, Paul R.
Williams, Spencer
Wilson, Ellis

1900–1909
Alston, Charles H.
Barthé, Richmond
Burke, Selma
Campbell, E. Simms
Delaney, Beauford
Delaney, Joseph
Hampton, James
Harris, Charles
Johnson, William H.

Jones, Frank
Jones, Lois Mailou
Lewis, Norman
Morgan, Sister Gertrude
Porter, James A.
Rowe, Nellie Mae
Washington, James W., Jr.
Wells, James Lesesne
Woodruff, Hale

1910–1919
Alexander, William
Artis, William E.
Bearden, Romare
Burroughs, Margaret Taylor
Catlett, Elizabeth
Clark, Claude
Commodore, Chester
Cortor, Eldzier
Crichlow, Ernest
Crite, Allan Rohan
DeCarava, Roy
Harrington, Ollie
Lawrence, Jacob
Lee-Smith, Hughie
McCullough, Geraldine
Ormes, Jackie
Parks, Gordon
Tolliver, Mose
White, Charles

INDEX

Boldface locators indicate major treatment of a topic. *Italic* locators indicate photos and illustrations.